"What a practical approach! June's compassionate counsel reflects decades of real-life experience helping people enjoy healed relationships. You'll find yourself reaching for this powerful resource again and again."

Dr. Gary Chapman
Author, *The Five Love Languages*

"June reveals God's heart for our relationships and then gives us a practical scriptural roadmap to show us how to handle difficult relationships…and how to heal from the damage they cause. Every pastor and Christian counselor should get two copies—one for their own bookshelf, and another to lend to someone who needs it."

Leslie Vernick
Licensed counselor, coach, speaker
Author, *The Emotionally Destructive Relationship*

"Everyone faces the challenge of difficult relationships—in the family, community, church, and workplace. June Hunt continues to be the go-to counselor for hurting people throughout the world. With her sensitive heart and sound biblical foundation, she helps those mired in difficulty identify problems and work systematically toward biblical solutions. Whatever your situation, June meets you there through this volume and other books in the series. She will help you with your struggles…and equip you to help others."

Dr. Dorothy Kelley Patterson
Professor of Theology in Women's Studies
Southwestern Baptist Theological Seminary

"God created us to be relational because He wants to relate to us. It grieves Him when we fail in our relationships, so we need to look for ways to mend what is broken and heal what is sick. June Hunt's work will help greatly!"

D. Stuart Briscoe
Cofounder, Telling the Truth Ministries
Author, *The One Year Devotions for Men*

"June Hunt has done it again! She provides readers with an excellent and practical book on how to deal with difficult relationships, all the while pointing directly to Scripture. It's a must-read for anyone in a difficult relationship or anyone helping those who deal with difficult relationships."

Dr. Beverly Rodgers
Author, *Becoming a Family That Heals*

"June gives us one of the most practical relationship books I've ever read. Filled with help and hope, it is a gold mine of biblically based insights and practical skills...showing how to not just survive, but actually *thrive*. As we navigate the rapids of differences and disagreements—the inevitable part of any relationship, we will learn to develop the trust and intimacy we all long for and that God created us to enjoy. I guarantee you that this is a book you'll want to read more than once, and a book you'll want to share with your friends."

Dr. Gary J. Oliver
Executive Director, The Center for Relationship Enrichment
Professor of Psychology & Practical Theology, John Brown University
Author, *Mad About Us: Moving from Anger to Intimacy with Your Spouse*

How to Deal with Difficult Relationships

June Hunt

HARVEST HOUSE PUBLISHERS
EUGENE, OREGON

Cover by Garborg Design Works, Savage, Minnesota

Cover photo © iStockphoto / beklaus

HOW TO DEAL WITH DIFFICULT RELATIONSHIPS
Copyright © 2011 by Hope for the Heart, Inc.
Published by Harvest House Publishers
Eugene, Oregon 97402
www.harvesthousepublishers.com

Library of Congress Cataloging-in-Publication Data

ISBN 978-0-7369-2816-8

12 13 14 15 16 17 18 19 20 / LB-KBD / 10 9 8 7 6 5 4 3 2 1

DEDICATION

With tremendous gratitude and respect, I dedicate this book to the Hope Care Center team of Hope for the Heart.

On the front lines of our ministry since 1986, our Hope Care Center representatives have provided *biblical hope and practical help* to callers each weekday morning from 7:30 to the next morning at 1:30. Whether those who write or call are requesting our practical resources, wise counsel, or personal prayer, I know of no more compassionate, competent and, yes, *caring* group of responders anywhere.

This gifted, trained team has assisted hundreds of thousands of callers (fielding our 500,000th call in 2011), helping them come to Christ...helping them become whole... helping them help others based on the practical principles of God's Word. I consider it my great honor to recognize the efforts of all Hope Care Center team members, both past and present:

Michael Allen	Sheila Guerra	Ruth Montenegro
Kevin Batista	Jack Hanks	Bob Mulima
Karen Billman	Kristina Hedges	Sherilyn Neudauer
Stacy Bledsoe	Ben Holland	Katie Nieder
Diedra Blosser	Courtney Hughes	Andrea Parisi
Glenn Bolton	Cheryl Hunter	Eric Puente
Kimberly Bousman	Dr. Steve Hunter	Haley Scully
Hannah Braswell	Dr. Morris Isara	Linda Seah
Jennifer Crow	Dr. Greg Jenks	Howard Smith
Shannon Donovan	Nate King	David Taylor
Ryan Doyle	Lenora Kizzee	Bryan Tripp
Dr. Joan Faubion	Kimberly Knighton	Paul Weaver
Dan Fries	Steve Light	Anita Wiggin
Andy Gingrich	Brandi Lim	Sandra Williamson
Ray Green	Matt McKinney	Meagan Yarbrough
Michael Gregg	Heike Middelmann	

...and all who came before them.

Please know, "I always thank my God for you...For in [Christ] you have been enriched in every way—with all kinds of speech and with all knowledge" (1 Corinthians 1:4-5).

ACKNOWLEDGMENTS

How grateful I am for the dedicated editorial team who helped me bridge the gap between the Hope for the Heart counseling resources we've created over the last 25 years...and the book you now hold in your hands. The close bond we've forged has made working together such a joy. Therefore, my great privilege is to acknowledge the expansive contributions of...

Angie White for being the project manager in charge of building this bridge from start to finish

Barbara Spruill for supporting the foundation of our efforts by skillfully editing the six *Biblical Counseling Keys* contained in this volume

Jill Prohaska for connecting ideas to illustrations through swaying sidebars and stories

Carolyn White and **Syl Mallette** for decking with perfect styles and layout for each chapter's Definitions, Characteristics, Causes, and Steps to Solution

Titus O'Bryant for inspecting facts and researching information to ensure each word is tied to truth

Phillip Bleecker, Karen Williams, and **Bea Garner** for passing over each page in a painstaking proofing process

Laura Lyn Benoit and **Karen Stebbins** for bearing the load of reading each chapter to ensure continuity

June Page, Karen Billman, and **Angie Todd** for suspending their regular activities in order to volunteer as sidebar editors

Kelley Basatneh for keying editorial changes throughout the span of this project

Kay Yates for supporting an enormous behind-the-scenes load of projects and people, freeing me to focus on the manuscript

Elizabeth Cunningham for tying the front matter of the book together with the manuscript and editing various other segments and sidebars

Steve Miller and **the entire Harvest House team** for joining us in our mission to link searching hearts with *biblical hope and practical help*

CONTENTS

Do you have a heavy heart…so heavy you feel isolated, separated, stuck off to the side? Do you feel discouraged, even emotionally disconnected due to a difficult person in your life?

Right now, are you looking—with deep longing—for true reconciliation, but the emotional distance is just too great and now you don't know what to do?

Do you know the pain of a broken relationship—the kind of pain filled with broken promises, the kind of betrayal that penetrates the very core of your being? The cords of trust have been completely severed so that the chasm seemingly can no longer be crossed. You want to close the gap, but conflict continually keeps you apart. If only you could find a way…to "bridge the gap."

As I recently looked back over the years at my own challenging relationships, I reflected on my attempts to bridge the gap (some failed, some didn't). I also learned a bit about bridges—I mean, *literal* bridges.

Deep in the jungles of India, in one of the world's wettest regions, indigenous people have been cultivating "living bridges" for more than 500 years. Planning 10 to 15 years in advance, members of the War-Khasis tribe decide where a bridge will be most useful. Then they begin the painstaking work of directing strong, resilient rubber tree roots to arch from one bank to another.

To start a new bridge, the tribespeople use native, bamboo-like vegetation to guide the direction of the roots to grow straight across, not down. It is also used to prevent the rubber tree roots from fanning out so that they create a tight, secure structure. After the roots have passed over the water, the people help the roots lodge themselves deep in the soil on the other side. Given enough time, a sturdy, *living bridge* takes hold and finds its shape. The more mature these bridges become, the more weight they can bear, with some spanning more than 100 feet and able to support 50 people crossing at once.[1]

Clearly this industrious group of people understands the extraordinary potential of a bridge. As a result, their daily lives are both enriched and eased.

A question we could all ask ourselves is this: "Am I a bridge builder, one who is firmly rooted and reaching out to reconcile with others?" If not, we are missing a major purpose in our lives.

Obviously, I'm not referring to bridge building in terms of beams, arches, or cantilevers. Not suspension cables either, nor rubber tree roots. I believe God is calling each of us to master something of greater value and eternal significance— He wants us to *become* living bridges that lovingly unite hearts and lives!

Actually, God is all about *relationships*...and all about *love*. Jesus said it this way: "'Love the Lord your God with all your heart and with all your soul and with all your mind.' This is the first and greatest commandment. And the second is like it: 'Love your neighbor as yourself'" (Matthew 22:37-39).

These two commandments, aligned together, reveal God's priority for our lives: loving relationships—first between Him and us, and then between others and us. To Him, nothing else is more important. Nothing else is worth Jesus' dying for.

God has firsthand knowledge of the heartache that results from broken relationships. That's exactly what He experienced when Adam and Eve rejected Him in the perfect garden He provided. At that moment, the heavenly Father suffered the sorrow of history's first "difficult relationship." The sad reality is that God—and everyone who has ever lived—has endured the excruciating pain of relationships marred by selfishness, sin, and strife.

But our loving Creator of Relationships didn't allow this rejection to stop His unquenchable quest for oneness *with* us and *between* us. Jesus' arrival on earth set into motion God's plan to bridge broken relationships. In fact, Jesus was the *Master* Bridge Builder. He created a way for us, undeserving as we are, and helped us to find our way across the otherwise insurmountable gap (caused by sin) that separates us from the Father's waiting, loving arms. (See pages 48-50.)

Because bridging broken relationships is God's priority, it needs to be our priority as well. Healing, recovery, and growth rarely occur outside the context of relationships. God is a *relational* God, and He has made us *relational*.

Perhaps you have heard this kind of conversation: "How do you like your job?" The reply: "It would be great...if it weren't for the *people*." But the truth is, if it weren't for people, there wouldn't be a fully functioning workplace, and there wouldn't be the opportunity to learn invaluable lessons from relating to different kinds of people.

If the Bible is our textbook for *learning*, relationships are our "laboratory" for *living*. Relationships provide us with opportunities to live out what we've learned from God's Word about life and love. Relationships force us to put theory into practice—ultimately, to test our bridge-building skills.

Apart from the random log that falls across a stream, bridges don't just "appear." They require designers and builders. So it is with relational bridges. Intention, design, and skillful implementation are required to build a living bridge toward the difficult people in our lives.

How to Deal with Difficult Relationships presents multiple "people problems" along with biblical principles for bridging the gaps. Filled with relevant Scripture passages, each chapter systematically explores *definitions, characteristics, causes,* and *solutions* concerning difficult relationships—and these are solutions I know can work!

Still, it's wise to remember: The complete resolution for difficult relationships requires *mutual effort* from everyone involved. Therefore, even if you are the world's most skilled bridge builder, there's no guarantee that your "bridge" will work, or that your relationship will be restored. Sometimes well-made bridges fail—eroding due to unnecessary neglect, buckling due to unpredicted pressure, collapsing due to unexpected catastrophes.

Romans 12:18 instructs us, "If it is possible, as far as it depends on you, live at peace with everyone." The "if" reminds us that bridging difficult relationships requires *two* willing people working in tandem toward the common goal of conflict resolution.

While we are called to reach out to others, we can't control their responses. We can, however, surrender our difficult relationships to God and allow Him to change whatever needs to be changed...in *us*!

In total candor, I remember times when I desperately needed to change. I was so codependent (although I didn't know the word *codependency*) that I continually caved into the *manipulation* of others—especially people with an angry *critical spirit*. Since healthy *confrontation* was foreign in my family, and since *forgiveness* wasn't "fair," *conflict resolution* completely eluded me. To put it mildly, my life was a mess...and I needed to change! (And that is why all of these topics are in this book.)

Personally, I've experienced the pain of unresolved relationships. I've experienced chasms a mile wide, separating me from certain family and friends. Yet today, most of those relationships have been restored—*because bridges were built*. Therefore, what I'm presenting in this book isn't mere theory. I'm sharing with you time-tested solutions from my own life.

But first, I was the one who needed to change. I needed a bridge—Jesus Himself, who bridged the chasm between the Father and me! Then He showed me how to bridge the gaps in my own difficult relationships. And, oh, did I need truth. I needed to know the truth (about Christ)...to face the truth (about me)...and then to act on the truth (about my relationships)—so, *the truth, indeed, could set me free*.

As we allow the Lord to change us, He calls us to extend a living bridge to those who are difficult to love. Then we leave the results in His hands...and live our lives in His peace.

Yours in the Lord's truth,

June Hunt

"Then you will know the truth, and the truth will set you free"
(John 8:32).

CRITICAL SPIRIT
Confronting the Heart of a Critic

1

CRITICAL SPIRIT

Confronting the Heart of a Critic

"Curse God and die!"

The words spew out of the mouth of an embittered wife who is stunned and stymied by tragedy. Gone—destroyed—are all their possessions and all their children as a result of God allowing Satan to test her godly husband in order to prove his faith.

Job mourns their losses but doesn't malign the goodness of God. Instead he submits himself to the sovereignty of God by declaring, "The Lord gave and the Lord has taken away; may the name of the Lord be praised" (Job 1:21).

But..."Curse God and die!" is her retort, especially after seeing her husband suddenly stricken—afflicted from head to toe with painful sores. She observes this once-respected man—so revered in the community—now scorned and reduced to sitting in a pile of ashes scraping his sores with a jagged piece of pottery.

Job's noble stance before the Lord is absolute nonsense to her. She doesn't want to hear one more word of devotion from her disease-ridden husband.

A critical spirit consumes the wife of the one whom God calls "the greatest man among all the people" (Job 1:3). However, she's had enough, and she wants Job—and God—to know it!

"Are you still maintaining your integrity?" she pounds, unleashing her toxic tongue: "Curse God and die!" (Job 2:9).

I. Definitions of a Critical Spirit

Everything is fine...until they open their mouths.

They are aghast at the sight before them. Their once highly respected friend is now horrifically humbled. Eliphaz, Bildad, and Zophar (Eli, Bill, and Zo for short) have set out from their homes to pour out words of comfort upon their troubled friend, but now they find themselves speechless. For seven days and seven nights they sit on the ground and commiserate, and "no one said a word to him, because they saw how great his suffering was" (Job 2:13).

But soon their sympathetic presence morphs into a barrage of stinging rebuke that further crushes the spirit of poor Job. He responds in deep emotional pain:

> *"Anyone who withholds kindness from a friend*
> *forsakes the fear of the Almighty"*
> (JOB 6:14).

Like Job's friends, has someone in your life assumed the role of your personal "heavenly sandpaper"—a self-appointed expert at finding fault and continually focusing on it in an attempt to refine you? The abrasive words are not helpful but hurtful, and qualify as verbal and emotional abuse. Such criticism grates against the grain of your soul, wearing you down, stripping you of your worth.

God holds all of us accountable for how we use our words, especially words that wound. Harsh, critical words don't pour out of the hearts of godly people. Jesus said,

> *"The mouth speaks what the heart is full of.*
> *A good man brings good things out of the good stored up in him,*
> *and an evil man brings evil things out of the evil stored up in him"*
> (MATTHEW 12:34-35).

A. What Is a Critical Spirit?

Eliphaz, most likely the eldest among the friends, is first to speak up ever so cautiously. But then his words take on a presumptive tone.

By the time Eli finishes, he insinuates that Job is being disciplined by God because of sin, and the wise way for Job to proceed is to submit to the discipline.

But there's a problem with his critical presumption—Job's torturous troubles have nothing to do with sin. Instead, they're all about a showdown between God and Satan over Job's testimony. Will Job stand? The Bible says,

> *"Blessed is the one who perseveres under trial because, having*
> *stood the test, that person will receive the crown of life*
> *that the Lord has promised to those who love him"*
> (JAMES 1:12).

At the Wimbledon tennis championship in England, a judge sits on an elevated chair to the side of the net between two competitors. The judge is hired for the prestigious match by earning a reputation for consistent fairness and accuracy. When a ball is served outside the boundary line, the judge yells, "Fault!" These judgment calls are appropriate and appreciated.

The person with a critical spirit, however, hasn't earned the reputation of being accurate or fair-minded. This judge sits uninvited and elevated above others, yelling "Fault...fault...fault!" These calls are inappropriate and unappreciated.

The Bible is not silent about those who have a critical spirit:

> *"You, then, why do you judge your brother or sister?*
> *Or why do you treat them with contempt?*
> *For we will all stand before God's judgment seat"*
> (ROMANS 14:10).

- A *critical spirit* is an excessively negative attitude characterized by harshness in judging.

  - *Criticizers* judge others severely and unfavorably.

  - *Hypercritical* people judge others with unreasonably strict standards.

  - *Faultfinders* look for and point out flaws and defects with nagging and unreasonable criticism.

For example, certain circumcised Jewish believers unjustly criticized the apostle Peter for fellowshipping with those uncircumcised. The issue of circumcision (was it necessary for salvation or not?) created sharp division in the early church.

> *"So when Peter went up to Jerusalem,*
> *the circumcised believers criticized him"*
> (ACTS 11:2).

- *Criticism* comes from the Greek word *kritikos*, which means "able to discern or skilled in judging."[1]

- *Criticism* has two different meanings:[2]
  - *Speaking fairly* with discernment in regard to merit or value. (A literary critic is expected to give a fair critique by accurately analyzing, judging, and reporting.)

– *Speaking unfairly* with trivial or harsh judgments. (A person with a *critical spirit* gives unfair criticism by faultfinding, nit-picking, and quibbling.)

The Bible stresses the powerful impact of our right and wrong words:

"The tongue has the power of life and death"
(Proverbs 18:21).

B. What Is a Caring Spirit?

Job's friends initially demonstrate a caring spirit, reflecting the deep, attentive love of God in the midst of suffering.

But then the misguided pride that accompanies a critical spirit consumes them to the degree that the three men are more concerned with delivering theological points than showing desperately needed compassion.

The Bible has much to say about pride, including God's heart attitude toward it:

"I hate pride and arrogance, evil behavior and perverse speech"
(Proverbs 8:13).

One of our deepest needs is for someone to care about us—our successes and failures, our strengths and weaknesses, our virtues and vices. We want people to be attentive to our likes and dislikes, our joys and sorrows, our dreams and disappointments. How blessed we are when we have people with caring spirits in our lives!

But how much more secure we feel when we come to know the breadth and the depth of God's love and care for us. The apostle Paul said,

"I pray that you, being rooted and established in love,
may have power, together with all the Lord's holy people,
to grasp how wide and long and high and deep is the love of Christ,
and to know this love that surpasses knowledge—
that you may be filled to the measure of all the fullness of God"
(Ephesians 3:17-19).

- *Caring* means giving watchful or painstaking attention based on desiring what is best for others.[3]

- *To care* means to be thoughtfully attentive and protective.
- *To care* means to be personally interested in or to feel affection toward someone else.
- *To care* means to be actively involved in doing what is best for another person.

The One who created you gives loving, watchful care toward you. This care is expressed in Scripture:

> *"What is mankind that you are mindful of them, a son of man that you care for him? You made them a little lower than the angels; you crowned them with glory and honor… The LORD is good, a refuge in times of trouble. He cares for those who trust in him"*
> (HEBREWS 2:6-7; NAHUM 1:7).

- *Caring* people are genuinely interested in showing concern for others. In the Bible we read about truly caring people such as…

  - The Good Samaritan, who took care of the savagely beaten traveler:

    > *"He [a Samaritan] went to him and bandaged his wounds, pouring on oil and wine. Then he put the man on his own donkey, brought him to an inn and took care of him"*
    > (LUKE 10:34).

  - The apostle Paul, who cared for the new Christians who were young in their faith:

    > *"We were like young children among you. Just as a nursing mother cares for her children"*
    > (1 THESSALONIANS 2:7).

  - The Christians in Philippi, who sent someone to care for the needs of Paul:

    > *"I think it is necessary to send back to you Epaphroditus, my brother, co-worker and fellow soldier, who is also your messenger, whom you sent to take care of my needs…*

> *he almost died for the work of Christ. He risked his life to*
> *make up for the help you yourselves could not give me"*
> (Philippians 2:25,30).

C. What Is Encouragement?

After Eliphaz's speech, Job replies in his own defense, expressing a need for sincere encouragement instead of words that wound.

"But my brothers are as undependable as intermittent streams, as the streams that overflow," Job laments (Job 6:15). His friends increase his burdens rather than help relieve them. He further responds,

> *"Now you too have proved to be of no help; you*
> *see something dreadful and are afraid"*
> (Job 6:21).

From our earliest years we have all yearned for approval; we have cried out for encouragement: "Mommy, look what I drew!" When we were learning to swim or play baseball, our hearts called out, "Daddy, look here! Look at me!" Just as children need encouragement, adults need encouragement. But not just occasionally—the Bible says we need this regularly:

> *"Encourage one another daily"*
> (Hebrews 3:13).

- *Encouragement* means inspiring another person with comfort, counsel, and confidence. *Encourage* literally means "to cause another to be confident."[4]

  - The prefix *en* means "to cause to be"; *courage* means "confidence."
  - The encourager causes others to have confidence to do what needs to be done and to make needed changes.
  - The Lord encouraged Joshua to "be strong and very courageous" in leading the Israelites to inherit the land God promised to give them (Joshua 1:7-8).

The Bible says we should all be encouragers:

> *"Encourage one another and build each other up"*
> (1 Thessalonians 5:11).

- In the Bible, the word "encouragement," as translated from the Greek word *paraklesis*, literally means "a calling to one's aid" to give comfort or counsel.[5]

  - *Para* means "beside"; *kaleo* means "to call."
  - We are called to come alongside and comfort others.
  - The Holy Spirit is the *paraclete*—our Comforter, our Counselor, our Advocate.

Jesus said,

> *"The Father...will give you another Counselor to be with you forever...The Comforter, which is the Holy [Spirit]...shall teach you all things...Let not your heart be troubled, neither let it be afraid"*
> (JOHN 14:16 HCSB; JOHN 14:26-27 KJV).

EMPOWERED BY THE SPIRIT

If you are an authentic Christian, consider this: The Holy Spirit has the power to comfort and counsel you to change. Because all true Christians have the indwelling presence of the Holy Spirit—the very presence of the Spirit of God—you are empowered to be an extension of the Comforter's ministry. The supernatural power of God can work through you to inspire others who *need* to change to have the *courage* to change!

However, if you sit in judgment of someone else, the exercise of a critical spirit may actually prevent the very changes you wish to see. The Bible is clear:

> *"There is only one Lawgiver and Judge, the one who is able to save and destroy. But you—who are you to judge your neighbor?"*
> (JAMES 4:12).

UPLIFTING ONE ANOTHER

Doesn't the way in which certain birds fly together in a V-shaped formation amaze you? Sometimes they will make sudden turns and dives—first heading one direction, then another, yet still maintaining their tight formation. Their fascinating flight patterns are a form of true beauty and a necessity for their survival.

Also remarkable is the fact they can travel hundreds of miles without stopping. At certain intervals—depending on the strength of the headwind—the lead bird, which is doing most of the work by breaking the force of the wind for the flock, suddenly leaves its position and drops back to the end of the formation.

Without missing a beat of the wings, another bird quickly moves into the lead position, taking on the task of meeting the wind head-on.

Ultimately, the V-formation is far more efficient than each bird flying independently. In fact, up to 65 percent less work is required! The flapping of all their wings produces an *uplift of air* that enables the birds at the back to glide and soar on the created air currents—thus the birds previously in the lead can recuperate by coasting on the current. In this way, the birds take turns "uplifting one another."[6]

By working in formation together, migrating birds can travel hundreds of miles—even thousands of miles—that they could never travel on their own. Even the strongest birds could not cross large bodies of water without the help of the flock *uplifting each other*.

Similarly, when we uplift one another through encouragement and prayer—by caring and sharing in true heart-to-heart friendships—all of us in the flock of God can go further in our journey than we ever could by trying to endure on our own. By uplifting one another, we are helping one another.

Our God is a God who cares. Psalm 145:14 says, "The LORD upholds all who fall and lifts up all who are bowed down." Your uplifting words can be used by God to give help to the helpless, to heal the brokenhearted, to give hope to the hopeless.

D. What Is God's Heart on a Critical Spirit?

Throughout the book of Job, God is mostly silent, speaking only at the beginning and the end. But make no mistake about it—He doesn't miss a single word of the conversation among Job and his three so-called friends.

Never assume that just because God is silent, that means He is absent. In the end, He speaks up, and reveals His heart response to a critical spirit:

> *"One who loves a pure heart and who speaks with grace*
> *will have the king for a friend"*
> (PROVERBS 22:11).

SEEING THE FATHER THROUGH JESUS

Jesus came to earth clothed in humanity in order to die for us, but He also came to show us the Father—in human flesh. He did that both by His actions and by His words. Therefore, if we want to know the Father's heart on the subject of a critical spirit, we need only examine the life of Jesus, or the way He behaved toward people and what He said to them. Clearly He confronted sin in people's lives, but He did it compassionately—not with a critical or condemning spirit. He did it as the Father did it then and as He still does it now...

> *"Jesus answered...*
> *'Anyone who has seen me has seen the Father.*
> *How can you say, "Show us the Father"?*
> *Don't you believe that I am in the Father,*
> *and that the Father is in me?*
> *The words I say to you*
> *I do not speak on my own authority.*
> *Rather, it is the Father, living in me,*
> *who is doing his work'"*
> (JOHN 14:9-10).

GOD'S HEART ON A CRITICAL SPIRIT, THROUGH THE WORDS OF JESUS

When it comes to interacting with others, Jesus wants us to examine our own conduct and motives. In Matthew 7:1-5, He spoke unforgettable words with unforgettable imagery:

- **Don't be judgmental** or you too will be judged.

  "Do not judge, or you too will be judged." . . . . verse 1

- **Don't judge others** or you will be judged in the same way and measured by the same standard.

  "In the same way you judge others, you will be judged, and with the measure you use, it will be measured to you." . . . . verse 2

- **Don't focus** on the small faults of others before focusing on your own big faults.

  "Why do you look at the speck of sawdust in your brother's eye and pay no attention to the plank in your own eye?" . . . . verse 3

- **Don't talk** to others about their faults while you ignore your own faults.

> *"How can you say to your brother, 'Let me take the speck out of your eye,'*
> *when all the time there is a plank in your own eye?"* . . . . verse 4

- **Don't be hypocritical**—correct your faults. Then you can correct someone else's faults.

> *"You hypocrite, first take the plank out of your own eye, and then you*
> *will see clearly to remove the speck from your brother's eye."* . . . verse 5

Luke, one of the Gospel writers, records Jesus saying very similar words:

> *"Do not judge, and you will not be judged.*
> *Do not condemn, and you will not be condemned.*
> *Forgive, and you will be forgiven"*
> (LUKE 6:37).

II. CHARACTERISTICS OF A CRITICAL SPIRIT

Bildad (Bill) can no longer contain himself; he is becoming increasingly frustrated that Job isn't owning up to his supposed "sins" and admitting that God is disciplining him.

"How long will you say such things? Your words are a blustering wind" (Job 8:2). Bill's compassion erodes into cruelty, and he even accuses Job's children of sinning and says that's why God allowed them to be killed. He makes the tragically wrong presumption, "When your children sinned against him, he gave them over to the penalty of their sin" (Job 8:4).

Is there someone in your life who has been especially hard on you? Notice how those with a critical spirit seek to cancel out their own "shortcomings" by focusing on their own "good intentions," but they will condemn you by focusing on your faults. Anyone can develop a critical spirit by focusing on the failures of others, and obviously no one is without fault. But with this selective vision, these faultfinders feel justified in playing dual roles: both judge and jury. Meanwhile, those being judged feel unjustly criticized, unjustly compared, unjustly condemned.

God, on the other hand, never calls attention to our faults in a way that wounds our spirit. Instead, His plan is to bring positive—though sometimes painful—conviction for this one purpose: to motivate us to change.

Those with a critical spirit deny the "weight" of their sin by measuring it with a different standard than they apply to others, and they need to be aware of these words from Proverbs:

> *"Who can say, 'I have kept my heart pure;*
> *I am clean and without sin'?*
> *Differing weights and differing measures—*
> *the LORD detests them both"*
>
> (PROVERBS 20:9-10).

A. What Are the Key Differences Between a Critical Spirit and a Caring Spirit?

A caring spirit...where can one be found?

The bombardment of criticism is getting to Job. He is slipping into despair and growing cynical concerning the justice of God. "It is all the same; that is why I say, 'He destroys both the blameless and the wicked.' When a scourge brings sudden death, he mocks the despair of the innocent. When a land falls into the hands of the wicked, he blindfolds its judges. If it is not he, then who is it?" (Job 9:22-24).

Job's desperate discouragement in the midst of righteous tribulation demonstrates the importance of manifesting a caring spirit to others in their deepest need:

> *"Walk in the way of love, just as Christ loved us*
> *and gave himself up for us as a fragrant*
> *offering and sacrifice to God"*
>
> (EPHESIANS 5:2).

Isn't it interesting how different people handle the same situation in completely opposite ways? Two people receive the same bad news: One reacts negatively and the other reacts positively. Two people see someone make a mistake: One person lacks mercy and the other extends mercy.

Those with a critical spirit rarely focus on the needs of others—they are too busy focusing on faults. A critical spirit and a caring spirit are on opposite ends of the spectrum; the one tears people down while the other builds people up. God continually manifests a caring spirit, and His desire is for us to do the same.

9 DISTINCT DIFFERENCES		
A CRITICAL SPIRIT		**A CARING SPIRIT**
Condemns the person as well as the action	*"The words of the reckless pierce like swords, but the tongue of the wise brings healing"* (PROVERBS 12:18).	**Condemns the action,** but not the person
Focuses on the faults of others	*"Why do you look at the speck of sawdust in your brother's eye and pay no attention to the plank in your own eye?"* (LUKE 6:41).	**Focuses on the faults of oneself**
Ridicules others	*"Whoever derides their neighbor has no sense, but the one who has understanding holds their tongue"* (PROVERBS 11:12).	**Encourages** others
Makes judgments based on **appearances**	*"Stop judging by mere appearances, but instead judge correctly"* (JOHN 7:24).	**Makes judgments** based on **facts**
Assumes the worst without first hearing from the accused	*"Does our law condemn a man without first hearing him to find out what he has been doing?"* (JOHN 7:51).	**Assumes the best** while waiting to hear from the accused

A CRITICAL SPIRIT		A CARING SPIRIT
Tears others down without seeing their unmet needs	*"Do not let any unwholesome talk come out of your mouths, but only what is helpful for building others up according to their needs, that it may benefit those who listen"* (EPHESIANS 4:29).	**Builds others up** according to their inner needs
Publicly criticizes those who have wronged them—without first going to them	*"If your brother or sister sins, go and point out their fault, just between the two of you. If they listen to you, you have won them over"* (MATTHEW 18:15).	**Privately confronts** those who have wronged them—by going to them first
Reacts pridefully when given advice	*"Where there is strife, there is pride, but wisdom is found in those who take advice"* (PROVERBS 13:10).	**Responds positively** when given advice
Lacks mercy toward others	*"Speak and act as those who are going to be judged by the law that gives freedom, because judgment without mercy will be shown to anyone who has not been merciful. Mercy triumphs over judgment"* (James 2:12-13).	**Extends mercy** toward others

> The old saying is true:
> "People don't care how much you know
> until they know how much you care."

Honor Your Father and Mother

QUESTION: "I want to be biblical, but...how can I honor my mother, who has a critical spirit and is verbally abusive toward me?"

ANSWER: Submitting to your mother's abuse is not honoring her, but rather is dishonoring because you are enabling her to continue a sinful habit. When you love someone, you want to do what is best for them.

You can honor your mother by...

- *Living a godly life* that reflects positively on her.
- *Not assuming false guilt* when blamed for situations in which you are blameless.
- *Becoming emotionally and spiritually healthy*, which will mean setting healthy boundaries for your relationship. You could respond in a manner similar to this:

  - "Mother, I genuinely care about you and love you. Right now I have a concern: If you speak negatively to me or about others, it reflects negatively on you.

  - "Therefore, it's not in *your* best interest to continue with negative comments, and it's not in *my* best interest to continue to hear the negative criticism.

  - "From now on, every time you speak with harsh criticism, I'm going to leave for a short time. I'll be back, but leaving will help me to have a more positive attitude.

  - "I want to honor you by expecting the best of you. I know we are capable of better and healthier ways of communicating, and I want us to have the best relationship possible."

With this caring spirit, you can adhere to God's command:

"Honor your father and your mother"
(EXODUS 20:12).

B. What Smoke Screens Serve to Camouflage a Critical Spirit?

Job is a *blameless* man, but he's not a *sinless* man.

Blamelessness signifies a lifestyle characterized by righteousness, but it does not mean that perfection has been achieved. Job's downward-spiraling despair turns his focus upon God, who is silent but not absent, and accusations begin to loom large. Rather than searching his heart to pursue greater righteousness, Job raises a smoke screen and begins to accuse God of injustice:

> *"I say to God: Do not declare me guilty, but tell me what charges you have against me...Are your days like those of a mortal or your years like those of a strong man, that you must search out my faults and probe after my sin—though you know that I am not guilty and that no one can rescue me from your hand?"*
> (Job 10:2,5-7).

Some criminals use smoke screens when they commit crimes. Setting off a smoke bomb serves as camouflage—a diversion and a covering for illegal behavior. Smoke screens are specifically designed to obscure, confuse, and mislead others.

Can you think of a time when you used a smoke screen to divert attention away from your own flaws—hiding your wrongs behind a "wall of smoke"? Having a critical spirit not only draws attention away from your own faults, but also focuses attention on the faults of others in an attempt to increase your sense of self-worth.

For example, if you are harboring bitterness, you might blame others for your bitter spirit. If you have selfish ambition and envy what others have, you could be overly critical of their success. These are both classic smoke screens. But look at what the Bible says:

> *"If you harbor bitter envy and selfish ambition in your hearts, do not boast about it or deny the truth"*
> (James 3:14).

THE SMOKE SCREEN

A critical spirit is evident based on a combination of classic characteristics that critical people exhibit. The following list will help you recognize and better understand those who have a critical spirit. In addition, you can use it as a personal test to gain insight into your own smoke screens.

S — **SPREADING** harmful gossip with the justification that "everyone ought to know"

M—**MAKING** others feel embarrassed about their success while secretly envying them

O—**OBJECTING** to criticism from others to avoid personal accountability

K— **KIDDING** someone with the intent to hurt

E— **ENGAGING** in "constructive" criticism when the criticism is in no way constructive

S— **SHIFTING** blame to someone else when you yourself are to blame

C—**CRITICIZING** someone's happiness because you are unhappy

R—**REMINDING** others of their past failures to avoid attracting attention to your failures

E— **EMPLOYING** sarcastic humor as a weapon to attack

E— **ELEVATING** yourself by putting others down

N—**NURTURING** perfectionistic tendencies to make yourself look better

What a picture Jesus paints of the faultfinder! Imagine a beam of wood embedded in your eye. It's too large for you to dislodge without immense pain. It's too terrifying to think of other people prying it out. The solution seems simple: Ignore it…deny it…create a smoke screen so no one will notice it. But you can't hide the beam from the Lord. That's why in the Gospel of Luke, Jesus says,

> *"Why do you look at the speck of sawdust in your brother's eye*
> *and pay no attention to the plank in your own eye?*
> *How can you say to your brother, 'Brother, let me take the speck out*
> *of your eye,' when you yourself fail to see the plank in your own eye?*
> *You hypocrite, first take the plank out of your eye, and then you*
> *will see clearly to remove the speck from your brother's eye"*
> (LUKE 6:41-42).

===== *A Wife's Faultfinding Friends* =====

QUESTION: "What can I say to friends who bad-mouth my husband? The things they say about him keep me focused on his faults."

ANSWER: Set boundaries with your friends as to what you will and will not listen to in regard to your husband.

- *Explain* that you have determined to switch your focus from your husband's faults to his needs...and to pray that your husband would let the Lord meet his deepest inner needs.

- *Elicit* their help—ask them to help you dwell on his positive traits. If your friends continue to be negative, they are not real friends, and you may need to limit your time with them.

- *Express* your concern with a pleasant voice: "I realize what you are saying is true, but I cannot change him; only God can do that."

- *Emphasize* your course of action: "I am choosing to thank God that (__mention a positive quality: He is a good provider, or he is good to the children__). Help me focus on his positive traits and pray that he will allow God to correct his faults, which is what God's Word tells me to do."

> *"Above all, love each other deeply,*
> *because love covers over a multitude of sins"*
> (1 PETER 4:8).

C. What Are Camouflaged Characteristics of a Critical Spirit?

Zophar (Zo) is tired of sitting on the sidelines—he wants to demonstrate his "superior" understanding of God's ways before Job.

With a harsher tone than the other two friends, and through the use of put-downs and slander, Zo wants to silence Job once and for all, hoping he'll finally admit gross sins have brought great tragedy to his life. "Are all these words to go unanswered? Is this talker to be vindicated? Will your idle talk reduce others to silence? Will no one rebuke you when you mock?" (Job 11:2-3).

And then slipping into vicious sarcasm, Zo insinuates Job is witless and that he has as much of a chance to become wise as a donkey has of giving birth to a person:

> *"But the witless can no more become wise than*
> *a wild donkey's colt can be born human"*
> (JOB 11:12).

Most people who display a critical spirit appear strong to the average observer because of the boldness with which they spew out their critical comments. In truth, criticism is more often the weapon of the weak than of the strong. It serves both to disguise their perceived inner deficiencies and to deceive others into thinking they are self-assured and confident.

Yet the Bible says,

> *"Blessed is the one whose sin the LORD does not count against them*
> *and in whose spirit is no deceit"*
> (PSALM 32:2).

People who possess a critical spirit have certain characteristics that are camouflaged—not evident to most people. These camouflaged characteristics include...

C—CONCEALING personal hurts and hopes out of distrust and fear of being abandoned

A—ALLOWING no one to get close enough to know the real person because of a fear of being rejected and scorned

M—MAKING others feel guilty when they are not in an effort to conceal or minimize their own guilt

O—OBTAINING revenge for personal offenses in order to even the score and feel a sense of power, control, and self-respect

U—USING put-downs and slander to hurt others in an attempt to feel superior and significant

F—FEELING they are better than others to increase self-esteem and diminish feelings of inferiority

L—LOVING to be "one up" on others to establish a position of control and to compensate for feeling vulnerable or like a victim

A—ASSUMING they are always right because being wrong is totally demeaning and demoralizing

G—GIVING little or no thought to the needs of others as a result of expending too much mental and emotional energy on meeting personal needs

E—ENJOYING few pleasures in life because the pressing need to be hypervigilant robs them of life's enjoyments

Those who attempt to conceal these classic characteristics constantly hide the truth from themselves and others. Unable to meet a certain standard, they attempt to pull others down to their level. They may succeed in hiding the truth from themselves and others, but they can never hide from God. He not only sees their sin, He also knows their need:

> *"You, God, know my folly;*
> *my guilt is not hidden from you"*
> (PSALM 69:5).

No Wire Hangers: The Joan Crawford Story[7]

This angry outcry ignites an image of a mother's meltdown. But not just any mother. To those familiar with the story, a famous film star displays an irrational repulsion to her daughter's dainty dress hanging on a cheap wire hanger. Who can forget the terrified look in her little girl's eyes as she succumbs to the stinging hits of the hangers?

But for Hollywood star Joan Crawford, image is everything and perfectionism permeates her life—perfection no matter what the cost. According to her adopted daughter Christina Crawford, "What my mother wanted was fans and puppies, not human beings...She was as close to being a totally manufactured person as I've ever met."[8]

Christina's depiction of her mother's erratic, hypercritical behavior rocked the literary world in her 1978 autobiography titled *Mommie Dearest*. The tell-all book cracked the Hollywood façade and spawned similar "bad parent" publications about Bette Davis and Bing Crosby. (Thirty years later, Christina rereleased an anniversary edition of her book with new material and photos.)

At age 13, Christina stopped believing her mother had any love for her. She simply couldn't escape painful memories of Joan grabbing her by the throat, punching her in the face, slamming her head against the floor. "You never forget that," Christina reflects. "It was up close and personal. She came this far from my face, and you could see it in her eyes, you can see if someone is trying to kill you."[9]

All the while, Christina was ordered to address her mother as Mommie Dearest. As Christina grew older, she resented the hypocrisy of her own public role in contrast to her private reality. "People fantasized about who or what I was; that I had this privileged, wealthy film-star family life. I didn't have any of that."[10]

Joan Crawford's critical spirit, her excessive control, had everything to do with her public image—after all, she perceived herself as a self-made woman who had much to lose. From an impoverished background, she became a leading Hollywood star in the 1940s with a film career spanning almost five decades, including an Academy Award for best actress. Her striking features and strong persona continually kept her in the forefront of the celebrity world.

Behind the scenes, Joan was a harsh, critical alcoholic prone to sporadic outbursts of violence that were usually aimed at Christina and her adopted brother, Christopher. With the later adoption of twin girls, this apparent benevolence brought Joan much sought-after publicity and impressive magazine spreads.

Lurking below the intriguing exterior, though, was this dark and overly critical side which was always more flagrant at Christmas. Celebrity magazines featured the piles of presents lavished upon the Crawford children. But in reality, they were only allowed to keep one gift. The rest were sent to charities and hospitals—a conspicuous example of generous giving, but in the eyes of an excessively criticized child, an example of cruel parenting.

Nonetheless, Joan made the children write thank-you notes for *all* the gifts, and then she painstakingly edited the cards and returned them to the children for correction. "The process was turned into a forced march," noted Christina. "It was all about power and deprivation. As a child, I was totally without trust. I felt entirely alone."[11] The tender truth is that a parent's critical spirit will crush the heart of any child.

Christina recalls her mother's violent mood swings. One moment she lavished her with new party dresses, then the next, she spanked her so hard with a hairbrush that it broke in two. Christopher was strapped into bed at night with a canvas harness to keep him from walking to the toilet. By age 11, he had run away several times.[12] Any infraction was always met with disproportionate punishment.[13]

Some public criticism surfaced, claiming Joan was excessively strict with her children. She responded: "I've tried to provide my children with what I didn't have: constructive discipline, a sense of security, a sense of sharing. Sloppiness has never been tolerated in our home, nor has rudeness. They're going into a world that isn't easy, a world where unless you're self-sufficient and strong, you can be destroyed."[14] How ironic that what Joan called "constructive discipline" was instead constant criticism (also called verbal and emotional abuse) which was the precursor to horrifying physical abuse.

After Joan Crawford died of a heart attack in May 1977 in her New York City apartment, Christina and Christopher learned they both had been disinherited. Joan's will stated, "It is my intention to make no provision herein for my son Christopher or my daughter Christina for reasons which are well-known to them."[15]

Unquestionably, Joan's own difficult childhood contributed to the harsh, critical spirit that sought retribution, even after death. Her own father abandoned the family shortly after Joan's birth. A stepfather—reportedly an embezzler or, even worse, a child abuser—also walked out. Then there was the harsh headmistress at the boarding school where Joan and her mother both worked to cover Joan's tuition. After being abandoned by yet another lover, Joan's mother was involved with a man who was alternately critical and crassly inappropriate with young Joan.[16]

Some who have been abused perpetuate the cycle of abuse as perpetrators themselves. And they attempt to justify their wrongful actions by rationalizing, "It's what I grew up with. I can't help it—it's all I know."

But think about it—do all abused children grow up to abuse others? No! Must all who have been overly criticized become overly critical? Again, no.

Therefore, is there anything that would eradicate all excessive criticism, all malicious mistreatment, all devastating abuse?

Rather than following the world's credo of "Do to others *what* has been done to you," or adopting the sarcastic humor of "Do to others *before* they do it to you," Jesus offers an altogether different alternative. It's known as the Golden Rule. He calls us all to "Do to others what you would have them do to you" (Matthew 7:12).

Quite simply, if this Scripture were lived out in people's lives, it would literally change the world.

III. Causes of a Critical Spirit

In exhibiting their critical spirits, Job's three friends seem to be struggling for a sense of superiority and a desire to be proven right in their allegation that Job is indeed a sinner who is a victim of God's disciplinary hand.

Might jealousy have been at play? At one time Job was labeled "the greatest man among all the people of the East" (Job 1:3). But as he holds on to his integrity, Job knows his status now has hit rock bottom:

> *"I have become a laughingstock to my friends,*
> *though I called on God and he answered—*
> *a mere laughingstock, though righteous and blameless!"*
> (Job 12:4).

A critical spirit is created and nurtured by past experiences—it doesn't just appear out of nowhere. But what kinds of experiences foster this flaw? When you associate with people with a critical spirit, first look beyond the present to the past. What could have produced their critical spirit, and what continues to perpetuate it? Scripture points to the source of ungodly behavior:

> *"What causes fights and quarrels among you?*
> *Don't they come from your desires that battle within you?*
> *You desire but do not have…"*
> (James 4:1-2).

A. What Was Modeled in Childhood?

What was life like for Eli, Bill, and Zo growing up? Were they nurtured in a loving environment, or did caustic words of criticism compose much of their days?

It's curious that none of the three friends rises to Job's defense in the midst of the verbal bombardment taking place. They seem to feed off of each other as they destroy an already-crushed man's spirit.

But the call of God's Word is…

> *"Defend the weak and the fatherless; uphold the cause*
> *of the poor and the oppressed. Rescue the weak and the*
> *needy; deliver them from the hand of the wicked"*
> (Psalm 82:3-4).

The most common cause of a critical spirit is living in a home where criticism abounds and where parents model a critical spirit before their children. Growing up in such a home can cause a child to become overly critical in adulthood. After all, with children, more is caught than taught.

Those who have a critical spirit cause others to have a heavy heart. What happens when children are continually crushed by critical words? Their sense of self-worth is suffocated, and eventually they get stuck in a self-defeated state.

Ultimately, critical parents provoke many children to anger—children who, under the weight of such provocation, develop caustic patterns of throwing critical stones at others. The book of Proverbs presents a poignant word picture of the damaging weight produced by a person who intentionally provokes others to feel or act negatively:

> *"Stone is heavy and sand a burden, but a fool's*
> *provocation is heavier than both"*
> (PROVERBS 27:3).

A critical spirit is molded under the weight of:

– Unanticipated anger	– Ungrounded guilt
– Unremitting stress	– Unjust rejection
– Undeserved condemnation	– Unmerited blame
– Undue pressure	– Unreasonable control
– Unending fear	– Unsubstantiated accusation
– Unfair comparison	– Unwarranted attacks

Typically those who live under the pressure of continual criticism feel the excess weight of false guilt. In truth, they could easily have written these words:

> *"My guilt has overwhelmed me like a burden too heavy to bear"*
> (PSALM 38:4).

B. What Are Childhood Wounds?

Job has discovered for himself that there is no bigger lie than the old childhood adage: "Sticks and stones may break my bones but words will never hurt me."

The accusing words of Eli, Bill, and Zo are delivering blow after blow to Job's spirit. They relentlessly accuse Job of being a sinner and associate shame with his contemptible condition. Zo misguidedly assures,

*"If you put away the sin that is in your hand and allow no
evil to dwell in your tent, then, free of fault, you will lift
up your face; you will stand firm and without fear"*
(Job 11:14-15).

"Sticks and stones may break my bones but words will never hurt me." Yes, what a lie! This old saying could not be further from the truth. Critical comments can cause extensive, even lifetime, harm. No visible wounds will show, but the damage to the spirit of a child can be devastating.

Many children who are assaulted with wounding words resort to criticism as a means of self-defense. To try to lessen the impact of emotional pain, they stay on the attack.

When painful words are played over and over in children's minds, they often want to retaliate. This explains why so many "hurt people...*hurt people*"! Children who are raised in an overly critical home experience great emotional pain.

"I am poor and needy, and my heart is wounded within me"
(Psalm 109:22).

Emotionally hurt children feel the pain of:

H—Harshness, which communicates, "You're not worth consideration."

U—Unconcern, which communicates, "You have no value."

R—Rejection, which communicates, "You're not acceptable."

T—Taunting, which communicates, "You deserve to be insulted."

A critical spirit is often a defense tactic. Typically, if one child hits another, the second hits back. Striking back when attacked is a natural defensive response.

Similarly, a child "hit" by criticism can become skilled in verbal attacks as a means of defense. However, if you want to be blessed with positive relationships, staying on the attack never solves a problem. That is why the Bible says,

*"Do not repay evil with evil or
insult with insult.
On the contrary,
repay evil with blessing,
because to this you were called so that you
may inherit a blessing"*
(1 Peter 3:9).

C. What Is the Cycle of Criticism?

Job has had enough, and hopes to quiet his friends-turned-accusers once and for all.

"You, however, smear me with lies; you are worthless physicians, all of you! If only you would be altogether silent! For you, that would be wisdom" (Job 13:4-5). But the cycle of criticism continues. All three friends keep up the verbal pounding, which prompts this battered man to plead before his God,

> *"Only grant me these two things, God, and then*
> *I will not hide from you: Withdraw your hand far from me,*
> *and stop frightening me with your terrors"*
> (JOB 13:20-21).

The painful situations we experience as children are processed by our soul—our mind, will, and emotions. Over time, we can develop a negative pattern of reacting to these painful situations (becoming critical), a pattern that can remain with us into and throughout our adulthood. We must rely on the transforming work of the Holy Spirit within us to help us overcome a critical spirit.

You may exclaim, "I can't help acting this way!" Yet your emotions are merely *responders* to what your mind thinks. Therefore, the cycle is this: Your negative thoughts produce your negative emotions, which in turn, produce your negative actions.

Since the cycle of criticism begins in our thoughts, we need to heed what the Bible tells us about renewing our minds and actually appropriate the mind of Christ. With God's help we can change our thoughts and then literally experience a changed life. Scripture says it this way:

> *"'Who has known the mind of the Lord so as to instruct him?'*
> *But we have the mind of Christ...*
> *Do not conform to the pattern of this world,*
> *but be transformed by the renewing of your mind"*
> (1 CORINTHIANS 2:16; ROMANS 12:2).

Whenever a negative situation occurs in your life, you have a choice as to how you will think about it (which will determine how you respond). Children develop patterns of thinking that dictate feelings and, as a result, actions. The natural progression occurs as follows:

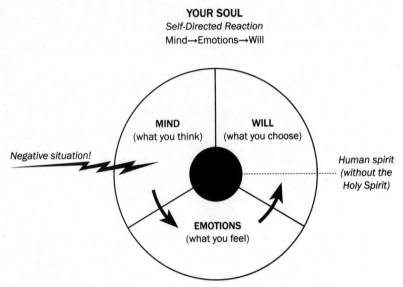

YOUR SOUL
Self-Directed Reaction
Mind→Emotions→Will

ILLUSTRATION #1

Negative Situation: Someone verbally cuts you down.

NATURAL HUMAN RESPONSE

- *Your mind* records the cruel words and thinks angry thoughts. ("He's so hateful.")
- *Your emotions* respond with angry feelings. ("I hate him.")
- *Your will* reacts with angry behavior. (You act in hateful ways.)

> *"Those who live according to the flesh have their minds set on what the flesh desires... The mind governed by the flesh is death"*
> (ROMANS 8:5-6).

- **Mind:** Many children develop a critical spirit because of the way they process the pain in their lives, and this process is naturally influenced by the ways the significant people in their lives have processed their own pain. (Children often do what was modeled before them.)

- **Emotions:** Because children are not physically or emotionally mature enough to analyze their thinking process, they base their decisions more on emotions than on reasoning. By the time children have developed their capacity for analysis and reasoning, their patterns of reacting are already established.

– **Will:** If you desire to change from being overly critical, you must begin by changing the way you think about God, people, and the events in your life. When you are led by the Spirit of God as to what is *right* to think, your emotional responses will be *right*, and then your choices will be *right*. You will respond in the Spirit, and your responses will be godly. The process will occur as follows:

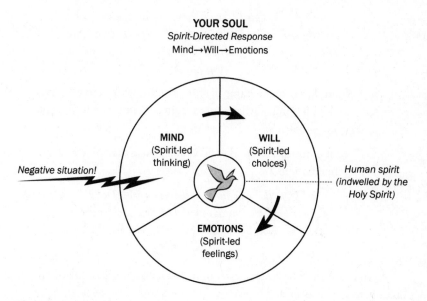

YOUR SOUL
Spirit-Directed Response
Mind→Will→Emotions

MIND
(Spirit-led thinking)

WILL
(Spirit-led choices)

Negative situation!

Human spirit
(indwelled by the Holy Spirit)

EMOTIONS
(Spirit-led feelings)

ILLUSTRATION #2

Negative Situation: Someone verbally cuts you down.

SPIRIT-LED RESPONSE

– **Your mind** records the unjust words, and the Holy Spirit, as your Counselor, teaches your mind how to think about the offense.

> *"The Counselor, the Holy Spirit—the Father will
> send Him in My name—will teach you all things
> and remind you of everything I have told you"*
> (John 14:26 hcsb).

"His words were so hateful. But there must be something painfully broken in his life. I will do what the Bible tells me to do—I need to 'pray for those who persecute [me]'"(read Matthew 5:44).

— **Your will** acts with prayer as the Spirit directs your will toward the right choice. As your conscience, He convicts you to pray, whether you feel like it or not.

> *"When he, the Spirit of truth, comes, he will guide you into
> all the truth. He will not speak on his own; he will speak
> only what he hears, and he will tell you what is yet to come"*
> (John 16:13).

"Lord, I pray that (_name of critic_) will allow You to meet the need for healing of whatever past pain is still causing (_name of critic_) problems."

— **Your emotions** respond with compassion as the Spirit controls your emotions.

> *"Hope does not put us to shame, because God's
> love has been poured out into our hearts through
> the Holy Spirit, who has been given to us"*
> (Romans 5:5).

As you pray, the Comforter evokes from you loving compassion toward the unjust person who is spiritually needy:

> *"Those who live in accordance with the Spirit
> have their minds set on what the Spirit desires...
> the mind governed by the Spirit is life and peace"*
> (Romans 8:5-6).

D. What Family Dynamics Foster a Critical Spirit?

The intolerant trio are relentless in their criticism of Job. Their destructive habits were no doubt nurtured in critical environments.

Eli inquires, "Would a wise person answer with empty notions or fill their belly with the hot east wind? Would they argue with useless words, with speeches that have no value?" (Job 15:2-3). Bill follows up with his own set of degrading questions: "When will you end these speeches? Be sensible, and then we can talk. Why are we regarded as cattle and considered stupid in your sight? You who tear yourselves to pieces in your anger, is the earth to be abandoned for your sake?" (Job 18:2-4).

And Zo makes an arrogant declaration: "My troubled thoughts prompt me to answer because I am greatly disturbed. I hear a rebuke that dishonors me, and my understanding inspires me to reply" (Job 20:2-3).

Job has two words for his three contentious counselors:

> *"Miserable comforters!"*
> (Job 16:2).

Dysfunctional families produce dysfunctional family members. Typically, a child growing up with a controlling, critical parent becomes either a controlling, critical adult or a controlled, cowering adult.

Children who have been powerless to stop unjust criticism can feel the need for power in order to keep from feeling powerless again. They feel the need to be controlling to keep from feeling out of control. Therefore, they adopt a critical spirit to maintain a sense of power and control. But beneath this detrimental demeanor is fearful insecurity.

Scripture gives this admonishment:

> *"Fathers, do not embitter your children,*
> *or they will become discouraged"*
> (Colossians 3:21).

THE OVERLY-CONTROLLED CRITICAL FAMILY[17]

- **The Structure:**

  - The tone is authoritative and dictatorial.
  - The emotional climate is rigid.
  - The parent (one or both) is faultfinding and critical.
  - The value of family members is based on their performance.
  - The love given within the family is conditional.
  - The child is fearful, angry, and task-oriented.

- **The Result:**

  The family members become fearful and insensitive—and can, by example, develop a critical spirit.

- **The Remedy:**

  "Fathers, do not exasperate your children; instead, bring them up in the training and instruction of the Lord" (Ephesians 6:4).

We cannot change the family into which we were born. However, God presents us with a unique, unparalleled opportunity—a remedy to keep us from being insecure and overly critical. The solution for fearful insecurity is to be adopted into another family—a balanced, healthy, functional family where love is unconditional, where our worth is God-given, where our value is inherent, where our security is eternal.

By God's design, our deepest need is to be adopted into His family. In fact, we are told that this is God's perfect plan for us:

> *"In love he predestined us for adoption to sonship*
> *through Jesus Christ, in accordance with his pleasure and will—*
> *to the praise of his glorious grace, which he has freely given*
> *us in the One he loves"*
> (Ephesians 1:4-6).

E. What Is the Root Cause of a Critical Spirit?

As Job is berated by his accusatory companions, he begins to develop a critical spirit toward God that borders on blasphemy.

He accuses God of denying him justice and makes a daring proclamation: "Oh, that I had someone to hear me! I sign now my defense—let the Almighty answer me; let my accuser put his indictment in writing. Surely I would wear it on my shoulder, I would put it on like a crown. I would give him an account of my every step; I would present it to him as to a ruler" (Job 31:35-37).

Self-centeredness and self-righteousness have surfaced in this man of God. The Bible warns,

> *"If we claim to be without sin, we deceive ourselves*
> *and the truth is not in us"*
> (1 John 1:8).

In essence, the sin committed by Adam and Eve in the Garden of Eden was *self-centeredness*—the desire for self-sufficiency and self-will apart from God's will, the desire to take on God's role and to be in total control. Self-will and desire for control has been passed on to everyone in the human family.

This inherent sin nature in unbelievers and the residual sinful patterns in believers cause those with a critical spirit to see others as inferior and in need of knowing when they are at fault. This is the essence of a critical spirit: assuming a superior role of faultfinding with a derogatory view of others.

In the Garden of Eden, God asked Adam to give an account of himself. Although Adam knew he had sinned, he first blamed God for giving him Eve, then blamed Eve for giving him the infamous forbidden fruit.

> *"The man said, 'The woman you put here with me—*
> *she gave me some fruit from the tree, and I ate it'"*
> (GENESIS 3:12).

Adam was the first but certainly not the last to shift blame to God—and then to someone else—rather than taking personal responsibility for his own wrong choice.

For some with a critical spirit, putting others down creates a false sense of significance—a sense of power, a sense of pride—at least temporarily. For them the Bible warns,

> *"When pride comes, then comes disgrace, but with*
> *humility comes wisdom"*
> (PROVERBS 11:2).

THREE GOD-GIVEN INNER NEEDS

We have all been created with three God-given inner needs: the needs for love, significance, and security.[18]

- **Love**—to know that someone is unconditionally committed to our best interest

> *"My command is this: Love each other as I have loved you"*
> (JOHN 15:12).

- **Significance**—to know that our lives have meaning and purpose

> *"I cry out to God Most High, to God who fulfills his purpose for me"*
> (PSALM 57:2 ESV).

- **Security**—to feel accepted and a sense of belonging

> *"Whoever fears the LORD has a secure fortress,*
> *and for their children it will be a refuge"*
> (PROVERBS 14:26).

THE ULTIMATE NEED-MEETER

Why did God give us these deep inner needs, knowing that people and self-effort fail us?

God gave us these inner needs so that we would come to know Him as our Need-meeter. Our needs are designed by God to draw us into a deeper dependence on Christ. God did not create any person or position or any amount of power or possessions to meet the deepest needs in our lives. If a person or thing *could* meet all our needs, we wouldn't need God! The Lord will use circumstances to bring positive people into our lives as an extension of His care and compassion, but ultimately, only God can satisfy all the needs of our hearts. The Bible says,

> *"The LORD will guide you always;*
> *he will satisfy your needs in a sun-scorched land*
> *and will strengthen your frame.*
> *You will be like a well-watered garden,*
> *like a spring whose waters never fail"*
> (ISAIAH 58:11).

The apostle Paul revealed this truth by first asking, "What a wretched man I am. Who will rescue me from this body that is subject to death?" He then answers his own question by saying he is rescued by "Jesus Christ our Lord!" (Romans 7:24-25).

All along, the Lord planned to meet our deepest needs for...

- **Love**—"I [the LORD] have loved you with an everlasting love; I have drawn you with unfailing kindness" (Jeremiah 31:3).
- **Significance**—"'For I know the plans I have for you,' declares the LORD, 'plans to prosper you and not to harm you, plans to give you hope and a future'" (Jeremiah 29:11).
- **Security**—"The LORD himself goes before you and will be with you; he will never leave you nor forsake you. Do not be afraid; do not be discouraged" (Deuteronomy 31:8).

The truth is that our God-given needs for love, significance, and security can be legitimately met—in Christ Jesus! Philippians 4:19 makes it plain:

> *"My God will meet all your needs according to*
> *the riches of his glory in Christ Jesus."*

- **Wrong Belief:**

"My sense of significance is increased when I point out the wrongs of others. The fact that I believe 'I am right' justifies my criticism of others." But the Bible says,

> *"You, therefore, have no excuse, you who pass*
> *judgment on someone else, for at whatever point you*
> *judge another, you are condemning yourself, because*
> *you who pass judgment do the same things"*
> (ROMANS 2:1).

- **Right Belief:**

"When I am critical of others, I am actually exposing my own sin. If Christ lives in me, continually extending His mercy toward me, I will reflect His compassion by caring about the needs of others rather than by criticizing them." The Bible says,

> *"Encourage the disheartened, help the weak, be*
> *patient with everyone. Make sure that nobody pays*
> *back wrong for wrong, but always strive to do what*
> *is good for each other and for everyone else"*
> (1 THESSALONIANS 5:14-15).

F. How Can You Escape Criticism Throughout Eternity?

In the midst of suffering, Job seems to sway between what he knows about God and what he feels about Him. Job *knows* God isn't unjust, but it *feels* like He's unjust. The book of Job is renowned for a mighty proclamation of faith that has inspired strugglers all around the world. Here, Job expresses what he knows about God:

> *"I know that my redeemer lives, and that in the end he will*
> *stand on the earth. And after my skin has been destroyed, yet in my*

will see God; I myself will see him with my own eyes—
and not another. How my heart yearns within me!"
(JOB 19:25-27).

If you're in despair from critical, caustic words, there is Someone right now who is eagerly waiting to have a relationship with you, and He will never, ever criticize. God is inviting you into His family, and be assured you'll never hear a single critical word in the heavenly home that awaits. God wants to bring you hope and healing, and He wants to save you from eternal condemnation.

When you enter into a right relationship with God, you are spiritually adopted into the family of Christ and will always be loved, esteemed, and honored. The Bible says,

> *"There is now no condemnation for those who are in Christ Jesus"*
> (ROMANS 8:1).

Scripture gives us four spiritual truths for beginning a relationship with God. He has graciously provided a way to bridge the spiritual gap that separates Him from us.

FOUR POINTS OF GOD'S PLAN: BRIDGING THE SPIRITUAL GAP

1. God's Purpose for You Is *Salvation*.

– What was God's motivation in sending Jesus Christ to earth?

To express His love for you by saving you! The Bible says,

> *"God so loved the world that he gave his one and only Son,*
> *that whoever believes in him shall not perish but have*
> *eternal life. For God did not send his Son into the world to*
> *condemn the world, but to save the world through him"*
> (JOHN 3:16-17).

– What was Jesus' purpose in coming to earth?

To bridge the gap that separates you from God, to forgive your sins, to empower you to have victory over sin, and to enable you to live a fulfilled life. Jesus said,

> *"I have come that they may have life, and that*
> *they may have it more abundantly"*
> (JOHN 10:10 NKJV).

2. Your Problem Is *Sin.*

– What exactly is sin?

Sin is the "gap" that separates you from God. Sin means living independently of God's standard—knowing what is right, but choosing what is wrong. The Bible says,

> *"If anyone, then, knows the good they ought to*
> *do and doesn't do it, it is sin for them"*
> (JAMES 4:17).

– What is the major consequence of sin?

Spiritual death, or eternal separation from God, with no way to reach Him. Scripture states,

> *"Your iniquities [sins] have separated you from*
> *your God... The wages of sin is death, but the gift*
> *of God is eternal life in Christ Jesus our Lord"*
> (ISAIAH 59:2; ROMANS 6:23).

3. God's Provision for You Is the *Savior.*

– Can anything remove the penalty for sin and build a bridge to God?

Yes! Jesus died on the cross to personally pay the penalty for your sins. He alone can bridge the sin gap that separates us from God. The Bible says,

> *"God demonstrates his own love for us in this:*
> *While we were still sinners, Christ died for us"*
> (ROMANS 5:8).

– What is the solution to being separated from God?

Belief in (entrusting your life to) Jesus Christ as the only way to God the Father. Jesus says,

> *"I am the way and the truth and the life. No one*
> *comes to the Father except through me...Believe*
> *in the Lord Jesus, and you will be saved"*
> (JOHN 14:6; ACTS 16:31).

4. Your Part Is *Surrender.*

– Give Christ control of your life, entrusting yourself to Him:

> *"Jesus said to his disciples, 'Whoever wants to be my*
> *disciple must deny themselves and take up their cross*
> *[die to your own self-rule] and follow me. For whoever*
> *wants to save their life will lose it, but whoever loses their*
> *life for me will find it. What good will it be for someone*
> *to gain the whole world, yet forfeit their soul?'"*
> (Matthew 16:24-26).

– Place your faith in (rely on) Jesus Christ as your personal Lord
and Savior and reject your "good works" as a means of earning
God's approval and bridging the sin gap.

> *"It is by grace you have been saved, through faith—*
> *and this not from yourselves, it is the gift of God—*
> *not by works, so that no one can boast"*
> (Ephesians 2:8-9).

The moment you choose to receive Jesus as your Lord and Savior—entrusting your life to Him—He builds a bridge enabling Him to live inside you forever. Then He gives you His power to live the fulfilled life God has planned for you. If you want to be fully forgiven by God and become the person God created you to be, you can tell Him in a simple, heartfelt prayer like this:

Prayer of Salvation

"God, I want a real relationship with You.
I admit that many times I've chosen to go my own way instead of Your way.
Please forgive me for my sins.
Jesus, thank You for dying on the cross to pay the penalty for my sins.
Come into my life to be my Lord and my Savior.
Change me from the inside out and make me the person
You created me to be.
In Your holy name I pray. Amen."

What Can You Now Expect?

If you sincerely prayed the above prayer, look at what God says about you!

"Very truly I tell you, whoever hears my word and believes him
who sent me has eternal life and will not be judged
but has crossed over from death to life"
(JOHN 5:24).

IV. STEPS TO SOLUTION

God is using Job's traumatic trials to bring sin to the surface and to transform Job into an even more blameless man of God. He is Job's "heavenly sandpaper," and as tough as Job's tragic experiences are, they will not lead to his death. In fact, blessing is just around the corner.

Like Job, everyone needs a little "heavenly sandpaper" in life, people who help gently point out the rough edges in us. But too much sanding can leave you feeling worn down and emotionally raw. Without a doubt, God will use our close relationships to teach us truths about ourselves—truths about our rough edges—but rather than wearing us down, He intends to raise us up. Rather than leaving us discouraged, He wants to encourage us toward positive change.

It's important to be receptive to the fact that constructive criticism can reveal specific areas in our lives that need to be refined. When you try to give constructive criticism, be absolutely certain God has directed your words and that they are spoken in truth and with love. And when *you* are criticized, ask God and perhaps others if a rough edge exists in you that needs to be sanded.

However, if criticism of you is incorrect, be calm, not critical or curt. The book of Proverbs makes this point plain:

"A person's wisdom yields patience; it is to one's glory
to overlook an offense"
(PROVERBS 19:11).

A. Key Verse to Memorize

All four men—Job and his fault-finding friends—three companions—failed to season their words with "salt" for the prevention of insipid, distasteful conversation (see Colossians 4:6). Rather than their conversations being full of grace, they were full of festering frustration. The unholy trio was determined to get Job to own up to his supposed guilt, and Job was just as determined to maintain his integrity.

Job describes his friends' words as "meaningless talk" (Job 27:12) and digs his heels in the sand: "I will never admit you are in the right; till I die, I will not deny my integrity. I will maintain my innocence and never let go of it; my conscience will not reproach me as long as I live" (Job 27:5-6).

Whether you give constructive criticism or receive it, the Bible says you are to

> *"let your conversation be always full of grace, seasoned with salt,*
> *so that you may know how to answer everyone"*
> (COLOSSIANS 4:6).

Known as "white gold" in ancient times, salt is still highly valued today. Previously used as money for commercial trade, today salt is used (1) to *season* food in homes and restaurants around the globe, (2) to *clean* cuts and abrasions as a disinfectant, (3) to *melt* ice on roads and sidewalks and help prevent accidents, and (4) to *preserve* food (in the absence of refrigeration) from quickly spoiling.

When the Bible says, "Let your conversation be...seasoned with salt," envision the "salt" of your words being used wisely to...

- *Produce* enhanced enjoyment within all your special relationships
- *Purify* your wounded relationships by speaking healing, grace-filled words
- *Prevent* the accidental slip of the tongue and the use of caustic, critical words
- *Preserve* your reputation and keeping it from being spoiled

Scripture reminds us:

> *"You are the salt of the earth. But if the salt loses its saltiness,*
> *how can it be made salty again?*
> *It is no longer good for anything, except to be thrown*
> *out and trampled underfoot"*
> (MATTHEW 5:13).

B. Key Passage to Read

The piercing power of the tongue is evidenced by Job and his jabbing friends, but it turns out there's been someone waiting in the wings for a chance to speak out, to use his own tongue in an attempt to impart truth.

Elihu (Hugh for short), the youngest of the friends who comes to visit Job, is "very angry" (Job 32:2) with all four men. Concerning his friends, none of the three had found a way to refute Job, yet they all condemned him. Hugh's issue with Job concerned the implications and outright declarations that God is unfair and unjust.

Hugh is the voice of reason amidst a torrent of emotion:

> *"So listen to me, you men of understanding. Far be it from God*
> *to do evil, from the Almighty to do wrong…It is unthinkable that*
> *God would do wrong, that the Almighty would pervert justice"*
> (Job 34:10,12).

Isn't it interesting how small objects can possess great power? The power of the tongue seems far out of proportion to its size. A large horse is controlled by a little bit in its mouth, and an enormous ship is controlled by a small rudder. James 3:5 says,

> *"Likewise, the tongue is a small part of the body,*
> *but it makes great boasts. Consider what a great*
> *forest is set on fire by a small spark."*

There is much we can learn from James 3:3-12. The tongue, though tiny, can be…

- **Powerful**—like a bit, turning a huge horse . . . . verse 3

- **Forceful**—like a rudder, steering a massive ship. . . . . verse 4

- **Dangerous**—like a spark, igniting a great forest . . . . verse 5

- **Devastating**—like a fire, burning the whole body . . . . verse 6

- **Corrupting**—like a force of evil, instigated by hell . . . . . . verse 6

- **Untamable**—like a restless evil, full of deadly poison. . . . . verse 8

- **Polluted**—like a hypocrite, both praising and
  criticizing others . . . . verse 10

- **Revealing**—like an instrument, showing whether the
  heart is impure . . . . verse 12

Based on the Bible, let's face this fact: Polluted water and pure water cannot pour out of the same stream. Yet if words of praise are ascending up to God from the same mouth as curses upon others, something is terribly wrong with the source. The heart is impure.

The main message is this: When you control your tongue, you control your body.

C. How to Stop Growing a Crop of Criticism

Even though Elihu (Hugh) eloquently espouses truths about the character and ways of God, he himself grows a crop of criticism where Job is concerned and wrongly assesses the cause of his tragic circumstances.

"Is there anyone like Job, who drinks scorn like water? He keeps company with evildoers; he associates with the wicked" (Job 34:7-8). Hugh, too, presses to move Job to conviction and repentance, making the following proclamation: "Now you are laden with the judgment due the wicked; judgment and justice have taken hold of you" (Job 36:17).

But the criticism will come to a stop when God speaks.

> *"God's voice thunders in marvelous ways;*
> *he does great things beyond our understanding"*
> (Job 37:5).

You can grow a "crop of criticism" even if you're usually not a critical person. These "crops" can suddenly sprout up based on circumstances in which you cast a critical eye or turn a critical ear. The source of your criticism is resentment toward others, so you're eager to point out the flaws of others. You may not recognize when you are being overly critical, but God does—and so do those who know you best. The Bible even says,

> *"All a person's ways seem pure to them, but motives*
> *are weighed by the LORD"*
> (Proverbs 16:2).

If you desire to quit growing your crop of criticism, first pray that you will see your "seeds" of criticism from God's perspective. Then ask yourself:

- What causes me to become critical?
- What kind of looks do I give when I'm being critical?
- How do I act when I'm being critical?
- Do I express a critical attitude…

  - When I'm around certain people (family, friends, coworkers, acquaintances, neighbors)? Who: _____
  - When I'm required to go to unpleasant places? Where: _____
  - When I must engage in undesirable activities (social, work, recreational)? What: _____

- When I feel unsettling sensations (anger, fear, frustration, grief, embarrassment, disgust, impatience)? Which one(s): _____

- When I have been unjustly treated (disrespected, ignored, misquoted, insulted)? How: _____

- When I think about those who are unlike me (educationally, physically, socially, racially, politically, spiritually)? Who: _____

- When I talk about controversial issues (political, religious, moral, or personal convictions)? Which issues: _____

• Why do I have a critical spirit toward (explore the reasons for each person, place, and situation listed)?

Once you have identified your crop of criticism, pray for God's discernment so you can...

• *Explain* your crops of criticism to someone spiritually mature who is able to support you in making godly changes.

• *Enlist* the help of an accountability partner in making two lists: first, those whom you need to forgive; and second, those of whom you need to ask forgiveness.

• *Exercise* your resolve to ask forgiveness of others and to extend forgiveness to others.

• *Enter* into an agreement with God to allow His Word to be your "critical spirit sifter."

• *Examine* your thought life in light of God's Word.

• *Expel* all thoughts, words, and deeds that do not pass through the grid of the guidelines set out in Scripture for your thoughts.

• *Exchange* your critical thinking for correct thinking:

> *"Whatever is true, whatever is noble, whatever is right,*
> *whatever is pure, whatever is lovely, whatever is admirable—*
> *if anything is excellent or praiseworthy—*
> *think about such things"*
> (PHILIPPIANS 4:8).

D. How to Hit the Target

Up until now, Job's judgmental trio has delivered speech after speech—rightly glorifying the greatness of God and wrongly accusing Job of being a flagrant sinner. God has been quiet, but it will soon be evident He hasn't missed a single word.

Now it's God's turn to impart truth; now there are important lessons to be learned to help each man hit the target by being conformed to the character of Christ, changing their thinking, and relying on Christ's strength to be all they are created to be.

Scripture assures us of God's faithfulness:

> *"Being confident in this, that he who began a good work in you*
> *will carry it on to completion until the day of Christ Jesus"*
> (PHILIPPIANS 1:6).

If you are aiming at nothing, you are sure to hit it every time. The truth is God wants you to set your sights on three separate targets and to take careful aim at each one. These aren't just any targets, but ones God has selected specifically for you—ones that will help to change your life, ones that will make you more Christlike. In addition, these targets will set your heart aglow, and will fill your soul with passion.

Like the apostle Paul, be mindful to take aim:

> *"Therefore I do not run like someone running aimlessly;*
> *I do not fight like a boxer beating the air.*
> *No, I strike a blow to my body and make it my slave*
> *so that after I have preached to others,*
> *I myself will not be disqualified for the prize"*
> (1 CORINTHIANS 9:26-27).

HITTING THE TARGET

Target #1—A New Purpose: God's purpose for me is to be conformed to the character of Christ.

> *"Those God foreknew he also predestined to be conformed to the image of his Son"* (Romans 8:29).

– "I'll do whatever it takes to be conformed to the character of Christ."

Target #2—A New Priority: God's priority for me is to change my thinking.

> *"Do not conform to the pattern of this world, but be transformed by the renewing of your mind"* (Romans 12:2).

> – "I'll do whatever it takes to line up my thinking with God's thinking."

Target #3—A New Plan: God's plan for me is to rely on Christ's strength, not my strength, to be all He created me to be.

> *"I can do all things through Christ who strengthens me"* (Philippians 4:13 NKJV).

> – "I'll do whatever it takes to fulfill His plan in His strength."

MY PERSONALIZED PLAN

Let's look now at how a critical heart can become a caring heart.

Suppose someone said to you, "When I think of you, I think of Jesus." How would you feel? In the deepest part of your heart, wouldn't you like to have the character of Christ show in your life? If so, what was He really like?

Do you perceive Jesus as having a critical spirit or a caring one? Did Jesus have a judgmental spirit toward people, or did the truth He spoke judge them? And when His words exposed the sinful reality of their hearts, were they not accompanied by a merciful offer of redemption?

People were drawn to Jesus because He was an encourager, not a critic. While He didn't ignore sinful behavior, He wasn't the classic faultfinder either. Instead, He was concerned with recognizing and meeting needs, most importantly our need to have our sins forgiven through His death and resurrection.

When you experience authentic salvation, the Bible says you have "Christ in you" (Colossians 1:27), therefore, you have the capacity to care rather than to criticize. If you truly want to be like Christ, don't be a critic. Instead, enlarge your heart and become an encourager.

> *"If you have any encouragement from being united with Christ,*
> *if any comfort from his love, if any common sharing in the Spirit,*
> *if any tenderness and compassion,*
> *then make my joy complete by being like-minded,*
> *having the same love, being one in spirit and of one mind"*
> (PHILIPPIANS 2:1-2).

How to Have a Caring Heart—The Heart of an Encourager

- **A caring heart sees** its own shortcomings.

  - Humble your heart to see your sin, your imperfections, and your immense need for God's mercy.

  - Rather than measuring yourself by human standards, measure yourself by God's standard—the perfect Savior.

  - Instead of making sure others see how significant you are, help them see *their* significance in God's eyes.

  - Pray, "Lord, may I see my sin as You see it, and may I hate my sin as You hate it."

    > *"Search me, God, and know my heart; test me and*
    > *know my anxious thoughts. See if there is any offensive*
    > *way in me, and lead me in the way everlasting"*
    > (Psalm 139:23-24).

- **A caring heart has active compassion** for others.

  - Look closely at the life of Christ to learn His compassionate way of confronting the truth.

  - Consider the woman caught in adultery—a crime which, in that day, was worthy of death. Jesus didn't focus on her fault. Instead of condemning her, He looked beyond her fault and saw her need. Then He compassionately met that need (read John 8:3-11).

  - Look at the woman at the well, who had been in multiple marriages and was living with yet another man. Although Jesus knew all about her, He didn't focus on her fault. Without ignoring her sin, He chose to focus on her need and then compassionately met that need (read John 4:5-42).

  - Pray that you will not be a critical stone-thrower, but a compassionate need-meeter.

    > *"As God's chosen people, holy and dearly loved,*
    > *clothe yourselves with compassion, kindness,*
    > *humility, gentleness and patience"*
    > (Colossians 3:12).

- **A caring heart draws** out the heartfelt needs of others.

  - Listen not only to what people say on the surface, but also for feelings beneath the surface—feelings of being unloved, insignificant, and insecure.

  - Learn the "language of love" that speaks to the heart—a thoughtful note, a favorite food, a surprising gift, a tender touch, or reaching out to one of their loved ones.

  - Ask, "What can I do to improve our relationship?" Listen carefully, then repeat back what you hear to make sure you understood correctly.

  - Reflect: "Are you saying _____? Is that what you said?"

    Clarify: "It sounds as if you feel…"

    Explore: "I'm not sure I understand what you are saying…"

    Extend: "Is there more?…What else are you feeling?"

    Offer: "What would be meaningful to you?"

  - Pray that God will give you a discerning spirit as you seek to draw others out.

    "The purposes of a person's heart are deep waters,
    but one who has insight draws them out"
    (PROVERBS 20:5).

- **A caring heart offers** acceptance to others.

  - Realize that everyone has an innate fear of rejection and a deep yearning for acceptance.

  - Recognize that God accepts you just as you are, even with your faults. You are His beloved child in whom He takes much pleasure.

  - Choose to be a channel through which God extends His acceptance to others.

  - Pray for God to reveal the ways you have rejected others and the ways you can reach out with a heart of acceptance.

    "Accept the one whose faith is weak, without quarreling
    over disputable matters…for God has accepted them"
    (ROMANS 14:1,3).

- **A caring heart sees** God-given worth in others.

  - Recognize that the worth of something is most often demonstrated by the price paid for it.

  - Look at how the Lord demonstrated the worth of every person by paying the highest possible price for them—His life. With His blood, He paid the necessary ransom to redeem people from the penalty of their sins.

  - Treat every person—including the most problematic—as someone with God-given worth. After all, God judges our hearts, attitudes, and actions toward others.

  - Pray that the Lord will not allow you to despise anyone He created. And pray that you will see others as God sees them, and value them as He values them.

  > *"Are not five sparrows sold for two pennies? Yet not*
  > *one of them is forgotten by God. Indeed, the very*
  > *hairs of your head are all numbered. Don't be afraid;*
  > *you are worth more than many sparrows"*
  > (LUKE 12:6-7).

- **A caring heart praises** the positives in others.

  - Refuse to be a pharisaical faultfinder. The Pharisees even found fault in the faultless Son of God.

  - Avoid the temptation to "catch" people doing something wrong. Instead, comment on what they are doing right.

  - Compliment outer characteristics (cleanliness, sweet countenance, modest clothing, etc.) and praise inner character: "I see that you have wisdom…perseverance…thoughtfulness… integrity."

  - Pray that you will see something positive in every person, then faithfully make that your focus.

  > *"The wisdom that comes from heaven is first of all*
  > *pure; then peace-loving, considerate, submissive, full*
  > *of mercy and good fruit, impartial and sincere"*
  > (JAMES 3:17).

- **A caring heart doesn't wound** others with words.
  - Understand the fallacy of saying, "Talk is cheap." Talk is costly when it tears others down. Consider that what you are criticizing in someone may be something God wants to deal with directly—and that God wants you to pray about and remain silent.
  - Before speaking words of criticism, ask a wise friend to evaluate your content and tone. Realize that after critical words are spoken, you can never take them back.
  - Inspire those needing to change with your belief that they *can* change: "Don't give up...God will guide you in the way you should go...I know you can make the right decisions...I believe you can experience God's best."
  - Pray that God will put His words into your mouth.

     *"Let the message of Christ dwell among you richly as you
     teach and admonish one another with all wisdom"*
     (COLOSSIANS 3:16).

- **A caring heart sees** the unmet needs of others.
  - Instead of judging the inappropriate actions of others, seek to understand the need behind their actions.
  - Realize that people who put down others have at least one unmet inner need—a need for love, for significance, or for security.
  - Realize that people don't always mean what they say or understand their own deepest needs.
  - Pray that your critics will allow the Lord to meet their deepest inner needs.

     *"My God will meet all your needs according
     to the riches of his glory in Christ Jesus"*
     (PHILIPPIANS 4:19).

- **A caring heart relies** on God's Word and God's Spirit for wisdom.
  - Seek God's wisdom by reading a chapter a day from the book of Proverbs. This book of wisdom was written by Solomon, whom God gifted with supernatural wisdom (read 2 Chronicles 1:7-12).

down every verse from Proverbs that pertains to the
___. Then look over the verses and determine whether you
are being wise with your words.

– See God at work in every circumstance and trust Him for wisdom to know how to respond. (Wisdom is the ability to look at life from God's point of view.)

– Pray that God's Spirit will teach you spiritual truths and lead you to speak these truths in love.

> *"This is what we speak, not in words taught us by*
> *human wisdom but in words taught by the Spirit,*
> *explaining spiritual realities with Spirit-taught words"*
> (1 CORINTHIANS 2:13).

E. How to Respond When You Are Confronted for Being Critical

God speaks—and the constructive criticism toward personal transformation begins.

Job had flooded the heavens with questions about his desperately despondent situation, but now God makes it clear as Job's Creator that He'll be asking all the questions. The pertinent, poignant truth is that God owes us no answers.

God also makes it crystal clear that Job's accusations have cast a shadow over the light of the truth of His counsel. If Job so wants to challenge God, God says, he does so at his own peril. (See what is said on page 224 regarding confrontation and Job.)

> *"Then the LORD spoke to Job out of the storm.*
> *He said: 'Who is this that obscures my plans with words without*
> *knowledge? Brace yourself like a man; I will question you,*
> *and you shall answer me'"*
> (JOB 38:1-3).

Being confronted about personal sins and shortcomings is never pleasant, but it is always necessary for spiritual growth and for developing healthy relationships. If you are to be conformed to the character of Christ, you must change. And change is the purpose of confrontation. God's heart for you is that you respond to confrontation with humility and wisdom, seeking God for keen discernment and the power to change if the criticism is legitimate. Change is never about pleasing people—it's about pleasing God, who commends those who heed constructive criticism:

"Whoever scorns instruction will pay for it,
but whoever respects a command is rewarded"
(PROVERBS 13:13).

Resolve to respond to criticism in a way that is biblical and reflects the character of Christ:

- **Make** your relationship a priority over your need to always be right.

  "The very fact that you have lawsuits among you means
  you have been completely defeated already. Why not
  rather be wronged? Why not rather be cheated?"
  (1 CORINTHIANS 6:7).

- **Demonstrate** a heart willing to understand the other person's perspective. Be willing to change where necessary and to heal any relational tension.

  "If it is possible, as far as it depends on
  you, live at peace with everyone"
  (ROMANS 12:18).

- **Listen** carefully even if you disagree with the other person's opinion. Give yourself time to consider what the other person says before you respond.

  "Everyone should be quick to listen, slow
  to speak and slow to become angry"
  (JAMES 1:19).

- **Respond** with humility. Give your reputation to God and ask Him to help you with your relationships.

  "Humble yourselves, therefore, under God's mighty
  hand, that he may lift you up in due time"
  (1 PETER 5:6).

- **Consider** those who confront you as being a gift from God. Flattery builds your pride, but confrontation helps you grow in the Lord.

> *"Wounds from a friend can be trusted,*
> *but an enemy multiplies kisses"*
> (PROVERBS 27:6).

- **Maintain** dignity and discernment. Allow God to speak to you through the other person. Your confronter may be someone who can help you overcome your critical attitudes. Even if you do not agree with your confronter, God may still use this opportunity for you to esteem the confronter for both the courage displayed in confronting you and for the value placed on your relationship.

> *"Those who disregard discipline despise themselves, but*
> *the one who heeds correction gains understanding"*
> (PROVERBS 15:32).

- **Consider** the counsel of your confronter without being defensive or reactive. God may be using this person to help you grow closer to Him. The benefits of confrontation may include coming closer to God, living a more loving lifestyle, and developing a better relationship with your confronter.

> *"Whoever remains stiff-necked after many rebukes*
> *will suddenly be destroyed—without remedy"*
> (PROVERBS 29:1).

F. How to Ask Forgiveness for Being Critical

Job's self-righteousness and critical spirit are met with a barrage of 72 questions from God Himself, all intended to greatly humble the man who so tightly holds on to his integrity. And several of the questions are laced with light sarcasm, further revealing the personality of Almighty God.

> *"Where were you when I laid the earth's foundation?*
> *Tell me, if you understand.*
> *Who marked off its dimensions? Surely you know!*
> *What is the way to the abode of light?*
> *And where does darkness reside? Can you take them to their places?*
> *Do you know the paths to their dwellings?*
> *Surely you know, for you were already born!*
> *You have lived so many years!"*
> (JOB 38:4-5,19-21).

If you've had a critical spirit, you need to ask forgiveness from those you've criticized. Why? Because you have a need to be forgiven—first by God, and then by those you have offended. However, asking for it can be difficult if you do not fully realize the depth of your need or the freedom it grants you. Jesus makes it clear that you are to go to those you have offended *before* you approach God and even before you offer Him a gift at church!

In Jesus' own words:

> *"If you are offering your gift at the altar*
> *and there remember that your brother or sister has*
> *something against you, leave your gift there in front of the altar.*
> *First go and be reconciled to them;*
> *then come and offer your gift"*
> (MATTHEW 5:23-24).

If there are people in your life you have wounded with your critical spirit, go to each one individually and…

- *Acknowledge your sin.*

  "I realize I've been wrong. My attitude has been wrong toward you, and I am genuinely sorry."

- *Acknowledge God's work in your life.*

  "God has absolutely convicted me. He has been doing a work in my heart and has made me aware of how I have wronged you."

- *Acknowledge your untrustworthiness.*

  "I realize you don't have any reason to trust me right now because I haven't proven myself trustworthy, but I hope one day to prove that I can be trusted."

- *Ask for clarification.*

  "You are important to me, and I can tell that I have wounded you. Would you please tell me in what other ways I have hurt you? I genuinely want to know."

- *Ask for further clarification.*

  "Are there other ways I have caused you pain?"

- *Acknowledge each offense.*

"I understand I have hurt you by…" (Using their words, mention every way you have hurt them.) For example, "I realize I have been insensitive to you."

• *Ask forgiveness.*

"I don't know whether you are willing to forgive me right now, and I understand if you aren't. I realize I don't deserve your forgiveness, but for my hurtful actions toward you, I would like to ask, 'Will you forgive me?'"

• *Acknowledge your commitment.*

"I am committed to allowing the Lord to continue working in my heart and life to change me. I thank you for helping me by having the courage to be honest with me."

• *Acknowledge your gratitude.*

"I thank you for talking with me and allowing me to apologize."

The Bible says to

> *"be kind and compassionate to one another,*
> *forgiving each other, just as in Christ God forgave you"*
> (Ephesians 4:32).

When You Can't Forgive Yourself

Question: "How can I forgive myself for continually criticizing the woman I love? Even though she has forgiven me, I have lost her."

Answer: When the consequences of sin are great, the difficulty with forgiving yourself is also great. If your sin had not cost you so much, you would likely have less difficulty forgiving yourself. The reality is that God and this woman have both forgiven you, and to not forgive yourself is to set yourself up as a higher judge than God.

• *Choose* not to focus on the past and what you have lost. This would only keep you angry with yourself and emotionally stuck.

• *Focus* on growing in your relationship with Jesus and conforming to His image. The result will be that God will change the way you relate to those you love, and He will make you into the godly, loving man you desire to be.

> *"Love is patient, love is kind.*
> *It does not envy, it does not boast, it is not proud"*
> (1 Corinthians 13:4).

G. How to Respond to Your Critic

God turns His attention to the tumultuous trio, Eli, Bill, and Zo. He states point-blank to presumably the eldest, Eli: "I am angry with you and your two friends, because you have not spoken the truth about me, as my servant Job has" (Job 42:7).

God instructs the three to take seven bulls and seven rams to Job, before whom they are to sacrifice a burnt offering to the Lord. Job will then pray for the men, and God says, "I will accept his prayer and not deal with you according to your folly" (Job 42:8).

Eli, Bill, and Zo are confronted by God for being critical and not speaking the truth about Him, and they respond with humble, teachable hearts. Like Job, they grow in spiritual understanding and wisdom.

To be Spirit-controlled rather than situation-controlled is not *natural* to human nature. Being Spirit-controlled is *supernatural*—it calls for yielding control of yourself to the indwelling Holy Spirit, whom you received at salvation. To return evil for evil is natural, and to return good for evil is the supernatural response God desires for you to have toward your critics.

Scripture gives a clear directive:

> *"Do not be overcome by evil,*
> *but overcome evil with good"*
> (Romans 12:21).

When you respond to criticism, do so by relying on the power of Christ's Spirit within you.

- **Be assured** you can accept others in the same way Christ accepts you.

> *"Accept one another, then, just as Christ accepted*
> *you, in order to bring praise to God"*
> (Romans 15:7).

Pray, "Lord, I thank You that You accepted me when I was undeserving and You continue to accept me even when I fail. Because of Your acceptance of me, I can accept others, even those who fail me. I will choose to accept my most severe critic as a divine creation of God."

- **Be open** to the slightest kernel of truth when you are criticized.

> *"A rebuke impresses a discerning person*
> *more than a hundred lashes a fool"*
> (PROVERBS 17:10).

Pray, "Lord, if there is any truth in the critical words said about me, please convict my heart so that I might confess it and cooperate with You to change it."

- **Be willing** to consider that the criticism may be true. Your critic may be God's megaphone to get your attention.

> *"The way of fools seems right to them,*
> *but the wise listen to advice"*
> (PROVERBS 12:15).

Pray, "Lord, I accept this criticism as Your way of teaching me something I need to know. Please reveal to me what it is You are saying to me through this criticism."

- **Be diligent** about receiving criticism without becoming defensive.[19]

> *"Mockers resent correction, so they avoid the wise"*
> (PROVERBS 15:12).

Pray, "Lord, I admit that I (__state the offense__). I agree I was wrong. Please continue to use others to put me on a correction course when I'm off track in my attitudes or actions. And please continue to transform me more and more into the character of Christ."

- **Be determined** not to speak ill of your critic.

*"Set a guard over my mouth, LORD; keep
watch over the door of my lips"*
(PSALM 141:3).

Pray, "Lord, I yield my tongue to You. I ask You to place a guard over my mouth so that I will speak only the truth in love to (name) and not speak ill of (name) to others. I pledge to focus on the good in (name) and not on the bad."

- **Be committed** to praying for your critic.

"Love your enemies and pray for those who persecute you"
(MATTHEW 5:44).

Pray, "Lord, I commit (name) into Your hands. I pray that (name) will learn of Your love and begin to love the way You love and have a peace that is Your peace. I pray that (name) comes to experience Your love, grace, and truth in profound ways and, in so doing, becomes a blessing to many."

- **Be aware** that as a follower of Christ, you will be criticized.

*"Blessed are you when people insult you, persecute you and
falsely say all kinds of evil against you because of me"*
(MATTHEW 5:11).

Pray, "Lord, I want to be like Christ. Just as Jesus was unjustly criticized, I should expect to be criticized. Rather than feeling rejected, I choose to rejoice in the privilege of suffering in this way, and I thank You for rewarding me by calling me blessed."

- **Be encouraged** that you will be disciplined by God because you are His child.

*"And have you completely forgotten this word of
encouragement that addresses you as a father addresses
his son? It says, 'My son, do not make light of the Lord's
discipline, and do not lose heart when he rebukes
you, because the Lord disciplines the one he loves,
and he chastens everyone he accepts as his son'"*
(HEBREWS 12:5-6).

Pray, "Lord, thank You for loving me and dealing with me as a loving Father by disciplining me when I need correction. I choose to receive all discipline from You as a sign of Your devotion to me and of Your acceptance of me as Your child."

- **Be dependent** on the Lord's perspective to determine your worth and value, not on the opinions of others.

> *"Am I now trying to win the approval of human beings,*
> *or of God? Or am I trying to please people? If I were still*
> *trying to please people, I would not be a servant of Christ"*
> (GALATIANS 1:10).

Pray, "Lord, thank You for demonstrating my worth and value by dying for me and adopting me into Your family. I will not live for the approval of people, for I have Your approval, and that is all I need. Thank You for loving me."

- **Be discerning** regarding the accuracy of the critical words of others.

> *"The wise in heart are called discerning, and*
> *gracious words promote instruction"*
> (PROVERBS 16:21).

Pray, "Lord, help me not to accept all critical words as true, nor to reject all critical words as lies. Enable me to discern the false from the true. Put a hedge of protection around my mind so that I reject the lies. Allow my heart to accept constructive criticism so that You may bring freedom to my life and change me."

H. How to Confront Someone Who Has a Critical Spirit

Based on the instructions of Jesus in Matthew 18:15-17, you should address an offense by confronting the offender in private and in love. The goal is repentance and restoration. Those who avoid confrontation aren't helping the one who needs help to change. The tragic result is that sin and pain continue, and relationships are destroyed.

Jesus stated the value of confrontation:

> *"If your brother or sister sins,*
> *go and point out their fault, just between the two of you.*
> *If they listen to you, you have won them over.*

> *But if they will not listen, take one or two others along,*
> *so that 'every matter may be established by the testimony*
> *of two or three witnesses'"*
> (MATTHEW 18:15-16).

- **Align your heart** and mind with God's heart.
  - Confess any sinful thought, motive, or deed on your part.
  - Ask God for discernment and direction as to what, if any, action you are to take.
  - Seek God's wisdom through prayer, His Word, and the godly counsel of others.

- **Ask permission** before you speak.
  - "Could I make a suggestion?"
  - "May I make an observation?"
  - "I have some thoughts on this situation, if you are interested."

- **Acquire a clear, accurate understanding** of the situation before you speak.
  - Gather the facts and leave out emotional reactions.
  - Listen to objective viewpoints.
  - Speak with only those involved.
  - Assume responsibility for any wrongful actions on your part.
    - » "I was wrong to have spoken to you as I did, and I ask your forgiveness."
    - » "I was wrong to have jumped to a hasty, inaccurate conclusion. I should have had all the facts before I formulated any opinion."
    - » "I was wrong to have taken my anger out on you. Will you please forgive me?"

- **Avoid analyzing** another person's feelings or actions.
  - Clarify actions: "Tell me, from your perspective, what happened and what you did."
  - Identify feelings: "Tell me what you were feeling when (_state_

<u>what happened   )." "How were you feeling when you…?" "How
are you feeling now?"

- Stick to the facts: "I saw you…" "I understood you to say…" "If
  I heard you correctly, you felt…"

- Apply the "sandwich approach" in voicing your criticism.

  » Give the person the bread of praise: "I appreciate your strong
    work ethic." "You are a very gifted and competent person." "I
    recognize that you are a hard worker."

  » Add the meat of the matter: "What I need from you right
    now is for you to speak to me without raising your voice. I
    feel disrespected and forced into a yelling match in order to
    resolve our differences."

  » Finish with the bread of encouragement: "I am confident you
    can work with me on this." "I know we can get through this
    together." "I know you can help me in this way."

- **Aim your criticism** at the specific problematic behavior, not at the
  person.

  - "I appreciate your tremendous efforts, but I am having a prob-
    lem with the sarcastic comments being made."

  - "I enjoy visiting with you, but I need to be able to talk with
    fewer interruptions so that I can keep my train of thought."

  - "I love your sense of humor, but I really don't enjoy off-color
    jokes and sexual innuendos."

- **Ax** any phrases that contain *always* or *never*.
  - Don't say, "You'll *never* change."
  - Don't say, "You *always* do this to me."
  - Don't say, "You *never* speak to me with respect."

- **Address only one** problematic behavior at a time.
  - Don't mention a list of offenses. Focus on just one.
  - Don't belabor your point or position; simply state it clearly and
    concisely: "I need you to be truthful with me about (state the

situation).” “I need you to speak to me in a calm and controlled manner.”

– Don't bring up incidents or problems from the past.

• **Allow emotions** to subside before confronting the problem.

– Realize that reason is not maximized in the heat of the moment.

– Wait until things are going well in the relationship before you choose a time to talk.

– Approach the subject calmly and objectively, with a positive, prayerful attitude.

– Assume some responsibility for finding a solution to the problem.

– Help formulate a plan for change: “What do you think we need to do?” “How do you think we can resolve this problem together and move on?” “I want to work with you on this in any way I can that will be helpful to you.”

– Consider the undesirable behavior/habit as the problem, not the person engaging in the behavior. “I'm not looking at this as *your* problem, but as *our* problem because it is affecting our relationship. I want us to have the best relationship possible.”

– Offer encouragement and emotional support: “What can I do to help?” “What do you need from me?”

• **Approach God together** with a united heart.

– Thank God together for His love, grace, and mercy and for the opportunity to honor Him in your relationship.

– Ask God to protect your relationship from petty differences, to guard your communication, and to increase your love for one another.

– Commit to God to being honest, open, and encouraging with one another and to faithfully seek God's wisdom in your decision making.

> *"Those who trust in themselves are fools,*
> *but those who walk in wisdom are kept safe"*
> (Proverbs 28:26).

Job is no insignificant person, formerly the most renowned man among all the people of the East, but the God of the universe recognizes that his critical spirit needs to be curtailed when it comes to defaming deity.

Reading the book of Job, there is no doubt that God takes great delight in what He has created, and He continues to glorify His magnificent wisdom and power before Job. "Look at Behemoth, which I made along with you and which feeds on grass like an ox. What strength it has in its loins, what power in the muscles of its belly!" (Job 40:15-16). Most believe "Behemoth" to be a hippopotamus.

Then God describes another intriguing creature, the Leviathan, which supposedly is a crocodile: "Can you pull in Leviathan with a fishhook, or tie down its tongue with a rope? Can you put a cord through its nose, or pierce its jaw with a hook?" His creation now fully exalted before His critical servant, Job, God inquires: "Who then is able to stand against me? Who has a claim against me that I must pay?" (Job 41:10-11).

And then God makes a statement that should silence all His critics:

> *"Everything under heaven belongs to me"*
> (Job 41:11).

I. How to Respond to Criticism from Significant People

Many people have a critical spirit, but sometimes the pain they inflict can be particularly excruciating. The tongue-lashing mother, the can-never-be-pleased coach, and other authority figures can make others become extremely vulnerable and sensitive to a critical spirit. Don't allow nonconstructive criticism to weaken your emotional or spiritual state. God promises He will bring good from everything, and that includes even negative circumstances. For the Christian, one inherent good in any unjust suffering is that it provides the opportunity to emulate Christ's example before the eyes of unbelievers who have yet to know Him:

> *"It is commendable if someone bears up under the pain*
> *of unjust suffering because they are conscious of God.*
> *But how is it to your credit if you receive a beating*
> *for doing wrong and endure it?*
> *But if you suffer for doing good and you endure it,*
> *this is commendable before God.*
> *To this you were called, because Christ suffered for you,*
> *leaving you an example, that you should follow in his steps"*
> (1 Peter 2:19-21).

FIVE SIGNIFICANT CRITICIZERS

Critical Parents

QUESTION: "My parents were critical of me in my childhood so when I became an adult, I withdrew physically and emotionally. I love my parents and have tried reconciliation, but how is this possible when there is no change? Now that I am expecting a child, I feel that I must withdraw again."

ANSWER: You are to be commended for seeking reconciliation even though your parents have not changed. Typically, people do not change unless something motivates them to act differently. Your pregnancy might possibly provide that motivation.

Schedule a time to talk with your parents about the kind of interaction you desire to have with them.

When you are all together…

- **Express your love** and appreciation for them.
- **Express your hurt** over their frequent critical words. Give specific examples.
- **Express your strong commitment** to creating a positive, encouraging environment for your child.
- **Express your decision** to spend time with them, but that you will leave, or they will have to leave, if they become negative and critical.
- **Express your resolve** to reflect the character and attitude of Christ toward them.
- **Express your desire** that they speak lovingly and positively to you and to their grandchild.

Remember, everyone has three God-given inner needs—the needs for love, significance, and security.[20]

When we feel like we are lacking in one or more of these areas, we often seek to get these needs met through negative behavior. A critical person is often seeking to meet a deep need for significance. Knowing this, you can seek to encourage and build up your parents in all you say and do.

> *"Let us therefore make every effort*
> *to do what leads to peace and to mutual edification"*
> (ROMANS 14:19).

Critical Spouse

QUESTION: "How can I deal with my critical, perfectionistic spouse? He was raised by a critical mother, and I was raised by a critical father."

ANSWER: Often, a person who is hypercritical has an underlying need to be in control or to feel significant. It may be that your husband is simply doing what he knows to do from the modeling he received growing up. Children who grow up with criticism learn to be critical. Children who grow up with encouragement learn to be encouraging. You cannot expect your husband to copy behavior he has not routinely seen.

- **Engage him in a conversation** in which you express your desire for the two of you to break the destructive patterns of interaction you both learned as children.

- **Turn this problem into a project.** Both of you must make a commitment to each other and to God to compliment each other about something different each day for the next 12 weeks—writing each compliment down. Over time, you'll see the transformation before your very eyes. You will learn to be encouraging and complimentary of one another.

The Bible says,

> *"Let us consider how we may spur one another*
> *on toward love and good deeds"*
> (HEBREWS 10:24).

Critical Church Leaders

QUESTION: "Several leaders in my church seem to have judgmental spirits and continually criticize other members. I try to be pleasant and forgiving, but is this the way the leaders in church should act?"

ANSWER: For a spiritual leader to be critical is contrary to Scripture. The Bible says the shepherds of the flock are to be humble examples of Christ. Examine yourself and the other people in your church. There is a possibility that you are in the wrong church. You could be in a church that is legalistic and therefore one that doesn't allow the grace of God or the love of Christ to flourish. The Bible says,

"To the elders among you...
Be shepherds of God's flock that is under your care,
watching over them—not because you must,
but because you are willing, as God wants you to be;
not pursuing dishonest gain, but eager to serve;
not lording it over those entrusted to you,
but being examples to the flock"
(1 PETER 5:1-3).

(Also, see the chapter on spiritual abuse in my book *How to Rise Above Abuse*.)

════════════════ *Critical Managers* ════════════════

QUESTION: "How can I deal with my manager, who is so critical of me that I feel beat up all the time?"

ANSWER: While we are to honor our authorities and heed their justifiable criticism, we are not called to submit to verbal or emotional abuse. Jesus confronted the religious leaders of His day, but, in doing so, He did not have a critical spirit toward them.

Prayerfully attempt to draw your superior out about your job performance and professional relationship. Humbly ask questions such as:

- Have I offended you in any way?
- Is there something I've done that you're displeased with?
- In what areas do I need to show improvement?

Your performance review would be an ideal time to raise these questions, but you could also request a private meeting with your manager and say, "I may have a blind spot that is causing me to not see what others see. I honestly want to be the very best employee I can be. What could I do to be a more valuable asset to our organization? I value your opinion and will work hard to improve." Then listen with an open heart to the answer, and bring what you hear before the Lord.

"Those who guard their mouths and their tongues
keep themselves from calamity"
(PROVERBS 21:23).

================= *Critical Friends* =================

QUESTION: "I have a major problem. How can I keep from being negatively affected by two people in my life who are verbally abusive and attack my Christian commitment?"

ANSWER: Realize you are not the one with a problem. The verbally abusive people are the ones with a problem.

Repeat out loud to yourself three times: "They have a problem. I am not going to let *their* problem be *my* problem."

- **Rehearse** these two statements every day for two weeks until these truths give you peace and your hurt and anger subside.

- **Recognize** the fact that their attacks on you are a reflection of their unmet needs and are not really about you at all.

- **Release** them and yourself to God and focus on praying for their relationship with Him.

- **Remember**, Jesus stated that we would be persecuted, but in the midst of the persecution, we would be blessed.

> *"Blessed are you when people hate you,*
> *when they exclude you and insult you and reject your name as evil,*
> *because of the Son of Man"*
> (LUKE 6:22).

J. How to Build Boundaries with Your Critic

The way in which Almighty God responds to Job makes it clear that Job has crossed some boundaries. God continues to fire off question after question to Job—questions that exalt His creation and His intimate involvement with it. Through all of this, Job had to have been thoroughly humbled.

> *"What is the way to the place where the lightning is dispersed, or*
> *the place where the east winds are scattered over the earth?*
> *...Can you bring forth the constellations in their seasons*
> *or lead out the Bear with its cubs?*
> *Do you hunt the prey for the lioness and satisfy the hunger of the*
> *lions when they crouch in their dens or lie in wait in a thicket?*

> *...Do you give the horse its strength or clothe*
> *its neck with a flowing mane?"*
> (Job 38:24,32,39-40; 39:19).

You can curtail the effects of criticism by developing a plan to prevent yourself from being controlled. You cannot change someone else, but you can change yourself so that tactics used on you are no longer capable of causing pain. Build appropriate boundaries with your critic, and realize that these boundaries are designed to protect your heart:

> *"Above all else, guard your heart,*
> *for everything you do flows from it"*
> (Proverbs 4:23).

First, determine your plan of action and set appropriate boundaries. Then...

1. **State clearly**, in a conversation or a letter, what you will accept and not accept from the criticizer.[21]

   Communicate your position in a positive way, in a pleasing manner, and at a pleasant time.

   – Don't justify yourself.

   – Don't be apologetic.

   – Keep your comments short and succinct. Simply state your boundaries.

   "I want us to have the best relationship possible. That means I need to make some changes. I have decided that..."

   » "...I will not listen to any more name-calling."

   » "...I will not listen to any more accusations concerning (name)."

   » "...I will no longer be controlled by the silent treatment."

The Bible says,

> *"The one who has knowledge uses words with restraint,*
> *and whoever has understanding is even-tempered"*
> (Proverbs 17:27).

2. **Announce the consequence you will enforce** if your critic violates your requests. Your response should be a matter of emotionally disengaging or even temporarily distancing yourself from your critic.

   – You cannot change your critic's behavior, but you can remove yourself from frequent exposure to unacceptable behavior.

   – Calmly and clearly state the consequences.

   "I want to be with you, but…"

   » "…If you choose to call me a name again, I will choose to leave for a period of time."

   » "…If you choose to make accusations, I will choose to end our conversation."

   » "…If you choose to give me the silent treatment, I will choose to go and enjoy time with others."

   Consequences are part of God's divine plan of sowing and reaping.

   "A man reaps what he sows"
   (GALATIANS 6:7).

3. **Enforce the consequence every single time** the criticism occurs.

   Don't bluff! Your critic needs to know that you are going to act consistently on your words.

   – Plan on being tested numerous times.

   – In your mind and heart, say *no.*

   » Say *no* to manipulation.

   » Say *no* to pressure.

   » Say *no* to control.

   Eventually your critic will stop the abusive tactic—but only after that tactic proves to be ineffective.

   "All you need to say is a simple 'Yes' or 'No'"
   (JAMES 5:12).

4. **Absolutely do not negotiate.**

   Since critics do not use words fairly, negotiation will not work.

   – Instead of "talking out" the problem, your critic will seek to wear you down.

- Simply state your intent to withdraw from the relationship as long as the criticism continues.

- Express your willingness to renew the relationship when the criticism stops.

  » "I am not willing to discuss this topic any longer at this time, but we can try another time."

  » "I have stated clearly what I will not accept, so we will have to resume this talk later."

  » "When you are ready to respect my requests, let me know. I look forward to enjoying being together at that time."

Keep your words brief and to the point:

> *"Sin is not ended by multiplying words, but*
> *the prudent hold their tongues"*
> (PROVERBS 10:19).

5. **Never react** when your boundary is violated. Instead, merely respond. A reaction will only lead to another reaction, and that will put you back under the control of the criticizer.

   - Expect your boundary to be violated, but determine not to react.

   - Expect your boundary to be violated again *and again*! But never react.

   - Respond by detaching yourself emotionally from your critic and by enforcing your repercussions.

     » Don't *cry* because of feeling hurt.

     » Don't *beg* because of feeling fearful.

     » Don't *explode* because of feeling frustrated.

Respond, be patient, and remember:

> *"The end of a matter is better than its beginning, and*
> *patience is better than pride. Do not be quickly provoked*
> *in your spirit, for anger resides in the lap of fools"*
> (ECCLESIASTES 7:8-9).

6. **Solicit the support of one or two people** to help you through this process. Having accountability and support is critical during this period of time.

   – Select people who are wise, objective, and know you well.

   – Include your supporters as you identify, analyze, and strategize regarding the problem.

     » Determine how to articulate your plan.

     » Enforce repercussions.

     » Resist being manipulated.

The Bible says,

> *"Listen to advice and accept discipline, and at the*
> *end you will be counted among the wise"*
> (PROVERBS 19:20).

7. **Remember, it takes only a short period** of time to renegotiate a relationship with someone who has a critical spirit.

   Just one change on your part will set into motion a series of changes throughout the entire relationship.

   – During this time, expect manipulative maneuvers and emotional ups and downs.

   – Assume that your actions will make your critic angry.

     » Allow your critic to react, but don't react yourself.

     » Don't seek to placate your critic; it won't work.

     » Compare this time to having surgery. It is painful, but you will recover.

Pain often provides the necessary motivation and the only hope for healing and having a new, healthy relationship.

> *"The soothing tongue is a tree of life…"*
> (PROVERBS 15:4).

K. How to Get Off the Critic's "Seesaw"

When it comes to God's "seesaw," it is wise to let Him control all activity—the ups and the downs—in His sublime sovereignty.

God is certainly "up high," so how will Job respond after being bombarded with questions that make his supposed wisdom look like foolishness? Will he jump off the seesaw in anger and rebellion? No, Job wisely decides to stay put and squint into the glaring light of infinite wisdom.

God inquires, "Will the one who contends with the Almighty correct him? Let him who accuses God answer him!" (Job 40:2).

And sitting very still on the seesaw, Job responds,

> *"I am unworthy—how can I reply to you?*
> *I put my hand over my mouth.*
> *I spoke once, but I have no answer—twice, but I will say no more"*
> (Job 40:4-5).

Insecure people use criticism like a seesaw—pushing others down so they can rise up. Rising up is empowering and creates the illusion of being better than those beneath them.

However, the emboldened moment can come to an abrupt end and the trip back down is jolting if the person on the low end jumps off the seesaw! Ultimately, if we are on the low end of the seesaw, we control the landing of the person on the high end, making it either hard or soft. We most definitely need to get off the seesaw, but we need to get off gently so that our critic doesn't rapidly drop and hit the ground hard, causing further injury to the relationship. Our behavior must be obedient to Scripture:

> *"Make sure that nobody pays back wrong for wrong,*
> *but always strive to do what is good for each other*
> *and for everyone else"*
> (1 Thessalonians 5:15).

If there is someone close to you who has you on a seesaw and keeps pushing you down, the following action steps will be helpful in getting off without destroying your relationship:

- *Go before the Lord*, asking Him to sensitize you to the pain your critic experienced while growing up—the pain that has yet to be healed.

- *Tell your critic:* "I have been thinking about the pain you experienced in your childhood. I know as a child you were hurt."

- *Express your desire:* "I feel like we've been going up and down on a seesaw at times, and I don't think it's best for either of us to be in this up-and-down cycle any longer. I don't want to push you down, and I don't want to be pushed down by you. I care about you so I'm going to get off the seesaw. When excessive criticism continues, we're not going to go up and down anymore."

- *State your plan:* "I am going to respect your position in my life and honor our relationship."

- *Offer your critic* an opportunity to give input: "What can I do in the future that will be meaningful to you and will change the dynamic of our relationship? Mention three specifics, and I will pick one to focus on."

- *State your goal:* "I'm going to seek to be right in God's sight in all of my interactions with you."

- *Pray* that you will do whatever it takes to reflect the character of Christ before your critic.

- *Ask the Lord* to bring to your mind strong, mature Christians who will provide you with the support and accountability you need to reach your goal of growing in Christlikeness.

- *Commit* to growing in your relationship with the Lord through prayer and in-depth Bible study and by cooperating with Him in conforming you to the character of Christ.

- *Thank God* for this person's good qualities, and then consistently focus on these qualities.

The Bible says,

> *"Devote yourselves to prayer, being watchful and thankful"*
> (COLOSSIANS 4:2).

L. How to Triumph with Truth

Truth has permeated Job to the core.

He is stunned, subjugated, and saddened. *What in the world was I thinking?* he undoubtedly laments. *Challenging the Most High God...I must have lost my mind along with everything else.*

God is satisfied. He stops parading His paradoxes of nature before Job because He has achieved His desired result. No longer is Job only humbled, now he is repentant. To his God he responds, "I know that you can do all things; no purpose of yours can be thwarted. You asked, 'Who is this that obscures my plans without knowledge?' Surely I spoke of things I did not understand, things too wonderful for me to know.

"You said, 'Listen now, and I will speak; I will question you, and you shall answer me.' My ears had heard of you but now my eyes have seen you" (Job 42:2-5).

And the revelation prompts a response from Job:

> *"Therefore I despise myself and repent in dust and ashes"*
> (Job 42:6).

Sailors often observe icebergs traveling in the opposite direction of strong, prevailing winds, a phenomenon that appears to be quite extraordinary. The explanation, however, is quite simple—the largest portion of icebergs is underwater, which makes them more subject to ocean currents than wind currents.

Likewise, when critical words are headed your way, you can move in the opposite direction, away from your offender and toward God. God doesn't identify Himself as an iceberg in the Bible, but He does use the metaphor of a rock, indicating that He is a strong, sturdy, immovable presence in our lives. In the face of extreme criticism, focus on what God says about you in His Word rather than on what your critic is saying. Triumph over criticism with truth.

Adopt the attitude of Jesus, who entrusted His life to the Father, the One who judges justly:

> *"When they hurled their insults at him, he did not retaliate;*
> *when he suffered, he made no threats.*
> *Instead, he entrusted himself to him who judges justly"*
> (1 Peter 2:23).

The question, then, becomes, "How?" How can we so have the mind and perspective of Christ that we are not pierced by sharp and penetrating words, not wounded by critical and sarcastic statements, not burned by blazing and fiery accusations? Jesus said,

> *"If you hold to my teaching, you are really my disciples.*
> *Then you will know the truth, and the truth will set you free"*
> (John 8:31-32).

Truth that Triumphs over Criticism

The Word of God teaches us that...

- **God provides** mercy, grace, and help in our time of need.

*"Let us then approach God's throne of grace with confidence, so that
we may receive mercy and find grace to help us in our time of need"*
(HEBREWS 4:16).

- **God suffered** for us and bids us to bear the disgrace He bore.

  *"Jesus also suffered outside the city gate to make the
  people holy through his own blood. Let us, then, go to
  him outside the camp, bearing the disgrace he bore"*
  (HEBREWS 13:12-13).

- **God brought** good from Jesus' bearing the brunt of cynical critics,
  and He will bring good from unjust criticism aimed at us.

  *"We know that in all things God works for the good of those
  who love him, who have been called according to his purpose"*
  (ROMANS 8:28).

- **God secured** our healing from the wounds of criticism by being
  wounded Himself.

  *"'He himself bore our sins in his body on the cross, so
  that we might die to sins' and live for righteousness;
  'by his wounds you have been healed'"*
  (1 PETER 2:24).

- **Enduring criticism** identifies us with Jesus, who endured criticism
  for us.

  *"...fixing our eyes on Jesus, the pioneer and perfecter of faith.
  For the joy set before him he endured the cross, scorning
  its shame, and sat down at the right hand of the throne
  of God. Consider him who endured such opposition from
  sinners, so that you will not grow weary and lose heart"*
  (HEBREWS 12:2-3).

- **Suffering the grief** of unjust criticism proves our faith.

  *"...for a little while you may have had to suffer grief in
  all kinds of trials. These have come so that the proven
  genuineness of your faith—of greater worth than gold,*

> *which perishes even though refined by fire—may result in*
> *praise, glory and honor when Jesus Christ is revealed"*
> (1 PETER 1:6-7).

- **Finding God's comfort** in the midst of criticism equips us to comfort others.

  > *"The Father of compassion and the God of all comfort…*
  > *comforts us in all our troubles, so that we can comfort those*
  > *in any trouble with the comfort we ourselves receive from*
  > *God. For just as we share abundantly in the sufferings of*
  > *Christ, so also our comfort abounds through Christ"*
  > (2 CORINTHIANS 1:3-5).

- **Bearing the pressure** of criticism reveals the life of Christ in us.

  > *"We are hard pressed on every side, but not crushed; perplexed,*
  > *but not in despair; persecuted, but not abandoned; struck down,*
  > *but not destroyed. We always carry around in our body the death*
  > *of Jesus, so that the life of Jesus may also be revealed in our body"*
  > (2 CORINTHIANS 4:8-10).

- **Facing the fiery trial** of criticism perfects perseverance and leads us to maturity and completeness of character.

  > *"Consider it pure joy, my brothers and sisters, whenever you face*
  > *trials of many kinds, because you know that the testing of your*
  > *faith produces perseverance. Let perseverance finish its work so*
  > *that you may be mature and complete, not lacking anything"*
  > (JAMES 1:2-4).

Throughout the centuries, Job has been heralded as a suffering saint. And, indeed, his struggles are monumental. But so is his reward.

At the conclusion of Job's fiery trial—with the critical clamor of his detractors silenced—the Bible tells us, "The Lord blessed the latter part of Job's life more than the former part. He had fourteen thousand sheep, six thousand camels, a thousand yoke of oxen and a thousand donkeys. And he also had seven sons and three daughters…After this, Job lived a hundred and forty years; he saw his children and their children to the fourth generation. And so Job died, an old man and full of years" (Job 42:12-13,16-17).

Full of years…and full of tested *faith* in God's goodness and grace.

On this side of eternity, we cannot comprehend the intricate tapestry God is weaving from the tormenting threads of criticism—deserved and otherwise—that He sovereignly grants entrance to our lives. However, we can know that, as we surrender to Him, we, like Job, will experience the refinement of our character and the very best God has to offer us…His perfect will for our lives.

As we tune out all other voices but His, what a joy it is to know that we will someday hear the words so dear to the heart of every child of God: "Well done, good and faithful servant!…Come and share your master's happiness!" (Matthew 25:23).

> *There are two sides of the coin of criticism:*
> *—When you give destructive criticism,*
> *the other person is hurt.*
> *—When you give constructive criticism,*
> *the other person is helped.*
>
> —JUNE HUNT

CRITICAL SPIRIT: ANSWERS IN GOD'S WORD

QUESTION: "Does God want us to encourage one another and to build each other up?"

ANSWER: *"Encourage one another and build each other up"* (1 Thessalonians 5:11).

QUESTION: "Why should I be aware of the power of the tongue?"

ANSWER: *"The tongue has the power of life and death, and those who love it will eat its fruit"* (Proverbs 18:21).

QUESTION: "According to the Bible, what defiles a person?"

ANSWER: *"Nothing outside a person can defile them by going into them. Rather, it is what comes out of a person that defiles them"* (Mark 7:15).

QUESTION: "What kind of a man derides his neighbor?"

ANSWER: *"Whoever derides their neighbor has no sense, but the one who has understanding holds their tongue"* (Proverbs 11:12).

QUESTION: "Why should we not pass judgment on someone else?"

ANSWER: *"You, therefore, have no excuse, you who pass judgment on someone else, for at whatever point you judge another, you are condemning yourself, because you who pass judgment do the same things"* (Romans 2:1).

QUESTION: "What enables us to know how to appropriately answer everyone?"

ANSWER: *"Let your conversation be always full of grace, seasoned with salt, so that you may know how to answer everyone"* (Colossians 4:6).

QUESTION: "What often stirs up anger?"

ANSWER: *"A gentle answer turns away wrath, but a harsh word stirs up anger"* (Proverbs 15:1).

QUESTION: "What is important to know about building others up?"

ANSWER: *"Do not let any unwholesome talk come out of your mouths, but only what is helpful for building others up according to their needs, that it may benefit those who listen"* (Ephesians 4:29).

QUESTION: "What typically happens to those who exalt themselves?"

ANSWER: *"For all those who exalt themselves will be humbled, and those who humble themselves will be exalted"* (Luke 14:11).

QUESTION: "What things should I think about to keep me from being anxious?"

ANSWER: *"Whatever is true, whatever is noble, whatever is right, whatever is pure, whatever is lovely, whatever is admirable—if anything is excellent or praiseworthy—think about such things"* (Philippians 4:8).

MANIPULATION
Cutting the Strings of Control

2

MANIPULATION
Cutting the Strings of Control

It's handed down from one generation…to the next…to the next…to the next. But this family trait has no genetic history of big ears or hazel eyes, no DNA for fair skin or brown freckles. This is something hurtful, something willful, something harmful. It's called *manipulation.*

This behavior—found in males and females alike—can also be called a character flaw. In fact, this pattern of conniving and cover-up periodically appears throughout the entire human family, even in the family line you would least suspect: the patriarchs of the Bible—Abraham, Isaac, and Jacob—then, in turn, in Jacob's descendants. All these men and women manipulated people and circumstances, attempting to dictate their own destinies or to circumvent some assumed negative consequences.

It's clear that sometimes the patriarchs faltered in their faith and even gave way to fear. Too many times, the results were grave: dishonor to their name and disgrace to their God. And all because of maniacal manipulation! Truly…

> *"There is a way that appears to be right,*
> *but in the end it leads to death"*
> (Proverbs 14:12).

I. Definitions of Manipulation

Abraham's wife, Sarah, has long been considered *submissive*; however, she can also be seen as *subversive.*

In the Bible, she is praised as a woman of inner beauty "who obeyed Abraham and called him her lord" (1 Peter 3:6). But she tarnishes that inner beauty by manipulating circumstances in an attempt to force God's promise to Abraham to be fulfilled—in *her* timing. God had assured Abraham that his descendants would be as numerous as the sand on the seashore, but now the couple is aged and they are still barren. Since Sarah is now well past childbearing years, she proposes a plan to be sure God's promise is on her calendar!

"Go, sleep with my slave; perhaps I can build a family through her" (Genesis 16:2). Abraham agrees and sleeps with Hagar, who, in turn, births a son named Ishmael—a son through whom the covenant promises were never intended and would never be fulfilled. Abraham and Sarah have not yet learned that

> *"the plans of the* LORD *stand firm forever,*
> *the purposes of his heart through all generations"*
> (PSALM 33:11).

A. What Is Manipulation?

She is 65 years old...and still stunning.

Since the life span of the patriarchs was twice that of people today, Sarai is doubtless in her prime, and that poses a serious threat to her husband, Abram (later called Sarah and Abraham).

The couple sets off for Egypt to escape a famine, but before setting foot into the foreign land, Abram decides to fabricate a tale, twisting the truth. This first patriarch of the faith fears for his life because if the Egyptians discover he is married to beautiful Sarai, they might kill him in order to take her into Pharaoh's harem.

So he twists the truth:

> *"I know what a beautiful woman you are...*
> *Say you are my sister, so that I will be treated well for your sake*
> *and my life will be spared because of you"*
> (GENESIS 12:11,13).

Bottom line: Abram manipulates the facts. Indeed, Sarai is his half-sister, but also fully his wife. Thus, rather than trusting God, the cycle of manipulation begins.

- *Manipulation* is the art of controlling people or circumstances by indirect, unfair, or deceptive means—especially to one's own advantage.[1]
- *Manipulation* happens to those who allow others to have excessive control over them—the control that God alone should have.

The Bible is clear about not giving others too much control, too much power, too much authority. We must not allow another person to take the place only God should have. Instead, we should apply the first of the Ten Commandments:

"You shall have no other gods before me"
(Exodus 20:3).

B. What Is Persuasion?

Although Sarai is indeed Abram's half-sister, this plan is all about a cover-up…and Sarai complies.

Once in Egypt, Sarai catches the eye of more than one court official and soon she is whisked away to Pharaoh's palace. Abram, of course, gets the royal treatment as well, acquiring "sheep and cattle, male and female donkeys, male and female servants, and camels" (Genesis 12:16).

But while Abram is pampered, Pharaoh is pummeled. God inflicts grave diseases on Pharaoh and his household because he has taken a woman who is Abram's wife, not merely his half-sister.

Sternly, Pharaoh confronts Abram. "'What have you done to me?' he said. 'Why didn't you tell me she was your wife? Why did you say, "She is my sister," so that I took her to be my wife? Now then, here is your wife. Take her and go!'" (Genesis 12:18-19).

How much better it would have been had Abram stuck with the truth, trusted God, and appealed to Pharaoh's mind, rather than trying to manipulate his actions through deception. Instead, Abram's deception was found out by Pharaoh.

"Whoever walks in integrity walks securely, but
whoever takes crooked paths will be found out"
(Proverbs 10:9).

- *Persuasion* is the act of convincing others by urging, reasoning, and appealing to their minds.[2]
- *Persuasion* is the process of winning over others by logical arguments and sound reasoning.

No other missionary for Christ is more well-known or more respected than the apostle Paul. He set the standard for how the gospel of Christ is to be shared with all people everywhere. And it is to be proclaimed not through manipulation, but through persuasion.

> *"Every Sabbath he reasoned in the synagogue,*
> *trying to persuade Jews and Greeks...*
> *'This man,' they charged, 'is persuading the people to worship God*
> *in ways contrary to the law'"*
> (Acts 18:4,13).

Manipulation or Persuasion

QUESTION: "What is the difference between manipulation and persuasion?"

ANSWER:

- *Those who manipulate* use dishonest methods of deception to achieve their goal.
- *Those who persuade* use honest reason to achieve their goal.

The Bible speaks plainly about our need to appeal to others by using accurate reasoning:

> *"Unlike so many...*
> *in Christ we speak before God with sincerity,*
> *as those sent from God...*
> *we have renounced secret and shameful ways;*
> *we do not use deception...*
> *by setting forth the truth plainly we commend ourselves*
> *to everyone's conscience in the sight of God"*
> (2 CORINTHIANS 2:17; 4:2).

C. What Is Spiritual Manipulation?

Now Sarah is 90 years old, and apparently still a knockout.

This time the king of Gerar is the recipient of Abraham and Sarah's conniving. After Abraham again identifies Sarah as his sister—out of fear for his own life—King Abimelek takes Sarah for his harem.

God intervenes this time, not with serious diseases as with Pharaoh, but with a most horrifying warning: "You are as good as dead because of the woman you have taken; she is a married woman" (Genesis 20:3).

Abimelek—petrified and perturbed—pleads his case before God. "LORD, will you destroy an innocent nation? Did he not say to me, 'She is my sister,' and didn't she also say, 'He is my brother'? I have done this with a clear conscience and clean hands" (Genesis 20:4-5).

In a dream the Lord acknowledges the king's innocence, and unveils His sovereign protection that had kept Abimelek from touching Sarah. Then the Lord gives this instruction:

> *"Now return the man's wife, for he is a prophet,*
> *and he will pray for you and you will live.*
> *But if you do not return her,*
> *you may be sure that you and all who belong to you will die"*
> (GENESIS 20:7).

Some lessons are hard to learn! It's been 25 years since Sarah and Abraham's first lesson, but trusting God doesn't always come easily. Manipulation, on the other hand, seems to come easily, even for the people of God—especially when it looks effective on the surface. Although *spiritual abuse* is a relatively new term, clearly spiritual manipulation has been occurring for a very long time.

Spiritual manipulation involves:

- **The use of religious words** or acts to manipulate someone for personal gain or to achieve a personal agenda, thereby harming that person's walk with God.

- **At the core of spiritual manipulation** is the control of others. Spiritual manipulation is acting "spiritual" to benefit oneself by using self-centered efforts to control others.

  A—Acting "spiritual" to…
  B—Benefit oneself by…
  U—Using…
  S—Self-centered…
  E—Efforts to control others.

Spiritual manipulation was a problem even in the earliest days of the Christian church.

> *"There are many rebellious people,*
> *full of meaningless talk and deception…*
> *They…are disrupting whole households by teaching*
> *things they ought not to teach"*
> (TITUS 1:10-11).

Examples:

- The *religious leader* who uses guilt to compel attendance, financial giving, or service

- The *religious counselor* who takes emotional or sexual advantage of a counselee in the name of "comfort" or "compassion"
- The *religious people* who accuse those who disagree with them of being rebellious toward God
- The *religious husband* who demands submission from his wife so that he can get her to violate her own conscience in order to satisfy his selfishness
- The *religious parent* who commands total, unquestioned compliance from children and uses harsh discipline without compassion or understanding
- The *religious employer* who micromanages employees, expecting them to work long hours without equitable monetary compensation.

Spiritual manipulators put confidence in their "position of authority" and their perceived right to use those under their influence to accomplish their own personal agenda. However, God alone has the wisdom, the power, and the right to accomplish His plans and purposes for those whom He has created.

> *"In their hearts humans plan their course,*
> *but the LORD establishes their steps"*
> (PROVERBS 16:9).

D. What Does It Mean to Manipulate Others?

King Abimelek returns Sarah, but not before confronting Abraham about his manipulative deception. "How have I wronged you that you have brought such great guilt upon me and my kingdom? You have done things to me that should never be done...What was your reason for doing this?" (Genesis 20:9-10).

Abraham fumbles with feeble excuses: "I said to myself, 'There is surely no fear of God in this place, and they will kill me because of my wife.' Besides, she really is my sister...I said to her, 'This is how you can show your love to me: Everywhere we go, say of me, "He is my brother"'"(Genesis 20:11-13).

Abimelek extends gracious gifts to the reunited couple, and Abraham prays on behalf of the king, for "the LORD had kept all the women in Abimelek's household from conceiving because of Abraham's wife Sarah" (Genesis 20:18). There are indeed negative consequences to deceptive manipulation. Sadly, wrong assumptions can lead to wrong actions, and manipulation of relationships is often the result.

- *To manipulate* is to unduly restrain, restrict, or rule in a relationship by use of deception.
- *To manipulate* is to suppress or oppress a person by subversive overt or covert tactics.
- *To manipulate* is to have excessive, cunning control.

However, God alone is to rule and reign over us. The Bible warns:

> *"You shall have no other gods before me"*
> (Deuteronomy 5:7).

E. What Does It Mean to Be Manipulated?

The town of Gerar is beset with guile—again.

This time Abraham's son, Isaac, will do the duping, and poor King Abimelek will become a victim of manipulation.

Isaac fears that the men of Gerar might kill him if he reveals that Rebekah is his wife, so he takes a page from his dad's playbook: "She is my sister" (Genesis 20:2; 26:7). The same deceptive words are uttered by father and son on two separate occasions—simply to shield the truth, simply because of fear.

The couple carries off the cover-up for a significant period of time, until King Abimelek "happens" to cast a downward glance through a window and sees Isaac and Rebekah—not having a sibling squabble, but caressing.

The king summons Isaac and fires off accusations and questions. "She is really your wife! Why did you say, 'She is my sister'?...What is this you have done to us? One of the men might well have slept with your wife, and you would have brought guilt upon us" (Genesis 26:9-10).

Like Abraham, Isaac expresses his fear for his life, and Abimelek gives orders throughout the land that anyone who harms Isaac and Rebekah will be killed. And also like Abraham, Isaac, the second patriarch of the faith, succumbs to fear—and resorts to manipulation.

Once more, faith is forgotten. Once more, someone is manipulated. Once more, someone is misled. Once more, someone suffers.

To be manipulated is to allow...

- *Another person* to dictate your thoughts, feelings, and behaviors
- *Decisions* to be made for you
- *Others* to have control over you, rather than allowing God to control you

Scripture tells us,

> *"The mind governed by the Spirit is life and peace"*
> (ROMANS 8:6).

F. What Is the Generational Maze of Manipulation?

The fabric of fear and the mantle of manipulation have passed from Abraham to Isaac and from Sarah to Rebekah, from father to son and from mother-in-law to daughter-in-law. And it does not stop there. This sin mushrooms into the third and fourth generations and beyond, leading to an even greater generational maze in time. Like all other sins, manipulation continues until it comes face-to-face with faith, the antithesis of fear.

> *"He [Jesus] said to his disciples,*
> *'Why are you so afraid? Do you still have no faith?'"*
> (MARK 4:40).

THE PATRIARCHS, THEIR WIVES, AND THEIR FAMILIES

- *Abram and Sarai manipulate Pharaoh* into thinking they are not husband and wife (Genesis 12:11-13,17-19).

- *Barren Sarai manipulates circumstances* to build a family for herself through her maidservant Hagar (Genesis 16:1-2).

- *Aged Sarah attempts to manipulate the Lord* by denying she had laughed when He said she would give birth to a son (Genesis 18:10-15).

- *Abraham and Sarah manipulate King Abimelek* into thinking they are not husband and wife (Genesis 20:2,4-5).

- *Jacob manipulates his brother Esau* by bartering a meal of lentil stew for Esau's birthright (Genesis 25:29-34).

- *Isaac and Rebekah manipulate King Abimelek* (of Gerar) into thinking they are not husband and wife (Genesis 26:7,9-10).

- *Rebekah and Jacob manipulate Esau and Isaac* to secure birthright blessings for Jacob (Genesis 27).

- *Rebekah manipulates Isaac,* persuading him to send Jacob to her brother Laban by claiming she feared he might otherwise marry a Hittite woman (Genesis 27:46).

- *Uncle Laban manipulates Jacob* on his wedding night by giving him the older sister, Leah, and not Rachel, as was agreed (Genesis 29:21-25).

- *Barren Rachel manipulates Jacob* to build a family for herself through her maidservant Bilhah (Genesis 30:1-3).

- *Leah, unable to continue bearing children, manipulates Jacob* to continue building her family through her maidservant Zilpah (Genesis 30:9-12).

- *Rachel manipulates Leah* into giving her some of her son's mandrakes, an aphrodisiac she hoped might help her become pregnant, in exchange for a night with Jacob (Genesis 30:14-16).

- *Laban manipulates Jacob's ability* to acquire a large herd from among his livestock as they agree to go their separate ways (Genesis 30:31-43).

- *Rachel manipulates Laban* by stealing his household gods and sitting on them inside her camel's saddle while he searches her tent in vain (Genesis 31:19,34-35).

- *Jacob manipulates Laban* by secretly leaving for Gilead with his family and all his possessions (Genesis 31:20,26-29).

- *Jacob's sons manipulate the Canaanites* to be circumcised so that while they are still weak in recovery the brothers can massacre their sister's rapist and all the men of the nearby town (Genesis 34:13-17,24-29).

G. What Is God's Heart on Manipulation?

Given the unsearchable wisdom and knowledge of God, the fact that His integrity is flawless and intact plus His inability to lie, the mere thought of being manipulative would never even enter His mind. He has no need to be anything less than honest and above board in His dealings with His creation.

We, on the other hand, all too often have to fight the temptation to be deceitful in an effort to get what we want or to not get what we don't want. If we are to be like the Lord and live a life of integrity, we must examine His ways and take to heart His invitation not to play games and see who can outwit who, but to...

"'Come now, let us reason together,' says the LORD"
(ISAIAH 1:18 ESV).

GOD'S HEART ON MANIPULATION

- **The world says** to slander another is acceptable; however, God's Word says to encourage one another and build each other up.

  "Therefore encourage one another and build each other up"
  (1 THESSALONIANS 5:11).

- **The world says** to hold a grudge against your brother is the way to get even; however, God's Word says to forgive whatever grievances you may have against someone.

  "Bear with each other and forgive one another if any of you has a grievance against someone. Forgive as the Lord forgave you"
  (COLOSSIANS 3:13).

- **The world says** make your own plans; however, God's Word says, "My plans are to prosper you, not to harm you, and to give you hope and a future."

  "'For I know the plans I have for you,' declares the LORD, 'plans to prosper you and not to harm you, plans to give you hope and a future'"
  (JEREMIAH 29:11).

- **The world says**, "Be the captain" of your soul; however, God says He will give you His Spirit so that you may follow His decrees and keep His laws.

> *"I will put my Spirit in you and move you to follow my decrees and*
> *be careful to keep my laws. Then you will live in the land I gave*
> *your ancestors; you will be my people, and I will be your God"*
> (Ezekiel 36:27-28).

- **The world says** whatever way you decide to act is acceptable; however, "the Lord weighs the heart."

> *"A person may think their own ways are*
> *right, but the Lord weighs the heart"*
> (Proverbs 21:2).

- **The world says** it is okay to save your own skin or lie to keep out of trouble; however, God cannot lie and does not want His children to lie.

> *"No one who practices deceit will dwell in my house; no*
> *one who speaks falsely will stand in my presence"*
> (Psalm 101:7).

- **The world says** it's okay to shirk individual responsibility; however, God's Word says you must account for your actions.

> *"Each one should carry their own load"*
> (Galatians 6:5).

- **The world says** get what you can any way you can; however, God's Word says ill-gotten gain will destroy you.

> *"A fortune made by a lying tongue is a*
> *fleeting vapor and a deadly snare"*
> (Proverbs 21:6).

- **The world says** a worldly lifestyle is to be sought after; however, God's Word says to present your body as a living sacrifice by the renewing of your mind.

> *"I urge you, brothers and sisters, in view of God's mercy, to*
> *offer your bodies as a living sacrifice, holy and pleasing to*

*God—this is your true and proper worship. Do not conform to
the pattern of this world, but be transformed by the renewing
of your mind. Then you will be able to test and approve
what God's will is—his good, pleasing and perfect will"*

(Romans 12:1-2).

The Master Manipulator: The Frank Abagnale Story

He was a con artist extraordinaire—a master manipulator who wrote a whopping $2.5 million in bad checks all around the world and became a millionaire…as a teenager.

"I was slipperier than a buttered escargot,"[3] Frank Abagnale recalled as he reflected on his five-year stretch of false identities. Inconceivably, Frank passed himself off as a pilot, a doctor, and a lawyer (among other occupations) and managed to stay a step ahead of the police until his capture at age 21. All the deception, all the manipulation, was driven by three motivations: the thrill, the money, and the *girls.*

Early on, Frank realized his minimum-wage job wouldn't finance his female fixation, so he asked his father for a gas credit card to loosen up his monthly budget. With card in hand, his first scam began—with Frank's own father becoming his first victim. This devious son manipulated the gas station attendants to financially give him back a portion of each sale while also encouraging them to pocket a portion themselves. He got away with the scheme at home by trashing the billing statements before his father saw them. Then an investigator for the gas company showed up at his father's workplace.[4]

Immediately, the interrogation began: "We are curious, sir…Just how…can you run up a $3,400 bill for gas, oil, batteries and tires for one 1952 Ford in the space of three months? You've put 14 sets of tires on that car in the last 60 days, bought 22 batteries in the past 90 days, and you can't be getting over two miles to the gallon on gas. We figure you don't even have an oil pan on the [darned] thing!"[5]

Frank's father could never have imagined being manipulated by his own flesh and blood. In fact, when he initially handed the gas card to Frank, he naively said, "All right, Frank, I trust you…I won't worry about your taking advantage of me.'"[6] (This merely highlights the danger of having misplaced trust in a manipulator.)

At age 16, Frank decided to leave home to make it on his own. After moving to New York City, he once again found himself struggling financially. This began his second season of scamming.

It was just too easy! Frank could cash checks in grocery stores, hotels, and other businesses with no one checking his account or detecting his doctored driver's license that added 10 years to his age. In no time, Frank officially became what is known on the streets as a "professional paperhanger"—a *check swindler.*[7] But he was also known on the streets as "hot"—*wanted by the police.*

Realizing he needed to fly under the radar, Frank sought to find another income source. That's when the string of false identities began. As soon as the police nipped at his heels in one profession, he switched to another. It was as though he was playing a game of *catch me if you can!*

Posing as a commercial airline pilot, Frank secured a uniform, faked a pilot's ID, forged an FAA license, and learned as much as he could about flying. The ruse enabled him to hitch rides on planes all around the world, earning him the nickname "The Skywayman."[8]

After this jig was up, Frank hightailed it to Atlanta and posed as a pediatrician, supposedly on sabbatical. He studied for his new role in a medical library at a nearby hospital, and before long, he was given the job of monitoring interns on the night shift. Next came his promotion to resident supervisor. Astoundingly, Frank received official authorization to practice medicine in Georgia. But when one of his patients—a child—almost died, he quit and left town. New Orleans became his next destination, where, while manipulating everyone he met, he posed as an attorney.[9]

Eventually this master of manipulation decided to skip the heat stateside and settle in France, but that turned out to be short-lived. He had bilked $300,000 out of French banks when a former girlfriend saw his face on a wanted poster and turned him in. He was arrested and imprisoned for a year in both Sweden and France before serving five years in a US penitentiary. After serving less than half his sentence, Frank was released on parole—but only on the condition that he shared his methods of manipulation and fraud with federal agents to help them catch other "Franks" in the future.

While working for more than 35 years for the FBI, Frank became one of the world's foremost authorities on check swindling, identifying forgeries, and busting embezzlers. In fact, he created the watermark that is placed on the back of bank checks, which made it more difficult for them to be altered or forged.

Frank also wrote two books and founded a consulting firm—all to educate people on how to avoid becoming victims of fraud.[10] And the 2002 film *Catch Me If You Can* nominated for numerous prestigious awards and starring Leonardo Dicaprio and Tom Hanks, memorializes this brazen bamboozler's manipulative years.

Frank Abagnale has been labeled both notorious and brilliant, but when he looks back on his past he sees nothing to boast about. In his own words, "I consider my past immoral, unethical, and illegal. It is something I am not proud of."[11]

Ultimately, Frank's life displays what God longs to see in every one of us—a repentant heart and a changed life. The simple truth is this: By living with a manipulative mind-set, *you want what you want when you want it...regardless of how you get it.* But getting your own way by means of manipulation is much too costly a pursuit. In the end, it will catch up with you! While you may get all that you think you want, you'll lose more than you ever bargained for.

The Bible's book of wisdom presents these words of warning for every manipulator to take to heart:

> *"Truthful lips endure forever, but a lying tongue lasts only a moment...*
> *The integrity of the upright guides them, but the*
> *unfaithful are destroyed by their duplicity"*

(PROVERBS 12:19; 11:3).

II. CHARACTERISTICS OF MANIPULATION

His name says it all.

After nine months of jostling in Rebekah's womb, Jacob comes into the world just behind Esau, his hand grasping Esau's heel. The name *Jacob* means "heel catcher," but its significance also stretches further into time when Jacob's character will one day mirror the name's additional meanings—"trickster" and "supplanter."[12] The two brothers couldn't be more different. Esau is extroverted and brash and a skillful hunter; Jacob is introverted and quiet, a cook who prefers spending his days at home. Esau is described as "hairy"; Jacob is described as "smooth." Esau has the favor of his father, Isaac; Jacob has the favor of his mother, Rebekah.

Jacob's manipulative ways will manifest themselves in adulthood when another jostling of sorts occurs—over Esau's birthright.

Esau would later say of Jacob,

> *"Isn't he rightly named Jacob?*
> *This is the second time he has taken advantage of me"*
> (GENESIS 27:36).

A. What Players Participate in the Game of Manipulation?

Esau has just returned from the countryside with one thing on his mind—his stomach. Once he gets a whiff of the thick red lentil stew Jacob is cooking, he is willing to satisfy his hunger pangs at all costs. "Quick, let me have some of that red stew! I'm famished!" (Genesis 25:30).

Esau does indeed get a delicious bowl of stew along with some bread and something to drink, but it costs him dearly. Jacob offers the stew on one condition: Esau must give him his birthright.

> *"Jacob said, 'Swear to me first.'*
> *So he swore an oath to him, selling his birthright to Jacob"*
> (GENESIS 25:33).

As their father, Isaac, is now aged and approaching death, the loss of the birthright blessing will soon leave Esau with a very bad taste in his mouth.

And so it generally goes with those who partake of the foul game of manipulation. Yet those who play the game have an entirely different perspective, as do Jacob and his mother, Rebekah.

MANIPULATIVE POWER PLAYERS[13]

- Use verbal and physical abuse to gain power

- Use put-downs to gain position

- Dominate conversations to gain control

- Use threats to intimidate

- Say anything to humiliate

Goal: To manipulate by implying, "I am right and you are wrong."

> *"They make their tongues as sharp as a serpent's;*
> *the poison of vipers is on their lips"*
> (PSALM 140:3).

MANIPULATIVE MARTYRS[14]

- Scold others to make them feel sad
- Blame others to make them feel bad
- Play the guilt game to make others feel at fault
- Shame others to make them feel sorry
- Play the victim to make others feel pity

Goal: To manipulate by implying, "It's all your fault. How could you treat me this way?"

> *"The soothing tongue is a tree of life, but a*
> *perverse tongue crushes the spirit"*
> (PROVERBS 15:4).

MANIPULATIVE RESCUERS

- Provide unsolicited help to make others feel obligated
- Assist others, even when not wanted, to gain a sense of indebtedness
- Help others to make them feel ingratiated
- Give exaggerated care to cause others to feel a commitment
- Extend aid in order to coerce others

Goal: To manipulate by implying, "After all I have done for you, now you owe me."

> *"A person may think their own ways are*
> *right, but the LORD weighs the heart"*
> (PROVERBS 21:2).

MANIPULATIVE PEOPLE PLEASERS[15]

- Use charm to gain the favor of others

- Praise others to gain approval
- Accommodate others to gain appreciation
- Extend favors to gain gratitude
- Do kind acts to gain loyalty

Goal: To manipulate by implying, "After all I've done to please you, you should please me."

"Charm is deceptive"
(PROVERBS 31:30).

B. What Are the Eight S's of Verbal Manipulation?

Like mother, like son.

The time has come, and Isaac is ready to bestow the birthright blessing upon his oldest son, Esau—apparently oblivious to the bartering between Jacob and Esau for a mere bowl of stew. Rebekah overhears Isaac telling Esau to go hunt some wild game and prepare him some "tasty food," and then he will give his first-born his blessing (Genesis 27:4).

Immediately Rebekah's manipulative mind begins strategizing, and she takes full advantage of one critical factor concerning her husband: He can no longer see.

No sooner has Esau walked out the door when Rebekah gives the following instructions to Jacob: "Now, my son, listen carefully and do what I tell you: Go out to the flock and bring me two choice young goats, so I can prepare some tasty food for your father, just the way he likes it. Then take it to your father to eat, so that he may give you his blessing before he dies" (Genesis 27:8-10).

Jacob's mind reels with questions: "But my brother Esau is a hairy man, while I have smooth skin. What if my father touches me?" (Genesis 27:11-12).

Jacob fears becoming the recipient of a curse rather than a blessing, but Rebekah accepts full responsibility and proceeds with her plot. And as it turns out, the goats will be useful for more than just tasty food.

And the scheming and conniving go on, with one verbal game after another.

VERBAL METHODS OF PLAYING THE GAME

1. SUBVERSIVE SCHEMERS

- Scheming to plot a deceptive plan
- Scheming to distort reality

  – Scheming by telling half-truths

  – Scheming by misrepresentation

The Bible addresses how God deals with schemers: "He [God] catches the wise in their craftiness, and the schemes of the wily are swept away" (Job 5:13).

The manipulator implies, "If you don't willingly do what I want, I will trick you into doing it."

2. SCHEMING SHOULDS

  – "You should show me respect."

  – "You should meet my needs."

  – "You should make me happy."

  – "You should give me security."

  – "You owe me…"

  – "You ought to…"

  – "You are expected to…"

  – "You are supposed to…"

The Bible says, "[Love] is not self-seeking" (1 Corinthians 13:5).

The manipulator implies, "If you don't meet my expectations, you are guilty of neglect."

3. STRIDENT SCREAMING[16]

  – Yelling to apply pressure

  – Yelling to unnerve

  – Yelling to publicly humiliate

  – Yelling to intimidate

The Bible says, "They sharpen their tongues like swords and aim cruel words like deadly arrows" (Psalm 64:3-4).

The manipulator implies, "If you don't do what I want, I'll make you wish you had."

4. SARCASTIC SWORDS[17]

  – Stabbing with cutting humor

  – Stabbing with jabbing words

  – Stabbing with put-downs

  – Stabbing with malicious mocking

The Bible says those who crucified Jesus "twisted together a crown of thorns and set it on his head. They put a staff in his right hand. Then they knelt in front of him and mocked him. 'Hail, king of the Jews!'" (Matthew 27:29).

The manipulator implies, "If you aren't what I want you to be, I will use words to wound you."

5. SEXUAL SEDUCTION[18]

- Seductive talk
- Suggestive clothing
- Sensual advertising
- Sexual body movements

The Bible warns about the manipulative, seductive woman: "With persuasive words she led him astray; she seduced him with her smooth talk. All at once he followed her like an ox going to the slaughter, like a deer stepping into a noose" (Proverbs 7:21-22).

The manipulator implies, "If you don't buy what I'm selling, you are not going to be popular or powerful, accepted or admired."

6. SHOWERING SENTIMENTS[19]

- Excessive praise to appeal to the ego
- Excessive gifts to create a sense of obligation
- Excessive affection to gain a sexual or emotional advantage
- Excessive money to buy control

The Bible says, "A flattering mouth works ruin" (Proverbs 26:28).

The manipulator implies, "If you don't respond to my generosity by doing what I want you to do, you are ungrateful."

7. SLY SUGGESTIONS[20]

- *Guilt Game #1:* A wife says, "John just bought Sara a new car. It must be nice to be so loved."

- *Guilt Game #2:* A husband says, "Mary encourages her husband to go out with the guys any time he wants, for as long as he wants. He's lucky to have such a wife."

- *Guilt Game #3:* A "friend" says to another friend: "Chris has a friend who will give him any amount of money—no questions asked. Now that is a true friend."

  – *Guilt Game #4:* A teenager says to parents, "None of my friends
  have a curfew. It must be nice to have such trusting parents."

The Bible describes the manipulator: "Enemies disguise themselves with their
lips, but in their hearts they harbor deceit" (Proverbs 26:24).

The manipulator implies, "You ought to meet my every need, and if you don't,
I'll make you feel guilty."

8. SYMPATHY SEEKERS[21]

  – Speaking and acting needy intentionally

  – Speaking and acting pitiful with pity parties

  – Speaking and acting helpless and childlike

  – Speaking and acting hopeless unless a rescuer arrives

The Bible says, "Each one should carry their own load" (Galatians 6:5).

The manipulator implies, "You should take care of my heart, and if you don't,
you are callous and cruel."

C. What Are the Eight S's of Nonverbal Manipulation?

Rebekah covers Jacob's hands and neck in goat hair and puts Esau's best
clothes on him. The ruse is now complete. Jacob is the personification of Esau,
down to the smell of the outdoors that wafts through Esau's clothing.

"Esau" presents himself before Isaac, who may be blind today but wasn't
born yesterday! Isaac inquires about the short time span it took "Esau" to find
and cook the game, and instantly recognizes Jacob's voice but is perplexed by his
"hairy hands."

As Jacob responds to his father's inquiries, the portrait of deceit becomes
colored with more than just manipulation. The quickly served-up meal? "The
LORD your God gave me success" (Genesis 27:20), Jacob lies. "'Are you really my son
Esau?'…'I am'" (Genesis 27:24), Jacob lies again.

And the birthright blessing ensues:

> *"May God give you heaven's dew and earth's richness—*
> *an abundance of grain and new wine.*
> *May nations serve you and peoples bow down to you.*
> *Be lord over your brothers,*
> *and may the sons of your mother bow down to you.*
> *May those who curse you be cursed*
> *and those who bless you be blessed"*
>
> (GENESIS 27:28-29).

Thus, this manipulative maze incorporates deceptive words and actions with blatant lies and "hairy hands."

NONVERBAL METHODS OF PLAYING THE MANIPULATION GAME

1. SITUATION SEIZER

– Uses the poor judgment of others to receive personal promotion

– Uses the poor health of others to receive personal profit

– Uses the problems of others to receive personal praise

– Uses the pain of others to receive personal progress

The Bible says, "Do nothing out of selfish ambition or vain conceit. Rather, in humility value others above yourselves" (Philippians 2:3).

The manipulator implies, "My wants and wishes supersede those of everyone else."

2. SILENT TREATMENT[22]

– Pouting, brooding, and ignoring

– Coldly turning away from your spouse

– Not answering the phone or door as punishment

– Refusing to speak to an offender

The Bible says, "So I remained utterly silent, not even saying anything good. But my anguish increased" (Psalm 39:2).

The manipulator implies, "If you don't do what I want, you don't get my approval, my communication, or me."

3. SLAM-BAM SLAMMING

– Slamming drawers

– Slamming doors

– Slamming phones

– Slamming books

The Bible says, "'In your anger do not sin': Do not let the sun go down while you are still angry" (Ephesians 4:26).

The manipulator implies, "If you don't meet my expectations, you don't deserve any dialogue with me, but I'll make my point in other intimidating ways."

4. SCORNFUL SNEER

- The curl of the lip
- The roll of the eyes
- The raising of the eyebrows
- The squinting of the eyes

The Bible says, "Who are you mocking? At whom do you sneer and stick out your tongue? Are you not a brood of rebels, the offspring of liars?" (Isaiah 57:4).

The manipulator implies, "If you don't do what I want you to do, you don't deserve my respect."

5. SARCASTIC SOUNDS

- Audible sighs
- Deep grunts
- Long groans
- Smacked lips

The Bible says, "All my longings lie open before you, Lord; my sighing is not hidden from you" (Psalm 38:9).

The manipulator implies, "If you don't meet my expectations, I will let you know how perturbed I am with you without saying a word to you."

6. SUPPRESSED SUPPORT[23]

- Withholding compliments
- Withholding gifts
- Withholding affection
- Withdrawing presence

The Bible says, via the apostle Paul, "We are not withholding our affection from you, but you are withholding yours from us" (2 Corinthians 6:12).

The manipulator implies, "If you don't meet my standards, you will suffer for it by not getting any attention whatsoever from me."

7. STRATEGIC STALLING

- Intentionally slow
- Intentionally late
- Intentionally "deaf" by ignoring
- Intentionally forgetful

The Bible says, "[Love] does not dishonor others" (1 Corinthians 13:5).

The manipulator implies, "If you don't give me control, I'll take control in other ways and frustrate you in the process."

8. SNIVELING SOBBER[24]

- Timed tears
- Subtle sniffles
- Tearful stories
- Extended crying

The Bible says, "They do not cry out to me from their hearts but wail on their beds. They slash themselves, appealing to their gods for grain and new wine, but they turn away from me" (Hosea 7:14).

The manipulator implies, "If you don't meet my emotional needs, I'll get your attention and make you feel guilty by falling apart."

D. What Are the Characteristics of Spiritually Manipulative People?

Exit "blessed" Jacob. Enter "beaten-to-the-punch" Esau.

He enters his father's presence with food in tow, eager for Isaac to begin eating—and expecting the blessing to be bestowed. But Esau's world gets turned upside down with the following question from his father: "Who are you?"

"'I am your son,' he answered, 'your firstborn, Esau.'"

"Isaac trembled violently and said, 'Who was it, then, that hunted game and brought it to me? I ate it just before you came and I blessed him—and indeed he will be blessed!'" (Genesis 27:32-33).

Esau breaks out with a loud and bitter cry, having no trouble identifying his impersonator and devising a dastardly plan of his own...

Every ruse has repercussions whether the initiator is relative, friend, or foe, but they are especially serious repercussions when the ruse affects a person's relationship with God.

A person with a heart for the Lord may struggle with the temptation to manipulate others. The following list identifies the traits of someone who may have developed such a habit or learned such a pattern of behavior:

- *Controlling* religious family members
- *Manipulative* church leaders/members (and equivalents in all religions)
- *Covert* occult practitioners
- *Mind-controlling* cultists

E. What Characterizes Spiritually Manipulative Groups?

Before Esau turns his attention to the "rightly named Jacob" (Genesis 27:36), he pleads with Isaac. "'Bless me—me too, my father!'...'Do you have only one blessing, my father? Bless me too, my father!' Then Esau wept aloud" (Genesis 27:34,38).

But Isaac's subsequent words for Esau are pitiful compared to what has been proclaimed for Jacob. "Your dwelling will be away from the earth's richness, away from the dew of heaven above. You will live by the sword and you will serve your brother. But when you grow restless, you will throw his yoke from off your neck" (Genesis 27:39-40).

The tragic turn of events leads Esau to look ahead to payback time. "The days of mourning for my father are near; then I will kill my brother Jacob" (Genesis 27:41).

Rebekah becomes aware of the planned revenge and decides to manipulate and deceive her husband once again. She concocts a story about how Jacob needs to be sent away to live with her brother Laban in order to "protect" him from marrying a Hittite woman because Esau's Hittite wives so grieve her:

> *"I'm disgusted with living because of these Hittite women.*
> *If Jacob takes a wife from among the women of this land,*
> > *from Hittite women like these,*
> > *my life will not be worth living"*
> (Genesis 27:46).

As the manipulative account concludes, Rebekah never sees her beloved son Jacob again, though the two brothers eventually reconcile.

The cost of manipulating people rather than trusting God, and of using deception rather than reason, is high indeed. Why, then, do certain individuals and groups succumb to manipulation?

Spiritually manipulative leaders are generally[25]...

- *Authoritarian*—Implying that God communicates with His people only through a hierarchy of power, not through an intimate personal relationship with each individual

- *Coercive*—Using any tactic available to persuade followers to disregard their own logic and do what the leaders demand

- *Condemning*—Heaping condemnation on outsiders and anyone who leaves the congregation

- *Discriminatory*—Telling members their needs are less important than are the needs of leaders

- *Image-conscious*—Seeking to present themselves as having perfect, unquestionable righteousness

- *Intimidating*—Threatening members routinely with punishment or excommunication in order to gain compliance

- *Isolating*—Encouraging members to minimize or discontinue contact with family, friends, and the outside world

- *Legalistic*—Expecting members to follow rigid rules and to make extreme sacrifices of money, time, and energy for the sake of the organization

- *Perfectionistic*—Condemning failure of any type or magnitude and ridiculing members who fail the organization in any area and to any degree

- *Suppressive of Criticism*—Maintaining that those who question anything about the organization are actually challenging God's authority

- *Terrorizing*—Blaming the ministry's problems on the sins of the members and threatening God's displeasure and discipline

- *Unbalanced*—Flaunting their distinctiveness to validate their claim of having a "special" relationship with God

Most spiritual leaders who use spiritual manipulation present God as a stern taskmaster—a judgmental *judge*. These spiritual manipulators have a misplaced confidence in themselves that often leads to frustration, failure, and self-condemnation. And their attitude toward others is one of prideful exclusivity, which produces frustration, fear, and resentment in others. The Bible tells us:

> *"Such people are false apostles,*
> *deceitful workers, masquerading as apostles of Christ"*
> (2 CORINTHIANS 11:13).

Love Turned Lethal: The Loverboy Story

She considers him her "loverboy"—smooth, sweet, soothing to her heart. At age 17, "Anna" is in love and ready to marry the man who has made every promise to her—especially to "love her for life."[26]

One day he exclaims, "Let's go to Greece!" Wooing her away from her Albanian home and the cultural oppression she feels, she simply cannot resist. The prospect of building a life together in Greece sounds like heaven on earth—until it becomes a living hell.

Upon their arrival in Greece, the man she loves—the man she trusts—does the unbelievable, the unimaginable, the unthinkable. In exchange for her devotion, he destroys every promise by selling her to a sex trafficker and stealing her passport.

This is the most horrifying form of manipulation anyone could experience. Anna's hopes are dashed, her body is debased, and her dreams are destroyed. She becomes yet another manipulated victim of the Loverboy Syndrome sweeping across Europe: young men feigning love to lure young women away from the security of family and friends, then callously selling them to depraved sex traffickers.

Anna's initiation into her dark new world begins with rape and beatings. Soon she is held hostage in a hotel with 30 other girls from different countries. All are forced to work the streets as prostitutes, and they experience torture upon torture.

Anna is expected to have sexual relations with 50 men a day. A full 24-hour cycle often leaves her body beaten and bloodied. Many times she tries to escape, but is always caught and then forced to endure even more torture. For two years Anna is viciously victimized—repeatedly day after day.

Eventually Anna comes across a computer and, on a social network, she makes a desperate plea to a woman she doesn't even know. This caring woman, who lives near the hotel, cannot ignore Anna's degrading plight and desperate cry for help. Together, they make arrangements for Anna to slip out of a back window and then flee to the woman's car for a fast getaway.

The escape is successful! Ultimately Anna makes it back to her native Albania, but the nightmare is far from over. Although she had been deceitfully victimized, Anna struggles with overwhelming guilt and shame resulting in several suicide attempts. Her former prostitution becomes a burden she can share with only one other person, her cousin, who had also been rescued from sex trafficking.

Tragically, Anna can't even tell her parents about her horrendous ordeal because within her culture is the disturbing premise "It's always the woman's fault." Women wrongfully bear the shame even when they've been bitterly abused. Anna also lives with continual fear—if her brother were ever to discover she had been a prostitute, he would probably kill her.

Because Anna's cousin had received compassionate help from a Hope for the Heart ministry partner in Albania (MEDIA 7),* Anna calls its live, daily talk show to share her story and seek hope and healing. Telling her tragic story is a huge step for Anna, because Albanians struggle with another premise deeply embedded within their culture: "People don't talk about their problems."

Yet Anna's tearful life story, broadcast on the radio, is so moving that God uses her pain to powerfully impact the lives of others. In fact, immediately after she shares the warning signs of manipulation and the steps to preventing it—how to avoid becoming a victim of the Loverboy Syndrome—two young women call the ministry for counseling, believing their boyfriends are in the process of trying to sell them.

Through this radio ministry, Anna becomes a Christian and now attends an Albanian university to become a teacher. Today, because of past pain, she can help others move out of manipulative relationships and cut the strings of controlling people. And because God rescued Anna in a mighty way, she can personally attest to these powerful words from her own life:

> *"He lifted me out of the slimy pit, out of the mud and mire; he*
> *set my feet on a rock and gave me a firm place to stand"*
> (Psalm 40:2).

---

* Media 7 consists of first-generation Christians who broadcast *Hope for the Heart* three times a day in both Albania and war-torn Kosovo. Hope for the Heart's Volume 1 *Biblical Counseling Keys* on Sex and Marriage topics was recommended to Albanians by the government on its book review television program, stating, "Every one of you need to read this!" This resulted in the availability of our other Albanian-language books in secular bookstores.

III. Causes of Manipulation

Where did this maze of manipulation begin, and how did it begin?

The guile began in the Garden of Eden.

God pronounced everything He had made to be "very good" (Genesis 1:31), but in time things became very bad. His perfect creation will be marred by manipulation, darkened by deception.

A creature "more crafty than any of the wild animals the LORD God had made" (Genesis 3:1) plays a part in tarnishing the crowning jewel of God's creation—man and woman—and the stain of sin will mark all who come after them. Eve is the first to be manipulated. She becomes mesmerized with what stands in the middle of the garden.

A. What Sets the Stage for Manipulation?

Satan speaks through a serpent—one that apparently stands upright. But its destiny is known for sure. The serpent is forever doomed to slither.

Cunning and clever, surreal and altogether satanic, the serpent draws Eve into a conversation that challenges the commands of God. "Did God really say, 'You must not eat from any tree in the garden'?" (Genesis 3:1).

The serpent's first strike is to cast doubt—to knock Eve off-kilter, to send her mind spinning as to *what God had actually said.* He attacks her confidence in God's command by altering and misquoting God's prohibition against eating the fruit to include all the trees in the garden.

The serpent's second strike is literally to lie about the consequences of eating the forbidden fruit from the tree of the knowledge of good and evil. God had said, "When you eat from it you will certainly die" (Genesis 2:17). However, Satan says, "You will not certainly die" (Genesis 3:4).

Eve is enticed in every way by the appeal of the fruit. It looks good, it will taste good, but more so, it will make her "like God," or so the serpent says (Genesis 3:5). Eve picks the fruit, tastes it, and passes it on to Adam.

"Therefore...sin entered the world through one man,
and death through sin, and in this way death came to all people"
(Romans 5:12).

Satan did a masterful job of manipulation, one that laid a solid foundation for sin and set the stage for manipulation to continue flowing through families from generation to generation to generation.

Background of Manipulation

In childhood, you...

- *Had an over-controlling parent:* domineering, critical, angry, punitive, or manipulative
- *Experienced* some type of abuse: verbal, emotional, physical, sexual, or spiritual
- *Grew up* in an abusive home environment
- *Had "no voice"* at home to share honest facts and feelings; you never dealt with your true feelings
- *Learned* about manipulation by watching your parents—with children, more is *caught* than *taught*
- *Grew up* in a "blaming home" that used guilt to control others
- *Accepted* blame for everything in childhood, a mind-set that easily set you up to be manipulated in adulthood
- *Blamed* everyone else for all of your wrongs, setting yourself up to become a manipulator
- *Thought* your "normal" was normal, but it was not
- *Wanted* to please others, but your "pleasing" was never pleasing enough

First Corinthians 13:11 tells us,

> *"When I was a child, I talked like a child,*
> *I thought like a child, I reasoned like a child.*
> *When I became a man, I put the ways of childhood behind me."*

Feelings of Being "Different"

Because you were...

- *Born* with a disability
- *Discriminated* against
- *A poor* student in school
- *Taunted* by schoolmates
- *Humiliated* by a teacher
- *Shamed* by a coach

- *Teased* by siblings
- *Taught* that God was ready to punish every bad thought
- *Told* that you could never please God

First Samuel 16:7 tells us:

> *"The* LORD *does not look at the things people look at . . .*
> *the* LORD *looks at the heart."*

B. What Motivates People to Manipulate Others?

There is no record that Adam wrestled with his conscience, or even attempted to wrestle the forbidden fruit from Eve's hand.

The Bible says, "She also gave some to her husband, who was with her, and he ate it" (Genesis 3:6). Period. Case closed. End of story. Well, not quite.

The sweetness of the fruit quickly sours as "the eyes of both of them were opened" (Genesis 3:7), and they realize—for the first time—they are naked. A flood of emotions sweep over them—discomfort with their nakedness, vulnerability, guilt, alienation, fear.

The devil accomplished his goal. He succeeded in bringing sin into God's creation and into the lives of His cherished couple. He challenged God's power and control, and now he feels he has won the battle, he has beaten God.

> *"You [Satan] said in your heart . . .*
> *I will make myself like the Most High"*
> (ISAIAH 14:13-14).

PEOPLE MANIPULATE OTHERS TO . . . [27]

- *Make* them feel guilty
- *Present* "reality" the way they want others to see it
- *Get* others to believe what they want them to believe
- *Control* others in order to protect themselves from being taken advantage of by others
- *Get* their own way
- *Maintain* a dependent friendship even when the relationship is unhealthy
- *Avoid* having to meet personal obligations and responsibilities in life

- *Appear* positive when they actually feel negative toward someone
- *Rescue* them or clean up their "messes"
- *Make* others feel sorry for them and take responsibility for them
- *Intentionally confuse* others with unclear messages
- *Get* others to do for them what they would not otherwise choose to do
- *Avoid* meeting personal obligations in life
- *Keep* them from moving away from the relationship
- *Force* others to feel responsible for them or for their welfare
- *Control* the emotions and reasoning of the ones being manipulated
- *Win* the battle for control

Scripture clearly tells us:

> *"The heart is deceitful above all things and beyond cure.*
> *Who can understand it?"*
> (JEREMIAH 17:9).

C. What Causes Someone to Succumb to Manipulation?

After succumbing to manipulation, Adam and Eve sew fig leaves together for clothing because they are uneasy with their nakedness. They hear the Lord walking in the garden and rather than respond to Him, they hide from Him.

"The LORD God called to the man, 'Where are you?'" (As if He has no clue!)

Then Adam answers, "I heard you in the garden, and I was afraid because I was naked; so I hid."

God replies, "Who told you that you were naked? Have you eaten from the tree that I commanded you not to eat from?" (Genesis 3:9-11).

The silver-tongued snake manipulates the first pair with a promise: The forbidden fruit will make them wise. Now, having succumbed to manipulation, the couple actually attempts to manipulate their Creator—proving that, rather than becoming wise, they have become merely weak-minded.

Typically, the manipulated don't understand why they are so easily baited. They fail to realize that it is as simple as choosing to whom they will respond—their manipulator or their Maker. Typically, they have a combination of the following:

MISPLACED DEPENDENCE ON THE MANIPULATOR[28]

- "*I must* have you in my life."
- "*I need* you to give meaning and purpose to my life."
- "*I have* to have your approval in order to feel significant."

Solution:

> "*Stop trusting in mere humans, who have but a breath*
> *in their nostrils. Why hold them in esteem?*"
> (ISAIAH 2:22).

MISPLACED PRIORITIES[29]

- "*What others think* is more important than anything else."
- "*The judgment and opinion* of others takes precedence over my own."
- "*The end justifies the means,* even if it involves violating my conscience."

Solution:

> "*I strive always to keep my conscience clear before God and man*"
> (ACTS 24:16).

FEAR OF DISAPPROVAL

- "*I can't* say 'no' for fear of making someone angry at me."
- "*I'm afraid* of being rejected."
- "*I can't* take a stand against someone whose approval I need."

Solution:

> "*Do not fear the reproach of mere mortals or*
> *be terrified by their insults.*
> *For the moth will eat them up like a garment;*
> *the worm will devour them like wool.*
> *But my righteousness will last forever,*
> *my salvation through all generations*"
> (ISAIAH 51:7–8).

PERFORMANCE-BASED ACCEPTANCE

- "*I am accepted* only because of what I do."

- "*I have value* only if my work is acceptable."
- "*I have worth* only if I please others."

Solution:

> *"The very hairs of your head are all numbered.*
> *Don't be afraid; you are worth more than many sparrows"*
> (LUKE 12:7).

DEFENSIVENESS ABOUT THE RELATIONSHIP

- "*I am* not seeing that the relationship is unhealthy."
- "*I am* not facing the need for a change in the relationship."
- "*I am* not willing to do anything about changing the relationship."

Solution:

> *"Search me, God, and know my heart;*
> *test me and know my anxious thoughts.*
> *See if there is any offensive way in me,*
> *and lead me in the way everlasting"*
> (PSALM 139:23-24).

LOSS OF INDEPENDENCE

- "*I am* not allowed to make independent plans."
- "*I am* not permitted to have 'alone time.'"
- "*I am* not encouraged to spend money on my own or to take time for myself."

Solution:

> *"My salvation and my honor depend on God;*
> *he is my mighty rock, my refuge"*
> (PSALM 62:7).

LOSS OF CONFIDENCE

- "*I lose* confidence when I am told the decision I made is wrong."
- "*I feel* uncomfortable when I am told my memory is wrong."
- "*I feel* stupid when I am told my perception is wrong."

Solution:

> *"Encourage one another and build each other up,*
> *just as in fact you are doing"*
> (1 THESSALONIANS 5:11).

LOSS OF IDENTITY (CONTROLLED BY THE MANIPULATOR'S PERSONALITY OR POWER)

- *"I am consumed* by the actions of the manipulator."
- *"I am consumed* by what the manipulator wants and desires."
- *"I am consumed* by what the manipulator threatens to do."

Solution:

> *"It is for freedom that Christ has set us free.*
> *Stand firm, then, and do not let yourselves*
> *be burdened again by a yoke of slavery"*
> (GALATIANS 5:1).

LOSS OF OBJECTIVITY (MAKES EXCUSES FOR THE MANIPULATOR)

- *"They don't mean* to act that way."
- *"They can't help* being that way."
- *"They are just trying* to make things better."

Solution:

> *"Better is open rebuke than hidden love"*
> (PROVERBS 27:5).

=== *Misplaced Dependency* ===

QUESTION: "How is my dependency misplaced if I am being manipulated?"

ANSWER: If you assume you must meet all the needs and fulfill all the expectations of someone else, then you are depending too much on yourself and expecting too much from yourself. You are taking the role God alone should have in that person's life. Likewise, if you assume someone must meet all your needs and fulfill all your expectations, then you are depending too much on them. You are putting a person in the role God alone should have in your life. This is what the Lord says:

> *"Cursed is the one who trusts in man,*
> *who draws strength from mere flesh*
> *and whose heart turns away from the LORD...*
> *But blessed is the one who trusts in the LORD,*
> *whose confidence is in him"*
> (JEREMIAH 17:5,7).

D. What Is the Connection Between Brainwashing and Manipulation?

Call it a classic case of passing the buck.

Adam admits eating the forbidden fruit, but not before he couches his confession in condemnation of Eve and even hints that God is at fault as well. Running from responsibility, Adam says, "The woman you put here with me—she gave me some fruit from the tree, and I ate it" (Genesis 3:12). You put her here, God. *She* gave me the fruit. *Then* I ate it.

Fortunately for Adam, God has patience with him and turns His gaze to Eve.

When God questions Eve, her index finger is likely stretched toward the serpent: "The serpent deceived me, and I ate" (Genesis 3:13).

Although the couple was not brainwashed, they did buy into Satan's deception—hook, line, and sinker. Then they found themselves scrambling to justify their behavior just like many who have been manipulated by maniacal brainwashing. While brainwashing may not always be associated with manipulation, by definition it can be considered an extreme form of manipulation.

To *brainwash* is to impose a set of usually political or religious beliefs on somebody through various coercive methods of indoctrination that are intended to destroy the victim's prior beliefs. It is to force someone to accept a particular set of beliefs by repeating the same idea many times so that the person can no longer think independently.[30]

THREE FORMS OF BRAINWASHING

- **Verbal Brainwashing**

  Intimidation. . . . . Implying that your failure to comply with all demands, attitudes, or beliefs of the manipulator will result in severe consequences

Indoctrination	Repeatedly implanting messages contrary to your presently held values
Discrediting.	Belittling your "outside" family and friends who disagree with the manipulator
Degrading.	Engaging in name-calling, insults, ridicule, and humiliation
Labeling	Claiming that your thoughts are childish, stupid, or crazy

Psalm 35:20 tells us, *"They do not speak peaceably, but devise false accusations against those who live quietly in the land."*

• Emotional Brainwashing

Isolation	Depriving you of all outside sources of emotional and social support
Induced exhaustion.	Keeping you up late, interrupting your sleep, causing sleep deprivation
Excessive compliance.	Enforcing trivial demands in a militant way
Ignoring	Withdrawing emotional support, but later denying that had been done
Forgetting	Breaking promises and agreements on purpose
Exploiting	Using you or someone close to you for self-interests or gain

Psalm 10:2 tells us, *"In his arrogance the wicked man hunts down the weak, who are caught in the schemes he devises."*

• Spiritual Brainwashing

Forced compliance	Requiring and reinforcing total adherence to prescribed behaviors, beliefs, doctrines, and teachings or face severe repercussions
Sacred writings	Repeatedly reading, memorizing, and quoting writings of an alleged supreme being or divinely appointed prophet,

	instilling messages conflicting with traditionally held values and beliefs
Repetitious prayers	Routinely reading or quoting memorized prayers acknowledging total allegiance to and praising some alleged supreme being
Rigid rules.............	Demanding complete obedience to religious laws that regulate actions, attitudes, and allegiances of group members
Religious rituals	Engaging in required rituals, ceremonies, or practices that reinforce sacred writ and allegiance to a particular supreme being

Matthew 7:15 tells us, *"Watch out for false prophets. They come to you in sheep's clothing, but inwardly they are ferocious wolves."*

E. What Is the Root Cause of Manipulation?

An omniscient God is nobody's fool, and soon catastrophic consequences befall all parties involved—consequences that are still being experienced by you and me today. Nature and the serpent are cursed, and the cunning creature is forced to crawl on its belly forever. Painful toil was pronounced for Adam, and increased pain in childbirth for Eve, among other judgments. But God's most devastating declaration of all is that *death* will become part of the human experience.

Satan's lie—"You can sin and get away with it"—is crushed by the weight of God's truth: "Sin will be punished."

But even in the midst of divine judgment, divine love and provision are declared for sinful mankind. Genesis 3:15 contains the first "good news" recorded in Scripture—the prophesying of a future victorious Savior. Here God addresses the serpent:

> *"I will put enmity between you and the woman,*
> *and between your offspring and hers;*
> *he will crush your head, and you will strike his heel"*
> (Genesis 3:15).

THREE GOD-GIVEN INNER NEEDS

We have all been created with three God-given inner needs: the needs for love, significance, and security.[31]

- **Love**—to know that someone is unconditionally committed to our best interest

> *"My command is this: Love each other as I have loved you"*
> (JOHN 15:12).

- **Significance**—to know that our lives have meaning and purpose

> *"I cry out to God Most High, to God who fulfills his purpose for me"*
> (PSALM 57:2 ESV).

- **Security**—to feel accepted and a sense of belonging

> *"Whoever fears the LORD has a secure fortress,*
> *and for their children it will be a refuge"*
> (PROVERBS 14:26).

THE ULTIMATE NEED-MEETER

Why did God give us these deep inner needs, knowing that people and self-effort fail us?

God gave us these needs so we would come to know Him as our Need-meeter. Our needs are designed by God to draw us into a deeper dependence on Christ. God did not create any person or position, or any amount of power or possessions to meet the deepest needs in our lives. If a person or thing *could* do that, we wouldn't need God! The Lord will use circumstances and bring positive people into our lives as an extension of His care and compassion, but ultimately only God can satisfy all the needs of our hearts. The Bible says,

> *"The LORD will guide you always;*
> *he will satisfy your needs in a sun-scorched land*
> *and will strengthen your frame.*
> *You will be like a well-watered garden,*
> *like a spring whose waters never fail"*
> (ISAIAH 58:11).

The apostle Paul revealed this truth by asking, "What a wretched man I am.

Who will rescue me from this body that is subject to death?" He then answered his own question by saying he is saved by "Jesus Christ our Lord!" (Romans 7:24-25).

All along, the Lord planned to meet our deepest needs for...

- **Love**—"I [the Lord] have loved you with an everlasting love; I have drawn you with unfailing kindness" (Jeremiah 31:3).

- **Significance**—" 'For I know the plans I have for you,' declares the LORD, 'plans to prosper you and not to harm you, plans to give you hope and a future' " (Jeremiah 29:11).

- **Security**—"The LORD himself goes before you and will be with you; he will never leave you nor forsake you. Do not be afraid; do not be discouraged" (Deuteronomy 31:8).

The truth is that our God-given needs for love, significance, and security can be legitimately met—in Christ Jesus! Philippians 4:19 makes it plain:

> *"My God will meet all your needs according to*
> *the riches of his glory in Christ Jesus."*

The couple in the Garden had been manipulated and deceived. They believed a lie, but God knew the truth.

- ### WRONG BELIEF OF THE MANIPULATOR:

"This is a dog-eat-dog world, a survival-of-the-fittest world. There-fore, I can't trust anyone to meet my needs. If I don't take control of the people and circumstances in my life, my needs for love, signifi-cance, and security will never be met.[32] It is up to me to take care of myself and to make sure my needs are satisfied in my way and in my time frame."

RIGHT BELIEF OF THE MANIPULATOR:

"God loves me sacrificially and has promised to meet my needs. There-fore, I will love others with His love rather than use others in an attempt to gain the love, significance, and security that only God can give me."

> *"Love one another. As I have loved you,*
> *so you must love one another"*
> (JOHN 13:34).

- **WRONG BELIEF OF THE ONE MANIPULATED:**

  "I must have the approval of others in order to feel good about myself."[33]

  RIGHT BELIEF OF THE ONE MANIPULATED:

  "I do not need the approval of others because God accepts me totally and loves me unconditionally, and He alone will meet all my inner needs."[34]

  "The LORD will guide you always; he will satisfy your needs in a
  sun-scorched land and will strengthen your frame. You will be like
  a well-watered garden, like a spring whose waters never fail"
  (ISAIAH 58:11).

IV. STEPS TO SOLUTION

What goes around comes around. And the sad saga of the manipulative patriarchs and their descendants continues…

After Jacob finagled Esau out of his birthright blessings, it is now Jacob's turn to be had.

Having fled to Haran to live with his uncle Laban, Jacob falls in love with Laban's beautiful daughter Rachel and strikes a deal with Laban. "So Jacob served seven years to get Rachel, but they seemed like only a few days to him because of his love for her" (Genesis 29:20).

Laban throws a feast and gives his daughter's hand to Jacob in marriage, but it isn't Rachel's hand that Jacob gets. The deceiver is deceived—this character trait obviously runs in the family. A master of manipulation, Laban lies and gives Rachel's older sister, Leah, to Jacob.

"When morning came, there was Leah! So Jacob said to
Laban, 'What is this you have done to me? I served you
for Rachel, didn't I? Why have you deceived me?'"
(GENESIS 29:25).

A. Key Verses to Memorize

"Why have you deceived me?" Jacob's father, Isaac, might have asked Jacob that very same question years before. Now the trickster himself has been tricked.

Laban explains it's not customary for a younger daughter to marry before the older. He instructs Jacob to finish the week of wedding festivities with Leah and then he'll get Rachel "in return for another seven years of work. And Jacob did so" (Genesis 29:27-28).

The tangled mess of manipulation ensnares all who seek to please either themselves or others rather than God.

FOR THE ONE MANIPULATED:

> *"Am I now trying to win the approval of human beings, or of God? Or am I trying to please people? If I were still trying to please people, I would not be a servant of Christ"*
> (GALATIANS 1:10).

FOR THE MANIPULATOR:

> *"His divine power has given us everything we need for a godly life through our knowledge of him who called us by his own glory and goodness. Through these he has given us his very great and precious promises, so that through them you may participate in the divine nature, having escaped the corruption in the world caused by evil desires"*
> (2 PETER 1:3-4).

B. Key Passage to Read

THE PASSAGE: 1 THESSALONIANS 2:3-8

- *"For the appeal we make does not spring from error or impure motives, nor are we trying to trick you"* . . . . .verse 3

- *"On the contrary, we speak as those approved by God to be entrusted with the gospel. We are not trying to please people but God, who tests our hearts"* . . . . .verse 4

- *"You know we never used flattery, nor did we put on a mask to cover up greed—God is our witness"* . . . . .verse 5

- *"We were not looking for praise from people, not from you or anyone else"* . . . . .verse 6

- *"As apostles of Christ we could have asserted our authority... we were like young children"* . . . . verses 6-7

- *"We loved you so much, we were delighted to share with you not only the gospel of God but our lives as well"* . . . . .verse 8

THE BIBLICAL MODEL

THE APPEAL: VERSE 3
- Without error
- Without impure motives
- Without trying to trick anyone

THE APPEALER: VERSE 4
- Approved by God
- Trustworthy
- Trying to please God, not men

THE METHOD OF APPEAL: VERSES 5-6
- Never use flattery.
- Don't put on a mask to cover up greed.
- Don't look for praise from men.

THE BASIS OF THE APPEAL: VERSES 6-8
- Not burdensome, but gentle
- Based on love
- Includes personal sharing and involvement

C. How to Turn Away from Manipulation by Trusting God

Rachel has much in common with her husband's grandmother, Sarah. Like Sarah, Rachel is beautiful, barren, and bereft of an heir.

Sarah attempted to solve her problem by offering her maidservant Hagar to Abraham in hopes of raising a family through her. The result was a son, but not the promised covenant son, Isaac. Rachel, wife of Sarah's grandson Jacob, is in the same desperate circumstances, compounded by the fact that her own sister Leah has borne Jacob not one, not two, but four sons. "When Rachel saw that she was not bearing Jacob any children, she became jealous of her sister. So she said to Jacob, 'Give me children, or I'll die!'" (Genesis 30:1).

As with Sarah, God was planning to bless Rachel with her husband's most blessed son of all (Joseph). But like Sarah, Rachel, too, offers her own maidservant, Bilhah, who gives Jacob two sons. And the manipulative cycle goes on—from generation to generation to generation, down through the annals of Hebrew history.

The solution to manipulation is never more manipulation, but is rather moving away from manipulation and moving toward God.

What is the first step away from manipulation?

The first step for you to take on the Lord's path *away* from manipulation is to enter into a loving relationship with Him. To help you understand the relationship God wants to have with you, see the four points from His Word that you need to know, which are listed on pages 48-50.

D. How to Hit the Target

Paul gazes throughout the teeming metropolis and finds himself "greatly distressed" (Acts 17:16).

Athens is a city flourishing on philosophical exchange and the free flow of ideas, but it is also a city "full of idols" (verse 16). Everywhere are statues of gold, silver, and stone, images made by man's design and skill. Paul preaches about an *invisible* God, one so powerful that He can never be contained in an inanimate object. How will the Athenians handle *that* idea?

Because many people in Athens spend their time "doing nothing but talking about and listening to the latest ideas" (verse 21), they undoubtedly are easy targets for manipulation and deception. But Paul's heart is to *persuade* the lost about the living Christ. As he *reasons* (verse 17) in the marketplace day after day, he gains the attention of a group of philosophers.

HITTING THE TARGET

Target #1—A New Purpose: God's purpose for me is to be conformed to the character of Christ.

> *"Those God foreknew he also predestined to be*
> *conformed to the image of his Son"*
> (ROMANS 8:29).

— "I'll do whatever it takes to be conformed to the character of Christ."

Target #2—A New Priority: God's priority for me is to change my thinking.

> *"Do not conform to the pattern of this world, but be*
> *transformed by the renewing of your mind"*
> (ROMANS 12:2).

– "I'll do whatever it takes to line up my thinking with God's thinking."

Target #3—A New Plan: God's plan for me is to rely on Christ's strength, not my strength, to be all He created me to be.

> *"I can do all things through Christ who strengthens me"*
> (Philippians 4:13 NKJV).

– "I'll do whatever it takes to fulfill His plan in His strength."

Up to this point, Paul has resisted any temptation to be manipulative, but now he must engage with philosophically minded unbelievers while avoiding manipulative conversation. If you find yourself in a similar situation with a stranger or even with someone you know quite well, walk through the following steps:

My Personalized Plan

With Christ as my anchor, I will take the necessary steps to stop being manipulated.

> *"We have this hope as an anchor for the soul, firm and secure"*
> (Hebrews 6:19).

1. *I will state clearly* what I am willing to accept and not willing to accept from the manipulator.

   – I will state my position in a positive way.

   – I will not justify myself. I will not be apologetic.

   – "I want our relationship to continue, but...

     ...I refuse to be controlled."

     ...I refuse to hear your accusations concerning (name) any longer."

     ...I refuse to endure the silent treatment from you."

   – I will keep what I say short and succinct.

Take to heart what the Bible says:

> *"The one who has knowledge uses words with restraint,*
> *and whoever has understanding is even-tempered"*
> (PROVERBS 17:27).

2. *I will tell the manipulator* the consequences I will enforce if the manipulator violates my request.

My response should serve to disengage me from the manipulator.

- I cannot change the manipulator's behavior, but I can remove myself from frequent exposure to unacceptable behavior.
- "I want to visit with you, but...

   ...if you call me a name again, I will leave for a period of time."

   ...if you persist in making that accusation, I will terminate our conversation."

   ...if you give me the silent treatment, I will find someone else to talk with."

- Consequences are part of God's divine plan that what we sow, we will reap.

Take to heart what the Bible says:

> *"A man reaps what he sows"*
> (GALATIANS 6:7).

3. *I will enforce the consequence* every single time manipulative behavior occurs.

- I will not bluff! The manipulator needs to know I am going to consistently act on my words.
- In your mind and heart...

   ...I will say *no* to manipulation.

   ...I will say *no* to pressure.

   ...I will say *no* to control.

- Eventually my manipulator will stop using manipulative tactics, but only after those tactics prove to be ineffective.

Take to heart what the Bible says:

> *"All you need to say is a simple 'Yes' or 'No'"*
> (JAMES 5:12).

4. *I will absolutely refuse to negotiate.*

- Since verbal manipulators do not use words fairly, negotiation will not work.
- Instead of being willing to talk out the problem, manipulators will seek to wear me down.
- I will state that I will look forward to a renewed relationship when the manipulative behavior stops.
    » "I am not willing to discuss this topic any longer."
    » "I have stated clearly what I will not accept."
    » "When you are ready to respect my requests, let me know. I look forward to enjoying being together at that time."
- I will keep my words brief and to the point.

Take to heart what the Bible says:

> *"Sin is not ended by multiplying words, but*
> *the prudent hold their tongues"*
> (PROVERBS 10:19).

5. *I will never "react"* when my boundary is violated—only respond.

- I will expect my boundary to be violated.
- I will expect my boundary to be violated again *and again*!
- If I react, I will find myself back under the control of the manipulator.
    » I will not *cry* in front of the manipulator when feeling hurt.
    » I will not *beg* when feeling fearful.
    » I will not *explode* when feeling frustrated.
- I will respond by detaching myself from the manipulator and enforcing my predetermined repercussions.

Take to heart what the Bible says:

> *"The end of a matter is better than its beginning, and patience is*
> *better than pride. Do not be quickly provoked*

> *in your spirit, for anger resides in the lap of fools"*
> (ECCLESIASTES 7:8-9).

6. *I will solicit the support* of one or two wise, objective people to help me through this process.

- I will include supporters as I analyze and identify the problem.
- I will include supporters as I determine how to articulate my plan.
- I will include supporters as I enforce the repercussions.
  - » I will discuss the situation with my supporters.
  - » I will discuss the tactics used on me.
  - » I will discuss the plan of action.
- I will include supporters—friend, mentor, counselor—to help me through this critical period.

Take to heart what the Bible says:

> *"Listen to advice and accept discipline, and at the*
> *end you will be counted among the wise"*
> (PROVERBS 19:20).

The time it takes to disassemble and disable a manipulative relationship is limited. But during that limited time, I will expect manipulative maneuvers and emotional ups and downs. I will assume my actions will anger the manipulator. I will allow the person to react without my reacting. I will not seek to placate this person—it won't work. I will think of this time period as comparable to having surgery. It is a painful experience, but it will provide the only hope for healing if I am to have a new, healthy relationship.

Take to heart what the Bible says:

> *"The words of the reckless pierce like swords,*
> *but the tongue of the wise brings healing"*
> (PROVERBS 12:18).

E. How to Discover Your Own Manipulative Maneuvers

King Ahab, a greedy Hebrew king, wants Naboth's vineyard, and the queen is going to make sure he gets it.

King Ahab tries to negotiate with Naboth for his vineyard near the palace, hoping to make it a vegetable garden. But Naboth refuses. "The LORD forbid that I should give you the inheritance of my ancestors," Naboth declares (1 Kings 21:3).

Angry and dejected, Ahab lies on his bed and sulks, refusing to eat. His wife, Jezebel, inquires about his sullen state and tells him to cheer up. She'll get that vineyard, no problem. She maneuvers people and devises a false accusation: "Proclaim a day of fasting and seat Naboth in a prominent place among the people. But seat two scoundrels opposite him and have them bring charges that he has cursed both God and the king. Then take him out and stone him to death" (1 Kings 21:9-10).

The queen's directive is obeyed, and Naboth is sacrificed for a vegetable garden. When Ahab goes to take possession of the property, he runs into God's man for the times, Elijah the Tishbite. Elijah doesn't have much to say about vegetables, but he does have a thing or two to say about dogs—*and divine punishment.* Elijah declares what the Lord says:

> "*In the place where dogs licked up Naboth's blood,*
> *dogs will lick up your blood—yes, yours!'...*
> *And also concerning Jezebel the* LORD *says:*
> *'Dogs will devour Jezebel by the wall of Jezreel'*"
> (1 KINGS 21:19,23).

While Ahab may have manipulated Jezebel to get the vegetable garden he wanted, there can be no doubt that Jezebel manipulated people and circumstances to arrange Naboth's death. Some manipulation is blatant. At other times, it is so subtle and covert that it is difficult to recognize, both by the manipulator and the manipulated. If you question whether you sometimes—or oftentimes—engage in manipulative maneuvers, read and honestly answer the following questions:

Have you ever been told…

____ You are manipulative or controlling?

____ You are too possessive or confining?

____ You do not take responsibility?

____ You are always "nicer" to others?

____ You tend to overreact?

____ You have difficulty admitting when you are wrong?

___ You usually insist on getting your way?

___ You use anger or blame to motivate others?

___ You have difficulty putting problems "on the table" for logical discussions?

___ You have a destructive style of interaction?

Scripture makes it clear how people feel about crafty manipulators:

> *"A quick-tempered person does foolish things,*
> *and the one who devises evil schemes is hated"*
> (PROVERBS 14:17).

F. How to Say *No* to Manipulators

He has beguiled an entire nation, but Hananiah's deception proves to be his doom.

The nation of Judah is facing 70 years of captivity in Babylon as discipline for a multitude of sins that were committed against the Lord. God's prophet Jeremiah wears a wooden yoke on his neck to symbolize the nation's subjection to Babylon's king, Nebuchadnezzar.

But Hananiah has a far more appealing message and manages to manipulate the nation with false prophecies. He foretells liberation from Israel's captors within two years, with all the exiles returning home and all articles from the temple safely restored. In addition, Hananiah removes the yoke from Jeremiah's neck and breaks it to "represent" the end of Nebuchadnezzar's reign over Judah.

However, Hananiah's sway over Judah leads to a squaring-off with the Sovereign One: "The prophet Jeremiah said to Hananiah the prophet, 'Listen, Hananiah! The LORD has not sent you, yet you have persuaded this nation to trust in lies. Therefore, this is what the LORD says: "I am about to remove you from the face of the earth. This very year you are going to die, because you have preached rebellion against the LORD"'" (Jeremiah 28:15-16).

Rather than taking the path of least resistance by going along with Hananiah, Jeremiah says *no* to his lies and says *yes* to God's truth—even when doing so is highly unpopular. Jeremiah's actions align with Jesus' admonition given hundreds of years later:

> *"All you need to say is simply 'Yes' or 'No'"*
> (MATTHEW 5:37).

You too can say *no* to manipulators by...[35]

- *Not buying* a certain product

  Affirm the item. . . . .   "I feel sure your product is very good..."

  Then say *no*. . . . .   "However, it does not fit within my budget, and I really don't have a need for it." (Repeat, if challenged.)

- *Not accepting* a certain assignment

  Affirm the project. . . . . .   "I think what you are doing is great, and I'm glad you have been able to make the time to do it."

  Then say *no*. . . . .   "However, I am so committed in other endeavors that I cannot in good conscience undertake another. I feel sure the Lord will put this project on the heart of someone else so that the need will be met."

- *Not agreeing* to meet a particular need of someone else

  Affirm the need. . . . .   "I know a great need exists for teachers with the young people."

  Then say *no*. . . . .   "However, I also know that I am not led by the Lord to do this. Therefore, God must have equipped and called someone else to meet this need, and I would not want to rob that person of the opportunity to fulfill God's will."

- *Not contributing* to a certain charity/church/ministry

  Affirm the charity. . . . . . .   "I'm sure the mission of (_____) is admirable."

  Then say *no*. . . . .   "However, God has already led me to support several other ministries. I feel sure you will find others who are not already as heavily committed, and it will bless them to give."

- *Not accepting* a date

  Affirm the person. . . . . . . "Thank you for asking me out."

  Then say *no*. . . . . "However, I need to say no. But I am honored that you would ask."

- *Not marrying* someone who says, "God told me you should."

  Affirm the person. . . . . . . "I'm highly complimented that you think God has told you we are to marry."

  Then say *no*. . . . . "However, I'm sure if God were truly speaking to you, He would have told me also. It sounds as though God might be preparing your heart for marriage. Therefore, I will pray that you will know who the right person is when the time is right."

- *Not continuing* in a relationship

  Affirm the person. . . . . . . "I want God's best for both of us."

  Then say *no*. . . . . "However, it's become apparent that we are not bringing out the best in each other. Therefore, I know our relationship should not continue."

- *Not submitting* in marriage to what violates your conscience

  Affirm the person. . . . . . . "I love you and want to be the best person I can be for you."

  Then say *no*. . . . . "However, I know God does not want me to do anything that would violate my conscience, even if it means displeasing you. I want you to always be able to trust me to do what is right. I cannot do what you want because I do not believe it is right for me in God's sight."

- *Not lying* for another person

  Affirm the feelings. . . . . . "I sincerely care about your feelings and want to help you in every way possible."

Then say *no*. . . . . "However, I have made a commitment to
Christ to be a person of integrity. There-
fore, I cannot lie and say you are not here,
but I can say you are unavailable and then
take a message."

> *"An honest witness gives honest testimony,*
> *but a false witness tells lies"*
> (PROVERBS 12:17).

As you prayerfully practice saying *no* to manipulators, practice saying *yes*
to God by consistently clinging to the Lord's promise to meet your inner needs
for...[36]

SACRIFICIAL LOVE

> *"The LORD appeared to us in the past, saying:*
> *'I have loved you with an everlasting love;*
> *I have drawn you with unfailing kindness'"*
> (JEREMIAH 31:3).

SIGNIFICANCE

> *"'I know the plans I have for you,' declares the LORD,*
> *'plans to prosper you and not to harm you,*
> *plans to give you hope and a future'"*
> (JEREMIAH 29:11).

SECURITY

> *"The LORD himself goes before you and will be with you;*
> *he will never leave you nor forsake you.*
> *Do not be afraid; do not be discouraged"*
> (DEUTERONOMY 31:8).

G. How to Answer Common Questions

Their words are sweet as molasses, rolling off their lips, but they should stick
like glue on their tongues.

They praise Jesus for having qualities they themselves do not have: "Teacher, we know you are a man of integrity. You aren't swayed by others, because you pay no attention to who they are; but you teach the way of God in accordance with the truth" (Mark 12:14).

It is a cunning commendation. The men are ready to trap Jesus so they can "catch him in his words" (Mark 12:13).

The Pharisees (the religious leaders of the Jews) and the Herodians (Jews who support Herod and Roman political authority) both despise Jesus, resenting His favor with the people, resenting His call to repentance. They hope to trip Jesus up over the issue of taxes, but He is fully aware of their manipulation and hypocrisy. Their snare comes encased in a question: "Is it right to pay the imperial tax to Caesar or not? Should we pay or shouldn't we?" (Mark 12:14-15).

Jesus asks them for a coin and then offers a few questions of His own: "Whose image is this? And whose inscription?

"'Caesar's,' they replied.

"Then Jesus said to them, 'Give back to Caesar what is Caesar's and to God what is God's'" (Mark 12:16-17).

The manipulators walk away...*marveling.*

While some snares come cloaked in a question, there are many questions regarding manipulation that are authentic and deserve a legitimate answer.

Ending a Manipulating Relationship

QUESTION: "I know I'm being manipulated. So why is it so hard for me to end the relationship?"

ANSWER: Probably because you fear losing the real or perceived benefits you are receiving in the relationship. Ask yourself what it will cost you to walk away. Even unhealthy relationships can provide a sense of feeling loved, significant, and secure.[37] A desperate fear of rejection often paralyzes a person who is trying to make healthy decisions. The belief is often that "any relationship is better than no relationship." In such cases it is helpful to remember the words of King David, and then to practice them:

> *"I sought the LORD, and he answered me;*
> *he delivered me from all my fears"*
> (PSALM 34:4).

QUESTION: "Is a wife still being submissive to her husband when she takes a stand against his manipulation?"

ANSWER: No wife is to submit to a husband's sinful request. And manipulation is a sin because faith is placed not in the Lord but in the manipulative tactics used. Therefore, if a wife perpetuates the sinful pattern of her husband by engaging in sin with him, she is not helping him but is rather hindering him. She is both endorsing and encouraging his sinful behavior because...

> *"...everything that does not come from faith is sin"*
> (ROMANS 14:23).

H. How to Maneuver Out of Being Manipulated

Clearly, Jesus did not yield to the manipulative maneuvers of the religious leaders of His day. Every tactic and trick they tried on Him, Jesus thwarted. None of them worked. He never yielded to their pressure or fell for their ploys. He was never sidelined by their schemes or sidetracked by their shenanigans. They never diverted His focus from His Father's will or His purpose.

> *"'My food,' said Jesus, 'is to do the will of him who sent me*
> *and to finish his work.'...*
> *'For I have come down from heaven not to do my will*
> *but to do the will of him who sent me'"*
> (JOHN 4:34; 6:38).

If it is your heart's desire to be like Jesus and no longer succumb to the shenanigans of selfish manipulators, apply the directives in the following acrostic on D-E-P-E-N-D-E-N-C-Y.

TEN MAJOR MANEUVERS

D—DECIDE not to be dependent on the manipulator.

- *Decide* that you have had an unhealthy, dependent relationship and confess it to God.
- *Decide* that you want a healthy relationship that glorifies God.
- *Decide* that you will be dependent on the Lord to meet your deepest needs.

For the Bible says,

> *"God will meet all your needs*
> *according to the riches of his glory in Christ Jesus"*
> (PHILIPPIANS 4:19).

E—EXPECT exasperation from the manipulator.

- *Don't expect* the manipulator to understand or agree with your decisions.
- *Don't expect* the manipulator to acknowledge being manipulative.
- *Don't expect* the manipulator to be willing to stop controlling you and to set you free.

For the Bible says,

> *"Since you are my rock and my fortress, for the sake*
> *of your name lead and guide me. Keep me from the*
> *trap that is set for me, for you are my refuge"*
> (PSALM 31:3-4).

P—PREPARE yourself for pain.

- *Accept* the fact that change is painful. In time, peace will reign in your heart and may also reign in your relationship.
- *Accept* the fact that the manipulator will resist change.
- *Accept* the fact that if you don't change, you will stay in pain and peace will elude you.

For the Bible says,

> *"I have no peace, no quietness; I have no rest, but only turmoil"*
> (JOB 3:26).

E—EXAMINE the methods of the manipulator.

- *Ask God* to open your eyes to the ways that you have been manipulated.
- *Ask yourself,* "How am I being manipulated?" Then write out your tactics for change.
- *Ask a trusted friend* to help you see your blind spots and develop a plan of action.

For the Bible says,

> *"The prudent see danger and take refuge, but the*
> *simple keep going and pay the penalty"*
>
> (PROVERBS 22:3).

N—NOTIFY the manipulator of the necessity for change.

- *State* that you have been wrong.
  "I've come to realize I've been wrong in the way I've related to you. At times I've not spoken up because I've been fearful. This is not healthy for either of us."

- *State* your commitment.
  "I really do care about you. I want you to know that I am committed to change. I believe we can ultimately have a much healthier relationship."
  Or, if it is not appropriate to continue in a relationship at all...

- *State* your resolve.
  "I cannot continue in a relationship with you and be the person I need to be before God."

For the Bible says,

> *"Since we are surrounded by such a great cloud of*
> *witnesses, let us throw off everything that hinders*
> *and the sin that so easily entangles. And let us run*
> *with perseverance the race marked out for us"*
>
> (HEBREWS 12:1).

D—DON'T defend yourself.

Although you will be accused of not being loving and caring...

- *You may choose* to be silent, but don't use silence as a weapon.

- *You may choose* to state the truth once or repeat it several times. "I'm so sorry you feel that way...What you've said is not true—it does not reflect my heart."

- *You may choose* to say, "I understand that you think I am being heartless, but my goal is to become healthy."

For the Bible says,

> *"There is...a time to tear and a time to mend,*
> *a time to be silent and a time to speak"*
>
> (ECCLESIASTES 3:1,7).

E—EXPECT experimentation with new strategies.

- *The manipulator may* resort to using other methods to control you.
- *The manipulator needs* to know you are aware of these new methods.
- *The manipulator needs* to see that these new methods will not succeed.

For the Bible says,

> *"Wisdom will save you from the ways of wicked*
> *men, from men whose words are perverse"*
> (PROVERBS 2:12).

N—NULLIFY your need to meet all the manipulator's needs.

- *Realize* that God didn't design for anyone to meet *all* the needs of another person.
- *Realize* that if you meet all the manipulator's needs, then the manipulator won't recognize his or her need for the Lord.
- *Realize* that you need to redirect the manipulator's focus onto the Lord as the only true Need-meeter.

For the Bible says,

> *"Take delight in the LORD and he will give you*
> *the desires of your heart. Commit your way to the*
> *LORD; trust in him and he will do this"*
> (PSALM 37:4-5).

C—COMMIT Galatians 1:10 to memory.

- *Recognize* the truth in Galatians 1:10 by saying it at least three times a day.
- *Realize* that the only approval you need comes from God.
- *Remember* to live out this truth because you are Christ's servant.

> *"Am I now trying to win the approval of human beings, or*
> *of God? Or am I trying to please people? If I were still trying*
> *to please people, I would not be a servant of Christ"*
> (GALATIANS 1:10).

Y—YIELD to pleasing the Lord first.

- *See* that Jesus was not a "peace at any price" person. He said, "Do not suppose that I have come to bring peace to the earth. I did not come to bring peace, but a sword" (Matthew 10:34).
- *See* that if you want to be like Jesus, you too must not be a "peace at any price" person.
- *See* that you are to keep your trust in God and to fear no one.

For the Bible says,

> *"In God I trust and am not afraid. What can man do to me?"*
> (PSALM 56:11).

I. How to Stop Being Spiritually Manipulated

And so the Athenians who are listening to the apostle Paul inquire: "May we know what this new teaching is that you are presenting? You are bringing some strange ideas to our ears, and we would like to know what they mean" (Acts 17:19-20).

What are the "strange ideas" Paul is preaching? The truths of the gospel, the death and resurrection of Jesus Christ. The Athenians have never heard of a god doing such a thing—dying and then coming back to life. Paul is brought before the Areopagus, the council that governs religious and educational matters, and begins his message by quoting an inscription. He says, "As I walked around and looked carefully at your objects of worship, I even found an altar with this inscription: TO AN UNKNOWN GOD. So you are ignorant of the very thing you worship—and this is what I am going to proclaim to you" (Acts 17:23).

Paul presents God as the all-powerful, self-sufficient Creator who governs the affairs of the world, gives all life its breath, calls people to repentance, and will one day judge the world through the One He has appointed—Jesus Christ. And Paul convincingly concludes that the true God is not some dreamed-up deity, a lofty image birthed in the recesses of man's imagination. "He has given proof of this to everyone by raising him from the dead" (Acts 17:31).

As Paul so powerfully points out, the God of the Bible, the God who created everything, is your Lord—your master, ruler, owner. Therefore, you are to...

- **Submit yourself to God's authority.** You are accountable to God first and human authorities second. As God's Word says,

"We must obey God rather than human beings!"
(ACTS 5:29).

- **Talk about your concerns with spiritual leaders** who are not involved in your manipulative situation. God desires peace, unity, and reconciliation between Christians. As God's Word says,

> "[We are to] *be completely humble and gentle; be patient, bearing with one another in love. Make every effort to keep the unity of the Spirit through the bond of peace"*
> (EPHESIANS 4:2-3).

- **Consider how the spiritually manipulative** attitude of others is affecting your spiritual life, your relationships with family members and friends, and your sense of personal value. As God's Word says,

> *"As iron sharpens iron, so one person sharpens another"*
> (PROVERBS 27:17).

- **Separate yourself** from manipulative situations and seek out people who are encouraging. As God's Word says,

> *"Encourage one another daily...so that none of you may be hardened by sin's deceitfulness"*
> (HEBREWS 3:13).

J. How to Stop Being a Manipulator

Many Jewish leaders believed in Jesus, but kept their belief hidden, "for they loved human praise more than praise from God" (John 12:42-43).

The Judaizers "want to impress people by means of the flesh"; thus, they *manipulate men into being circumcised* in order "to avoid being persecuted for the cross of Christ" (Galatians 6:12).

Paul, Silas, and Timothy, on the other hand, care nothing about accolades or *manipulating circumstances to draw attention to themselves.* Their focus is on the One who tests the heart. "With the help of our God we dared to tell you his gospel in the face of strong opposition. For the appeal we make does not spring from error or impure motives, nor are we trying to trick you. On the contrary, we speak as those approved by God to be entrusted with the gospel. We are not trying to please people but God, who tests our hearts" (1 Thessalonians 2:2-4).

If you want to move from manipulating people and circumstances to becoming a pleaser of God and worthy of His trust, then you need to...

- **Face the Facts**

  – *Admit* you have been a manipulator.

  – *Admit* you have used people and circumstances to your own benefit.

  – *Admit* you have hurt yourself and others by manipulation.

  – *Admit* you need to change.

  (Write out ways you have manipulated others and what needs to change.)

Pray...

> "*Create in me a pure heart, O God, and*
> *renew a steadfast spirit within me*"
> (PSALM 51:10).

- **Tell the Truth**

  – *Tell* God you have sinned against Him by manipulating people and circumstances to your own advantage.

  – *Tell* God you know you need a changed heart in order to fully please Him.

  – *Tell* others that you have wronged them by manipulating them for self-centered reasons.

  – *Tell* those you have wronged that you are genuinely sorry and ask for their forgiveness for your wrongful actions toward them.

Pray...

> "*Have mercy on me, O God, according to your unfailing love;*
> *according to your great compassion blot out my transgressions.*
> *Wash away all my iniquity and cleanse me from my sin. For*
> *I know my transgressions, and my sin is always before me*"
> (PSALM 51:1-3).

- **Consider the Causes**

  - *Examine* your childhood experiences of relating within your family.

  (What were the family dynamics?)

  - *Examine* the patterns of relating among your family members.

  (Who was manipulative in your family?)

  - *Examine* your previous patterns of manipulating in your relationships.

  (What were your earliest memories of manipulating others?)

  - *Examine* your life based on the three inner needs for love, significance, and security.[38]

  (What needs were unmet? What needs did you seek to meet through manipulation?)

Pray...

> *"Yet you desired faithfulness even in the womb;*
> *you taught me wisdom in that secret place"*
> (Psalm 51:6).

- **Pardon the Past**

  - *Forgive family members* for wronging you in your childhood. (Make a list of your offenders and appropriate the power of God to forgive each person and each offense, giving it all to God.)
  - *Forgive others* for wronging you in your childhood. (Make a list of offenders outside your family and forgive each person and each offense, giving it all to God.)
  - *Forgive those* who have had unhealthy, manipulative relationships with you in the past. (Make a list of offenders from childhood to the present and forgive each offender and each offense.)
  - *Forgive yourself* for being manipulative in your past relationships. (Make a list of those whom you have manipulated and the ways in which you manipulated them. Confess it all to God, then accept God's forgiveness for each one.)

Pray for God's power to enable you to…

> *"Bear with each other and forgive one another*
> *if any of you has a grievance against someone.*
> *Forgive as the Lord forgave you"*
> (COLOSSIANS 3:13).

- **Focus on Faith**

  - *Realize* that your manipulative ways have demonstrated a lack of faith in God to meet your needs.

  - *Realize* that your manipulative ways have resulted in idolatry on your part.

  - *Realize* that the basis for change is your commitment to rely on God, rather than on others, to meet your needs for love, significance, and security.[39]

  - *Realize* as you move from manipulation to faith that your actions will need to be Spirit-led rather than need-driven.

Realize…

> *"If by the Spirit you put to death the misdeeds of the body, you will*
> *live. For those who are led by the Spirit of God are the children of*
> *God. The Spirit you received does not make you slaves, so that you*
> *live in fear again; rather, the Spirit you received brought about*
> *your adoption to sonship. And by him we cry, 'Abba, Father'"*
> (ROMANS 8:13-15).

- **Grow in Grace**

  - *Embrace* the grace of God (His unmerited favor) as the means by which you have been forgiven of your sins and the means by which you can walk in forgiveness toward others.

  - *Embrace* the grace of God as the means by which God will meet your needs through Christ Jesus.

  - *Embrace* the grace of God as the means by which the Spirit of God will work in your life to bring about change.

  - *Embrace* the grace of God as the means by which you will be able to appropriate the power of God operating within you.

Personalize and pray the following prayer:

"I pray that out of his glorious riches he may strengthen you with power through his Spirit in your inner being, so that Christ may dwell in your hearts through faith...Now to him who is able to do immeasurably more than all we ask or imagine, according to his power that is at work within us, to him be glory in the church and in Christ Jesus throughout all generations, for ever and ever! Amen" (EPHESIANS 3:16-17,20-21).

- **Oust the Old**
  - *Refuse old ways* of thinking that lead to the development of manipulative patterns in your relationships.
  - *Refuse old messages* from the past that leave you feeling worthless, shameful, defeated, and like a failure.
  - *Refuse old relationships* that keep you in bondage to the past and offer no encouragement for the future.
  - *Refuse old patterns* of behavior that are based on fear and not on faith in God and His sufficiency in your life.

Personalize and pray the following verses:

"In Christ all the fullness of the Deity lives in bodily form, and in Christ you have been brought to fullness. He is the head over every power and authority. In him you were also circumcised with a circumcision not performed by human hands. Your whole self ruled by the flesh was put off when you were circumcised by Christ, having been buried with him in baptism, in which you were also raised with him through your faith in the working of God, who raised him from the dead" (COLOSSIANS 2:9-12).

- **Mold Your Mind**
  - *Replace* lies about yourself from the past with truths from God's Word about who you are in Christ.
  - *Replace* self-defeating messages from the past with encouraging messages of hope and victory from God's Word.
  - *Replace* your old perspective of life with God's perspective of life as found in His Word.

— *Replace* your worldly way of thinking with God's way of thinking as revealed in the Bible.

Personalize and practice the following verses:

> *"I urge you, brothers and sisters, in view of God's mercy, to offer*
> *your bodies as a living sacrifice, holy and pleasing to God—*
> *this is your true and proper worship. Do not conform to the*
> *pattern of this world, but be transformed by the renewing*
> *of your mind. Then you will be able to test and approve*
> *what God's will is—his good, pleasing and perfect will"*
> (ROMANS 12:1-2).

• **Live to Love**

— *Focus* on loving God as the highest aim of your life and the motive behind your service to Him and to others.

— *Focus* on loving your friends as the motive behind building healthy relationships with them.

— *Focus* on loving your family as the goal of your service to them.

— *Focus* on loving your "enemies" as being the Christlike thing to do and as the motivation for doing whatever is in *their* best interests.

Personalize the following prayer:

> *"I pray that [I], being rooted and established in love, may*
> *have power, together with all the Lord's holy people, to grasp*
> *how wide and long and high and deep is the love of Christ,*
> *and to know this love that surpasses knowledge—that [I]*
> *may be filled to the measure of all the fullness of God"*
> (EPHESIANS 3:17-19).

At times, the most spiritual sacrifice you can make is to stop being a people-pleaser. This means you must choose not to please another person so that you can please the Lord.

> *To stop being manipulated,*
> *you must sometimes say* no *to people*
> *so you can then say* yes *to God.*
>
> —JUNE HUNT

MANIPULATION: ANSWERS IN GOD'S WORD

QUESTION: "What does God say about letting a person be too important? Is that like putting other gods before Him?"

ANSWER: God says, *"You shall have no other gods before me"* (Exodus 20:3).

QUESTION: "What will happen if I continue to live in fear of man?"

ANSWER: *"Fear of man will prove to be a snare, but whoever trusts in the LORD is kept safe"* (Proverbs 29:25).

QUESTION: "What will happen if I try to win the approval of other people and try to please them?"

ANSWER: *"Am I now trying to win the approval of human beings, or of God? Or am I trying to please people? If I were still trying to please people, I would not be a servant of Christ"* (Galatians 1:10).

QUESTION: "What should I not do when I'm around a hot-tempered person?"

ANSWER: *"Do not make friends with a hot-tempered person, do not associate with one easily angered"* (Proverbs 22:24).

QUESTION: "Why should I test my own actions instead of comparing myself to somebody else?"

ANSWER: *"Each one should test their own actions. Then they can take pride in themselves alone, without comparing themselves to someone else"* (Galatians 6:4).

QUESTION: "How does the Bible contrast a perverse tongue with one that is soothing?"

ANSWER: *"The soothing tongue is a tree of life, but a perverse tongue crushes the spirit"* (Proverbs 15:4).

QUESTION: "How does God view the person who trusts in the Lord and puts confidence in Him?"

ANSWER: *"Blessed is the one who trusts in the LORD, whose confidence is in him"* (Jeremiah 17:7).

QUESTION: "What is the difference between giving in to someone out of love and giving in out of fear?"

ANSWER: *"There is no fear in love. But perfect love drives out fear, because fear has to do with punishment. The one who fears is not made perfect in love"* (1 John 4:18).

QUESTION: "Why should I guard my heart?"

ANSWER: *"Above all else, guard your heart, for everything you do flows from it"* (Proverbs 4:23).

QUESTION: "How can I have the power and self-discipline to stand up to a manipulator?"

ANSWER: *"The Spirit God gave us does not make us timid, but gives us power, love and self-discipline"* (2 Timothy 1:7).

CODEPENDENCY
Balancing an Unbalanced Relationship

3

CODEPENDENCY
Balancing an Unbalanced Relationship

When God gave us His Ten Commandments, He began with these words: "You shall have no other gods before me" (Exodus 20:3). He knew that if we were to be all He created us to be and receive all He planned for us to receive, we would have to make our relationship with Him our top priority. He knew He would then be free to bless our lives and bless the lives of others through us.

Codependent relationships violate the heart of God's first commandment. In a codependent relationship, you allow someone else to take the place God alone should have in your heart—you allow another person to be your "god." If you have a *misplaced dependency*, you will have neither *peace with God* nor the *peace of God*.

But if you trust His love for you and do what He asks of you— if you put Him first, loving Him foremost—you will have God's peace as well as His blessing because you will have Him as the center of your life.

Scripture directs us concerning the scope of our love for God:

*"Love the Lord your God with all your heart and with all your soul
and with all your strength and with all your mind"*
(LUKE 10:27).

And Scripture reveals to us the scope of God's love for us:

*"This is how we know what love is:
Jesus Christ laid down his life for us...
For God so loved the world that he gave his one and only Son,
that whoever believes in him shall not perish but have eternal life"*
(1 JOHN 3:16; JOHN 3:16).

I. DEFINITIONS OF CODEPENDENCY

Life is a series of choices. We can choose to believe God loves us and operates in our best interest, or we can choose to believe the lie that He is against us, the same lie that Adam and Eve believed. We can choose to love and obey Him, or we can choose to rebel against Him. We can choose to seek Him as our Need-meeter, or we choose to seek somewhere else or someone else to get our needs met.

Scripture makes it clear that these choices are ours because God gives them to us to make. In creating us as free-willed individuals, He grants us the choice of acknowledging Him as God, accepting Him as the lover of our souls, and loving Him in return…or the choice of rejecting Him.

> *"He has shown you, O mortal, what is good.*
> *And what does the LORD require of you?*
> *To act justly and to love mercy*
> *and to walk humbly with your God"*
> (MICAH 6:8).

A. What Is Dependency?

From conception to death, God created us to be dependent—not on another person or on another of His creations, but on Him alone. We need Him in every area of life—physical, emotional, mental, spiritual, and relational. He alone knows the number of hairs on our heads, our thoughts before we think them, our words before we speak them, and our needs before we voice them. His knowledge of us is thorough and our need of Him is total.

Our problem is that we refuse to accept the truth of our dependence on Him and our subsequent great need of Him, and we then set about to replace Him with another created being…like ourselves. We reject the truth and we believe the lie that we can take care of ourselves and one another, that we can be "god" in our own lives and in the lives of others, or that we can make another god of our own liking.

> *"Since the creation of the world God's invisible qualities*
> *—his eternal power and divine nature—*
> *have been clearly seen, being understood from what has been made,*
> *so that people are without excuse.*
> *For although they knew God,*
> *they neither glorified him as God nor gave thanks to him,*
> *…they became fools and exchanged the glory of the immortal God*

> *for images made to look like a mortal human being*
> *and birds and animals and reptiles"*
> (Romans 1:20-23).

- *Dependency* is a reliance on something or someone else for support or existence.

  "I have to have this to live."

- *Dependency* can be either negative or positive, such as being dependent on cocaine versus being dependent on Christ.

  "This is necessary for my life."

- *Dependency* can be an addiction to any object, behavior, or person that represents an underlying attempt to get emotional needs met.[1]

  "I must do this to meet my needs, to make me happy, to make me significant."

YOU CAN BE DEPENDENT ON...

Objects
- A chemical addiction to drugs (alcohol, tobacco, cocaine)
- A sexual addiction to erotic items (pornographic magazines, videos, and sex toys)

Behaviors
- An addiction to behaviors generally considered to be corrupt, those that are not widely socially acceptable and can be harmful (premarital and extramarital sex, gambling, excessive spending, compulsive eating)
- An addiction to behaviors generally considered to be good, those that are widely socially acceptable but may be equally harmful (perfectionism, workaholism, caregiving, extreme weight loss to the extent of anorexia or bulimia)

People
- A "love addiction" in which you feel your identity is in another person (A weak "love addict" is emotionally dependent on someone considered strong.)
- A "savior addiction" in which you feel your identity is in your

ability to meet the needs of another person (A strong "savior" needs to be needed by someone considered weak.)

Because addictions can provide a momentary high, good feelings are usually associated with them. However, the book of Proverbs gives this poignant warning:

> *"There is a way that appears to be right,*
> *but in the end it leads to death"*
> (PROVERBS 14:12).

=== *Interdependence* ===

QUESTION: "What is wrong with people depending on other people?"

ANSWER: We should have a healthy *interdependence* on others in the sense that we value and enjoy each other and love and learn from each other, but we should not be totally dependent on each other. Essentially, an interdependent relationship involves a healthy, mutual give-and-take where neither person looks to the other to meet each and every need.

Many people, however, have a *misplaced dependence* on others. These relationships are not healthy, for God intends for us to live in total dependence on Him. Over and over, the Bible portrays how godly people learn to have a *strong dependence* on the Lord rather than a *weak dependence* on each other. The apostle Paul said we should

> *"not rely on ourselves but on God"*
> (2 CORINTHIANS 1:9).

B. WHAT IS CODEPENDENCY?[2]

In our quest of the true God or a fabricated false god, we encounter many candidates along the way. There are a myriad of possibilities for us to choose from—all the way from the hosts of heaven to the inhabitants of the earth and anywhere in between. Once we lose our grip on God and our trust in Him, we are at the mercy of the wind and likely to be blown from one philosophy to another, or from one person to another. The Bible puts it this way:

> *"The one who doubts is like a wave of the sea,*
> *blown and tossed by the wind.*
> *That person should not expect to receive anything from the Lord.*

Such a person is double-minded
and unstable in all they do"
(JAMES 1:6-8).

Many people have heard others use the word *codependent*, but they can't really define it. So let's take a look at the background of this word.

- **Codependent people** today are those who are dependent on another person to the point of being controlled or manipulated by that person.

- *Codependent*—the term—was first used in the 1970s to describe a family member living with someone dependent on alcohol. The prefix *co-* means "with" or "one associated with the action of another."

- *Codependency* became a word used to describe the dysfunctional behavior of family members seeking to adapt to the destructive behavior of the alcoholic.

- **Codependency** is a relationship addiction. Just as the alcoholic is dependent on alcohol, the codependent is dependent on *being needed* by the alcoholic, or by someone who is problematic. Today, a codependent is anyone who is dependent on trying to help someone to the point of being controlled or manipulated by that person.

- **Codependent "enablers"** enable addicts or the dysfunctional people in their lives to continue with their addictions without marking and maintaining boundaries. Codependency can be compared to the sin of depending on false gods that are powerless to help or depending on a broken water well that won't hold water. It simply won't work!

"My people have committed two sins:
They have forsaken me, the spring of living water,
and have dug their own cisterns, broken
cisterns that cannot hold water"
(JEREMIAH 2:13).

Enablers

QUESTION: "How can I know whether or not I'm an enabler?"

ANSWER: You are an enabler if you perpetuate another's destructive behavior by protecting that person from painful consequences that could actually serve as a motivation for change.

> – The *enabling parent* allows the teenager's drug habit to continue with no repercussions, even to the detriment of other family members.
>
> – The *enabling wife* calls her husband's boss to say he has the flu when in fact he has a hangover.

Ask yourself: *How many lies have I told to protect the reputation of someone with a destructive habit?* The Bible has strong words to say about those who protect the guilty.

> *"Whoever says to the guilty, 'You are innocent,'*
> *will be cursed by peoples and denounced by nations"*
> (Proverbs 24:24).

C. What Are Common Codependent Relationships?

In a codependent relationship, one person is perceived as weak and the other as strong. The weak one appears totally dependent on the strong one. But the one who appears strong is actually weak because of the excessive *need to be needed* by the weak one. In fact, the strong one needs the weak one to *stay* weak. This, in turn, keeps the strong one feeling strong.

The ultimate solution—God's solution—for both people is not to draw strength in a dysfunctional way from each other, but rather to draw their strength from God. The Bible says,

> *"He gives strength to the weary and increases the power of the weak"*
> (Isaiah 40:29).

Common Codependent Relationships

In the examples below, the first person is dependent on the second person and the second person is actually the codependent one in the relationship, or the one needing to be needed.

- A *wife* is excessively helpless around her *husband*...and the husband needs his wife to stay helpless.
- A *husband* is excessively needy in how he relates to his *wife*...and the wife needs him to stay needy.

- A *student* is excessively tied to a *teacher*…and the teacher needs the student to stay tied to them.
- A *child* is excessively pampered by the *parent*…and the parent needs the child to stay in need of pampering.
- A *parent* is excessively protected by the *child*…and the child needs the parent to stay in need of protection.
- An *employee* is excessively entangled with an *employer*…and the employer needs the employee to stay entangled.
- A *friend* is excessively fixated on another *friend*…and that person needs the friend to stay fixated.
- A *counselee* is excessively clinging to a *counselor*…and the counselor needs the counselee to continue clinging.
- A *disciple* is excessively dependent on a *discipler*…and the discipler needs the disciple to stay dependent.
- A *victim* is excessively vulnerable to a *victimizer*…and the victimizer needs the victim to stay vulnerable.
- A *spiritual seeker* is excessively leaning on a *spiritual leader*…and the leader needs the seeker to continue leaning.

When we have *misplaced dependency*, we have a misplaced trust. We are excessively trusting in the relationship to provide more than God intended. The book of Psalms describes a misplaced trust:

> *"Some trust in chariots and some in horses,*
> *but we trust in the name of the* Lord *our God"*
> (Psalm 20:7).

=========== *Changing Dynamics* ===========

Question: "When I was a struggling addict, my wife held our home together. Now that I have truly changed, why is she continually upset and threatening divorce?"

Answer: You changed the dynamic! It is common knowledge, for example, that after an alcoholic becomes healthy and whole, the *strong* codependent mate is no longer needed in the same way. The new dynamic changes the balance in the relationship. The *strong one*, who no longer feels needed in the same way, could choose to divorce and remarry another needy mate in order to feel needed again. Obviously, divorce is *not* God's solution. Both of you becoming emotionally balanced and spiritually healthy is God's solution. Just as every alcoholic needs to overcome alcoholism, every codependent needs to overcome codependency. The Bible says,

> *"Do not conform to the pattern of this world,*
> *but be transformed by the renewing of your mind.*
> *Then you will be able to test and approve what God's will is*
> *—his good, pleasing and perfect will"*
> (ROMANS 12:2).

D. What Is Biblical Dependency?

David, an Israeli shepherd boy, knows the "giants" in his life are no match for his God. Time and time again he expresses complete dependence on the Lord for His provision and protection, no matter how daunting the tasks or how enormous the enemy. One such formidable foe is a giant of a man who stands more than nine feet tall. The Philistine warrior flaunts his strength and taunts the army of Israel, daring just one man to fight him. Without hesitation, David rises to the call—unmoved by the popular opinion that he is destined for destruction!

David's muscles are no match for the so-called strong man, but his spiritual might will deliver the final blow. "What will be done for the man who kills this Philistine and removes this disgrace from Israel? Who is this uncircumcised Philistine that he should defy the armies of the living God?" (1 Samuel 17:26). While the Israeli army cowers in fear, David conquers the blustering behemoth by faith.

With just a sling and five smooth stones, David approaches Goliath and declares the giant's doom. "You come against me with sword and spear and javelin, but I come against you in the name of the LORD Almighty, the God of the armies of Israel, whom you have defied. This day the LORD will deliver you into my hands, and I'll strike you down and cut off your head" (1 Samuel 17:45-46).

With that, David slings a stone into the forehead of Goliath, who instantly drops to the ground...dead. Afterward, David is brought before Israel's King Saul to herald Goliath's death. David holds the giant's head in his hand, proclaiming his total dependence upon God.

In David's own words:

> *"My salvation and my honor depend on God;*
> *he is my mighty rock, my refuge"*
> (PSALM 62:7).

BIBLICAL DEPENDENCY— GOD WANTS YOU TO DEPEND ON HIM

- **To totally rely** on Him, not on people or things or self-effort.

  > *"My flesh and my heart may fail, but God is the
  > strength of my heart and my portion forever"*
  > (PSALM 73:26).

- **To believe** that He will meet all of your needs. You can safely reveal your hurts, your fears, and your needs to God. He will be your Need-meeter.

  > *"The LORD will guide you always; he will satisfy your needs in a
  > sun-scorched land and will strengthen your frame. You will be like
  > a well-watered garden, like a spring whose waters never fail"*
  > (ISAIAH 58:11).

- **To trust** in Him to take care of your loved ones.

  > *"Trust in him at all times, you people; pour out
  > your hearts to him, for God is our refuge"*
  > (PSALM 62:8).

- **To rely on Christ**, whose life in you will enable you to overcome any destructive dependency.

  > *"The one [Christ] who is in you is greater than
  > the one [Satan] who is in the world"*
  > (1 JOHN 4:4).

=== *Unhealthy vs. Healthy Marriage* ===

QUESTION: "What is the difference between a codependent marriage and a healthy marriage?"[3]

ANSWER:

- An Unhealthy, Codependent Marriage
  - The *weak* spouse has a deep-seated need for security and continually looks to the *strong* spouse to meet all needs. This means the weak one stays weak.

– The supposedly *strong* spouse has a deep-seated need for significance and tries to meet all the needs of the *weaker* partner in
order to keep that mate dependent on the relationship.

- A Healthy, Interdependent Marriage

  – Each emphasizes the other's strengths and encourages the other
  partner to overcome personal weaknesses.

  – Each encourages the other to be dependent on the Lord while
  being responsive to the legitimate needs of the other.

> *"Let each of you look not only to his own interests,*
> *but also to the interests of others"*
> (PHILIPPIANS 2:4 ESV).

E. What Is God's Heart on Codependency?

If you live your life with a *misplaced dependency* on others, you will miss the
extraordinary relationship that God planned for you to have with Him.

In order to break a pattern of codependent relationships, you need to be able
to recognize the lies you believe that perpetuate the pattern and replace them
with God's truth so you can live your life in dependence on Him!

In King David's own words:

> *"My salvation and my honor depend on God;*
> *he is my mighty rock, my refuge"*
> (PSALM 62:7).

GOD'S HEART ON CODEPENDENCY

- **Lie:** I need people I can trust and depend on to feel good about
myself.

  Truth: I need to put my trust and confidence completely in the
  Lord.

  > *"This is what the LORD says: 'Cursed is the one who trusts*
  > *in man, who draws strength from mere flesh and whose*
  > *heart turns away from the LORD. But blessed is the one*
  > *who trusts in the LORD, whose confidence is in him'"*
  > (JEREMIAH 17:5,7).

- **Lie:** I need the approval of others to feel good about myself.

  Truth: I am to desire the approval of God, not men.

  > *"Am I now trying to win the approval of human beings, or of God? Or am I trying to please people? If I were still trying to please people, I would not be a servant of Christ"*
  > (Galatians 1:10).

- **Lie:** I need to change who I am.

  Truth: I am a new person in Christ, and He is changing me from the inside out and is making me into the person He created me to be.

  > *"If anyone is in Christ, the new creation has come; the old has gone, the new is here!"*
  > (2 Corinthians 5:17).

- **Lie:** I can expect people to meet all my needs.

  Truth: I am to look to God alone to meet my needs.

  > *"My God will meet all your needs according to the riches of his glory in Christ Jesus"*
  > (Philippians 4:19).

- **Lie:** My thinking does not need to change.

  Truth: I am to use God's Word to transform my thinking.

  > *"Do not conform to the pattern of this world, but be transformed by the renewing of your mind. Then you will be able to test and approve what God's will is—his good, pleasing and perfect will"*
  > (Romans 12:2).

- **Lie:** I need someone to lead me.

  Truth: I am to rely on the Lord to guide me.

  > *"He guides me along the right paths for his name's sake"*
  > (Psalm 23:3).

- **Lie:** Everything I need for life and happiness can be found in a relationship with a significant person.

  Truth: I have everything I need for life and godliness in my relationship with God alone.

> *"His divine power has given us everything we need for a*
> *godly life through our knowledge of him who called us by*
> *his own glory and goodness. Through these he has given us*
> *his very great and precious promises, so that through them*
> *you may participate in the divine nature, having escaped*
> *the corruption in the world caused by evil desires"*
>
> (2 PETER 1:3-4).

- **Lie:** My security and safety come from my relationships with others.

  Truth: I am to depend on God for my security and safety.

> *"You are my hiding place; you will protect me from*
> *trouble and surround me with songs of deliverance"*
>
> (PSALM 32:7).

Who Am I Trying to Please? The Story of Patricia

After 11 years of conflict, turmoil, and tears, Patricia finally finds the courage to end an on-again, off-again relationship with her chemically addicted boyfriend. Yet instead of feeling relieved, she is overwhelmed with sadness and confused by thoughts of taking him back. Desperate for direction, she calls *Hope in the Night*,* my live two-hour call-in counseling broadcast, to share her heart:

"I know I did the right thing by walking away, but all I can feel is sorrow," she says. "Why can't I feel angry for how he treated me? Why can't I just say, 'Thank You, God—he's finally gone!'?"

When I ask Patricia to tell me more about the relationship, she describes an enmeshed bond with a man whose substance abuse causes chronic conflict and chaos. Early in their relationship, Patricia began regretting their choice to live together and asked him to move out. He moved alright—straight into another woman's apartment. But four months later, he was back on Patricia's doorstep.

"He vowed he'd always love me, so I allowed him back into my life," she says. "But he still smokes marijuana and abuses pills. Now I've told him I can't do this anymore."

---

* *Hope in the Night* is heard Monday through Friday from 11:00 pm to 1:00 am Central time. Contact Hope for the Heart at 1-800-488-HOPE (4673) or visit www.hopefortheheart.org for broadcast information.

Clearly, Patricia is yearning for God's strength as she tries to make a fresh start, but her emotions have overtaken her reasoning, erasing memories of all the pain he caused her.

"In my head, I know breaking up is right, but I can't get my heart to follow. I still love him. How can I get to the point where my heart follows my head?"

"True love—in its highest form—seeks the very best for another person," I remind Patricia. "As long as you support this man in his destructive lifestyle, you are *not* loving him. To make matters worse, he will drag you down with him."

Like so many codependent relationships, this one is founded on control and manipulation. Over time, Patricia's unhealthy attachment has become obsessive as she compulsively slaves to help, please, and rescue her boyfriend. A childhood history of being controlled and abandoned serves as the perfect setup for her dysfunctional relationships.

I remind Patricia of the Scripture so meaningful to me that I had it etched on a window inside my office door: "Am I now trying to win the approval of human beings, or of God? Or am I trying to please people? If I were still trying to please people, I would not be a servant of Christ" (Galatians 1:10). To expand on this, I add:

"The message is clear. We mustn't allow any person to become our 'god'—to take the place that He alone must occupy in our heart. A life of being *controlled* by another person's needs, desires, and well-being causes a misplaced dependency. A codependent relationship always leads to a destructive cycle of control and manipulation. And it keeps you from being all God created you to be."

"But June, I'm so afraid of the pain I'll feel if I let him go," Patricia confides, her voice soft and unsteady.

"The truth is: You're going to experience pain either way. If you continue in this codependent relationship, there will be pain. If you break it off, there will be pain. But by doing the hard thing—the right thing—now, you'll position yourself to experience lasting peace *without* the pain. And that, my friend, is priceless."

I then ask Patricia to imagine a key and lock, explaining that a twisted key will only fit into a similarly twisted lock. But when you repair the lock, the twisted key will no longer fit. "It's that way with codependent relationships. When you become healthy, no matter how many broken men approach you wanting to be in a relationship, they will no longer fit with the new you!"

To experience the fullness of God's peace, Patricia will first need to place her total trust in the Lord alone. With relief in her voice, she says she understands and wants to make a fresh start. She tells me she already has trusted Jesus as her Savior. And now, in her desire to surrender to Him, she wants to allow the Lord to truly *be Lord* of her life.

Colossians 1:27 speaks of "Christ in you, the hope of glory." I say, "Count on this Scripture to counter your fear of abandonment. Realize that you will never be abandoned. With Christ in you, you are never alone, never overlooked, never forgotten."

By the end of our conversation, Patricia confirms her desire to begin a new life without her destructive, unfaithful boyfriend, and give full control of her life to the Lord. She affirms that whenever she starts to feel controlled by emotion or to be drawn back into codependency, she will immediately say out loud, "I reject that feeling," and then she will fill her mind with truths from God's Word.

She also makes a commitment to join a codependency support group at her church and to seek out godly women who can support her in her journey. Together we pray, thanking God for His promise: "The LORD himself goes before you and will be with you; he will never leave you nor forsake you. Do not be afraid; do not be discouraged" (Deuteronomy 31:8).

Patricia is well on her way to understanding that freedom from codependency represents the highest and best thing we can do for ourselves...and for those we love. And though the road to recovery from codependency—like any addiction—is often walked with two steps forward and one step back, still, those who undertake this journey can be "confident of this, that he who began a good work in you will carry it on to completion" (Philippians 1:6).

II. CHARACTERISTICS OF CODEPENDENCY

Can children be conditioned to become codependent? The definitive answer is yes. In the Bible, Rebekah shows a blatant bias toward her second-born son, Jacob, probably because he stays close to hearth and home. Isaac, her husband, favors their firstborn son, Esau, largely because he is an outdoorsman with a prowess for hunting.

Because no two children have identical skills, all children should be recognized for their differences and respected for their distinctive abilities. Oh, but Rebekah does not love in this way! She is driven toward division—thus the conniving begins. Rebekah wants Jacob to receive the birthright of the firstborn, a gateway toward great blessing. And so she dupes her dying husband into giving that birthright to Jacob instead of his older brother, Esau.

Because of the *enmeshed relationship* between Rebekah and Jacob, she finds it easy to persuade her son to defraud his father. She plots...she schemes...she secretly plans. Rebekah covers Jacob's hands and part of his neck with the skin of a young goat so that, when Isaac reaches for his firstborn, Jacob's skin will feel like Esau's, who is described as "hairy" (Genesis 27:11). She even dresses Jacob in Esau's best clothes. Because of old age and weak eyes, Isaac is fooled.

Although Rebekah deems the scheme a success—Jacob, her favorite, receives the firstborn blessings—Esau soon uncovers the fraud, forcing Jacob to flee for his life. Even so, Jacob does not escape his *passive dependency*. All too soon, he again becomes manipulated by others. His father-in-law switches women on him, and Jacob experiences a classic case of "what goes around comes around." He feels conned and controlled, but such is the misery in adulthood when one is enmeshed in childhood (see Genesis chapters 27–30).

Scripture addresses the sure consequences of sin:

> *"Do not be deceived: God cannot be mocked.*
> *A man reaps what he sows"*
> (GALATIANS 6:7).

A. What Is the Codependent Person Profile?

Codependent people may appear capable and self-sufficient, but in reality they are insecure, self-doubting, and in need of approval. This need for approval often results in an excessive sense of responsibility and a dependence on people-pleasing performances. The Bible, however, says our primary focus should not be on pleasing people, but rather on pleasing God.

> *"We instructed you how to live in order to please God,*
> *as in fact you are living. Now we ask you and urge*
> *you in the Lord Jesus to do this more and more"*
> (1 THESSALONIANS 4:1).

THE CODEPENDENT PERSON PROFILE[4]

Consider whether or not any of these statements are reflections of you. Check (✓) everything that applies to you.

- ☐ I feel responsible for the feelings, needs, and actions of another person close to me.
- ☐ I try to fix the problems of this person, even to the detriment of my own well-being.
- ☐ I can discern the thoughts of this person but cannot identify my own.
- ☐ I know the feelings and needs of this person but do not know my own.
- ☐ I do things for others that they are capable of doing for themselves.
- ☐ I feel angry when my help is not wanted.
- ☐ I tend to be rigid and judgmental in the eyes of others.
- ☐ I judge myself more harshly than I judge others.
- ☐ I deny my own feelings and needs—so I've been told.
- ☐ I feel guilty when I stand up for myself.
- ☐ I feel good about giving, but have difficulty receiving.
- ☐ I try to be perfect in order to avoid anger or criticism.
- ☐ I look for my worth in the approval of others.
- ☐ I find I am attracted to needy people, and needy people are attracted to me.

"Those who are in the flesh cannot please God"
(ROMANS 8:8 NKJV).

============ *Criteria for Dating* ============

QUESTION: "Should I date a woman who is secure, confident, and competent, or someone who is insecure, from a difficult background, and really needs me?"

ANSWER: You can be a knight in shining armor and rescue a damsel in distress. But if you make a habit of rescuing her, she will not value you as a person—only as a rescuer. You need to be wanted and loved for who you are, not for having rescued an emotionally unhealthy female who is unable to extend unconditional love to you in return.

- Someone who is emotionally healthy can love you out of strength and will be able to accept you unconditionally and offer you security in a relationship.
- Someone who is emotionally needy is typically self-focused and limited in ability to be unselfishly sensitive to the needs of others.
- Emotionally needy people are more often *takers* rather than *givers* in relationships and tend to "use people up" emotionally.

Seek someone with emotional maturity and spiritual wisdom, someone who can help you to grow more and more in your relationship with the Lord.

> *"Walk with the wise and become wise..."*
> (Proverbs 13:20).

B. What Is the Codependent Relationship Profile?

They share a strong spiritual connection, a covenant oath of friendship. And it all begins the day David kills Goliath.

The king's son Jonathan "became one in spirit with David, and he loved him as himself" (1 Samuel 18:1). Jonathan protects David from his jealous, murderous father. And though he is the rightful heir to the throne, he commits to helping David become the next king because he recognizes him as God's anointed. Their relationship is characterized by strength, sacrifice, and support. There's not even a hint of codependency.

Jonathan and David model a healthy relationship. By contrast, in a codependent relationship, both people are insecure and become entangled in a web of emotional bondage. The two combine to produce a destructive cycle of manipulation and control, draining joy and happiness out of life. Because this destructive dynamic is often subconscious, both parties can feel innocent of any wrongdoing. Yet God knows legitimate emotional needs are being temporarily met in illegitimate ways.

Scripture discloses the keen discernment of God:

> *"All a person's ways seem pure to them,*
> *but motives are weighed by the Lord"*
> (Proverbs 16:2).

=== *The Codependent Relationship Profile*[5] ===

Both…

- *Are in denial*
- *Have difficulty establishing* healthy, intimate relationships
- *Have difficulty setting* boundaries
- *Have one other addiction* other than the relationship
- *Have a false sense* of security
- *Become jealous* and possessive
- *Control* and manipulate
- *Struggle* with low self-worth
- *Violate* their consciences
- *Experience* extreme ups and downs
- *Fear* abandonment
- *Feel a loss* of personal identity
- *Feel trapped* in the relationship

> *"I find more bitter than death the [person] who is a snare,*
> *whose heart is a trap and whose hands are chains"*
> (ECCLESIASTES 7:26).

=== *Unhealthy vs. Healthy Friendships* ===

QUESTION: "Is a friendship codependent when two friends depend on one another?"

ANSWER: No, if the friendship is interdependent (reciprocal with balanced sharing), then it is healthy. If the friendship is codependent (out of balance), then it is unhealthy.

> *"As iron sharpens iron, so one person sharpens another"*
> (PROVERBS 27:17).

- **An Unhealthy, Codependent Friendship**
  - One friend is *weak* and troubled; the other friend is *strong* and

competent. (There is an imbalance of power and of give-and-take.)

– One friend desires freedom to enjoy other significant relationships but is fearful of doing so.

– The one friend desires exclusivity and becomes easily jealous or threatened.

– Both may put the other friend in the place of Christ, and neither is bettered by the friendship.

- **A Healthy, Interdependent Friendship**

  – Both come together as equals with a balance of power and of give-and-take.

  – Both pursue and enjoy other significant relationships and avoid exclusivity.

  – Both friends are better because of each other. Each strengthens the other spiritually.

Biblical Illustration: During a difficult time in his life, David did not try to draw Jonathan to himself, nor did Jonathan try to draw David to himself. Instead, the Bible says, "Jonathan...helped him [David] find strength in God" (1 Samuel 23:16).

C. What Is the Codependency Checklist Test?

Those caught up in codependency are often too emotionally entangled with someone and too emotionally driven to recognize their personal unhealthiness and the unhealthiness of their relationships. Generally, the emotional highs and lows that characterize their lives hold them captive and only through the eyes of an insightful caring person are they able to see the truth of their dilemma and the reality of their sin.

And it is only in the strength of the Lord and with the strong support of healthy individuals that they are able to move from being codependent to interdependent people.

> *"It is God who arms me with strength*
> *and keeps my way secure...*
> *The Lord is my strength and my shield;*
> *my heart trusts in him, and he helps me"*
> (Psalms 18:32; 28:7).

THE CODEPENDENCY CHECKLIST TEST

Are you unsure about someone who is significant in your life? Is it possible you are in a relationship others would call "codependent"? If so, how would you know? Read through the Codependency Checklist and check (✓) everything that applies to you.

- ☐ Do you struggle with feeling unloved; therefore, you look for ways to be needed?
- ☐ Do you throw all of your energy into helping someone else?
- ☐ Do you say *no* when you should say *yes*, and say *yes* when you should say *no*?
- ☐ Do you feel compelled to take charge of another person's crisis?
- ☐ Do you feel drawn to people you think need to be rescued from their problems?
- ☐ Do you have difficulty setting boundaries with others and then keeping those boundaries?
- ☐ Do you find it difficult to identify and express your true feelings?
- ☐ Do you rely on the other person in your relationship to make most of the decisions?
- ☐ Do you feel lonely, sad, and empty when you are alone?
- ☐ Do you feel threatened when the person closest to you spends time with someone else?
- ☐ Do you think other people's opinions are more important than yours?
- ☐ Do you refrain from speaking in order to keep peace?
- ☐ Do you fear conflict because the other person could abandon you?
- ☐ Do you become defensive about your relationship with another person?
- ☐ Do you feel stuck in a relationship with another person?
- ☐ Do you feel that you have lost your personal identity in order to "fit into" another person's world?
- ☐ Do you feel controlled and manipulated by another person?
- ☐ Do you feel used and taken advantage of by another person?
- ☐ Do you plan your life around another person?

☐ Do you prioritize your relationship with another person over your relationship with the Lord?

If you responded with a *yes* to four or more of these questions, you may be involved in a codependent relationship!

When we find ourselves in unhealthy patterns of relating, we need to change our focus, change our goals, and change what is hindering us from running the race God has planned for us. Our primary focus should be not on another person, but on Jesus.

> *"Let us throw off everything that hinders and the*
> *sin that so easily entangles. And let us run with*
> *perseverance the race marked out for us"*
> (Hebrews 12:1).

═══════════ *Codependency and the Workplace* ═══════════

QUESTION: "As an employee, how can I keep codependency out of my workplace?"

ANSWER:

- *Don't* be afraid to establish and maintain appropriate boundaries.
- *Don't* try to be your employer's "all-in-all"—the one who will always do everything.
- *Don't* be controlled by manipulation and fear.
- *Don't* let staying late be a detriment to your God-given, personal priorities.
- *Don't* fail to speak up if the workload is too great to accomplish what you have been hired to do in the time allowed. You can express an accurate picture to your employer in this way:

    "(Employer's name), thank you for the opportunity to work on this assignment. We seem to have run into a problem. You have employed me to be here 40 hours a week; however, there are at least 85 hours of work to be done. How do you want me to prioritize my tasks and utilize my 40 hours this week?"

- *Don't* be afraid to say *no* when it's appropriate to say *no*.

> *"All you need to say is simply 'Yes' or 'No' "*
> (Matthew 5:37).

Desperate No More: The Laurie and Lance Story

They appear to be the perfect couple.

Both highly educated, Laurie and Lance attended a renowned seminary and seemingly shared a calling to full-time ministry. Laurie worked several years for a Christian ministry, teaching people how to study the Bible. I had casually known Laurie for more than ten years and saw her as intelligent, competent, and assured. What I did *not* see that both shocked and grieved me was that she was also abused.

Lance is now divorcing Laurie to be with another woman, and they are in the midst of a custody battle over their two young sons. The judge rules that until a decision is made as to which parent will have custodial care, this arrangement is to be followed: The children are to stay in the home, and each parent will rotate in and out every other week. So every other week for about a year and a half, Laurie stayed in my home.

We had many late-night talks. The one that stands out most in my memory is the evening I asked whether she had any pictures to prove to the judge that her husband was violent. Immediately she went to my guest bedroom and returned with pictures of herself—*actual police photos*—depicting her severely bruised head and swollen eyes. I was absolutely stunned.

Lance had enacted the typical pattern of abuse: first inflicting verbal and emotional abuse, which later escalated into physical abuse. Laurie became a victim of repeated domestic violence, oblivious to the fact that a codependent mind-set is the foundation on which an abusive relationship is built. For too long, she had kept herself in harm's way—her codependency had her trapped in a dangerous situation.

This codependent mind-set resides within anyone who is controlled or manipulated by someone else. They become people-pleasers, looking for worth from the approval of others. They likely felt powerless and insignificant as children. Laurie grew up in a dysfunctional, alcoholic home and therefore became skilled at "doing." This pattern, which made her feel empowered and significant, continued into adulthood and marriage.

She wants to feel significant, so she becomes overly dependent on Lance, desperately seeking his approval to validate her worth. He, too, desperately seeks significance, feeling empowered by having her under his complete control. Not knowing that each person has intrinsic value given by God allows the abuse to flourish.

Like so many abused wives caught up in codependency, Laurie thinks it is her duty to maintain appearances for the sake of their good name and Christian image. To the outside world, their family looks perfect. While Laurie appears competent and content outside her home, within its walls, Lance controls everything...their finances, their schedule, their friends—*everything*.

If others were to know how dysfunctional our so-called "Christian marriage" is, she reasons, *they might stumble in their faith.* How can she tell anyone?

Codependent women like Laurie become further victimized because they dare not disclose their abuse to others. They fear that well-meaning people could wonder, *What did you do to cause it?* Many times, those who are abused ask themselves the same question, sadly believing they have caused the inexcusable abuse. Suffering with a full-blown case of false guilt, they tend to blame themselves. After all, he tells her repeatedly, "It's all your fault!" As with Lance, since he is supposedly *never* wrong, he is also *never* repentant and *never* says "I'm sorry."

When I gave Laurie our *Biblical Counseling Keys* on Wife Abuse, she quickly identified with Lance's "Scripture twisting." This simply means that most batterers are adept at manipulating their wives with the Scripture "Wives, submit yourselves to your own husbands..." (Ephesians 5:22), but they refuse to look at that verse in context. The prior verse states, "Submit to one another out of reverence for Christ." The subsequent verses say husbands are to demonstrate sacrificial love to their wives. However, following Lance's skewed interpretation, Laurie spirals downward from faith-based *submission* to fear-driven *subservience*.

Rather than recognizing her own unhealthy dependence on Lance and rather than realizing how she is enabling his belittling abuse to continue, Laurie justifies this plight as being her cross to bear. She thinks, *If only I could do everything right, he might be pleased.* Though she is sincere, she is sincerely wrong.

For so long she has misplaced her deepest dependence on her husband. Laurie has become entirely dependent on Lance, naively believing that God would intervene because of her faith. She doesn't realize that God has given her active authority to use her *mind* to know this is wrong and must not continue, and to use her *mouth* to say, "No. If you continue, I'll move out of harm's way," and to use her *motivation* (the Bible) to strengthen her resolve: "Do not make friends with a hot-tempered person, do not associate with one easily angered" (Proverbs 22:24).

Regrettably, it is not until after Lance divorces Laurie that she finally begins to discover hope and healing from the crippling codependency she had unwittingly been enslaved to throughout her marriage. Looking back, she wishes she had learned to be more assertive much sooner.

But looking forward, Laurie has now learned to place her dependence on God first and foremost—and to depend on Him to help her relate to others. She has allowed God to prove Himself to be her all-sufficient Need-meeter. Today, Laurie is free to be all God created her to be because she not only *knows* the truth and verbally *admits* the truth, but she also *acts* on the truth. Jesus says,

> *"You will know the truth, and the truth will set you free"*
> (JOHN 8:32).

III. Causes of Codependency

What draws people into destructive, codependent relationships? The answer is most often found in childhood pain—a past pain that impacts today's choices. In reality, codependent people are grown-ups who have never grown up emotionally.

The Bible refers to immature grown-ups by using the analogy of infants feeding on milk instead of solid food:

> *"Though by this time you ought to be teachers,*
> *you need someone to teach you the elementary truths*
> *of God's word all over again.*
> *You need milk, not solid food!*
> *Anyone who lives on milk, being still an infant,*
> *is not acquainted with the teaching about righteousness"*
> (HEBREWS 5:12-13).

A. What Causes Codependency to Develop in Children?[6]

All children progress through five developmental stages on their way to maturity and adulthood. God designed the family to provide the necessary structure for the healthy completion of each of these stages. If we fail to progress successfully from one stage to another in childhood, our development will be stunted and we will grow up to be emotionally and spiritually immature adults. We will develop adult bodies, but—like children—we will be underdeveloped emotionally and spiritually. As a result, we will be inclined to be drawn into codependent, needy relationships. Out of tender concern for the protection of children, Jesus gave this strong warning to adults:

> *"If anyone causes one of these little ones—those who*
> *believe in me—to stumble, it would be better for*
> *them to have a large millstone hung around their*
> *neck and to be drowned in the depths of the sea"*
> (MATTHEW 18:6).

FIVE STAGES OF CHILDHOOD DEVELOPMENT

God bestows on parents the major responsibility of nurturing their children so that they will not be *love-starved*—an emotional state that sets them up to look for love in all the wrong places.

1. THE HELPLESS STAGE

Babies need to bond with their parents because they are helpless and totally dependent for all of their basic needs (including the three inner needs for love, significance, and security).[7] If your parents did not meet your needs, you may have grown into a needy adult who *feels "empty" inside*—as if there is a hole in your heart.

2. THE PUSHING AWAY STAGE

Toddlers need to begin to push away from their parents as a way of exploring their environment and setting boundaries. If your parents did not allow separation, you may have grown into an adult who *manipulates others* in order to gain some sense of control.

3. THE CONFLICT STAGE

Young children need to learn proper ways of resolving conflict as they begin to test their parents' rules. If you did not learn healthy conflict resolution skills, you may have grown into an adult who *lacks problem-solving skills* in your adult relationships.

4. THE INDEPENDENT STAGE

Preadolescent children need to grow in independence, but they still need direction and support from their parents. If your parents stifled your assertiveness, you may have grown into a *needy, unassertive* adult who is dependent on others to validate you.

5. THE SHARING STAGE

Adolescents need to learn mutual give-and-take and even sacrificial sharing from their parents as they begin to pursue involvement within their own groups. If you did not see a healthy give-and-take between your parents or see ways of sacrificially helping others, you may have grown into a *self-focused* adult who forms unequal relationships in order to feel some sense of significance.

Children who grow up being emotionally needy and who are not allowed to learn the skills necessary for forming healthy adult relationships experience great challenges in learning healthy independence. They have difficulty speaking the truth, asking for what they want, and setting boundaries. They become codependent adults who are addicted to unhealthy relationships because they never learned anything different. Ultimately, they are desperately trying to finish what they started in infancy—to grow up!

> *"Brothers and sisters, stop thinking like children.*
> *In regard to evil be infants, but in your thinking be adults"*
> (1 CORINTHIANS 14:20).

=========== *Parenting Healthy Children* ===========

QUESTION: "As a parent, how can I keep my children from having an unhealthy dependence on me?"

ANSWER:

- *Begin early* to model good decision-making principles for your children.

- *Teach* your children to pray about their decisions and to depend on God to guide them.

- *Allow* your children (early on) to choose between two or three options regarding the clothing they would like to wear or tasks they would like to perform.

- *Praise* your children for making good decisions. They will want to repeat actions that are praiseworthy.

- *Allow* your children to experience the repercussions of making poor decisions. (Rather than finding a way to rescue them, maintain the boundary line. Some of the most memorable lessons are learned the hard way.)

- *Teach* your children the practical principles of decision making in regard to age-appropriate topics, such as boundaries, chores, friends, curfews, money, dating, and goals.

- *Encourage* your children to develop friendships with other children and to learn to give-and-take in relationships.

- *Teach* your children to take care of their possessions, to perform routine household chores, and to prepare meals.

- *Show* your children how to budget their money and establish spending priorities.

- *Enroll* your children in group activities or clubs that will expose them to new experiences, enhance their life skills, and develop their self-confidence.

- *Identify* your children's strengths and find avenues in which they can succeed in developing those strengths.

"Start children off on the way they should go,
and even when they are old they will not turn from it"
(Proverbs 22:6).

God meant for us to grow physically, emotionally, mentally, and spiritually. By God's design, you can change and grow in maturity in every area of your life.

More specifically, you can have mature relationships. By God's grace and power, what has been ravaged can be restored. What has been ruined can be redeemed.

Ask the Lord to transform your mind with His truth. Realize that the tree rooted in truth will bear much fruit:

"That person is like a tree planted by streams of water,
which yields its fruit in season and whose leaf does not wither—
whatever they do prospers"
(Psalm 1:3).

═══════════ *Bonding vs. Enmeshment* ═══════════

Question: "In the parent-child relationship, what is the difference between bonding and enmeshment?"

Answer:

- *Healthy bonding* occurs when parents are connected with their children by being God's instruments to meet their basic physical, emotional, and spiritual needs. With healthy bonding, nurturing flows naturally *from parent to child*, leaving the child emotionally fulfilled and whole.

- *Unhealthy enmeshment* occurs when parents need an excessive connection with their children in order to get their own emotional needs met. With enmeshment, nurturing flows unnaturally *from child to parent*, leaving the child emotionally drained and empty.

> *"Children should not have to save up for their parents,*
> *but parents for their children"*
> (2 CORINTHIANS 12:14).

B. What Causes Repeated Cycles of Codependency?

Why do some people go from one codependent relationship to another? Your friend escapes one controller only to be attracted to another controller. Why move from one negative relationship to another? Have you yourself been caught up in this cycle? If so, you may have spoken words expressing your perplexity, just like the apostle Paul:

> *"I do not do the good I want to do, but*
> *the evil I do not want to do—this I keep on doing"*
> (ROMANS 7:19).

WHAT CHILDHOOD SETUP LEADS TO ADULT LOVE ADDICTION?

- ### As children, their "love buckets" were empty.

No one sets out to be emotionally addicted to another person, to constantly crave love from another person. These cravings were created in childhood because there was "no water in the well"—their "love buckets" were and still are empty. They are truly *love-starved*.

When unloved children receive a rare moment of attention or affection from their unloving parents, the result is both exhilarating and confusing. They feel confused as to why they can't be consistently loved, and they become fixated on how to get that feeling of being loved again. Rejected children live for any moment of acceptance. Any hint of love becomes an emotional high that temporarily relieves their pain. These children may become adult *love addicts* because they…

- Did not receive enough positive affirmation as children

- Grew up feeling unloved, insignificant, and insecure

- Experienced a traumatic separation or a lack of bonding

- Felt and continue to feel intense sadness and a profound loss as a result of being abandoned

- Experienced repeated rejection from their parents

- Felt and continue to feel extreme fear, helplessness, and emptiness

- **As adults, they find their "love buckets" have holes in them.**

   Children with empty "love buckets" create a fantasy about some "savior" who will remove their fear and finally make them feel whole. But no matter how much love they receive, it's not enough because they themselves are not whole.

   As adults, they are still emotionally needy "children" who…

   - Believe being loved by someone—anyone—is the solution to their emptiness

   - Enter relationships believing they cannot take care of themselves

   - Assign too much value and power to the other person in a relationship

   - Have tremendously unrealistic expectations of the other person

   - Try to "stick like glue" to the other person in order to feel connected

   - Live in fear that those who truly love them will ultimately leave them

The plight of love addicts would seem without solution were it not for the Lord, who is the only true Savior, the One who loves unconditionally and eternally. The Lord gives this assurance:

"I have loved you with an everlasting love;
I have drawn you with unfailing kindness"
(JEREMIAH 31:3).

THE CYCLE OF THE WEAK ONE[8]

SCENARIO #1

A woman appears weak because as a child her emotional needs were never met. She fantasizes about her knight in shining armor who will one day sweep her away into romantic bliss. This love addict constantly yearns for someone to complete her as a person. She is drawn to caregivers, yet at the same time, she is terrified at the thought of true intimacy.

Feeling the Pain of Abandonment

Fascination
The *weak one* is attracted to the power, praise, and adulation of the *strong one*, feeling; *I need your strength to become strong.*

Fantasy
The *weak one* fantasizes that the *strong one* will be "the savior." The more the *strong one* fights being engulfed, the more fantasy the *weak one* needs to keep from feeling abandoned.

Frenzy
In a frenzy, the *weak one* compulsively pursues the *strong one* again...or abandons the relationship for someone else who could be a "savior."

Fog
Looking through "rose-colored glasses," the *weak one* lives in a fog, not seeing that the *strong one* is distancing and that their relationship is seriously flawed.

Fixation
Out of fear of being abandoned, the *weak one* obsesses over some other addictive behavior in order to get relief from the painful reality of rejection.

Fear
The *strong one* retreats further, throwing the *weak one* into withdrawal, generating fear of abandonment and triggering previous abandonment issues.

THE CYCLE OF THE STRONGER ONE[9]

SCENARIO #2

A man appears strong because as a child he was in an enmeshed relationship with his mother. He was his mother's "caregiver" and surrogate husband. (His father was emotionally or physically absent.) Now, as an adult, he is drawn to women who need to be "taken care of," but he is terrified at the thought of being smothered again.

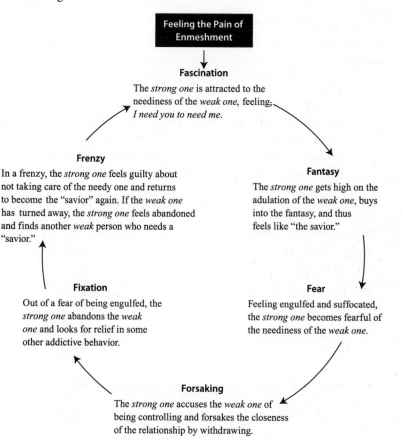

Feeling the Pain of Enmeshment

Fascination
The *strong one* is attracted to the neediness of the *weak one*, feeling, *I need you to need me.*

Frenzy
In a frenzy, the *strong one* feels guilty about not taking care of the needy one and returns to become the "savior" again. If the *weak one* has turned away, the *strong one* feels abandoned and finds another *weak* person who needs a "savior."

Fantasy
The *strong one* gets high on the adulation of the *weak one*, buys into the fantasy, and thus feels like "the savior."

Fixation
Out of a fear of being engulfed, the *strong one* abandons the *weak one* and looks for relief in some other addictive behavior.

Fear
Feeling engulfed and suffocated, the *strong one* becomes fearful of the neediness of the *weak one.*

Forsaking
The *strong one* accuses the *weak one* of being controlling and forsakes the closeness of the relationship by withdrawing.

Codependent relationships are formed by two people who are addicted to each other yet are in denial about their addiction. Both the weak and the strong persons can be either male or female. Both have abandonment issues and enmeshment issues. They generally flip-flop between being the weak one and the strong one—sometimes even within the same relationship. The intensity of their relationship and the intensity of their pain are immense as they swing from one extreme to the other, from suffocating one another to distancing from one another. They fail to focus on this simple, but wise, counsel:

> *"Avoid all extremes"*
> (ECCLESIASTES 7:18).

C. What Is the Root Cause of Codependency?

If we expect or demand that another person meet all our needs and fulfill us or if we become dependent on another person to do so, we have a *misplaced dependency*. The Bible gives us this clear directive:

> *"See to it that no one takes you captive through hollow and deceptive philosophy, which depends on human tradition and the elemental spiritual forces of this world rather than on Christ. For in Christ all the fullness of the Deity lives in bodily form, and in Christ you have been brought to fullness"*
> (COLOSSIANS 2:8-10).

THREE GOD-GIVEN INNER NEEDS

In reality, we have all been created with three God-given inner needs: the needs for love, significance, and security.[10]

- **Love**—to know that someone is unconditionally committed to our best interest

> *"My command is this: Love each other as I have loved you"*
> (JOHN 15:12).

- **Significance**—to know that our lives have meaning and purpose

> *"I cry out to God Most High, to God who fulfills his purpose for me"*
> (PSALM 57:2 ESV).

- **Security**—to feel accepted and a sense of belonging

> *"Whoever fears the LORD has a secure fortress, and for their children it will be a refuge"*
> (PROVERBS 14:26).

THE ULTIMATE NEED-MEETER

Why did God give us these deep inner needs, knowing that people and self-effort fail us?

God gave us these inner needs so that we would come to know Him as our Need-meeter. Our needs are designed by God to draw us into a deeper dependence upon Christ. God did not create any person or position or any amount of power or possessions to meet the deepest needs in our lives. If a person or thing *could* meet all our needs, we wouldn't need God! The Lord will use circumstances and bring positive people into our lives as an extension of His care and compassion, but ultimately, only God can satisfy all the needs of our hearts. The Bible says,

> *"The LORD will guide you always;*
> *he will satisfy your needs in a sun-scorched land*
> *and will strengthen your frame.*
> *You will be like a well-watered garden,*
> *like a spring whose waters never fail"*
> (ISAIAH 58:11).

The apostle Paul revealed this truth when he said, "What a wretched man I am. Who will rescue me from this body that is subject to death?" He then answered his own question by saying he is saved by "Jesus Christ our Lord!" (Romans 7:24-25).

All along, the Lord planned to meet our deepest needs for...

- **Love**—*"I* [the Lord] *have loved you with an everlasting love; I have drawn you with unfailing kindness"* (Jeremiah 31:3).

- **Significance**—*"'For I know the plans I have for you,' declares the LORD, 'plans to prosper you and not to harm you, plans to give you hope and a future'"* (Jeremiah 29:11).

- **Security**—*"The LORD himself goes before you and will be with you; he will never leave you nor forsake you. Do not be afraid; do not be discouraged"* (Deuteronomy 31:8).

The truth is that our God-given needs for love, significance, and security can be legitimately met—in Christ Jesus! Philippians 4:19 makes that clear:

> *"My God will meet all your needs according to*
> *the riches of his glory in Christ Jesus."*

- **WRONG BELIEF FOR THE DEPENDENT:**

"I need to be connected to a *stronger* person who will provide me with a sense of love and emotional security."

RIGHT BELIEF FOR THE DEPENDENT:

"While God often expresses His love through others, He doesn't want me to live my life depending on another person. I need to live dependently on Jesus, who will meet my needs, give me healthy relationships, and make my life fruitful." Jesus said,

> *"I am the vine; you are the branches. If you remain in me and I in you, you will bear much fruit; apart from me you can do nothing"*
> (JOHN 15:5).

- **WRONG BELIEF FOR THE CODEPENDENT:**

"I am responsible for meeting all the needs of this person whom I love, and that gives me a real sense of significance."

RIGHT BELIEF FOR THE CODEPENDENT:

"If I try to meet all the needs of another person, I'm taking the role that God alone should have. My need for significance cannot be met by pleasing another person, but it is met by pleasing God and finding my significance in Him."

> *"We make it our goal to please him [God]..."*
> (2 CORINTHIANS 5:9).

D. What Are Dangerous Dependencies?

When God created you, He planned for you to enter into a tender, trusting relationship with Him. He is so trustworthy that you can totally depend on Him to meet all of your needs. Any other dependency is dangerous. He designed you to live in *dependence on Him*—not on anyone else—to complete you, to fulfill you.

To avoid developing a dangerous dependency, heed the following scriptures:

> *"Trust in the LORD with all your heart*
> *and lean not on your own understanding;*

> *in all your ways submit to him,*
> *and he will make your paths straight"*
> (PROVERBS 3:5-6).

HOW TO BEGIN DEPENDING ON GOD ALONE

If you have struggled with codependency, God has a solution for you—a solution that can be spelled out in four points, which are listed on pages 48-50.

IV. STEPS TO SOLUTION

In the beginning, everything is perfect.

God creates a man and a woman, Adam and Eve, and He enjoys perfect fellowship with the pair. As Adam and Eve interact with one another in healthy, holy ways, their relationship can be described as nothing other than perfect. God places Adam and Eve in a perfect environment, the Garden of Eden, filled with provision and pleasure.

The scenario truly is the picture of perfection—that is, until a crafty serpent empowered by Satan leaves a lasting stain that has sullied the world to this day.

The Bible warns,

> *"Be strong in the Lord and in his mighty power.*
> *Put on the full armor of God, so that you can take*
> *your stand against the devil's schemes"*
> (EPHESIANS 6:10-11).

A. Key Verse to Memorize

The wily serpent woos Eve away from her primary relationship with God, causing her to doubt and challenge the truth He has instilled in her life.

Rather than trusting and depending on God to guide her, Eve develops a misplaced dependency upon the serpent, choosing to believe his lies over God's truth. Satan inquires of Eve: "Did God really say, 'You must not eat from any tree in the garden?'" (Genesis 3:1). It is a question designed to plant doubt about the goodness of God and to test how firmly she is grounded in His truth.

Eve's response is *almost* right. She replies to the serpent that she and Adam can eat from any tree in the garden except for the one in the middle, the tree of the knowledge of good and evil, and if they eat from it, they will die. *Correct.* But Eve also adds that if she and Adam touch the tree they will die. *Incorrect.*

Satan takes note of the erroneous addition and detects vulnerability and weakness. Eve's focus and dependence aren't fully on God and His word, on believing Him and pleasing Him, on loving Him. The serpent's cunning response is crafted to create strife between the couple and God. Jesus aptly describes Satan in this way:

> *"He was a murderer from the beginning, not holding to the*
> *truth, for there is no truth in him. When he lies, he speaks*
> *his native language, for he is a liar and the father of lies"*
> (JOHN 8:44).

One of the key Scripture passages in the Bible that points to the problem of codependency is Galatians 1:10. It redirects our focus and dependence from the people around us onto God, whose approval and pleasure we must seek foremost, and whom we must love foremost. The apostle Paul is emphatic about our priority relationship and declares his disinterest in pleasing people. Like Paul, we must put first things first, or else our relationships will never have the peace and fulfillment that God desires for us.

> *"Am I now trying to win the approval of human beings, or of God?*
> *Or am I trying to please people?*
> *If I were still trying to please people,*
> *I would not be a servant of Christ"*
> (GALATIANS 1:10).

B. Key Passage to Read

"You will not certainly die" (Genesis 3:4).

It is a bold-faced lie, completely contrary to the truth God had spoken. And then Satan tempts Eve to disobey God's clear command: "God knows that when you eat from it your eyes will be opened, and you will be like God, knowing good and evil" (Genesis 3:5).

Eve's misplaced dependency for wisdom and guidance apart from God draws her to the forbidden tree...and she takes a fatal bite. The first woman is disobedient to the following scripture regarding God:

> *"You have laid down precepts that are to be fully obeyed"*
> (PSALM 119:4).

Notice the two thoughts in the following key passage that seem to be in opposition to one another:

> *"If someone is caught in a sin,*
> *you who live by the Spirit should restore that person gently.*
> *But watch yourselves, or you also may be tempted.*
> *Carry each other's burdens,*
> *and in this way you will fulfill the law of Christ.*
> *If anyone thinks they are something when they are not,*
> *they deceive themselves.*
> *Each one should test their own actions.*
> *Then they can take pride in themselves alone,*
> *without comparing themselves to someone else,*
> *for each one should carry their own load"*
>
> (GALATIANS 6:1-5).

Note that verse 2 says, "Carry each other's burdens," and verse 5 says, "Each one should carry their own load." At first glance these two clear-cut directives seem contradictory to each other. So which one is true? When you carefully analyze what is being said, there is no contradiction. In actuality, both are true.

- *Verse 1*—Gently encourage another person to change from negative behavior, and at the same time, beware of the possibility that you yourself might be tempted.

- *Verse 2*—In the original Greek text, the word translated "burden" is *baros*, which means "weight," implying a load or something that is pressing heavily.[11] When you help carry what is too heavy for someone else to bear alone, your caring response fulfills the law of Christ.

- *Verse 5*—The Greek word for "load" is *phortion*, which means "something carried."[12] Clearly, when you carry what others *should* carry, you are not wise. You are not called by God to relieve others of their rightful responsibilities, nor are you to require others to take on your God-given responsibilities.

Conclusion: Those who are codependent try to get their needs met by *carrying loads that others should be carrying.* To move out of a codependent relationship, both individuals need to quit trying to be the other person's "all-in-all" and instead encourage each other to take responsibility for their own lives, *to carry their own loads and to live dependently on God's strength.*

=========== *Healthy Counseling* ===========

QUESTION: "As a counselor, how can I keep my clients from developing an unrealistic dependency on me?"

ANSWER: There are several ways to discourage your clients from developing an overly dependent relationship with you. Remember, you are the one who sets the tone for your sessions.

- *Don't* have a session without first praying for God's wisdom. Then let your client know that you will be depending on the discernment God will give the two of you.
- *Don't* allow yourself to be your client's "savior"—there is only one Savior, and you are not Him!
- *Don't* be available at all times—set boundaries and make it clear you have other responsibilities that are important priorities as well.
- *Don't* strive to impress your client or be a hero, but rather present and model how to have an intimate relationship with the Lord.
- *Don't* rely on your own sufficiency based on your education or experiences. Instead, rely on the Lord's sufficiency and encourage your client to do the same.
- *Don't* merely quote Scripture but open up God's Word and have the person read aloud the passage and apply it to the present problematic circumstance.

> *"Blessed are those whose help is the God of Jacob,*
> *whose hope is in the LORD their God"*
> (PSALM 146:5).

C. How to Hit the Target

If Adam's dependency had been solely on God, he would have repudiated his wife's mistake since he was there with her. But Adam exhibits a misplaced dependency on Eve, allowing her to lead him down the path of rebellion. He, too, partakes of the forbidden fruit, and the initial consequence suggests both shame and vulnerability. Adam and Eve realize they are naked and sew fig leaves together to cover themselves. Their once-perfect relationship is stained by sin, and their nakedness becomes a source of deep embarrassment.

Misplaced dependencies mar Adam and Eve's perfect relationship with God and with each other. The couple undoubtedly has a cry similar to that of the psalmist:

> *"Oh, that my ways were steadfast in obeying your decrees! Then I*
> *would not be put to shame when I consider all your commands"*
> (PSALM 119:5-6).

Codependency does not originate from a personality flaw or a genetic defect. A codependent relationship is rooted in immaturity, a fact that speaks to the possibility of freedom from a codependent lifestyle. While change is never easy, no one ever has to remain forever codependent and forego the opportunity to move from immaturity to maturity. The first step toward maturity is acknowledging and confronting your own codependency.

The key to change is *motivation*. When your pain in the relationship is greater than your fear of abandonment, the motivation for change is powerful. Moving away from the pain of codependency then becomes a matter of choice and commitment. If you feel that the relationship you are in is more of a curse than a blessing—that it brings more death to your soul than life—this can be strong motivation for change.

God makes it clear which path He wants us to choose:

> *"I have set before you life and death, blessings and curses.*
> *Now choose life, so that you...*
> *may love the LORD your God, listen to his*
> *voice, and hold fast to him"*
> (DEUTERONOMY 30:19-20).

HITTING THE TARGET

With the motivation to change comes the need to establish three new targets and a systematic strategy for hitting them.

Target #1—A New Purpose: God's purpose for me is to be conformed to the character of Christ.

> *"Those God foreknew he also predestined to be*
> *conformed to the image of his Son"*
> (ROMANS 8:29).

– "I'll do whatever it takes to be conformed to the character of Christ."

Target #2—A New Priority: God's priority for me is to change my thinking.

> *"Do not conform to the pattern of this world, but be*
> *transformed by the renewing of your mind"*
> (ROMANS 12:2).

– "I'll do whatever it takes to line up my thinking with God's thinking."

Target #3—A New Plan: God's plan for me is to rely on Christ's strength, not my strength, to be all He created me to be.

> *"I can do all things through Christ who strengthens me"*
> (PHILIPPIANS 4:13 NKJV).

– "I'll do whatever it takes to fulfill His plan in His strength."

MY PERSONALIZED PLAN

Through the strength of Christ, I will confront my codependency and take the necessary steps to regain balance in my life.

- **I will confront** the fact that I am codependent.[13] I will...

  – *Admit the truth* to myself. I will be honest with myself about my pattern of being emotionally addicted to another person.

  – *Admit the truth* to someone else. I will identify the beliefs and behaviors that have perpetuated my emotional addiction and share them with an objective, trusted friend.

  – *Admit the truth* to God. I will realize my emotional addiction is a serious sin in the eyes of God, and I choose now to confess it to Him.

> *"Confess your sins to each other and pray for each*
> *other so that you may be healed. The prayer of a*
> *righteous person is powerful and effective"*
> (JAMES 5:16).

- **I will confront** the consequences of my codependency. I will...

  - *Accept responsibility* for how my codependent behaviors have hurt my adult relationships (by becoming manipulative, controlling, possessive, or angry).

  - *Accept responsibility* for the pain I have caused myself because of my codependency (by becoming jealous, envious, selfish, or obsessive).

  - *Accept responsibility* for the ways my codependency has weakened my relationship with God (by a loss of quality time, quantity of time, and intimacy with the Lord).

    > *"Whoever conceals their sins does not prosper, but the one who confesses and renounces them finds mercy"*
    > (PROVERBS 28:13).

- **I will confront** my painful emotions. I will...

  - *Understand* that I'll have pain no matter what I choose. If I leave the codependent relationship I will hurt now, but if I stay I will hurt later. Clearly, the only hope for future healing is leaving the codependent lifestyle forever.

  - *Understand* that when the intensity of the relationship diminishes I will experience emotional withdrawal from the exhilarating highs.

  - *Understand* that I'll need the support of others to get through the initial pain of withdrawal and to help me avoid anesthetizing my pain with a secondary addiction.

    > *"The pleasantness of a friend springs from their heartfelt advice"*
    > (PROVERBS 27:9).

- **I will confront** my secondary addictions.[14] I will...

  - *Recognize* that in an effort to numb the emotional pain of the relationship, codependency often leads to other addictions, such as a chemical dependency, sexual addiction, compulsive eating, excessive spending, or gambling.

  - *Recognize* my existing secondary addictions and then seek counseling and spiritual support to overcome them.

    — *Recognize* that my recovery from a secondary addiction is dependent on recovery from my primary addiction to codependent relationships.

> *"The heart of the discerning acquires knowledge,*
> *for the ears of the wise seek it out"*
> (PROVERBS 18:15).

- **I will confront** my current codependent relationship.[15] I will...

    — *Acknowledge* my codependent role in the relationship and cease relating through codependent patterns.

    — *Acknowledge* my destructive behaviors (write them down), and replace them with constructive behaviors (write them down).

    — *Acknowledge* the natural pain of emotional withdrawal (common to the healing of addictions) and focus on God's supernatural purpose (conforming me to the character of Christ).

> *"Those God foreknew he also predestined to be*
> *conformed to the image of his Son"*
> (ROMANS 8:29).

- **I will confront** my codependent focus. I will...

    — *Stop focusing* on what the other person is doing and start focusing on what I need to do in order to become emotionally healthy.

    — *Stop focusing* on the other person's problems and start focusing on solving my own problems (those resulting from my neglect of people and projects in my life).

    — *Stop focusing* on trying to change the other person and start focusing on changing myself.

> *"The wisdom of the prudent is to give thought to*
> *their ways, but the folly of fools is deception"*
> (PROVERBS 14:8).

- **I will confront** my codependent conflicts.[16] I will...

    — *Not allow* myself to become trapped in heated arguments or to become emotionally hooked by the bad behavior of the other person. Instead, I will say several times, "I will not argue"—and then disengage from the conflict. I will decide ahead of time that, when agitation begins, I will distance myself.

- *Not defend* myself when I am unjustly blamed. Instead, I'll say only once, "I'm sorry you feel that way. That doesn't reflect my heart."

- *Not be afraid* to leave if the conflict continues. I'll say, "I will be gone for a while," then calmly walk away.

> *"Don't have anything to do with foolish and stupid*
> *arguments, because you know they produce quarrels"*
> (2 TIMOTHY 2:23).

- **I will confront** my codependent responses.[17] I will...

- *Remind myself* that problem people are free to choose wrong. I will not react to their problem behavior—they are independent of me.

- *Remind myself* not to return insult for insult. I will refuse to raise my voice.

- *Remind myself* that my Christlike role is to respond with respect, even when others are disrespectful.

> *"Do not repay evil with evil or insult with insult. On the*
> *contrary, repay evil with blessing, because to this you were*
> *called so that you may inherit a blessing...But do this*
> *with gentleness and respect, keeping a clear conscience,*
> *so that those who speak maliciously against your good*
> *behavior in Christ may be ashamed of their slander"*
> (1 PETER 3:9,15-16).

- **I will confront** what I need to *leave* in order to receive.[18] I will...

- *Leave* my childhood and my dependent thinking ("I can't live without you."), then enter into healthy adulthood ("I want you in my life, but if something were to happen, I could live without you."). I'll face the truth and reality and refuse falsehood and fantasy.

— *Leave* my immature need to be dependent on someone else and embrace my mature need to be dependent on the Lord, who will make me whole within myself.

— *Leave* my fantasy relationships (thinking, *You are my all-in-all*) and instead nurture several balanced relationships (in which a healthy give-and-take attitude exists).

> *"Wounds from a friend can be trusted,*
> *but an enemy multiplies kisses"*
> (Proverbs 27:6).

- **I will confront** my need to build mature non-codependent relationships.[19] I will...

  — *Establish* several interdependent relationships, not just one exclusive relationship. I need mature relationships in which my codependency issues can be resolved and my needs can be met in healthy ways through multiple people.

  — *Establish* emotionally balanced relationships without being needy of the extreme emotional highs and lows of codependent relationships.

  — *Establish* personal boundaries in all of my relationships, saying *no* when I need to say it and holding to my *no*.

> *"Let us...be taken forward to maturity"*
> (Hebrews 6:1).

To strengthen your resolve to conquer codependency and bring balance to your life, be sure to work through the following recovery steps.

D. How to Regain Balance: Recovery Step #1

Adam and Eve need to regain balance, to find restoration in their relationship with one another and with God. The Creator confronts the pair about their sinful actions—and dire consequences follow. The serpent, believed by many to have been a beautiful, upright creature, is cursed to crawl on its belly all of its days. Furthermore, God declares to Satan (who inhabits the serpent), "I will put enmity between you and the woman, and between your offspring and hers; he will crush your head, and you will strike his heel" (Genesis 3:15).

Known as *protoevangelium*, this is the Bible's first mention of God making a way, through the death and resurrection of Jesus, to have a restored relationship with mankind. This gospel message foretells God making the move to regain a balanced relationship, as Scripture explains:

> *"For God did not send his Son into the world to condemn the world, but to save the world through him"*
> (JOHN 3:17).

EXAMINING YOUR PAST LOVE ADDICTIONS

One effective way to assess your predisposition for codependency is by examining past codependent love relationships through journaling. Detailing your thoughts, feelings, and experiences in writing can enhance your perspective and help you detect patterns of codependent behavior. Putting your life on paper is not easy, but until you are ready to take an in-depth look at your past love addictions you cannot expect to have healthy relationships in the future.

Before you begin, ask God to bring to mind what you need to acknowledge in order for change to begin, and ask Him to lead you as you take action steps toward growth. He will give you both the wisdom and power to free yourself from your addictions and to begin developing healthy relationships.[20]

Scripture esteems those who pursue wisdom:

> *"The one who gets wisdom loves life; the one who cherishes understanding will soon prosper"*
> (PROVERBS 19:8).

QUESTIONS TO ASK YOURSELF

Make a list of every person with whom you have had a codependent relationship. Think about your family and friends. Put each name at the top of a separate page and then answer the following questions for each relationship:

1. WRITE OUT...

– How did you meet and how were you attracted to this person?

– How did you pursue and draw this person to you?

– How did you feel and what did you fantasize about this person?
Conclude by answering...

– How do you think God felt about your choices?

Realize that the Lord is ready to meet your deepest emotional needs. When you live with misplaced priorities, according to the Bible, you commit spiritual adultery.

> *"I have been grieved by their adulterous hearts, which have turned away from me, and by their eyes, which have lusted after their idols. They will loathe themselves for the evil they have done and for all their detestable practices"*
> (EZEKIEL 6:9).

2. WRITE OUT...

– How did the relationship progress through various stages (fascination, fantasy, fog, fear, forsaking, fixation, frenzy)?

– How did you feel in each stage?

– How did you act during each stage?

Conclude by answering...

– How did you fail to involve God in your life during each stage?

Realize how ready the Lord has been to intervene:

> *"When I came, why was there no one? When I called, why was there no one to answer? Was my arm too short to deliver you? Do I lack the strength to rescue you? By a mere rebuke I dry up the sea, I turn rivers into a desert; their fish rot for lack of water and die of thirst. I clothe the heavens with darkness and make sackcloth its covering"*
> (ISAIAH 50:2-3).

3. WRITE OUT...

– How did you become preoccupied with the relationship?

– How did you start neglecting yourself and start focusing on taking care of the other person?

– How did you come to expect that person to meet all of your needs?

Conclude by answering...

– How did you start neglecting God? When did you stop relying on Him?

Realize how ready the Lord has been to make you fruitful:

"I had planted you like a choice vine of sound and reliable stock.
How then did you turn against me into a corrupt, wild vine?"
(JEREMIAH 2:21).

4. WRITE OUT…

- How has this relationship replicated your painful childhood experiences?

- How were you mistreated in the relationship, and how did you react?

- How does the relationship impact you today?

  Conclude by answering…

- How is God replacing (or wanting to replace) your self-destructive, love-addicted patterns with constructive, healthy, holy patterns?

  Realize how ready the Lord is to "re-parent" you in order to meet your deepest needs and heal your deepest hurts:[21]

"Though my father and mother forsake
me, the LORD will receive me"
(PSALM 27:10).

5. WRITE OUT…

- How have you experienced fear, envy, jealousy, abandonment, and anger in the relationship?

- How did you come to assign a higher priority to this person than to everything else?

- How have you made this person the focus of your thought life?

  Conclude by answering…

- How can you appropriate "the mind of Christ" so that you can overcome destructive feelings and live out of your resources in Christ?

  Realize how ready the Lord is to align your thinking with His will:

> *"We have the mind of Christ"*
> (1 CORINTHIANS 2:16).

6. WRITE OUT...

– How do you feel about the person and the relationship now?

– How has your perspective changed?

– How did things, people, and circumstances become factors in changing your perspective?

Conclude by answering...

– How do you think God has been involved in changing your perspective?

Realize how ready the Lord is to complete His perfect plan for your life:

> *"Being confident of this, that he who began a good work in you*
> *will carry it on to completion until the day of Christ Jesus"*
> (PHILIPPIANS 1:6).

E. How to Regain Balance: Recovery Step #2

Adam and Eve's misplaced dependencies result in history's first recorded eviction—the pair is forever banished from their home, the Garden of Eden. And there are other dire consequences from the hand of God. Eve's pain in childbearing will greatly increase, and Adam will fight thorns and thistles as he tends the ground.

But the greatest consequence of all is God's proclamation of physical death: "By the sweat of your brow you will eat your food until you return to the ground, since from it you were taken; for dust you are and to dust you will return" (Genesis 3:19).

In all this, Adam and Eve can relate to the psalmist:

> *"You, God, know my folly; my guilt is not hidden from you"*
> (PSALM 69:5).

DEVELOPING HEALTHY INTERDEPENDENT RELATIONSHIPS

We all love to see pictures of babies and then observe their "stair step" growth into young adulthood. Built within little, immature children is the ability to grow to both physical and emotional maturity. This is no less true for emotionally immature adults—they too can grow to develop healthy interdependent relationships.

Once we understand the goals for each developmental stage of establishing healthy relationships, we can set out to accomplish those goals—even without the aid of earthly parents from whom many of our codependent issues were birthed. Many have done this by taking the hand of the heavenly Father and allowing Him to re-parent them.

You too can do this by having a plan and then working your plan with the caring support of others. It is a truly important journey with enormously gratifying rewards. This is the journey God intended for you to take from the beginning. This is His goal for you now—to grow from immaturity to maturity, from childhood to adulthood by developing healthy, interdependent relationships.

Scripture provides this sound exhortation:

> *"When I was a child, I talked like a child,*
> *I thought like a child, I reasoned like a child.*
> *When I became a man, I put the ways of childhood behind me"*
> (1 CORINTHIANS 13:11).

MAKING HEALTHY INTERDEPENDENT RELATIONSHIPS HAPPEN

- **Make it your goal** to develop an intimate relationship with God and to form interdependent relationships with significant people in your life.

    - *Commit* to becoming actively involved in a group Bible study and in group prayer.

    - *Commit* to reading God's Word on a daily basis and memorizing Scripture.

    - *Commit* to finding an accountability group and a Christian "relationship mentor" who will be available to you, spend time with you on a regular basis, be honest with you, and coach you in your relationships.

> *"Let us consider…not giving up meeting*
> *together…but encouraging one another"*
> (HEBREWS 10:24-25).

- **Make a plan** to move toward maturity in your relationships.
  - *Ask God* to help you discern where you are stuck in the relationship developmental stages.
  - *Ask your mentor* or another wise person to help you identify your relationship needs (for example: sharing, problem solving, listening, negotiating).
  - *Ask your accountability group* to hold you responsible to establish appropriate goals in order to meet each of your relationship needs.

    "Let perseverance finish its work so that you may be mature and complete, not lacking anything"
    (JAMES 1:4).

- **Make your relationship** with your parents healthy.
  - *Choose* to resolve any unhealthy patterns with your parents. Break any unhealthy bonds and, if possible, establish mature, adult bonds with each parent.
  - *Choose* to not be emotionally enmeshed, needy, or controlled by your parents. If necessary, separate yourself emotionally until you can respond in a healthy way with no strings attached.
  - *Choose* to identify and process your "family of origin" problems, forgive your offenders, and grieve your losses. Say, "That was then; this is now."

    "Do not say, 'I'll do to them as they have done to me; I'll pay them back for what they did'"
    (PROVERBS 24:29).

- **Make a vow** to be a person of integrity in thought, word, and deed.
  - *Learn* to free yourself of any family secrets—refuse to carry them any longer.
  - *Learn* to listen, to say *no*, to set boundaries, to give and receive, and to ask for what you need from people. Then practice, practice, practice these new, healthy patterns.
  - *Learn* to feel your feelings, to express hurt, and to withdraw and

think about what you need to do or say. Write out your action plan, rehearse it, then do it.

> *"Therefore, with minds that are alert and fully sober, set your hope on the grace to be brought to you when Jesus Christ is revealed at his coming. As obedient children, do not conform to the evil desires you had when you lived in ignorance. But just as he who called you is holy, so be holy in all you do"*
> (1 PETER 1:13-15).

- **Make a new job** description.
  - *My job* is to discern the character of a person and to respond accordingly with maturity.
  - *My job* is to be a "safe" person for my friends and family and to be present and attentive in my relationships.
  - *My job* is to take care of myself and to be responsible for myself without hurting, punishing, attacking, getting even, or lying to myself or to others.

> *"I will maintain my innocence and never let go of it; my conscience will not reproach me as long as I live"*
> (JOB 27:6).

- **Make a new commitment** to yourself.
  - *I will* let go of the old, self-centered me because I am growing into a new, Christ-centered me.
  - *I will* exchange the lies I've believed about myself for God's truth about me according to His Word.
  - *I will* no longer betray myself by making immature choices, and I will redeem my past, bad choices by making good, mature choices.

> *"If anyone is in Christ, the new creation has come: The old has gone, the new is here!"*
> (2 CORINTHIANS 5:17).

- **Make mature** relationships your highest goal.
  - *Focus* on forming friendships in which you are free to learn,

grow, and mature as opposed to emotional attachments that lead to roller-coaster relationships.

— *Focus* on any relationships that have the potential to trigger your codependent tendencies and guard your heart from the emotional highs and lows.

— *Focus* on building relationships with trustworthy, mature Christians whose goal is Christlikeness.

During a time of severe trial, Paul offered this encouragement to Timothy, his son in the faith:

> *"You then, my son, be strong in the grace that is in Christ Jesus"*
> (2 TIMOTHY 2:1).

F. How to Regain Balance: Recovery Step #3

Despite Adam and Eve's misplaced dependencies, God graciously provides for them and assures them of His unchanging love. He makes garments out of skin for the couple, and later blesses them with offspring.

But His greatest provision in regaining balance in their relationship will be the future death and resurrection of Jesus, who will pay for Adam and Eve's sins and provide the way to receive eternal life. It is Jesus who once again makes everything perfect.

Scripture draws a parallel between Adam and Jesus:

> *"For if, by the trespass of the one man,*
> *death reigned through that one man,*
> *how much more will those who receive*
> *God's abundant provision of grace*
> *and of the gift of righteousness reign in life*
> *through the one man, Jesus Christ!"*
> (ROMANS 5:17).

FINDING THE ROAD TO FREEDOM

When you are behaving in a codependent way, you are trying to get your needs met through a drive to "do it all" or to be another person's "all-in-all." However, you can find the road to freedom by *releasing* your desire to control or change the person you love.

When you give the Lord control of your life and release to Him the desire to change the person you love, you can rest in His assurance:

"My grace is sufficient for you, for my power
is made perfect in weakness"
(2 CORINTHIANS 12:9).

If your heart's desire is to develop healthy, interdependent relationships, apply the directives in the following acrostic on R-E-L-E-A-S-E.

RELEASE

R–RECOGNIZE that you are overly dependent on another person, then choose to place your dependency on God.

- *Admit* that your codependency is a sin.
- *Pray* that God will give you the desire to put Him first and to please Him in all your relationships.
- *Determine* to look to the Lord to meet your needs for love, significance, and security.
- *Realize* that God did not create you to meet all the needs of another person.

"Love the Lord your God with all your heart and with all your
soul and with all your mind and with all your strength"
(MARK 12:30).

E–EXAMINE your patterns of codependent thinking.

- *Don't* believe that pleasing people is always Christlike.
- *Don't* think you should always assume the role of peacemaker.
- *Don't* fear losing the love of others when you allow them to suffer the consequences of their negative actions.
- *Don't* say *yes* when you really believe you should say *no*.

"You desired faithfulness even in the womb; you
taught me wisdom in that secret place"
(PSALM 51:6).

L–LET go of your "super responsible" mentality.

- *Confess* that you are trying to be like God in the life of another person.
- *Trust* God to be actively working in the life of your loved one.
- *Realize* you cannot make another person become dependable or responsible.
- *Rest* in God's sovereign control over all people, events, and circumstances.

> *"What you are doing is not good. You and these people*
> *who come to you will only wear yourselves out. The work*
> *is too heavy for you; you cannot handle it alone"*
> (EXODUS 18:17-18).

E–EXTEND forgiveness to those who have caused you pain.

- *Reflect* on any type of abuse you have experienced in the past—verbal, emotional, physical, spiritual, or sexual.
- *What* has been unjust and painful in your life?
- *Whom* do you need to forgive?
- *Would* you be willing to release this person and your pain to God?
- *Choose* to forgive again whenever your angry feelings resurface.

> *"Bear with each other and forgive one another if any of you has*
> *a grievance against someone. Forgive as the Lord forgave you"*
> (COLOSSIANS 3:13).

PRAYER OF FORGIVENESS

"God, You know the pain I have experienced in my past.
I don't want to keep carrying all this pain for the rest of my life.
I release (_list hurts_) into Your hands,
and I ask You to heal my emotional pain.
Lord, You know what (_name of person_) has done to hurt me.
As an act of my will, I choose to forgive (_name_).
I take (_name_) off of my emotional hook and put (_name_) onto
Your emotional hook.

> Thank You, Lord Jesus, for setting me *free*.
> In Your holy name I pray. Amen."

A–APPROPRIATE your identity in Christ.

- *Learn* to live out of your resources in Christ Jesus.

- *Know* the truth: "I can be emotionally set free because Christ lives in me."

> *"If the Son sets you free, you will be free indeed"*
> (JOHN 8:36).

- *Believe* the truth: "I can change from having my dependency on people to having my dependency on God through the power of Christ in me."

> *"I can do all this through him who gives me strength"*
> (PHILIPPIANS 4:13).

- *Appropriate* the truth: "I will nurture only healthy, godly relationships because I have been given a new nature in Christ."

> *"His divine power has given us everything we need for a godly life through our knowledge of him who called us by his own glory and goodness. Through these he has given us his very great and precious promises, so that through them you may participate in the divine nature, having escaped the corruption in the world caused by evil desires"*
> (2 PETER 1:3-4).

S–SET healthy boundaries.

- *Communicate* the necessity for change.

  "I realize I have not been responding to you in a healthy way. I have been far too dependent on you to meet my needs, and I have sought to meet all of your needs. I am committed to having healthy relationships and to putting God first in my life. I know I have had negative responses to you, and I intend to begin having positive responses by making decisions based on what is right in the eyes of God."

- *Establish* what you need to ask forgiveness for.

  "I realize I was wrong for _____ (not speaking up when I should have, not being the person I should have been in this relationship). Will you forgive me?"

- *Establish* what your limits of responsibility will be.

  "I feel responsible for _____. But I am not responsible for _____ (making you happy, making you feel significant). I want you to be happy, but I don't have the power to make you happy."

- *Establish* your limits of involvement.

  "I want to do _____ with/for you, but I don't feel led by God to do _____."

> *"The prudent see danger and take refuge, but the*
> *simple keep going and pay the penalty"*
> (Proverbs 27:12).

E–EXCHANGE your emotional focus for spiritual focus.

- *Make* God and your spiritual growth your first priority.
- *Attend* an in-depth Bible study in order to learn the heart of God and to grow spiritually with the people of God.
- *Memorize* sections of Scripture in order to put God's Word in your heart and to learn the ways of God.
- *Redirect* your thoughts to focus on the Lord and take prayer walks (talking out loud to the Lord as you walk regularly in your neighborhood or on a trail).

> *"Direct me in the path of your commands, for there I*
> *find delight. Turn my heart toward your statutes and not*
> *toward selfish gain. Turn my eyes away from worthless*
> *things; preserve my life according to your word"*
> (Psalm 119:35-37).

The primary problem with codependency is idolatry—that is, giving greater priority to a person than to God Himself. God is the One who created you and has a perfect plan for your life. He is the Lord who loves you and knows how to fulfill you. If you are in a codependent relationship, your...

- *Excessive care* causes you to compromise your convictions.
- *Excessive loyalty* leaves you without healthy boundaries.
- *Excessive "love"* leads you to say *yes* when you should say *no*.

God alone has the right to have primary rule in your heart and over your life. Any other substitute is simply idolatry. The Bible says,

> *"Love the LORD your God with all your heart*
> *and with all your soul and with all your strength"*
> (DEUTERONOMY 6:5).

MAKING IT ALL POSSIBLE THROUGH CHRIST'S POWER

The cure for codependency is rooted in developing an ever-deepening relationship with the Lord. Your increased intimacy with Him will naturally conform you to His character. When you let the Lord live inside you, *you can live in His power.* This means that, because Christ was not codependent, you have His power to overcome codependency.

> *"In this world you will have trouble.*
> *But take heart! I have overcome the world"*
> (JOHN 16:33).

RELEASING YOU

Releasing is not to stop loving you,
but is to love enough to stop leaning on you.

Releasing is not to stop caring for you,
but is to care enough to stop controlling you.

Releasing is not to turn away from you,
but is to turn to Christ, trusting His control over you.

Releasing is not to harm you,
but is to realize my "help" has been harmful.

Releasing is not to hurt you,
but is to be willing to be hurt for healing.

Releasing is not to judge you,
but is to let the divine Judge judge me.

Releasing is not to restrict you,
but is to restrict my demands of you.

Releasing is not to refuse you,
but is to refuse to keep reality from you.

Releasing is not to cut myself off from you,
but is to prune the unfruitful away from you.

Releasing is not to prove my power over you,
but is to admit I am powerless to change you.

Releasing is not to stop believing in you,
but is to believe the Lord alone will build character in you.

Releasing you is not to condemn the past,
but is to cherish the present and commit our future to God.

—*June Hunt*

CODEPENDENCY: ANSWERS IN GOD'S WORD

QUESTION: "What does the Lord say about making people like gods, putting them before my relationship with Him?"

ANSWER: *"You shall have no other gods before me"* (Exodus 20:3).

QUESTION: "Can the Son of God set me free from a codependent relationship?"

ANSWER: *"So if the Son sets you free, you will be free indeed"* (John 8:36).

QUESTION: "Doesn't God want me to trust in and depend on the strength of significant people?"

ANSWER: *"This is what the LORD says: 'Cursed is the one who trusts in man, who draws strength from mere flesh and whose heart turns away from the LORD'"* (Jeremiah 17:5).

QUESTION: "How do I forgive whatever grievances I have toward someone who drains me emotionally?"

ANSWER: *"Bear with each other and forgive one another if any of you has a grievance against someone. Forgive as the Lord forgave you"* (Colossians 3:13).

QUESTION: "Am I to put my trust in the Lord or put my confidence in people?"

ANSWER: *"Blessed is the one who trusts in the LORD, whose confidence is in him"* (Jeremiah 17:7).

QUESTION: "Don't I need someone to depend on to be my rock of strength, my refuge?"

ANSWER: *"My salvation and my honor depend on God; he is my mighty rock, my refuge"* (Psalm 62:7).

QUESTION: "When someone pretends to need help, should I insist that he carry his own load?"

ANSWER: *"Each one should test their own actions. Then they can take pride in themselves alone, without comparing themselves to someone else, for each one should carry their own load"* (Galatians 6:4-5).

QUESTION: "Is there something wrong with seeking to please men in order to win their approval?"

ANSWER: *"Am I now trying to win the approval of human beings, or of God? Or am I trying to please people? If I were still trying to please people, I would not be a servant of Christ"* (Galatians 1:10).

QUESTION: "Can God give me strength to break away from a codependent relationship?"

ANSWER: *"I can do all this through him who gives me strength"* (Philippians 4:13).

QUESTION: "Why should I cast my anxiety on the Lord when I'm trying to become more independent?"

ANSWER: *"Cast all your anxiety on him because he cares for you"* (1 Peter 5:7).

CONFRONTATION
Challenging Others to Change

4

CONFRONTATION

Challenging Others to Change

"Adam, Eve, where are you?" The probing voice of God pierces the evening air, confronting the two pounding hearts hiding in the foliage. Scant hours before, all was so perfect, so peaceful. But then they ate the forbidden fruit, and everything changed. They chose to disobey God—to defy His authority—and now they flinch in fear as they hear His voice come nearer and nearer.

As they step out of their hiding place, how will God confront the guilty couple? Things could have been so different. He created them—this first man and woman—and placed them in a perfect environment where He planned to meet all of their needs. If only they had listened to Him! If only they had trusted Him! If only they had obeyed Him! But in making their fatal choice, they forfeited His perfect plan. Now what will He say to them? How will He approach them? How will He confront their sin?

For the first time ever, rather than being at peace with God, the couple cowers in fear in His presence. Finally, as though in reluctant acceptance of the unavoidable, Adam manages a weak response to God's call: "I heard you in the garden, and I was afraid because I was naked; so I hid" (Genesis 3:10). God responds with questions: "Who told you that you were naked? Have you eaten from the tree that I commanded you not to eat from?" (Genesis 3:11).

God then asks Eve, "What is this you have done?" Although God clearly knew all that had transpired in their lives that day, He chose to confront both of them with questions—questions that would expose their sin and establish the truth, that would expose wrong and establish right (Genesis 3:9,11,13).

I. DEFINITIONS OF CONFRONTATION

Like Adam and Eve, we do not enjoy having our sin exposed. Like them, we try to cover it up—to hide all the evidence—in an effort not to get caught. Often, we do whatever we possibly can to avoid having to face the consequences of our bad choices. Our preference is to figure out how to get away with it, to somehow make it go away, or, at the very least, not to have to take responsibility for it.

How then do we face our own sinful actions, and how do we handle the sins of others? Clearly, the answer is not by ignoring, avoiding, hiding, or covering up offenses. If we use the way God dealt with Adam and Eve as our model, then we must acknowledge bad behavior, face the consequences, and yield to God as He empowers us to change what we otherwise cannot. We must expose what is wrong to establish what is right. We must expose the problem to establish the solution. That process is called *confrontation*, and it requires wisdom and discernment:

> *"Wisdom reposes in the heart of the discerning*
> *and even among fools she lets herself be known"*
> (PROVERBS 14:33).

A. What Constitutes Confrontation?

Adam and Eve *do* what God tells them *not to do*—eat from the forbidden tree. The couple dies spiritually, and God could have taken their lives physically, with no chance for change. Thus the story of Adam and Eve could have ended just as quickly as it began.

The history of humanity might have been contained in one brief chapter.

However, God has a plan for the ages, and it begins with the cowering couple hiding in fig leaves and foliage. He confronts Adam and Eve to expose wrong and to establish right. His questions are direct, like projectiles to the heart, intended to penetrate deeply for soulful reflection and to lead to repentance.

> *"Who told you that you were naked?*
> *Have you eaten from the tree that I commanded you*
> *not to eat from?... What is this you have done?"*
> (GENESIS 3:11,13).

- *Confrontation* is the act of challenging a person in order to expose what is wrong and establish what is right.[1]

- *Confronting* a person helps establish the truth for the purpose of conviction, correction, and a changed life.
  - The Hebrew word *tokhot* means "to correct, rebuke."[2] Solomon, the wisest man who ever lived, understood the value of confrontation when he wrote, "Correction and instruction are the way to life" (Proverbs 6:23).
  - At times God will guide you to confront so that others can *see* their need to change as well as know what and how to change.

> *"The grace of God...It teaches us to say 'No' to ungodliness and worldly passions, and to live self-controlled, upright and godly lives in this present age...These, then, are the things you should teach. Encourage and rebuke with all authority"*
> (Titus 2:11-12,15).

B. What Are Five Methods of Confrontation Used in the Bible?

Unfortunately, many people are fairly opinionated about how God confronts mortal human beings in the Bible, and God's love is generally not what first comes to mind. Typically, people picture God sitting behind an enormous judge's bench, pounding a huge, celestial gavel with eyes blazing and a bony finger pointing at some puny, helpless human while meting out severe judgment upon the poor soul. However, this is not an accurate portrait of the true character of God.

Our loving God created the human race with immense diversity, and He also uses diverse methods to confront. From questions asked of Adam and Eve in the book of Genesis to His rebuke of the churches in Revelation, we see God tailoring His confrontation to the people and the need.

God not only confronts directly, but works through others to confront, including His anointed people, the nation of Israel. Throughout the Old and New Testaments, God uses His people to confront ungodliness in a variety of ways. Each method, whether direct or indirect, is used with the loving intent of confronting what is wrong and establishing what is right so that those being confronted can become all He created them to be. As with Adam and Eve, such confrontations require a response and are to be valued, not despised.

> *"My son, do not despise the LORD's discipline, and do not resent his rebuke, because the LORD disciplines those he loves, as a father the son he delights in"*
> (PROVERBS 3:11-12).

METHOD #1: CONFRONTING WITH A QUESTION (INDIRECT)—JOB 38–42:6

Have you witnessed the wisdom of those who ask many questions of others even though they already know the answers? These intuitive individuals have discovered a powerful secret: Asking wise questions helps others gain insight into truth through inner reflection. In the Bible, Job begins reflecting on his wrong thinking, *knowing* that God will confront him.

> *"What will I do when God confronts me?*
> *What will I answer when called to account?"*
> (JOB 31:14).

- **The purpose of wise questioning** is to encourage people to think seriously about their attitudes and actions. This method of confrontation is less about asking questions to evoke answers and more about issuing challenges to induce changes.

    - *Wise questioning* can cause people to rethink their thoughts and reconsider their conclusions.

    - *Wise questioning* can cause people to acknowledge their actions and examine their intentions.

It can lead people to realize that...

> *"God is exalted in his power. Who is a teacher like him?*
> *Who has prescribed his ways for him, or said to him, 'You*
> *have done wrong'?... The Almighty is beyond our reach*
> *and exalted in power; in his justice and great righteousness,*
> *he does not oppress. Therefore, people revere him, for*
> *does he not have regard for all the wise in heart?"*
> (JOB 36:22-23; 37:23-24).

- **The power of wise questioning** is used by the Lord God Almighty. In all literature, the most dramatic example of wise questioning is found in the book of Job. Job begins to doubt God's goodness and sense of justice. In turn, God begins His inquisition of Job with this question: "Who is this that obscures my plans with words without knowledge? Brace yourself like a man; I will question you, and you shall answer me" (Job 38:2-3).

    - *Pertinent questions* can be powerful. Through one question after another—literally 72 questions—God reveals His very nature to Job.

– *Pertinent questions* can be convicting. After hearing God's questions, Job is so deeply moved with conviction that he says, "I despise myself and repent in dust and ashes" (Job 42:6).

- **The skill of wise questioning** is used by wise counselors. If you are one who understands and utilizes this technique, you have learned an essential counseling skill. God, our ultimate Counselor, demonstrates throughout Scripture that questions effectively draw others out to think *about* themselves and *for* themselves. Some questions that appeal to the conscience are...

  – "Do you want to live your life with true contentment?"

  – "Do you want to be a person of total integrity?"

  – "Do you want to fulfill God's purpose for your life?"

  – "Do you want to have God's blessing on your life?"

Clearly...

> *"The purposes of a person's heart are deep waters,*
> *but one who has insight draws them out"*
> (PROVERBS 20:5).

METHOD #2: CONFRONTING WITH A PARABLE (INDIRECT)—LUKE 20:9-19

Parables have long been recognized as food for thought and refreshing nourishment for the soul. Simple parables appeal to young and old alike. No wonder these memorable stories have passed the test of time to remain classic lessons through the centuries.

> *"Jesus spoke all these things to the crowd in parables;*
> *he did not say anything to them without using a parable"*
> (MATTHEW 13:34).

- **A parable is a short, fictitious illustration**—A parable is an earthly story with a heavenly meaning, focusing on one moral or spiritual truth. The Greek word *parabole* means "comparison" or "illustration."[3] The parable, when used in Scripture, illustrates a moral or spiritual truth by using simple, everyday objects and settings.

- **A parable shines a probing light on the darkness** within our hearts and challenges us to change. Parables can have unending value in developing godly character in our lives. A parable of a vineyard owner was used by Jesus to expose the dark motives within the hearts of Jewish leaders—the scribes and Pharisees (see Luke 20:9-19).

  The owner of a vineyard rents out his land. At harvest time, the owner sends one servant after another to obtain some of the fruit. The tenants, however, beat and treat each servant shamefully. Finally, when the long-suffering owner sends his beloved son, the tenants plot and kill him. Then Jesus said, "What then will the owner of the vineyard do to them? He will come and kill those tenants and give the vineyard to others" (Luke 20:15-16).

  – In telling this parable, Jesus exposes the truth—He knows the scribes and Pharisees are plotting to kill Him. The tenants in the parable represent the Jewish leaders. The owner's servants represent the prophets of God whom Israel has murdered throughout the ages, and the owner's son represents Jesus.

  – Through this parable, Jesus confronts the Jewish leaders' abuse of the oversight God has entrusted to them. Rather than allowing the truth within the parable to convict them and seeing it as an opportunity to correct their wrong ways, they seek to kill Jesus.

  *"The teachers of the law and the chief priests looked for a way
  to arrest him immediately, because they knew he had spoken
  this parable against them. But they were afraid of the people"*
  (LUKE 20:19).

METHOD # 3: CONFRONTING WITH A TRUE-TO-LIFE STORY (INDIRECT)— 2 SAMUEL 12:1-13

A well-told story has the power to move our emotions to anger or move our hearts to tears. When people are blind to the truth of their own sin, telling them a story paralleling their own story of sin can be powerfully convicting. A compelling true-to-life story is hard to ignore.

The true story of King David's adulterous affair with Bathsheba is one of the most potent and well-known stories recorded in the Bible. David, in his amorous pursuit of Bathsheba, impregnates her, arranges her husband's murder, and then marries her to cover up his sinful actions. David's position as king allows him to escape the legal consequences of his crimes—consequences he would have surely enforced on any of his subjects who had committed such acts, for Scripture says,

"A king's wrath strikes terror like the roar of a lion;
those who anger him forfeit their lives"
(Proverbs 20:2).

- **A true-to-life story can have a spiritual purpose.** The Lord sends Nathan to confront David through a skillfully told story about two men. One is rich, and the other is poor. The rich man has many flocks of sheep, but the poor man has only one beloved pet lamb. When preparing a meal for a traveler, the rich man refuses to pick a sheep from his own large flock and instead takes the poor man's little lamb to serve to his guest. After Nathan tells this story, David passes severe judgment on this rich man: "David burned with anger against the man and said to Nathan, 'As surely as the Lord lives, the man who did this must die!' " (2 Samuel 12:5).

- **A true-to-life story can be powerful.** David's instant judgment against the rich man was absolutely justified. So what could he say when Nathan turned the tables on him saying, "You are the man!" (2 Samuel 12:7)?

- **A true-to-life story can be convicting.** In listening to Nathan's words, David realized how his lust had led to adultery, his adultery to deceit, and his deceit to murder. As a result of this confrontation, he repented and said, "I have sinned against the Lord" (2 Samuel 12:13).

- **A true-to-life story can cause a change of life.** Convicting stories can serve to create a hunger to have a pure heart before God. After his moral failure with Bathsheba and Nathan's subsequent confrontation, David said, "Create in me a pure heart, O God, and renew a steadfast spirit within me" (Psalm 51:10).

Method #4: Confronting with an Admonition (Direct)—John 8:1-11

We are all created with a conscience by which we gauge whether an attitude or action is right or wrong. Christians also have the convicting work of the Holy Spirit within their hearts. Feeling guilt is appropriate when we stray from the truth and engage in wrongful acts—this is true guilt. If we stay in sin for a long time without responding to appropriate guilt, we can develop a seared conscience. At times, however, God appeals to our conscience by sending someone to confront us.

> *"Acknowledge those who work hard among you,*
> *who care for you in the Lord and who admonish you"*
> (1 THESSALONIANS 5:12).

- **An admonition is a gentle confrontation.** It is a warning or counsel given for the purpose of correction. To admonish in a gentle, earnest manner means to warn or counsel a person who is in the wrong.

  - The Greek word *noutheteo* means to "admonish" or literally "to put in mind" (*nous* = mind, *tithemi* = to put).[4]

  - An admonition is an earnest warning given in order to train a person's mind to think differently so that the person will act differently.

  The apostle Paul said,

> *"Let the message of Christ dwell among you richly as*
> *you teach and admonish one another with all wisdom*
> *through psalms, hymns, and songs from the Spirit,*
> *singing to God with gratitude in your hearts"*
> (COLOSSIANS 3:16).

- **An admonition can convict a person's conscience.** Consider this example: After a woman is caught in the act of adultery, the religious leaders bring her before Jesus. They want Him to pronounce the death sentence so they can stone her. But rather than confront the woman, Jesus confronts the judgmental attitudes of the scribes and Pharisees by appealing to their conscience. Jesus cleverly turns the tables on these accusers by highlighting their focus on the letter of the law and their obvious lack of grace. Jesus challenges them to first judge themselves and their own actions in light of the law: "He who is without sin among you, let him throw a stone at her first" (John 8:7 NKJV). No one moves. Convicted by their consciences, they all depart—one by one—leaving only Jesus and the woman standing alone.

- **An admonition can encourage a change of life.** Now, for the first time, Jesus addresses the woman and her wrongful actions. "When Jesus had raised Himself up and saw no one but the woman, He said to her, 'Woman, where are those accusers of yours? Has no one condemned you?' She said, 'No one, Lord.' And Jesus said to her, 'Neither do I condemn you; go and sin no more' " (John 8:10-11 NKJV).

When you are confronting someone caught in sin, use some of these examples to lovingly appeal to the conscience:

- – "Would you like to know the way God has provided for you to gain and maintain a clear conscience?"
- – "Would you allow me the honor of helping you?"
- – "Would you like to have God's power over temptation and not be continually hooked and defeated?"
- – Follow the example of Paul, who said,

> *"Although in Christ I could be bold and order you to do what you ought to do, yet I prefer to appeal to you on the basis of love"*
> (PHILEMON 8-9).

METHOD #5: CONFRONTING WITH A REBUKE (DIRECT)—MATTHEW 16:21-23

At times, the most appropriate way to confront is to be direct and definite, as when someone does something flagrantly wrong or when a bad role model corrupts a child's conscience. Directly exposing someone when they offend does risk alienating them, but at times this method is necessary to turn hearts and to correct a negative situation.

> *"Those who are sinning rebuke in the presence of all, that the rest also may fear"*
> (1 TIMOTHY 5:20 NKJV).

- **A rebuke** is a stern, strict reprimand or a convincing, convicting reproof used in order to correct a fault. To *rebuke* is to confront those in the wrong directly with the aim of *charging* or *challenging* them to do what is right.
  - – The Greek word *epitimao* is translated "rebuke."[5] During the

crucifixion of Christ, one repentant thief *rebuked* the other thief—he *challenged* him to change:

> *"The other criminal rebuked him. 'Don't you fear God,'*
> *he said, 'since you are under the same sentence?'"*
> (Luke 23:40).

— To *rebuke* can also mean to confront those in the wrong with the aim of *convincing* or *convicting* them to do right. The Greek word *elengcho*, which is often translated "rebuke," also means "to convict, convince or reprove."[6] Scripture gives this reminder:

> *"Have you completely forgotten this word of encouragement*
> *that addresses you as a father addresses his son? It says,*
> *'My son, do not make light of the Lord's discipline,*
> *and do not lose heart when he rebukes you'"*
> (Hebrews 12:5).

• **A double rebuke** occurred after Jesus told His followers that He must be killed and that He would rise again three days later. Not grasping God's plan, Peter rebuked Jesus:

> *"Peter took him aside and began to rebuke him. 'Never,*
> *Lord!' he said. 'This shall never happen to you!'"*
> (Matthew 16:22).

Subsequently, there is no more powerful rebuke than the one that followed from Jesus to Peter:

> *"When Jesus turned and looked at his disciples, he rebuked*
> *Peter. 'Get behind me, Satan!' he said. 'You do not have in*
> *mind the concerns of God, but merely human concerns'"*
> (Mark 8:33).

• **A correct rebuke** requires the direct confrontation be balanced with great patience and careful instruction in order to bring about change.

> *"...correct, rebuke and encourage—with great*
> *patience and careful instruction"*
> (2 Timothy 4:2).

C. What Distinguishes Positive Confrontation from Negative?

The goal of confrontation is not to point a pious finger at someone else's sin, but to point to the truth that *correction is necessary.* This truth sets us free, turns us around, and puts us on a correction course.

Have you ever unknowingly been walking the wrong way, pursuing a direction in life that dishonored God and discredited you? Did you not later wish someone had cared enough to intervene, to challenge you, to confront you, to put you on a correction course?

At times we all need to be confronted with truth in a way that can result in conviction, correction, and a change of direction. Confrontation, if wisely handled and heeded, is often used by God to correct us from going the wrong way and to cause us to start going the right way.

> *"The way of fools seems right to them,*
> *but the wise listen to advice"*
> (PROVERBS 12:15).

THE PURPOSE OF POSITIVE CONFRONTATION

The Spirit of God confronts sin in the life of a nonbeliever in order to bring that person to confession, repentance, and salvation. Likewise, the Spirit of God confronts sin in the life of a Christian in order to produce confession, repentance, and Christlikeness.

Jesus died not just to save us from the penalty of sin (eternal separation from God), but also to save us from the power of sin in our lives now. Therefore, sin must be confronted so that we can be set free from its bondage. Confrontation is necessary both for salvation and for victorious living.

What God's love does:

– God confronts us in order to keep us walking within His will and in close relationship with Him.

> *"Know then in your heart that as a man disciplines his son, so*
> *the LORD your God disciplines you. Observe the commands of the*
> *LORD your God, walking in obedience to him and revering him"*
> (DEUTERONOMY 8:5-6).

– God gives us the task of wise confrontation in order to help others see their need to have a personal relationship with Christ or to become more Christlike.

> *"He is the one we proclaim, admonishing and*
> *teaching everyone with all wisdom, so that we may*
> *present everyone fully mature in Christ"*
> (Colossians 1:28).

– God confronts us because He loves us as a father loves his child. He wants to make us holy, as He is holy, so we can live at peace with others.

> *"They disciplined us for a little while as they thought best;*
> *but God disciplines us for our good, in order that we may*
> *share in his holiness. No discipline seems pleasant at the*
> *time, but painful. Later on, however, it produces a harvest of*
> *righteousness and peace for those who have been trained by it"*
> (Hebrews 12:10-11).

– God confronts us by using His Word to equip us for life…

> *"All Scripture is God-breathed and is useful for teaching, rebuking,*
> *correcting and training in righteousness, so that the servant*
> *of God may be thoroughly equipped for every good work"*
> (2 Timothy 3:16-17).

THE PERIL OF NEGATIVE CONFRONTATION

Confrontation, which should be helpful and healing, can miss the mark by becoming harmful and hostile when the motive is self-centered and the method is self-serving.

While positive confrontation is used to benefit the person being confronted, negative confrontation is used to benefit the person doing the confronting. It is rooted in love for self rather than in love for others.

What our desires do:

– We use harmful confrontation in order to keep others walking within our will and in subjection to our opinions without regard for their circumstances or feelings.

Righteous Job lamented that his friends were wrong to confront him in the midst of his intense suffering. After they confronted him, he cried out to them,

> *"Miserable comforters, all of you!...I also could speak like*
> *you, if you were in my place; I could make fine speeches*
> *against you and shake my head at you. But my mouth would*
> *encourage you; comfort from my lips would bring you relief"*
> (Job 16:2-5).

— We use hostile confrontation to eliminate any opposition to our personal goals or desires without any regard for the rights or respect for the dreams of others.

David, too, wrote about how the Lord delivered him from the hostile confrontation of his enemies and specifically from the hand of King Saul:

> *"The cords of the grave coiled around me; the snares of death*
> *confronted me...He rescued me from my powerful enemy,*
> *from my foes, who were too strong for me. They confronted me*
> *in the day of my disaster, but the Lord was my support"*
> (2 Samuel 22:6,18-19).

D. What Are Four Styles of Confrontation?

Does the thought of confronting someone make you want to run for cover? Awkward situations that require confrontation can cause great emotional strain—even ruining a close relationship. Have you tiptoed around a problem, hoping it will go away? Have you stuffed your anger only to have it build and later erupt like a volcano in the face of your offender? Ultimately, you need to overcome your fear and have the courage to lovingly confront others by living in the light of God's truth:

> *"The Lord is my light and my salvation—*
> *whom shall I fear?*
> *The Lord is the stronghold of my life—*
> *of whom shall I be afraid?"*
> (Psalm 27:1).

David's life illustrates four distinct styles of dealing with difficult people.

1. **The Passive Style:** The *avoider* confronts indirectly by using silence or nonspecific language to communicate needs and desires.

- Shuns direct interaction with others because of fear
- Expects others to figure out what is wanted

  Goal: Avoid confrontation to ensure self-protection

  Disadvantages: Produces no long-term solution and leads to bigger problems

  Example: At one time David chose to be silent and avoid saying anything at all around his offenders. However, his passive approach only increased the anguish and anger within his heart:

  > *"I [David] said, 'I will watch my ways and keep my tongue from sin; I will put a muzzle on my mouth while in the presence of the wicked.' So I remained utterly silent, not even saying anything good. But my anguish increased; my heart grew hot within me. While I meditated, the fire burned; then I spoke with my tongue"*
  > (PSALM 39:1-3).

2. **The Aggressive Style:** The *attacker* confronts by overtly attacking the character of the other person in order to gain power.

- Threatens and intimidates others to get needs met at any cost
- Violates the rights of others

  Goal: Gain power and control through anger or force

  Disadvantages: Produces only short-term solutions and makes enemies by hurting feelings

  Example: Many of David's enemies levied all-out attacks in order to bring David down:

  > *"My adversaries pursue me all day long; in their pride many are attacking me"*
  > (PSALM 56:2).

3. **The Passive-Aggressive Style:** The *ambusher* confronts by covertly ambushing the other person as a power play.

- Uses sarcasm and sniping rather than direct, specific language
- Tries to get even for actual or imagined slights

Goal: Avoid direct responses and accountability while getting even

Disadvantages: Produces no solutions and expresses destructive anger in indirect ways

Example: Repeatedly, David was verbally *ambushed* with indirect attacks from his passive-aggressive offenders.

> *"Hide me from the conspiracy of the wicked... They sharpen*
> *their tongues like swords and aim cruel words like deadly*
> *arrows. They shoot from ambush at the innocent..."*
> (PSALM 64:2-4).

4. **The Assertive Style:** The *activator* confronts by directly affirming the truth that positive change needs to take place.

- Uses direct, specific language to express factual information
- Confronts directly in a way that expresses value for the opinions and feelings of others

Goal: Present the facts, correct untruths, and change behavior

Advantages: Produces effective solutions and builds long-term trust and respect

Example: On two separate occasions David had the opportunity to put to death his enemy King Saul, but rather than act aggressively or passively, David chose to spare Saul's life and confront him assertively:

> *"Why do you listen when men say, 'David is bent on harming*
> *you'? This day you have seen with your own eyes how the LORD*
> *delivered you into my hands in the cave. Some urged me to*
> *kill you, but I spared you; I said, 'I will not lay my hand on*
> *my Lord, because he is the LORD's anointed.'...May the LORD*
> *judge between you and me. And may the LORD avenge the*
> *wrongs you have done to me, but my hand will not touch you"*
> (1 SAMUEL 24:9-10,12).

E. What Examples of Confrontational Styles Exist in the Gospels?

The four Gospels shine a spotlight on the four different *styles* of confrontation, as seen just prior to the crucifixion of Christ. We can see each style highlighted because of memorable individuals who have shaped the course of human history. One of those individuals is Peter, who was confronted not with strong words, but with a single glance.

> *"Peter replied, 'Man, I don't know what you're talking about!'*
> *Just as he was speaking, the rooster crowed.*
> *The Lord turned and looked straight at Peter.*
> *Then Peter remembered the word the Lord had spoken to him:*
> *'Before the rooster crows today, you will disown me three times.'*
> *And he went outside and wept bitterly"*
> (LUKE 22:60-62).

THE PASSIVE AVOIDER: PONTIUS PILATE

Pilate was a peace-at-any-price person. This Roman governor was faced with a difficult dilemma: What should he do with Jesus? Condemn Him or free Him? His personal fear of losing his powerful position—if mounting public unrest erupted into violence—was being pitted against the fate of an innocent man. He affirmed Jesus' innocence, but in the end he was too afraid to free Him from the snares of death. Rather than asserting himself, Pilate tried to quickly end his conflict by passing Jesus off to Herod. When that didn't work, he handed Jesus over to an angry mob—literally washing his hands of the matter.

> *"When Pilate saw that he was getting nowhere, but*
> *that instead an uproar was starting, he took water and*
> *washed his hands in front of the crowd. 'I am innocent of*
> *this man's blood,' he said. 'It is your responsibility!'"*
> (MATTHEW 27:24).

THE AGGRESSIVE ATTACKERS: THE SELF-RIGHTEOUS PHARISEES

Envious and exasperated, Israel's religious leaders incited the crowd into a murderous frenzy. Capitalizing on Pilate's character flaws, they coerced him into surrendering Jesus for crucifixion. This "brood of vipers" tested, tempted, and taunted Jesus at every turn, attacking Him openly. They remained completely unwilling to embrace His teachings or the possibility that His claims might be true. In doing so, they not only missed their Messiah, but used Rome to crucify Him.

> *"The chief priests and the elders persuaded the crowd to ask for*
> *Barabbas and to have Jesus executed... 'What shall I do, then,*
> *with Jesus who is called the Messiah?' Pilate asked. They all*
> *answered, 'Crucify him!'... Then he released Barabbas to them.*
> *But he had Jesus flogged, and handed him over to be crucified"*
> (Matthew 27:20,22,26).

The Passive-Aggressive Ambusher: Judas Iscariot

For three years, Judas masqueraded as a devoted disciple...cloaking dark motives with his privileged position. His protests against Mary's "wasting" expensive perfume to anoint Jesus' feet—funds that he said would be better spent on the poor—were a decoy to disguise his own greed. In a secret meeting with those conspiring to kill Jesus, he accepted 30 pieces of silver as payment for betraying the Son of God. Even when it was time to identify Jesus to his enemies, this *ultimate ambusher* remained covert—going under the cover of darkness and sealing the Lord's fate with a kiss.

> *"'The betrayer had arranged a signal with them: 'The*
> *one I kiss is the man; arrest him.'...but Jesus asked him,*
> *'Judas, are you betraying the Son of Man with a kiss?'"*
> (Matthew 26:48; Luke 22:48).

The Assertive Activator: Jesus Christ

The Savior came that we "may have life, and that [we] may have it more abundantly" (John 10:10 NKJV). No motive has been more pure; no action more unselfish. His mission led Him to confront evil at every turn—dishonest money changers, hypocritical religious leaders, corrupt government officials, common sinners. With each encounter, Jesus remains the only person in history who *always* assertively confronted sin with total integrity, flawless discernment, and perfectly chosen words.

> *"'I have spoken openly to the world,' Jesus replied. 'I always*
> *taught in synagogues or at the temple, where all the Jews come*
> *together. I said nothing in secret. Why question me? Ask those*
> *who heard me. Surely they know what I said.' When Jesus*
> *said this, one of the officials nearby struck him in the face.*
> *'Is this the way you answer the high priest?' he demanded. 'If*

*I said something wrong,' Jesus replied, 'testify as to what is
wrong. But if I spoke the truth, why did you strike me?' "*
(JOHN 18:20-23).

F. What Is God's Heart on Confrontation?

The Bible is a relational book. It reveals God's holy standard for the way we
are to interact with one another. You, therefore, have scriptural support to confront when someone violates God's standard and steps over your moral, physical, or emotional boundaries—or those of another person.

*"LORD, who may dwell in your sacred tent? Who may live
on your holy mountain? The one whose walk is blameless,
who does what is righteous, who speaks the truth from
their heart; whose tongue utters no slander, who does no
wrong to a neighbor, and casts no slur on others"*
(PSALM 15:1-3).

THE 12 COMMANDMENTS OF CONFRONTATION

1. God declares you are **to show respect** and to be treated with respect.

   "Show proper respect to everyone"
   (1 PETER 2:17).

2. God declares you are **to speak truthfully** from your heart and others are to speak truthfully to you.

   *"Each of you must put off falsehood and
   speak truthfully to your neighbor"*
   (EPHESIANS 4:25).

3. God declares you are **to listen to others** and others should listen
   to you.

   *"Everyone should be quick to listen, slow to
   speak and slow to become angry"*
   (JAMES 1:19).

4. God declares you are **to express appropriate anger** and to have
   anger appropriately expressed toward you.

"In your anger do not sin"
(EPHESIANS 4:26).

5. God declares you are **to both give and receive** only justifiable rebukes.

> *"Whoever heeds life-giving correction will*
> *be at home among the wise"*
> (PROVERBS 15:31).

6. God declares you are **to value and protect your conscience** by treating others in a Christlike way.

> *"I strive always to keep my conscience clear before God and man"*
> (ACTS 24:16).

7. God declares you are **to say *no* to selfish or self-serving motives** or actions…

> *"Say 'No' to ungodliness and worldly passions…"*
> (TITUS 2:12).

8. God declares you are **to remove yourself** from angry, hostile, or harmful confrontation.

> *"Do not make friends with a hot-tempered person,*
> *do not associate with one easily angered"*
> (PROVERBS 22:24).

9. God declares you are **to bring opposing parties together** to determine the truth.

> *"The first to speak seems right, until someone*
> *comes forward and cross-examines"*
> (PROVERBS 18:17).

10. God declares you are **to both seek and give** emotional and spiritual support.

> *"Let us consider how we may spur one another on*
> *toward love and good deeds, not giving up meeting*
> *together…but encouraging one another"*
> (HEBREWS 10:24-25).

11. God declares you are **to appeal to a higher authority** when necessary.

> *"If the charges brought against me by these Jews are not true, no*
> *one has the right to hand me over to them. I appeal to Caesar!"*
> (ACTS 25:11).

12. God declares you are **to confront and be confronted** with all wisdom.

> *"Let the message of Christ dwell among you richly as*
> *you teach and admonish one another with all wisdom*
> *through psalms, hymns, and songs from the Spirit,*
> *singing to God with gratitude in your hearts"*
> (COLOSSIANS 3:16).

II. CHARACTERISTICS OF CONFRONTATION

Do you confront when you shouldn't, and do you avoid confronting when you should?

A story in the Bible highlights this struggle when a strong religious leader confronts a woman who is behaving as though drunk, but she is actually in anguish, crying out to God because she can't conceive a child. The leader aggressively confronts her based only on appearances and before he knows the facts (see 1 Samuel 1:9-18).

This same leader who confronts when he shouldn't is later guilty of *not* confronting when he *should*. He fails to confront his two contemptible sons when they abuse their position as priests and take advantage of God's people (see 1 Samuel 2:12-36). God rebukes Eli for his passivity because he fails to protect the people under his care.

So, back to the original question: Do you confront when you shouldn't, and do you avoid confronting when you should? Fear of conflict can make you passive so that you do nothing, and misunderstanding can cause you to confront inappropriately. Knowing when and how to confront requires wisdom.

In his old age, Eli finally confronts his sons—but by then it's too late. Eli pays a high price for being too passive for too long. God tells Eli He will

> *"judge his family forever because of the sin he knew about;*
> *his sons blasphemed God, and he failed to restrain them"*
> (1 SAMUEL 3:13).

A. What Determines When You Should Confront?[7]

There are times when confronting someone does more damage than good, and there are times when confronting someone serves God's purpose. How can you know whether it's the right time or the wrong time to confront?

> *"There is a proper time and procedure for every matter…"*
> (ECCLESIASTES 8:6).

YOU SHOULD CONFRONT…

1. **When someone is in danger.** Some people say or do things that hurt themselves or others to the extent that lives are at risk. God opposes all abusive behavior, whether it is self-inflicted or inflicted upon others. You need to intervene when you see any behavior that puts people in harm's way.

> *"Rescue those being led away to death; hold back those staggering toward slaughter. If you say, 'But we knew nothing about this,' does not he who weighs the heart perceive it? Does not he who guards your life know it? Will he not repay everyone according to what they have done?"*
> (PROVERBS 24:11-12).

2. **When a relationship is threatened.** Relationships are vulnerable to damaging words or actions. You need to confront when necessary to preserve the relationship.

> *"I plead with Euodia and I plead with Syntyche to be of the same mind in the Lord. Yes, and I ask you, my true companion, help these women since they have contended at my side in the cause of the gospel, along with Clement and the rest of my co-workers, whose names are in the book of life"*
> (PHILIPPIANS 4:2-3).

3. **When division exists within a group.** One of the enemy's tactics is to cause quarrels, strife, and jealousy among believers. God calls us to unity, agreement, and peace. He charges us to guard and protect the precious relationships we have with brothers and sisters in Christ.

> *"Let us therefore make every effort to do what leads to peace and to mutual edification"*
> (ROMANS 14:19).

4. **When someone sins against you.** Difficult though it may be, God gives you a clear directive to confront anyone who does something to you that clearly violates God's will in regard to how you are to be treated.

> *"If your brother or sister sins, go and point out*
> *their fault, just between the two of you. If they*
> *listen to you, you have won them over"*
> (MATTHEW 18:15).

5. **When you are offended.** Sometimes you can be offended by someone's actions even when the actions are not sinful. For the sake of the relationship, confronting in humility and expressing your concern provides the other person the opportunity to be sensitive to you in the future and to avoid offending you by discontinuing the offensive actions.

> *"Be completely humble and gentle; be patient, bearing*
> *with one another in love. Make every effort to keep the*
> *unity of the Spirit through the bond of peace"*
> (EPHESIANS 4:2-3).

6. **When someone is caught in a sin.** At times you will see sin in others to which they are blind. While guarding against the possibility of the same sin in your own life, God wants to use you to expose the sin and help the one trapped to overcome it.

> *"When I [God] say to a wicked person, 'You will surely die,' and*
> *you do not warn them or speak out to dissuade them from their*
> *evil ways in order to save their life, that wicked person will die*
> *for their sin, and I will hold you accountable for their blood"*
> (EZEKIEL 3:18).

7. **When others are offended.** Sometimes confronting on behalf of others is appropriate. In cases of prejudice, injustice, or violence toward those unable to defend themselves, God expects you to take up their cause and speak out against the wrong done to them. Even the apostle Paul confronted Peter when it was necessary to do so:

"I opposed him to his face, because he stood condemned. For
before certain men came from James, he used to eat with
the Gentiles. But when they [the Jews] arrived, he began to
draw back and separate himself from the Gentiles because
he was afraid of those who belonged to the circumcision
group. The other Jews joined him in his hypocrisy, so that
by their hypocrisy even Barnabas was led astray"
(GALATIANS 2:11-13).

Forgive, then Confront

QUESTION: "Why can't I just forgive and forget? Why do I have to confront someone when they offend me?"

ANSWER: Undisclosed forgiveness benefits you by keeping you from becoming bitter, but it does not necessarily benefit your offender, who is in need of correction. Yes, you need to forgive and not dwell on the offense, but you also need to confront in order to make your offender aware of a problem in need of being addressed.

Forgiving without confronting can later result in your offender resenting you for not caring enough to make the offense known so that the bad behavior could be changed. Your offender could then develop a bitter root that later bears bitter fruit.[8]

"See to it that no one falls short of the grace of God and that
no bitter root grows up to cause trouble and defile many"
(HEBREWS 12:15).

B. What Determines When You Should Not Confront?[9]

Confrontation can create unity, but it can also divide, especially when done at the wrong time, in the wrong way, under the wrong circumstances, by the wrong person, or to the wrong person. For example, the Bible gives this instruction as to how to properly confront an older person:

"Do not rebuke an older man harshly, but
exhort him as if he were your father"
(1 TIMOTHY 5:1).

To avoid needless damage:

YOU SHOULD NOT CONFRONT...

1. **When you are not the right person to confront.** If you are not the one offended or not responsible for the one offended, you may not be the one who should confront. However, God might use you to help the person who bears the responsibility of confronting.

> *"Like one who grabs a stray dog by the ears is someone*
> *who rushes into a quarrel not their own"*
> (PROVERBS 26:17).

2. **When it's not the right time to confront.** You may be the right person to do the confronting, but it may not be the right time or your heart may not be right.

> *"There is a time for everything...a time*
> *to be silent and a time to speak"*
> (ECCLESIASTES 3:1,7).

3. **When you are uncertain of the facts.** Be sure you are fully informed of what is happening. Sometimes asking the right questions and listening objectively will reveal that you are simply misperceiving the situation.

> *"To answer before listening—*
> *that is folly and shame"*
> (PROVERBS 18:13).

4. **When it's best to overlook a minor offense.** You may find that overlooking minor offenses allows God to convict others of their errors. When in doubt, erring on the side of restraint and mercy is generally best.

> *"Whoever would foster love covers over an offense"*
> (PROVERBS 17:9).

5. **When you are committing the same sin.** Paradoxically, you can be most offended by people who are engaging in the very behaviors

with which you yourself struggle. You would be hypocritical in correcting others when you are guilty of doing the same thing. First, correct your own behavior. Then you can help correct the behavior of someone else.

> *"Why do you look at the speck of sawdust in your brother's eye and pay no attention to the plank in your own eye? How can you say to your brother, 'Let me take the speck out of your eye,' when all the time there is a plank in your own eye? You hypocrite, first take the plank out of your own eye, and then you will see clearly to remove the speck from your brother's eye"*
> (MATTHEW 7:3-5).

6. **When your motive is purely to satisfy your own rights, not to benefit the other person.** A "my rights" attitude will only damage the spirit of a positive confrontation. Therefore, consider another's interests over your own.

> *"Do nothing out of selfish ambition or vain conceit. Rather, in humility value others above yourselves, not looking to your own interests but each of you to the interests of the others"*
> (PHILIPPIANS 2:3-4).

7. **When you have a vindictive motive.** Before you confront, genuine forgiveness of the offender is imperative. In your heart, release the offender into the hands of God. You must not confront out of a secret desire to take revenge or to get even.

> *"Do not repay anyone evil for evil. Be careful to do what is right in the eyes of everyone"*
> (ROMANS 12:17).

8. **When the consequences of the confrontation outweigh those of the offense.** Look at the degree of the offense before you confront. Some battles pay little dividends and are just not worth the fight!

> *"Better a dry crust with peace and quiet than a house full of feasting, with strife"*
> (PROVERBS 17:1).

9. **When the person you want to confront has a habit of foolishness and quarreling.** Avoid confronting people who are unwilling to recognize their offense. If you cannot avoid the confrontation, you may need to take others with you to help in confronting these persons.

> *"Don't have anything to do with foolish and stupid*
> *arguments, because you know they produce quarrels. And*
> *the Lord's servant must not be quarrelsome but must*
> *be kind to everyone, able to teach, not resentful"*
> (2 TIMOTHY 2:23-24).

10. **When setting aside your rights will benefit an unbeliever.** Jesus modeled suffering for righteousness' sake and exhorts you to endure unjust hardship for the sake of exposing God's character to an unbeliever. Allow room for God to work in another person's heart by showing restraint.

> *"It is commendable if someone bears up under the pain of*
> *unjust suffering because they are conscious of God...To this*
> *you were called, because Christ suffered for you, leaving*
> *you an example, that you should follow in his steps"*
> (1 PETER 2:19,21).

11. **When the person who offended you is your enemy.** Sometimes it is best not to confront those who oppose you but to seek to win them over by praying for them and blessing them with unexpected kind acts. You and your offender are ultimately responsible to God for your actions. The path to peace might mean forgiving and blessing your offender without ever confronting the offensive behavior.

> *"Love your enemies and pray for those who persecute*
> *you, that you may be children of your Father in heaven.*
> *He causes his sun to rise on the evil and the good, and*
> *sends rain on the righteous and the unrighteous"*
> (MATTHEW 5:44-45).

12. **When confrontation will be ineffective and reprisal severe.** You may not be able to effectively confront a person who has a violent temper and who is likely to exact severe retribution on you or on

someone you love. However, with such a person you still need to have and enforce proper boundaries.

> *"Whoever corrects a mocker invites insults;*
> *whoever rebukes the wicked incurs abuse"*
> (PROVERBS 9:7).

Confronting Fellow Believers

QUESTION: "If I have a Christian friend who is continuing to live in sin, am I obligated to confront this friend?"

ANSWER: Realize that you may be God's agent to help your friend change and then grow to become more Christlike. If you care enough to confront, God can use you to encourage and support loved ones in overcoming habits that enslave them or alienate them from others. At times He will call you to directly and lovingly intervene in the lives of fellow believers who have wandered from the truth and become ensnared by sin.

> *"If one of you should wander from the truth and someone*
> *should bring that person back, remember this: Whoever*
> *turns a sinner from the error of their way will save them*
> *from death and cover over a multitude of sins"*
> (JAMES 5:19-20).

C. What Is the Difference Between Constructive and Destructive Confrontation?

Glaring differences separate constructive confrontation from destructive confrontation, and rightly so. One delivers hope, the other dashes hope. One dignifies the recipient, the other devastates the recipient. One delights God, the other displeases God. Choose wisely which one you use because God holds you accountable for what you do.

> *"Everyone will have to give account on the day of judgment*
> *for every empty word they have spoken"*
> (MATTHEW 12:36).

DESTRUCTIVE CONFRONTATION... FOCUSES ON CHARACTER	CONSTRUCTIVE CONFRONTATION... FOCUSES ON BEHAVIOR
Uses degrading, accusing, or threatening words to motivate change	Uses loving, hopeful, and encouraging words to motivate change
Assumes a negative motive is behind offensive behavior	Assumes a desire exists to grow and become more like Christ
Gives no opportunity for apology or restitution	Invites confession and is eager to forgive and seek reconciliation
Demands immediate correction as a condition for continued fellowship	Allows for time to mature, learn better behaviors, and grow in Christlikeness
Imposes either no consequences or disproportionate consequences	Offers appropriate consequences that develop character and responsibility
Puts total responsibility for correction on the offender	Accepts responsibility for accountability through the change process

"Love is patient, love is kind.
It does not envy, it does not boast, it is not proud.
It does not dishonor others, it is not self-seeking, it is not easily
angered, it keeps no record of wrongs.
Love does not delight in evil but rejoices with the truth.
It always protects, always trusts, always hopes,
always perseveres. Love never fails"
(1 CORINTHIANS 13:4-8).

D. What Characterizes the Four Confrontational Styles of Relating?

Successful confrontation is contingent first on the successful identification of the relational style of the one being confronted, then on the realization that different styles require different approaches. If you walk blindly into a confrontation without taking into account the type of individual you are approaching, you may walk away scratching your head, wondering what just happened and where you went wrong. Wisdom with good judgment calls for discernment when dealing with the problematic actions of others.

"Wisdom is found on the lips of the discerning,
but a rod is for the back of him who has no sense"
(PROVERBS 10:13).

As you seek to make a general assessment of your own or someone else's style of relating, the following chart will be of much help to you:[10]

Passive AVOIDER	Aggressive ATTACKER	Passive-aggressive AMBUSHER	Assertive ACTIVATOR
Fears confrontation	Incites confrontation	Resents confrontation	Values confrontation
Rarely expresses personal needs and desires to others	Demands personal needs and desires be met by others	Covertly tries to get personal needs and desires met by others	Willingly and openly expresses needs and desires to others
Communicates by saying what others want to hear	Communicates by using self-serving statements	Communicates by using silence as a weapon	Communicates by speaking the truth directly and correcting errors with facts
Agrees with everything, but acts on nothing	Disagrees excessively and acts selfishly	Appears to agree, but acts to get even	Agrees to disagree respectfully and acts with impartiality
Holds others accountable for own happiness, sadness, anger without communicating desires	Holds others accountable for own happiness, sadness, anger through coercion and intimidation	Holds others accountable for own happiness, sadness, anger through manipulation with sympathy and guilt	Holds self accountable for own happiness, sadness, anger through positive choices
Speaks only when forced to communicate	Speaks with accusations and open attacks	Speaks behind your back and conspires against you	Speaks directly and with respect
Acts unsure of the truth	Acts certain of the truth	Acts unconcerned about the truth	Acts on the truth
Wants the interaction over quickly	Wants to control the interaction	Wants to win through indirect interaction	Wants direct interaction for resolution
Expects others to pick up on hints and to be mind readers	Expects others to respond to demands	Expects to defuse confrontation with jokes and sarcasm	Expects to get to the source of the problem

Passive AVOIDER	Aggressive ATTACKER	Passive-aggressive AMBUSHER	Assertive ACTIVATOR
Sees losing as inevitable	Sees winning as everything	Sees covert attacks as the way to win	Sees a way for everyone to win
Justifies having a fear-based mentality toward others	Justifies open attacks on others	Justifies covert attacks on others	Justifies God-given responsibility to confront others
Aims to avoid conflict in relationships	Aims to dominate relationships	Aims to manipulate relationships	Aims to have healthy relationships
"Fear of man will prove to be a snare, but whoever trusts in the LORD is kept safe" (PROVERBS 29:25).	*"Fools give full vent to their rage, but the wise bring calm in the end"* (PROVERBS 29:11).	*"Whoever scorns instruction will pay for it, but whoever respects a command is rewarded"* (PROVERBS 13:13).	*"The wise in heart are called discerning, and gracious words promote instruction"* (PROVERBS 16:21).

E. What Are the Four Confrontational Strategies?[11]

If you are involved in a conflict and you realize you need to confront, use good judgment and be careful not to make the mistake of using one of three negative strategies: *avoiding, attacking,* or *ambushing.*

> *"The tongue of the righteous is choice silver…*
> *The lips of the righteous nourish many,*
> *but fools die for lack of sense"*
> (PROVERBS 10:20-21).

- **If You Are a *Passive Avoider*…**

  – Your strategy is to completely *avoid* the problem without ever addressing the person directly.

  – You have a fear-based mentality, perhaps learned in childhood, that makes you feel unworthy or inadequate to confront.

  – You are overly compliant because you want to avoid disagreement, and you cower out of fear.

  – By avoiding confrontation, you allow the sinful behavior of the other person to continue creating relational conflicts.

The Bible records King Saul's confession:

> *"Then Saul said to Samuel, 'I have sinned. I violated*
> *the LORD's command and your instructions. I was*
> *afraid of the men and so I gave in to them'"*
> (1 SAMUEL 15:24).

- **If You Are an *Aggressive Attacker*...**

    – Your strategy is to *attack* the other person, not the problem.

    – You build up your own self-esteem by attacking and suppressing others.

    – You feel entitled to cross the personal boundaries of another person's space, work, time, or personal life. You seek to control others by intimidation.

    – By attacking, you may win the momentary battle, but you lose the ultimate war. Your inappropriate attacks harm the relationship and provide no lasting resolution for correcting offensive behavior.

The Bible says,

> *"The LORD detests all the proud of heart. Be sure*
> *of this: They will not go unpunished"*
> (PROVERBS 16:5).

- **If You Are a *Passive-aggressive Ambusher*...**

    – Your strategy is to *ambush* the other person without confronting the problem.

    – You are afraid and prefer hiding, manipulating, and ambushing in order to gain power rather than directly confronting.

    – You keep a record of real or imagined offenses to justify getting even. You find it difficult to accept responsibility for hurting others, and you act as a "sniper," shooting slander, sarcasm, and mockery from a distance.

    – By ambushing, you avoid a direct confrontation. At the same time, you look for subtle ways to make a power play. Your relational conflicts are never resolved because you never deal with them.

The Bible says,

> *"Mockers resent correction, so they avoid the wise"*
> (PROVERBS 15:12).

- **If you are an *Assertive Activator* (a positive approach!)...**
  - Your strategy is to actively *assert* yourself by confronting in order to resolve the problem.
  - You deal fairly and respectfully with everyone involved by listening carefully, stating the truth, correcting untruth directly, and exposing areas where people differ or misunderstand one another.
  - You make requests, taking the needs of others into account by courageously giving words of admonishment, rebuke, or encouragement when appropriate.
  - By asserting yourself, you make positive relationships possible because you speak with discernment and confidently confront with sound judgment.

> *"My son, do not let wisdom and understanding out of your*
> *sight, preserve sound judgment and discretion...for the LORD*
> *will be at your side and will keep your foot from being snared"*
> (PROVERBS 3:21,26).

Certain other strategies may seem right for the moment, but they will not bring about godly results and will ultimately fail. Only an *assertive strategy* based on truth and applied with love will succeed and stand the test of time.

The Bible says,

> *"The words of the reckless pierce like swords, but*
> *the tongue of the wise brings healing"*
> (PROVERBS 12:18).

III. Causes of Confrontation

Do you know someone who is arrogant, rude, and cruel, yet continues to get away with it? While you wish he would change, deeper still, you wish he would get what he deserves!

That is exactly why one man refused to deliver a life-changing message to people he considered to be enemies. They were arrogant and cruel. He didn't want to confront them because they just might change, and then they wouldn't have to pay for their cruelty.

God tells Jonah to go and confront the rebellious people of Nineveh. If they don't repent, God will destroy them—but Jonah *wants* them to be destroyed, so he *refuses* to warn them. Instead, he boards a boat and heads in the opposite direction. That's when God uses a big storm and a big fish to reveal a big mistake. Finally, Jonah obeys God and confronts the people. But when they all repent and receive God's mercy, is Jonah grateful and glad? No, he resents God's mercy and carries a grudge. He wants them wiped out; he wants revenge. In response, he sits down and sulks (see Jonah 1:1–4:11).

Jonah has a *passive-aggressive* mind-set:

- He *passively* remains silent so that the people will not repent.
- He *aggressively* does everything possible to keep them from receiving God's mercy.

Jonah's mind-set needs a major overhaul; he needs a boatload of mercy. Jonah could receive the blessing of God if only he would offer the mercy of God. He needs to both hear and heed the words of Jesus:

> *"Blessed are the merciful, for they will be shown mercy"*
> (MATTHEW 5:7).

A. What Makes Confrontation Difficult?

Although the Bible says much about the benefits of confrontation, we frequently avoid confronting those who offend us. Why do we sidestep a one-on-one encounter when it could restore a strained relationship? The apostle Paul faced this dilemma with the Christians in the church at Corinth, and his confrontation led to repentance and restoration.

> *"Even if I caused you sorrow by my letter, I do not regret it.*
> *Though I did regret it—*
> *I see that my letter hurt you, but only for a little while—*
> *yet now I am happy, not because you were made sorry,*
> *but because your sorrow led you to repentance.*
> *For you became sorrowful as God intended*
> *and so were not harmed in any way by us"*
> (2 CORINTHIANS 7:8-9).

It Is Difficult to Confront When...

- **You are a shy person.** Confrontation does indeed take boldness and strong faith in the Lord.

  - *However*, take heart, God will always give you His strength to do what is right.

    > *"I can do all things through him who strengthens me"*
    > (Philippians 4:13 esv).

- **You risk more damage to the relationship.** If the offender does not respond properly, there is legitimate danger that the relationship may be damaged.

  - *However*, by confronting with the proper spirit and in the proper way, you can trust God to bring about His purposes through your confrontation.

    > *"Those who disregard discipline despise themselves, but the one who heeds correction gains understanding"*
    > (Proverbs 15:32).

- **You may hurt someone's feelings.** Sometimes confrontation does inflict temporary emotional pain.

  - *However*, your intervention may help a person avoid suffering severe consequences of persistent, harmful behavior. It is better to hurt a little now for a short time than to hurt a lot throughout a lifetime. Honesty in a friendship is more valuable than excessive praise and flattery.

    > *"Whoever rebukes a person will in the end gain favor rather than one who has a flattering tongue"*
    > (Proverbs 28:23).

- **You could risk advancement or career opportunities.** If you confront a coworker or even a supervisor, you do risk earning a reputation as a confrontational or contentious person.

  - *However*, if you confront in love and with a correct attitude, your offenders are likely to see that you are not trying to hurt them, but to help them.

> *"Let your conversation be always full of grace, seasoned with*
> *salt, so that you may know how to answer everyone"*
> (COLOSSIANS 4:6).

- **You know you have faults and don't want to appear hypocritical.**
  It is true, no one is perfect.

  - *However*, if you wait until you are perfect before you try to help
    others with their imperfections, you will never confront the sin
    in anyone's life. The requirement for confrontation is not per-
    fection, but a desire and willingness to overcome personal sin
    while compassionately reaching out to others who are struggling
    in sin.

  > *"Whoever conceals their sins does not prosper, but the*
  > *one who confesses and renounces them finds mercy"*
  > (PROVERBS 28:13).

- **You have never seen proper, biblical confrontation.** Angry arguments and inappropriate accusations were the patterns modeled for
  you as a child.

  - *However*, don't allow negative examples from your past to dis-
    suade you from learning and practicing biblical confrontation
    today.

  > *"Do not conform to the pattern of this world, but be transformed*
  > *by the renewing of your mind. Then you will be able to test and*
  > *approve what God's will is—his good, pleasing and perfect will"*
  > (ROMANS 12:2).

B. What Keeps People from Confronting Others?

Despite his fear of damaging the relationship he enjoyed with the church
in Corinth, the apostle Paul weighed the risk and decided not to keep silent.
Instead, he chose to chance disfavor in order to set those he loved and cherished on a needed correction course. Just as the Lord corrects those He loves, He
expects us to follow His example and confront sin in the lives of those we love—
not to hurt them, but to help them.

> *"I am jealous for you with a godly jealousy.*
> *I promised you to one husband, to Christ,*

> *so that I might present you as a pure virgin to him.*
> *But I am afraid that just as Eve was deceived by the*
> *serpent's cunning, your minds may somehow be led astray*
> *from your sincere and pure devotion to Christ"*
> (2 CORINTHIANS 11:2-3).

PEOPLE FAIL TO CONFRONT WHEN...

- **They think they do not have the right to confront.** Many people hesitate to say anything to those who irritate or mistreat them in some way because they think it's not their place to say anything.
  - *However*, the problem with that mind-set is that often there is no one else who can say something. This is particularly true when no one else is troubled by the person's behavior. The result is that nothing changes, and no one matures.

> *"Blessed is the one whom God corrects; so do not*
> *despise the discipline of the Almighty"*
> (JOB 5:17).

- **They think people don't need to be confronted.** These nonconfronters say people with troublesome behavior surely must be aware when someone is displeased with them, so it is pointless to tell them what they already know.
  - *However*, the problem with this logic is that often people do not know how others are reacting to them but would want to know so they could do something about it. Rarely do people derive pleasure in constantly offending those with whom they associate.

> *"When a righteous person turns from their righteousness and*
> *does evil, and I put a stumbling block before them, they will die.*
> *Since you did not warn them, they will die for their sin...and I*
> *will hold you accountable for their blood. But if you do warn the*
> *righteous person not to sin and they do not sin, they will surely live*
> *because they took warning, and you will have saved yourself"*
> (EZEKIEL 3:20-21).

- **They think hurtful emotions might arise and damage the relationship.** In reality, people do sometimes become defensive and lash out, resulting in the confronter becoming offended and reacting in anger.

  - *However,* the problem with keeping silent for fear of having an emotional outburst is that it prevents potential confronters from both confronting offenders and from making the necessary effort to resolve whatever buried anger is behind their emotional outbursts. The result is that no one makes needed changes and no one is further conformed to the image of Christ. Fear of anger replaces fear of God and prevents kindness from being extended in the form of a compassionate confrontation.

    "Anyone who withholds kindness from a friend
    forsakes the fear of the Almighty"
    (Job 6:14).

- **They prefer complaining over confronting.** These people are self-focused rather than other-focused and find emotional relief in telling everyone about the offenses committed against them—everyone, that is, except the offender. They thrive on sharing their woes and expend all their emotional energy complaining rather than compassionately confronting.

  - *However,* the problem with complainers is that they never resolve conflicts with others because they never address them with anyone who could solve them. The result is that offensive behavior continues and offended people continue to be offended without taking any responsibility for stopping it.

    "Do everything without grumbling [complaining] or arguing,
    so that you may become blameless and pure, 'children of
    God without fault in a warped and crooked generation.'
    Then you will shine among them like stars in the sky"
    (Philippians 2:14-15).

- **They prefer avoiding over confronting.** Sadly, these folks will do just about anything to keep from having to confront bad or hurtful

behavior, even to the point of avoiding their offenders. They expend a great deal of emotional energy making sure they don't run into someone they don't want to see rather than dealing with why they don't want to see them.

— *However*, the problem with this tactic is that the offender remains oblivious to offenses committed against others, and the offended person becomes a slave to avoidance. All the while, God sees everything because nothing escapes His eye.

> *"His eyes are on the ways of mortals; he sees their every step. There*
> *is no deep shadow, no utter darkness, where evildoers can hide"*
> (Job 34:21-22).

- **They prefer pretending over confrontation.** While pretense can be a temporary stress reliever, it is not a productive approach to resolving conflicts and stopping the offensive behavior of others. Sadly, these pretenders put a lot of stress on their bodies by living in denial and stuffing legitimate concerns that will never go away on their own.

  — *However*, the problem with this approach is that the pretender develops health problems and the offender never knows the truth—the truth God wants to use to bring about needed changes.

> *"But whoever lives by the truth comes into the light,*
> *so that it may be seen plainly that what they have*
> *done has been done in the sight of God"*
> (John 3:21).

C. What Is the Root Cause for Confusion Concerning Confrontation?

If you are unwilling to confront, you are living with the wrong assumption that confronting an offender means our basic inner needs will not be met. The right assumption is that God will meet those needs:

> *"God will meet all your needs according to*
> *the riches in his glory in Christ Jesus"*
> (Philippians 4:19).

THREE GOD-GIVEN INNER NEEDS

We have all been created with three God-given inner needs: the needs for love, significance, and security.[12]

- **Love**—to know that someone is unconditionally committed to our best interest

> *"My command is this: Love each other as I have loved you"*
> (JOHN 15:12).

- **Significance**—to know that our lives have meaning and purpose

> *"I cry out to God Most High, to God who fulfills his purpose for me"*
> (PSALM 57:2 ESV).

- **Security**—to feel accepted and a sense of belonging

> *"Whoever fears the LORD has a secure fortress,*
> *and for their children it will be a refuge"*
> (PROVERBS 14:26).

THE ULTIMATE NEED-MEETER

Why did God give us these deep inner needs, knowing that people and self-effort fail us?

God gave us these inner needs so that we would come to know Him as our Need-meeter. Our needs are designed by God to draw us into a deeper dependence on Christ. God did not create any person or position or any amount of power or possessions to meet the deepest needs in our lives. If a person or thing *could* meet all our needs, we wouldn't need God! The Lord will use circumstances and bring positive people into our lives as an extension of His care and compassion, but ultimately, only God can satisfy all the needs of our hearts. The Bible says,

> *"The LORD will guide you always;*
> *he will satisfy your needs in a sun-scorched land*
> *and will strengthen your frame.*
> *You will be like a well-watered garden,*
> *like a spring whose waters never fail"*
> (ISAIAH 58:11).

The apostle Paul revealed this truth by first asking, "What a wretched man I am. Who will rescue me from this body that is subject to death?" He then answers his own question by saying he is saved by "Jesus Christ our Lord!" (Romans 7:24-25).

All along, the Lord planned to meet our deepest needs for...

- **Love**—"I [the Lord] have loved you with an everlasting love; I have drawn you with unfailing kindness" (Jeremiah 31:3).

- **Significance**—"'I know the plans I have for you,' declares the Lord, 'plans to prosper you and not to harm you, plans to give you hope and a future'" (Jeremiah 29:11).

- **Security**—"The Lord himself goes before you and will be with you; he will never leave you nor forsake you. Do not be afraid; do not be discouraged" (Deuteronomy 31:8).

The truth is that our God-given needs for love, significance, and security can be legitimately met in Christ Jesus! Philippians 4:19 makes it plain:

> *"My God will meet all your needs according to the riches of his glory in Christ Jesus."*

Wrong Beliefs About Confronting:

The *passive* person believes, "If I confront others, the end result will be bad. I will hurt, they will hurt, and our relationship will be hurt. By avoiding confrontation, I can protect my basic needs from being threatened. The only way I can please those around me is to keep silent."

The *aggressive* person believes, "If I don't strongly confront others, the end result will be bad. I will lose, they will win, and my goals will not succeed. By strongly confronting, I can ensure my basic needs are met. The only way I can reach my goals is to dominate others."

The *passive-aggressive* person believes, "If I confront, I could be rejected. If I don't confront, I could be belittled. By masking my discontent, I can still find ways to make my point without risking personal loss. The only way I can reach my goals is to avoid direct confrontation but covertly attack from a safe distance."

Right Belief About Confronting:

The *assertive* person believes, "I will neither be afraid of nor exaggerate opportunities to confront. Knowing I am deeply loved, eternally secure, and truly significant, I am willing to confront with confidence, knowing confrontation can produce positive growth and change. I will also keep uppermost in my mind that my goal is to please God, not myself or someone else."

> *"Am I now trying to win the approval of human beings, or*
> *of God? Or am I trying to please people? If I were still trying*
> *to please people, I would not be a servant of Christ"*
> (GALATIANS 1:10).

D. What Is God's Cause for Confrontation?

You will never be ready and fully able to confront someone else effectively until you've confronted yourself, from the inside out. You, like everyone else, were created to have a personal relationship with God, but sin has caused that relationship to be broken. There is only one way to a restored relationship with God—through His Son, Jesus. In order to be in right standing with God, you must confront the fact that you have sinned and you need God's mercy, the free gift He is graciously offering to you through Jesus.

> *"The gift of God is eternal life in Christ Jesus our Lord"*
> (ROMANS 6:23).

RECEIVE GOD'S FREE GIFT TO YOU

The first step toward having a good relationship with God is understanding four important points from God's Word, which are listed on pages 48-50.

A Confrontation That Changed a Country:
The William Wilberforce Story

This is a confrontation that changed a country: "In my investigation of the slave trade, I confess to you sir, so enormous, so dreadful, so irremediable did its wickedness appear that...I from this time determined that I would never rest till I had effected its abolition."[13]

And rest he does not! As a young man, William Wilberforce begins to confront the horrendous slave trade throughout the British Empire, displaying not only perseverance but other admirable qualities—all for the cause of right. A long battle continues to be fought, because the slave trade is so lucrative—and money talks! But for many Brits, the issue is "oceans away" from their everyday lives. With the bulk of the slave trade conducted in the colonies, their eyes are blind to the beatings and their ears deaf to the crying of the slaves.[14]

Wilberforce is determined, however, to bring these horrific realities back home—front and center. After sending eyewitnesses to report back on the living conditions aboard the slave ships, this highly gifted orator creates vivid mental images to sting the collective conscience of his colleagues. So compelling is his confrontation that he says, "You may choose to look the other way, but you can never say again that you did not know."[15]

Wilberforce reveals devastating, startling statistics about the slaves on these trans-Atlantic ships. On average, "not less [than] 12% perish in the passage…4% die on the day of the sale…33% more die in their first season… here is a mortality of 50%."[16]

Then Wilberforce takes his passionate plea from the Parliament to the public. He enlists the support of Joseph Wedgewood—the famous pottery maker—to design relatively large pieces of jewelry, or anti-slavery medallions, depicting a kneeling slave in chains with the poignant inscription, "Am I not a man and a brother?" The popularity of this decorative pin, along with other such figurines in bronze, furthers his pro-freedom/anti-slavery influence.

In addition, Wilberforce collaborates with a well-known poet to pen two poems describing the plight of slaves—"The Negro's Complaint" and "Pity for Poor Africans." Between the poems and the medallions, he has made inroads into the worlds of both literature and fashion. Finally, a new awareness begins to stir the souls of those who had been numb to the brutal mistreatment of slaves.[17]

But when pocketbooks begin to be affected, painful repercussions multiply! Publicly attacked in the newspapers, Wilberforce loses many so-called "friends," and even faces death threats, which necessitates the hiring of an armed bodyguard.

Although this tenacious freedom fighter founds the Society for the Abolition of the Slave Trade in 1787, it takes 20 years for him to chalk up one real political victory. At long last in 1807, both the Lords and the Commons pass the Slave Trade Act—a monumental accomplishment. Still, this law eliminates only *slave trade*, not *slave ownership*. Thus, Wilberforce continues his campaign to fight against the inhumane treatment of slaves and to have them set free.

Not until 1833 does his courageous confrontation move Parliament to pass the Abolition of Slavery Bill, which calls for the end of slavery in all of the British colonies and establishes apprenticeships to help support the slaves as free people.[18] Finally, just days before his death, he gets word that the Abolition Act will pass both houses and receive royal approval.

What an inspiration! Millions of lives were changed—all because of the perseverance of one man who creatively confronts the cultural norms of his day in Britain. One man who directly impacts the end of slavery in the United States, as well as in other countries. One man who ultimately allows God to work through him for the good of many.

Could this be an overstatement? Consider that slavery dates back to the earliest references within recorded history, existing as a common part of the earliest cultures in civilization. It is even mentioned over 20 times in the first book of the Bible, thousands of years before the birth of Christ. Slavery has been a fixture throughout human history.

Then enters William Wilberforce to confront politicians, pastors, and the populace. Because of his unusual Christian conviction, exceptional compassion, and uncompromising courage, this godly man does change the world.

Wilberforce explains the motivation for his actions and convictions through these poignant words: "When we think of eternity and of the future consequences of all human conduct, what is there in this life that should make any man contradict his conscience, the principles of justice, the laws of religion and of God?"[19]

Confrontation possesses extraordinary potential, especially when based on the Word of God and empowered by the Spirit of God. In the future, if God should call you to confront, make the decision *now* to do it—even if you don't yet know the end results God has planned.

Indeed, the Bible exhorts you in this way:

> *"Speak up for those who cannot speak for themselves,*
> *for the rights of all who are destitute.*
> *Speak up and judge fairly; defend the rights*
> *of the poor and needy"*
> (Proverbs 31:8-9).

IV. Steps to Solution

Life is full of confrontations—from birth to death. Parents confront the misbehavior of their children, couples confront the problematic behavior of their spouses, peers confront the unacceptable behavior of friends, employers confront the unsatisfactory behavior of employees, law enforcement officers confront the illegal behavior of citizens, and God confronts the sinful behavior of everyone.

Confrontation is inevitable and impossible to escape. Therefore, the question is not "Will confrontation occur?" but "How will it occur?" How will you choose to confront troublesome behavior in your own life, and how will you confront it in the lives of others? Will you let emotions—fear, anger, frustration—dictate your actions? Or will you let God rule over your emotions and allow Him to direct your actions? If the Spirit of God indwells you, then you have everything you need to confront assertively.

As you study and learn God's ways of confronting, He will enable you to put His ways into practice:

> *"His divine power has given us everything we need for a godly life*
> *through our knowledge of him who called us*
> *by his own glory and goodness"*
> (2 Peter 1:3).

A. Key Verses to Memorize

In the beginning, the Lord confronted Adam and Eve directly when they disobeyed Him, and today He charges those who live by His Spirit to confront those who disobey Him. Paul referred to such a confrontation as restorative, and he issued a statement as to the seriousness—and a warning as to the danger—involved in such a noble cause. But more importantly, Paul identified confrontation as fulfilling the beloved "law of Christ":

> *"Brothers and sisters, if someone is caught in a sin,*
> *you who live by the Spirit should restore that person gently.*
> *But watch yourselves, or you also may be tempted.*
> *Carry each other's burdens,*
> *and in this way you will fulfill the law of Christ"*
> (Galatians 6:1-2).

B. Key Passage to Read

Clearly, the Lord intends for us to confront sin as we would confront any enemy seeking to destroy us and those we love. But we tend to focus more on the possible unpleasantry of confrontation to us than the gross unpleasantry of sin to God—sin that separates us from Him and from one another, sin that keeps us from being all He created us to be and receiving all He has for us, sin that crucified His Son!

> " 'He himself bore our sins' in his body on the cross,
> so that we might die to sins and live for righteousness"
> (1 PETER 2:24).

To help us, He has laid out a simple three-step blueprint to follow when confronting those caught up in sinful behaviors, and we find it in Matthew 18:15-17.

SPIRITUAL STEPS FOR CONFRONTING OFFENDERS

- **Step One: Confront Alone.** . . . . verse 15

  "If your brother or sister sins, go and point out their fault, just between the two of you. If they listen to you, you have won them over."

  – To preserve the dignity of the other person

  – To show your personal concern for the other person

  – To give occasion for clarifying motives

  – To offer opportunity for repentance

  – To provide the possibility of complete reconciliation

- **Step Two: Confront with Witnesses** . . . . verse 16

  "But if they will not listen, take one or two others along, so that 'every matter may be established by the testimony of two or three witnesses.' "

  – To show the seriousness of the offense

  – To express that other people have concern

  – To confirm and clarify the accusation

  – To offer a second opportunity for repentance

  – To provide accountability and hope for change

- **Step Three: Confront Before the Church Body.** . . . . verse 17

  "If they still refuse to listen, tell it to the church; and if they refuse to listen even to the church, treat them as you would a pagan or a tax collector."

  – To reveal the severity of the offense

— To demonstrate proper confrontation to the entire church body

— To provide yet another opportunity for repentance

— To offer restoration of the person to the entire church body

— To discipline the unrepentant person for the sake of Christian unity

C. How to Hit the Target

Before establishing a plan for confronting someone else, plan to confront yourself. Honest self-examination is necessary before you can build a strong case for confronting another person's behavior.

> *"By the grace God has given me,*
> *I laid a foundation as a wise builder…*
> *But each one should build with care"*
> (1 Corinthians 3:10).

Hitting the Target

Target #1—A New Purpose: God's purpose for me is to be conformed to the character of Christ.

> *"Those God foreknew he also predestined to be*
> *conformed to the image of his Son"*
> (Romans 8:29).

— "I'll do whatever it takes to be conformed to the character of Christ."

Target #2—A New Priority: God's priority for me is to change my thinking.

> *"Do not conform to the pattern of this world, but be*
> *transformed by the renewing of your mind"*
> (Romans 12:2).

— "I'll do whatever it takes to line up my thinking with God's thinking."

Target #3—A New Plan: God's plan for me is to rely on Christ's strength, not my own, so I can be all He created me to be.

"I can do all things through Christ who strengthens me"
(PHILIPPIANS 4:13 NKJV).

– "I'll do whatever it takes to fulfill His plan in His strength."

MY PERSONALIZED PLAN

- **I will make** sure my heart is right.[20]

  "Search me, God, and know my heart; test me and know my anxious thoughts. See if there is any offensive way in me, and lead me in the way everlasting"
  (PSALM 139:23-24).

- **I will look** at the conflict from the offender's perspective.

  "Do nothing out of selfish ambition or vain conceit. Rather, in humility value others above yourselves, not looking to your own interests but each of you to the interests of the others. In your relationships with one another, have the same mindset as Christ Jesus"
  (PHILIPPIANS 2:3-5).

- **I will listen** in order to gain insight into thoughts, feelings, and concerns.

  "My dear brothers and sisters, take note of this: Everyone should be quick to listen, slow to speak and slow to become angry"
  (JAMES 1:19).

- **I will take** responsibility for my emotional reactions.

  "Better a patient person than a warrior, one with self-control than one who takes a city"
  (PROVERBS 16:32).

- **I will keep my tongue under control.** You may not realize that you have been offended until you are tempted to hurt someone with words. If you find yourself being sarcastic, giving subtle hints or jabs, talking behind someone's back, tearing down someone's reputation, lying, grumbling, or complaining, you are not in a position to confront in a loving way.[21]

"A good man brings good things out of the good stored up in his
heart, and an evil man brings evil things out of the evil stored
up in his heart. For the mouth speaks what the heart is full of"
(LUKE 6:45).

- **I will ask forgiveness of my offender.**[22] When you ask forgiveness
  for your own failures, often others are able to see and feel convicted
  of their own failure and will respond with, "Yes, and would you also
  forgive me?"[23]

"Confess your sins to each other"
(JAMES 5:16).

- **I will forgive my offender.**[23] Forgiveness does not mean forcing
  yourself to feel good about the person or the offense. Rather, it is the
  act of releasing that person from their obligation to you. Forgiveness
  goes beyond justice—it is what God did for you when He accepted
  Christ's death in your place! You can forgive someone who offends
  you even if they never know they have offended you.

"Bear with each other and forgive one another if any of you has
a grievance against someone. Forgive as the Lord forgave you"
(COLOSSIANS 3:13).

- **I will pray for my offender.**[24] Pray for God to intervene and help
  the offender recognize sinful behavior and turn from it so that God
  will be glorified in the person's life.

"Far be it from me that I should sin against the LORD by failing to
pray for you. And I will teach you the way that is good and right"
(1 SAMUEL 12:23).

- **I will care about my offender.** Make sure you approach the person
  you are seeking to correct with a prayerful and tender heart. A good
  sign you really care about the person is that you find confronting
  difficult—this can show you have thought through the issue from
  the offender's perspective.

"Administer true justice; show mercy and
compassion to one another"
(ZECHARIAH 7:9).

- **I will be sensitive to the pain of my offender.** There is an adage that says: "Hurt people hurt people." Don't make your pain the central issue of a confrontation, but seek to acknowledge the hurt felt by your offender and to offer encouragement.

> *"Mourn with those who mourn...if you were*
> *in my place...my mouth would encourage you;*
> *comfort from my lips would bring you relief"*
> (Romans 12:15; Job 16:4-5).

- **I will make the level of the confrontation match the level of the offense.** You might be tempted to exaggerate the offense because you have not found comfort for your hurt. The severity of the encounter must be balanced to match the severity of the offense.

> *"He has shown you, O mortal, what is good. And*
> *what does the LORD require of you? To act justly and to*
> *love mercy and to walk humbly with your God"*
> (Micah 6:8).

- **I will complete the task and comfort my offender.** Are you willing to do what it takes to work with the offender to overcome sin patterns for the sake of your relationship and in obedience to God? Before you confront, make sure you are willing to invest the time and energy necessary to encourage the offender to overcome the offensive behavior.

> *"The punishment inflicted on him by the majority*
> *is sufficient. Now instead, you ought to forgive and*
> *comfort him, so that he will not be overwhelmed by*
> *excessive sorrow...reaffirm your love for him"*
> (2 Corinthians 2:6-8).

D. How to Apply the Three Approaches for Confrontation[25]

After you decide that you are going to confront, you must decide the best way to confront so the person can receive the maximum benefit. Since different methods produce different results, consider the following scenarios and how you can best use them to help the one you are confronting.

The apostle Paul used both face-to-face and written confrontation in his ministry to the early churches. His example of assertive confrontation through these two approaches is seen throughout his epistles and can be of great value to you as you seek to confront others in a godly way.

> *"Even when we were with you, we gave you this rule:*
> *'The one who is unwilling to work shall not eat.'*
> *We hear that some among you are idle and disruptive.*
> *They are not busy; they are busybodies.*
> *Such people we command and urge in the Lord Jesus Christ*
> *to settle down and earn the food they eat"*

(2 THESSALONIANS 3:10-12).

FACE-TO-FACE
(generally the first choice)

ADVANTAGES	DISADVANTAGES
• Most personal form of communication	• Most threatening to both the offender and the confronter
• Allows you visually to…	• Gives little time for offender to ponder your words and to process before responding
– Express your concern in person	
– See immediate reaction	• Can be more emotional
– Read body language	• Offers less control over what is heard and what is said— may lead to regrettable statements
• Allows you to…	
– Hear tone of voice	
– Receive immediate feedback	• Risks temptation if you have engaged in a sexually immoral relationship with the one you are confronting
– Clarify misunderstanding	
– Determine the acceptance or rejection of the confrontation	
• Allows the offender to visually see your concern and care through your facial expressions, eyes, and body language	

"I must speak and find relief;
I must open my lips and reply"
(Job 32:20).

TELEPHONE
(generally the second choice)

ADVANTAGES

- Less formal than face-to-face
- Usually easier to set up the meeting
- Allows you direct confrontation with less intensity
- Sometimes provides more privacy than trying to meet in person
- Allows you to...
  - Hear immediate reaction
  - Focus on tone of voice
  - Receive immediate feedback
  - Clarify misunderstandings
- Provides safety by allowing both parties the option of terminating the conversation and physically relieving tension through pacing or facial expressions
- Provides a better opportunity for repeated contact and follow-up

DISADVANTAGES

- Immediacy perhaps most threatening to the offender
- Gives offender little time to process before reacting
- Doesn't allow you to express warmth or concern through your body language
- Can be more easily terminated by the offender before the conflict is resolved
- Prevents possibility of communicating through body language or physical gestures

"Bear with me while I speak,
and after I have spoken, mock on"
(Job 21:3).

WRITTEN
(generally the third choice)

ADVANTAGES	DISADVANTAGES
• Offers the most objective scenario because it is not done in haste	• Such an established permanent record cannot be rescinded
• Provides control of wording, timing, and expression	• Certain negative behaviors need a more personal confrontation in order to address the need for change
• Provides a healthy distance from a physical, sexual, or emotional abuser	• The offender can choose not to respond or can misinterpret intent behind written words
• Allows for repeated reading of the letter for better understanding	• Follow-up conversation may be necessary to resolve conflict and pursue mutual forgiveness
• Sometimes makes your feelings known without the need to confront face-to-face	• Copies of any written correspondence can be sent to others who are not involved in the difficult relationship

*"I wrote you out of great distress and anguish of
heart and with many tears, not to grieve you but
to let you know the depth of my love for you"*
(2 CORINTHIANS 2:4).

E. How to Use the Sandwich Technique

When confronting someone who needs to be corrected, the Sandwich Technique has proved to be an effective way to both instruct and encourage at the same time. We all know how it feels to have plans fail for lack of preparation, information, or skills—and to have relationships fail for lack of insight, discernment, or communication. We also know how it feels to fail because of blatant wrongdoing on our part, reacting angrily when disappointed, forcing compliance when pressured, or seeking retaliation when rejected. In such times, we need someone to come alongside us and, in a gentle, nonthreatening way, set us straight before we do even more harm.

*"Brothers and sisters, if someone is caught in a sin,
you who live by the Spirit should restore that person gently"*
(GALATIANS 6:1).

The Sandwich Technique

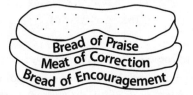

- **Bread of praise:** Begin with a positive statement, a sincere compliment, or a genuine statement of loving care. Accentuate the positive aspect of the situation.

  Example: "I know this is a very difficult time for you, but I know you have the God-given courage and ability to rise above this situation and turn it around. I would love to help you if you will let me."

  > *"The wise in heart are called discerning, and*
  > *gracious words promote instruction"*
  > (Proverbs 16:21).

- **Meat of correction:** Clarify the desired goal. Objectively recount the chain of events that led up to the present problem, examining what might have gone wrong and why. Problem-solve by brainstorming about possible options presently available for correcting the situation. Then determine a future course of action.

  Example: "Let's look at the situation and ask God to help us figure out what happened and how we can work on establishing a new strategy that will set you on a correction course and improve your chances of being successful."

  > *"Whoever loves discipline loves knowledge,*
  > *but he who hates correction is stupid"*
  > (Proverbs 12:1).

- **Bread of encouragement:** Conclude with a statement expressing confidence and assurance of future success.

  Example: "I've seen you overcome difficulties in the past, and I know you can do this. I'm extremely proud of you. I believe in you, and I believe in God, who lives within you. If you follow His leading and rely on Him for your sufficiency, you will succeed at everything He calls you to do."

> *"Encourage one another and build each other*
> *up, just as in fact you are doing"*
> (1 THESSALONIANS 5:11).

F. How to Conduct a One-on-One Confrontation

A chance for change is given to the churches in the book of Revelation.

Jesus Himself models how to effectively confront to expose wrong and to establish what is right as He addresses seven churches in Asia Minor, all representative of churches in our world today.

He begins with praise for their positive strides, then He tracks their pitfalls. And finally, Jesus provides a promise "to him who overcomes" (Revelation 2:7 NKJV)—to all those who experience conviction, correction, and a changed life.

SET YOUR GOALS FOR CONFRONTATION[26]

- **Don't** choose any setting where interruptions or distractions could easily occur. Suggest a place. "Let's meet in the conference room where we can have privacy and not be interrupted."

  Do control the time and place as much as possible to minimize distractions and to maximize privacy and focus.[27] A neutral setting is best where there are no telephone interruptions, television, music, or Internet distractions.

  > *"There is a time for everything, and a season*
  > *for every activity under the heavens"*
  > (ECCLESIASTES 3:1).

- **Don't** become angry or defensive at the negative reaction of those confronted. Avoid saying things like, "Don't get mad at me. You're the one in the wrong!"

  Do speak directly and honestly, but also gently and respectfully, knowing that the one you are speaking to needs a changed heart. "I realize this is difficult to hear, but we can work it out and get things resolved between us."

  > *"The one who has knowledge uses words with restraint,*
  > *and whoever has understanding is even-tempered"*
  > (PROVERBS 17:27).

- **Don't** speak for others. "Some people feel like you…"

  Do keep the conversation personal. "I have noticed…"

  > *"The wise in heart are called discerning, and*
  > *gracious words promote instruction"*
  > (PROVERBS 16:21).

- **Don't** attack character. "You're lazy…dishonest…greedy…hateful…irresponsible!"

  Do address behavior-specific problematic patterns. "I'm concerned that you're not following through on your commitments. You're consistently late (getting your homework done…getting to work…getting to meetings)."

  > *"The words of the reckless pierce like swords, but*
  > *the tongue of the wise brings healing"*
  > (PROVERBS 12:18).

- **Don't** use generalities or inference. "You just need to change!"

  Do speak in concrete, specific terms. "I'm concerned about the direction your life is going. When I (heard, saw) (action, behavior), I felt (sad, disappointed) because (state the reason)."

  > *"The teaching of the wise is a fountain of life,*
  > *turning a person from the snares of death"*
  > (PROVERBS 13:14).

- **Don't** use shaming tactics. "Remember when you (failed…forgot…were caught)? You should feel horrible."

  Do help the offender process any guilt or shame. "I know you must feel bad about your actions, and I do too. But God doesn't want you to be guilt-ridden, and neither do I. Can we talk about it and turn it over to Him?"

  > *"Be kind and compassionate to one another, forgiving*
  > *each other, just as in Christ God forgave you"*
  > (EPHESIANS 4:32).

- **Don't** focus on your own pain. "I continue to (__feel angry, hurt,__ __frustrated__)."

    Do focus on the offender's need to repent and change. "I am concerned about our relationship being damaged if some positive changes aren't made."

    > *"He [the Lord] is patient with you, not wanting anyone*
    > *to perish, but everyone to come to repentance"*
    > (2 PETER 3:9).

- **Don't** shut off conversation or objectivity. "I don't want to hear anything you have to say."

    Do listen to the offender, and be prepared to change your perspective of the offense. "I am genuinely interested in what you think and how you feel about what I am saying."

    > *"The heart of the righteous weighs its answers,*
    > *but the mouth of the wicked gushes evil"*
    > (PROVERBS 15:28).

- **Don't** say, "You're hopeless" or act as though no hope exists.

    Do offer hope. Realize there are no hopeless people—only those who feel hopeless. God offers hope to everyone. "I realize you may be feeling discouraged and down right now, but God is so much bigger than this problem, and He is on your side."

    > *"'I know the plans I have for you,' declares the*
    > *LORD, 'plans to prosper you and not to harm you,*
    > *plans to give you hope and a future'"*
    > (JEREMIAH 29:11).

- **Don't** put people "in cement," assuming they will *never* change. "You'll never change! You'll *always*…"

    Do be patient, praying that as you plant seeds of truth, in time the person will change. Realize that people don't change overnight. "The task ahead of you may seem daunting, but God has promised to conform you to the character of Christ, and He will keep that promise to you. As you cooperate with Him, He will change you from the inside out in His time and in His way."

"Be patient with everyone"
(1 Thessalonians 5:14).

- **Don't** assume that a confrontation is wasted just because it ends in anger or rejection. "I guess this was just a waste of time and energy."

  Do be prepared for hostility and lack of cooperation. Some people need time to process a confrontation before they can take responsibility. Leave open an opportunity for further communication. "I realize this has been a difficult conversation and will take some time to digest. I will be available if you have any questions or need anything clarified. I want us to resolve this together, but I respect your right to make that decision."

"The Lord's servant must not be quarrelsome but must be kind to everyone...Opponents must be gently instructed, in the hope that God will grant them repentance leading them to a knowledge of the truth, and that they will come to their senses and escape from the trap of the devil, who has taken them captive to do his will"
(2 Timothy 2:24-26).

G. How to Answer Common Questions About Confrontation

The church in Ephesus is warned not to rebuff Jesus' rebuke.

After Jesus tells the church members what they're doing right, He succinctly and directly confronts them on what they're doing wrong: "Yet I hold this against you: You have forsaken the love you had at first" (Revelation 2:4).

The church has forsaken Jesus Himself. Hearts once warmed with deep devotion for God have chilled, and monotonous undertones are streaming through the ministry. If their hearts aren't rekindled and ablaze with love for God again, Jesus warns He will "remove your lampstand from its place" (Revelation 2:5).

The light of their testimony runs the risk of being extinguished.

═══════ *Responding to Defensiveness or Anger* ═══════

QUESTION: "How do I respond to someone who reacts defensively or with anger when confronted?"

ANSWER: You cannot control the responses of others. If you lovingly and responsibly confront, yet people fail to respond appropriately, you may need to let them go by releasing them to God. Each person is directly accountable before God for their wrong behavior, and ultimately, He will judge them justly.

> *"Each of us will give an account of ourselves to God"*
> (ROMANS 14:12).

Continuing Wrong Behavior

QUESTION: "If I have confronted someone for wrong behavior and that person continues to rebuff my words, should I continue to bring it up?"

ANSWER: If no change occurs after repeated attempts to confront someone who is clearly wrong, don't continue confronting. The Bible says,

> *"If anyone will not welcome you or listen to your words,*
> *leave that home or town and shake the dust off your feet"*
> (MATTHEW 10:14).

Litigation

QUESTION: "If someone refuses to take responsibility when confronted, can I take that person to court? What can I do legally when someone has wronged me in a way that costs me materially or psychologically?"

ANSWER: The goal of confrontation is to correct someone who is at fault in the hopes of bringing unity and peace. Litigation is used when rights have been violated and a person refuses to accept responsibility. Litigation rarely results in unity or peace. That is why Scripture instructs Christians to settle their conflicts outside of court (1 Corinthians 6:1-7).

Some disputes can best be settled with the help of others who will listen to both parties and then mediate a settlement (Matthew 18:15-17). With an unbeliever, although civil action is not forbidden, God's heart is still for reconciliation.

> *"As you are going with your adversary to the magistrate,*
> *try hard to be reconciled on the way,*
> *or your adversary may drag you off to the judge,*

and the judge turn you over to the officer,
and the officer throw you into prison"
(Luke 12:58).

H. How to Know What You Can Say, and How You Can Say It

There is commendation for the congregation in Ephesus.

Jesus assesses the church's ministry efforts and acknowledges its hard work and perseverance, as well as its commitment to sound doctrine. "You have persevered and have endured hardships for my name, and have not grown weary" (Revelation 2:3).

And there is a promise for those who rightly respond to Jesus' confrontation, resulting in conviction, correction, and a changed life. It is a reminder of the gift of heaven and eternal life, which is extended to all true believers.

"To the one who is victorious, I will give the right to eat
from the tree of life, which is in the paradise of God"
(Revelation 2:7).

As with Jesus, deciding you need to confront is one thing. Deciding what you need to say is another. Preparing your words in advance will help you speak clearly and caringly when the occasion for confrontation arises.

"Like apples of gold in settings of silver is a ruling rightly given.
Like an earring of gold or an ornament of fine gold
is the rebuke of a wise judge to a listening ear"
(Proverbs 25:11-12).

- **Confronting unjust treatment** on behalf of a coworker
  - "Maybe he was not doing his job adequately, but do you think it is fair to fire him without allowing him an opportunity to change?"
  - "You might challenge him by pointing out the improvements that need to take place within his area of responsibility and instructing him to devise a plan to make those improvements."

- **Confronting a friend** who is excessively late
  - "I thought we were to meet for lunch at 1:00. I have been waiting for an hour."

— "Did I misunderstand the time we agreed on?"

- **Confronting a friend** who violates your personal phone boundaries
  - "Please know that I enjoy talking with you, but we need to talk earlier in the evening."
  - "Since I really need to get to sleep earlier, let's not call each other after 9:00 pm, okay?"

- **Confronting a spouse** for repeated failure to call when late for dinner
  - "I've had dinner ready at 6:30 for the last five days, yet you've not called to say you would be late. I need you to call me by 6:15 if you are not going to be on time."
  - "If you haven't called by 6:30, I'll assume you're on your way, and the children and I will go ahead and eat."

- **Confronting a coworker** for gossip and slander
  - "Would you tell me what you said about the project I've just finished? I heard that you don't respect my work."
  - "It would be helpful if you'd come directly to me with your concerns. I will value your comments. I sincerely want to do my best."

- **Confronting others** to help them see their blind spots
  - "Since you felt betrayed by your friend, do you think it's wise to keep trusting him?"
  - "Do you think it's wise to put all your emotional eggs in one basket and not develop other relationships?"

- **Confronting to set or enforce boundaries**
  - "I thought you weren't going to eat any more sweets after 7:00 pm."
  - "Do you still want me to hold you accountable for that?"

Be aware that the Bible says,

> *"Those who disregard discipline despise themselves,*
> *but the one who heeds correction gains understanding"*
> (PROVERBS 15:32).

I. How to Confront Assertively

Two goals must be kept in balance when confronting someone: On the one hand, you need to *expose the negative behavior*. On the other hand, you need to *maintain a respectful relationship*. Three of the four following approaches yield poor results because they do not keep this balance. Only one approach addresses the behavior problem and, at the same time, preserves the relationship. [28]

> *"There is a way that appears to be right,*
> *but in the end it leads to death"*
> (PROVERBS 14:12).

- **The Passive Approach:** "Running Away, Staying Away"

  If you *avoid* confrontation because of fear, you resign yourself to maintain the mind-set "I lose, you win."

  Instead...

  – Face your offender and set boundaries for the relationship. This will give a greater opportunity for you to eventually earn respect.

  – Be willing to give up the relationship if the offense is serious or the offender is dangerous. This will help you to protect yourself and could potentially motivate the offender to change.

  > *"Do not rebuke mockers or they will hate you;*
  > *rebuke the wise and they will love you"*
  > (PROVERBS 9:8).

- **The Aggressive Approach:** "My Way or the Highway"

  If your confrontation turns into an *attack* because you must be in charge, you assume the position "I win, you lose!"

  Instead...

  – Look beyond the short-term argument to win a mutually caring long-term relationship, which is the greater goal of successful confrontation. Seek to understand the deeper needs of your offender represented by wrong behavior.

  – Look for healthy compromise to produce necessary behavioral change in order to preserve a relationship with your offender.

> *"Do not take revenge, my dear friends, but leave*
> *room for God's wrath, for it is written: 'It is mine*
> *to avenge; I will repay,' says the Lord"*
> (ROMANS 12:19).

- **The Passive-Aggressive Approach:** "Have It Your Way, but You'll Pay"

  If you *ambush* the character of another person because you feel powerless, your goal is "I lose, but you lose too!"

  Instead...

  - Avoid the trap of undermining the character of another rather than confronting directly. The temptation to slander or gossip is a passive-aggressive approach that fails to resolve the offensive behavior.

  - Retreat temporarily from your offender, if necessary, but don't let your need to collect your thoughts be a reason to avoid confronting directly.

  > *"A wise son heeds his father's instruction, but*
  > *a mocker does not respond to rebukes"*
  > (PROVERBS 13:1).

- **The Assertive Approach:** "God's Way, the Best Way"

  When you *assertively* confront because you care about the relationship, thereby offering hope for a change in behavior, your goal is a win-win solution: "We both win!"

  Realize...

  - The reward of an assertive confrontation is greater trust and respect, which results in a deeper and more satisfying relationship. And confrontation is a means for greater unity in the body of Christ.

  - Assertive confrontation may produce short-term conflict, but it is often the means for long-term gain. Relationships can be strengthened and people's lives can be changed when you learn to confront assertively.

> *"I appeal to you, brothers and sisters, in the name of our*
> *Lord Jesus Christ, that all of you agree with one another*
> *in what you say and that there be no divisions among you,*
> *but that you be perfectly united in mind and thought"*
> (1 Corinthians 1:10).

J. How You Can Master the Assertive Style

The secret to mastering confrontation is to learn not only how to confront assertively, but also how to interact effectively with the different ways people respond. For example, your approach toward a passive person should be different from your approach toward an aggressive person.

> *"The wisdom of the prudent is to give thought to their ways,*
> *but the folly of fools is deception"*
> (Proverbs 14:8).

THE KEY COMPONENTS OF ASSERTIVE CONFRONTATION

- *Begin with a positive statement*—a sincere compliment.
    - "I value our relationship. I appreciate your (name good character traits)."
- *Describe the unacceptable behavior and how it made you feel.* (Address only the facts. Make no personal attacks.)
    - "The last three times we agreed to leave at 8:45, you arrived late, and we didn't leave until after 9:00. Truthfully, being late makes me feel not only bad but also disrespected."
- *Present expectations.*
    - "I would like for us to go together, but no matter what you choose to do, I have decided to be on time from this point forward."
- *Communicate consequences with a plan of accountability.*
    - "In order to be on time next week, we need to leave by 8:45. If you're not here by then, I will leave without you. However, I'm hoping we can leave together."

> *"Instruct the wise and they will be wiser still;*
> *teach the righteous and they will add to their learning"*
> (PROVERBS 9:9).

The following examples are possible ways to handle a confrontation with people who are repeatedly late:

1. **Confronting Avoiders—***The Assertive Approach to Passive People*

   Deal gently, but firmly with passive people. Fear of failure causes them to avoid taking responsibility. Your goal as an assertive confronter is not to push passive people out of their comfort zone, but to elicit their cooperation and to get an agreed-upon plan with accountability for a change of behavior. (Realize that acting assertively may feel aggressive to those who are passive.) Consider this example of confrontation with a passive person who is repeatedly late.

   - *Involve the person in the problem and offer solutions.* Counter objections with encouragement that a change of behavior is possible.
     - "How do you feel about being late?" (Wait for a response.) "I'm glad to hear that you don't want to be late. What are you doing before coming here that causes you to be late? What creative alternative do you think would bring about a solution? What do you think about *planning* to be here at 8:30 instead of at 8:45? You could set your clock ahead fifteen minutes to help you be on time."

   - *Declare what is to be expected* in specific, measurable terms.
     - "If we are to go together, I need you to be here by 8:45 or to call me by 8:30 if you see that you cannot make it so that I can make other arrangements."

   - *Give the person simple choices* to help ease decision making.
     - "Would you rather be here at 8:45 so we can go together, or would you like for me to make other arrangements and just meet you there?"

   - *Obtain their agreement* to follow through, and hold them accountable.

- "Are we in agreement that you will be here no later than 8:45?" (Wait for a response.) "Thank you! That means a lot to me. To make sure we're on the same track, will you call me at 8:30 to assure me you are leaving on time? I am confident you're not trying to be late and in your heart you really do want to be on time."

> *"Let the wise listen and add to their learning,*
> *and let the discerning get guidance"*
> (PROVERBS 1:5).

2. Confronting Attackers—*The Assertive Approach to Aggressive People*

Deal directly with aggressive people because they respond well to those who stand up to them. Consciously choose to be calm, yet bold. Determine that you will not be intimidated by fear or provoked to anger. The goal is not to win an argument, but to gain agreement that a change of behavior is necessary and then to devise a plan for change.

- *Reclaim control* of your life that you should not have given away.
  - "Until now, I have not said anything about your being late. However, being on time is an important value to me. In the future I plan to be on time even if it means going by myself; therefore, if we are going to go together, you need to be on time."

- *Give the aggressive person* time to talk. Then say back what you heard.
  - "What I'm hearing you say is _____. Is that right? Is there anything else you want to say about that?"

- *Defuse a competitive* atmosphere openly.
  - "I realize we don't see eye-to-eye on this subject. My wanting to be on time is not a personal attack against you. To me, repetitive lateness is an issue of integrity—a destructive habit only you have the power to change. Do you understand why this is important not just to me, but to you as well?" (Wait for a response.) "Good!"

- *Draw the line in the sand:* State the principle and maintain it.

— "I need you to make a commitment to be on time. If you won't make this a priority, I will make other arrangements to go by myself. You may not see this as an issue of integrity, but I do. Integrity involves being reliable and faithful to keep your word. Because I know you want to be a person of integrity, you need to develop the habit of being on time."

> *"Whoever walks in integrity walks securely"*
> (PROVERBS 10:9).

3. Confronting Ambushers—*The Assertive Response to Passive-aggressive People*

Deal directly and transparently with passive-aggressive people. Because they are afraid to state their desires through direct interaction, your goal is to confront their indirect attacks and motivate them to be open and direct with you.

- *Expose their offensive behavior* while holding them accountable for the truth.

  — "You've been over thirty minutes late the last three times. Do you agree this is true?"

- *Confront their covert issues* with you by inviting direct and open criticism.

  — "Is there a reason why you want to be late? Have you considered it might be intentional? Have I done something to offend you? Have I done something to cause you to be afraid of me?"

- *Hold them accountable* to ask for what they want.

  — "I want you to talk with me directly and state explicitly what you want—I need that. I can't read your mind. Will you do that for me and, more importantly, for yourself?"

- *State your expectation* of having direct communication between the two of you, along with the consequences of not doing so.

  — "I see the underlying problem is not your lateness, but a lack of direct communication between the two of us. I realize being late may not be an issue of integrity for you, but it is an issue of integrity to me. In the future, I will need you to be on time if we are to go together. Otherwise, we will go separately. But more importantly, I am expecting you to come to me about any problems you have with me. Can we agree on that?"

> *"The integrity of the upright guides them,*
> *but the unfaithful are destroyed by their duplicity"*
> (Proverbs 11:3).

K. How to Conduct a Crisis Confrontation for Chronic Problems[29]

What can you do when you confront a loved one who has a chronic problem—an addiction, a bad habit, or another behavior that is self-destructive or dangerous to others—and that person refuses to change? When *personal* confrontations are ineffective at bringing about changed behavior, you may need to turn to a *group* confrontation—there is power in numbers!

Many times, personal confrontations and earnest appeals fall on deaf ears. Even when several individuals confront one-on-one, each plea is summarily dismissed. As individuals, you are each a little firecracker. But as a group, you are dynamite. As an individual, you are viewed as popping off and making a little noise, whereas a united group can be empowered by God to move the immovable. God's Word lays out the blueprint for such an intervention:

> *"If your brother or sister sins,*
> *go and point out their fault, just between the two of you.*
> *If they listen to you, you have won them over.*
> *But if they will not listen, take one or two others along,*
> *so that 'every matter may be established*
> *by the testimony of two or three witnesses' "*
> (Matthew 18:15-16).

- **Pray for wisdom** and understanding from the Lord.

> *"The Lord gives wisdom; from his mouth*
> *come knowledge and understanding"*
> (Proverbs 2:6).

- **Educate yourself** regarding the offender's particular addiction or besetting sin.

> *"The heart of the discerning acquires knowledge,*
> *for the ears of the wise seek it out"*
> (PROVERBS 18:15).

- **Enlist the aid of key people** affected by the offender's harmful behavior—people who are willing to confront (caring family, friends, employer, coworkers, a spiritual leader).

> *"A truthful witness saves lives"*
> (PROVERBS 14:25).

- **Hold a first meeting in absolute confidentiality and *without the offender present,*** in which these key people rehearse what they will say, how they will say it, and the order in which they will speak when confronting.

> *"Better is open rebuke than hidden love.*
> *Wounds from a friend can be trusted"*
> (PROVERBS 27:5-6).

- **Hold a second meeting *with the offender present,*** in which each key confronter—one at a time—communicates genuine care for the offender and then shares the rehearsed confrontations (The Six P's of an Appeal).

> *"The soothing tongue is a tree of life, but a*
> *perverse tongue crushes the spirit"*
> (PROVERBS 15:4).

THE SIX P'S OF AN APPEAL[30]

1. The Personal

Affirm rather than attack.

- "I want you to know how much I value you (or love or care about you), and I am genuinely concerned about your behavior."

> *"Do not let any unwholesome talk come out of your mouths,*
> *but only what is helpful for building others up according*
> *to their needs, that it may benefit those who listen"*
> (EPHESIANS 4:29).

2. The Past

Give a recent, specific example describing the offender's negative behavior and the impact it had on you.

– "Yesterday, when you were drunk and slurred your speech in front of my friend, I felt humiliated."

> *"An honest witness tells the truth"*
> (PROVERBS 12:17).

– Be brief, keeping examples to three or four sentences.

> *"The one who has knowledge uses words with restraint,*
> *and whoever has understanding is even-tempered"*
> (PROVERBS 17:27).

3. The Pain

Emphasize the painful impact the addict's behavior has had on you by using "I" statements.

– "I felt deeply hurt and degraded because of the way you yelled at me."

> *"The hearts of the wise make their mouths prudent,*
> *and their lips promote instruction"*
> (PROVERBS 16:23).

4. The Plea

Make a personal plea for your loved one to receive treatment.

– "I plead with you to get the help you need to overcome (<u>offensive behavior</u>). If you are willing, you will have my help and deepest respect."

> *"The tongue has the power of life and death"*
> (PROVERBS 18:21).

5. The Plan

Be prepared to implement an immediate plan if treatment is agreed on.

— "Your bags have been packed, and you have been accepted into the treatment program at _____."

> *"Rescue those being led away to death; hold back those*
> *staggering toward slaughter. If you say, 'But we knew nothing*
> *about this,' does not he who weighs the heart perceive it?*
> *Does not he who guards your life know it? Will he not*
> *repay everyone according to what they have done?"*
> (PROVERBS 24:11-12).

6. The Price

If treatment is refused, detail the repercussions.

— "We cannot allow you to come home or to be with our family until you have been free of this negative behavior for (name a specific period of time)."

> *"Stern discipline awaits anyone who leaves the*
> *path; the one who hates correction will die"*
> (PROVERBS 15:10).

L. How to Respond When You Are Confronted[31]

Hear and heed is what Jesus was seeking from the church members in Ephesus when He said, "Whoever has ears, let them hear what the Spirit says to the churches" (Revelation 2:7). Jesus' confrontation was intended to bring about change—that what the believers hear with their ears will directly impact their hearts, restoring the deep love and devotion for Christ that they once had.

Jesus knew that deaf ears will only result in dull hearts.

> *"Whoever heeds correction is honored"*
> (PROVERBS 13:18).

• **Make your relationship a priority** over your personal rights.[32]

> *"The very fact that you have lawsuits among you means*
> *you have been completely defeated already. Why not*
> *rather be wronged? Why not rather be cheated?"*
> (1 CORINTHIANS 6:7).

- **Understand the other person's perspective.** Be willing to change where necessary and to heal any relational tension.

> *"If it is possible, as far as it depends on*
> *you, live at peace with everyone"*
> (ROMANS 12:18).

- **Listen carefully** even if you disagree with the other person's perspective. Give yourself time to consider what the other person says before you respond.

> *"Everyone should be quick to listen, slow to*
> *speak and slow to become angry"*
> (JAMES 1:19).

- **Respond with humility.** Give your reputation to God, and ask Him to help you with your relationships.

> *"Humble yourselves, therefore, under God's mighty*
> *hand, that he may lift you up in due time"*
> (1 PETER 5:6).

- **Consider your confronter as a gift from God.** Flattery builds your pride, but confrontation helps you grow in the Lord.

> *"Whoever rebukes a person will in the end gain favor*
> *rather than one who has a flattering tongue"*
> (PROVERBS 28:23).

- **Maintain dignity and discernment.** Allow God to speak to you through the other person. Your confronter may be someone who can help you get past an obstacle in your life. Even if you do not agree with your confronter, God may still use this opportunity for you to esteem the confronter for the courage displayed in confronting you and for the value placed on your relationship.

> *"Those who disregard discipline despise themselves, but*
> *the one who heeds correction gains understanding"*
> (PROVERBS 15:32).

- **Do not be defensive or reactive,** but consider the counsel of your confronter. God may be using that person to help you grow closer to Him. The benefits of confrontation may include coming closer to God, living a more loving lifestyle, and improved communication with your confronter.

> *"Whoever remains stiff-necked after many rebukes*
> *will suddenly be destroyed—without remedy"*
> (PROVERBS 29:1).

The sculptor's hammer and chisel
can change a block of stone into an admired masterpiece.
You become a chisel
in the Master Sculptor's hand when you carefully confront
the one who clearly needs to change.

—JUNE HUNT

CONFRONTATION: ANSWERS IN GOD'S WORD

QUESTION: "Why are you to confront someone about the error of his way?"

ANSWER: *"Remember this: Whoever turns a sinner from the error of their way will save them from death and cover over a multitude of sins"* (James 5:20).

QUESTION: "In what way do a fool and a wise man differ?"

ANSWER: *"The way of fools seems right to them, but the wise listen to advice"* (Proverbs 12:15).

QUESTION: "What would help motivate me to rebuke a wise man?"

ANSWER: *"Do not rebuke mockers or they will hate you; rebuke the wise and they will love you"* (Proverbs 9:8).

QUESTION: "Why should you not lose heart when the Lord rebukes you?"

ANSWER: *"Have you completely forgotten this word of encouragement that addresses you as a father addresses his son? It says, 'My son, do not make light of the Lord's discipline, and do not lose heart when he rebukes you, because the Lord disciplines the one he loves, and he chastens everyone he accepts as his son' "* (Hebrews 12:5-6).

QUESTION: "What should you do if someone sins against you?"

ANSWER: *"If your brother or sister sins, go and point out their fault, just between the two of you. If they listen to you, you have won them over"* (Matthew 18:15).

QUESTION: "What will you gain if you heed correction?"

ANSWER: *"Those who disregard discipline despise themselves, but the one who heeds correction gains understanding"* (Proverbs 15:32).

QUESTION: "Before you confront, what should you remove from 'your own eye'?"

ANSWER: *"How can you say to your brother, 'Let me take the speck out of your eye,' when all the time there is a plank in your own eye? You hypocrite, first take the plank out of your own eye, and then you will see clearly to remove the speck from your brother's eye"* (Matthew 7:4-5).

QUESTION: "Should you trust a friend who 'wounds' you with the truth?"

ANSWER: *"Wounds from a friend can be trusted, but an enemy multiplies kisses"* (Proverbs 27:6).

QUESTION: "How should I confront someone caught in a sin?"

ANSWER: *"Brothers and sisters, if someone is caught in a sin, you who live by the Spirit should restore that person gently. But watch yourselves, or you also may be tempted"* (Galatians 6:1).

QUESTION: "What is the difference between the one who disregards discipline and the one who heeds correction?"

ANSWER: *"Whoever disregards discipline comes to poverty and shame, but whoever heeds correction is honored"* (Proverbs 13:18).

CONFLICT RESOLUTION
Solving Your People Problems

5

CONFLICT RESOLUTION

Solving Your People Problems

Gather two or more people together and you can have a montage of differing personalities, priorities, perceptions, and preferences—a concoction ripe for fascinating conversations but also for formidable *conflict*. Rather than hands shaking in agreement, the result can be fingers pointing in accusation. Welcomed words of blessing can be replaced by caustic words of bitterness.

From the very beginning, the first people God created—Adam and Eve and their offspring—experienced conflict. The Bible clearly shows that all who came after them certainly experienced conflict. All through the ages and even today, similar struggles have continued to occur anywhere and everywhere people gather. Who hasn't at times wanted to throw their hands up in the air and exclaim, "Why can't we all just get along?" Well, we can—when we live with pure hearts and pure motives and pure principles. The Word of God provides principles for peace that can result in lasting reconciliation and resolution. One of those principles is:

"Encourage one another and build each other up"
(1 THESSALONIANS 5:11).

I. DEFINITIONS OF CONFLICT RESOLUTION

Living in obscurity as a Jewish orphan, she seems the least likely candidate to be the mediator—the *only* mediator—to save her people from sure destruction. However, the Lord knows her heart. He knows that Esther will face the most critical conflict of her life with complete humility and total confidence in His provision.

The conflict arises because a conniving official in the king's court named Haman devises a plot to murder all the Jewish people in the empire. His fury has been flamed by a man who refuses to bow down to him—namely, Esther's cousin Mordecai, who has raised her. Little does Esther know she will carry the fate of the Jewish people on her shoulders as she faces and seeks to resolve a conflict of epic proportions. Yet Mordecai aptly poses this thought-provoking question:

> *"Who knows but that you have come to your royal position*
> *for such a time as this?"*
> (ESTHER 4:14).

How does young, obscure Esther become involved in this critical conflict? The book of Esther recounts her story. After days of feasting, King Ahasuerus (King Xerxes) is "in high spirits from wine" (Esther 1:10), and he wants to show off the stunning beauty of his wife before the people and nobles. He sends seven attendants to summon her; however, Queen Vashti does the unthinkable and refuses to come. The king is furious because of her refusal and his advisors feel action has to be taken—otherwise, "there will be no end of disrespect and discord" (Esther 1:18).

Heeding the advice of his closest counselors, the king immediately issues a royal decree: Queen Vashti can never again enter into the king's presence, and she will be replaced (Esther 1:19-21)! With this new edict, the outward conflict between the king and queen appears to be "resolved." But the resolution of one conflict gives rise to another: Now the king has no queen.

A. What Is a Conflict?

Throughout the kingdom a major search ensues to find a distinguished queen for the disgruntled king. All the beautiful young virgins in the land are rounded up so that "the young woman who pleases the king" can be selected as queen (Esther 2:4). Esther, described as a young woman who "had a lovely figure and was beautiful" (Esther 2:7), quickly gains favor. At cousin Mordecai's instruction, she does not reveal her Jewish heritage. Meanwhile, wise Mordecai saves the king's life by reporting an assassination plot against him. The event is recorded in the annals of the king.

After a full year of preparation and pampering, Esther finally stands before the king, who "was attracted to Esther more than to any of the other women… and made her queen instead of Vashti" (Esther 2:17).

Esther's feet are now firmly planted on the path of God's divine purpose. But she's also on a collision course with a colossal conflict, a challenge far greater than replacing a dishonored queen.

- **Conflicts** are disagreements, struggles, or battles over opposing issues or principles.[1]
- *Conflictus,* the Latin word, means an "act of striking together" or clashing with.[2]
- **Conflict**, in the letters of Paul, is often presented by using forms of the Greek word *agon*, from which the English word "agony" developed.[3] Originally used to describe a gathering of spectators for the Greek athletic games, this word changed over time to refer to various types of conflict and became a metaphor in the New Testament to describe spiritual conflict, intense labor, or trial.[4] The apostle Paul said, "I want you to know how hard I am contending for you and for those at Laodicea, and for all who have not met me personally" (Colossians 2:1).

B. What Is the Difference Between Resolution and Reconciliation?

Soon a personal power struggle begins when corrupt Haman, the top royal official, becomes infuriated with Mordecai, who day after day refuses to bow down to him when Haman passes by the royal gate. When he discovers Mordecai is a Jew, he manipulates the king and convinces him to order an official decree mandating the massacre of all the Jews—every man, woman, and child. Haman thinks he has won the conflict, but he will never get the homage his insatiable ego pursues. In fact, he will one day pay for his actions at a very high and *horrific* cost.

> *"When Haman saw that Mordecai would not kneel down*
> *or pay him honor, he was enraged.*
> *Yet having learned who Mordecai's people were,*
> *he scorned the idea of killing only Mordecai.*
> *Instead Haman looked for a way to destroy all Mordecai's people,*
> *the Jews, throughout the whole kingdom of Xerxes"*
> (Esther 3:5-6).

Once the king's decree is pronounced throughout the provinces, the fate of the Jewish people seems doomed. No constructive conflict resolution is in sight. However, Mordecai appeals to Esther for help, and she can't believe what he asks her to do—approach the king unannounced and uninvited! He knows the law: "Any man or woman who approaches the king in the inner court without being summoned by the king has but one law: that they be put to death unless the king extends the gold scepter" (Esther 4:11).

Since Esther has not been summoned by the king for 30 days, how can she go to the king to plead on behalf of her people? What if the king becomes displeased with her? Clearly, going to the king will mean putting her life on the line, to which Mordecai responds that her life is on the line anyway:

> *"Do not think that because you are in the king's house*
> *you alone of all the Jews will escape"*
> (ESTHER 4:13).

RESOLUTION VS. RECONCILIATION

Resolution and reconciliation are different. Here's how:

- *Resolution* means finding the answer or analyzing a complex notion into simpler ideas.
- *Reconciliation* means 100 percent restoration to harmony, to bring together again.[5]

Some differences may never be resolved, but you can still be reconciled to those with whom you differ. At other times, resolution of differences may be possible, but reconciliation may be inappropriate, such as in the case of adultery or cult entrapment. God requires only that, as much as it is possible, you seek to be at peace with everyone.

> *"Make every effort to live in peace with everyone and to be holy;*
> *without holiness no one will see the Lord"*
> (HEBREWS 12:14).

════ *Forgiveness and Reconciliation* ════

QUESTION: "Is forgiveness the same as reconciliation?"

ANSWER: No. Forgiveness is not the same as reconciliation.

- Forgiveness focuses on the offense; reconciliation focuses on the relationship.
- Forgiveness requires no relationship, while reconciliation requires nurturing a relationship—two people, in agreement, walking together toward the same goal.

The Bible asks,

> *"Do two walk together unless they have agreed to do so?"*
> (AMOS 3:3).

C. What Are Some Different Types of Conflict?

Suddenly, Esther is facing an *inner conflict* just as heavy, just as grave, and just as deadly as the *outer conflict* caused by Haman.

On multiple levels, Esther has a conflicted soul. Where will she find the strength, the courage, to do what needs to be done...what *must* be done? This scripture could apply to Esther's critical situation:

> *"Destruction and violence are before me;*
> *there is strife, and conflict abounds"*
> (HABAKKUK 1:3).

1. Intrapersonal Conflict[6]

– A struggle within a person to decide *between two or more choices*

– Does Esther approach the king in an attempt to save the Jewish people from annihilation—which could earn her a death sentence—or does she remain silent and take her chances of being spared since she is now queen? She has no illusions about the risk.

> *"All the king's officials and the people of the royal provinces*
> *know that for any man or woman who approaches the king*
> *in the inner court without being summoned the king has*
> *but one law: that they be put to death unless the king extends*
> *the gold scepter to them and spares their lives. But thirty*
> *days have passed since I was called to go to the king"*
> (ESTHER 4:11).

2. Interpersonal Conflict

– A clash of ideas or interests *between two or more people*

– In the book of Esther, malicious Haman plots to have Mordecai murdered only because Mordecai refuses to bow down to him.

> *"When Haman saw that Mordecai would not kneel*
> *down or pay him honor, he was enraged"*
> (ESTHER 3:5).

3. Intraorganizational Conflict

- A competitive or opposing action *within a group* (a family, department, church, political party, state, or nation)
- In the book of Esther, the king's chief noble and the king's queen are on a collision course that will cost one of them dearly. One of them will die—not by the hand of an outsider, but by the hand of their own king (Esther 4:11). The king becomes enraged after realizing that Haman has manipulated him into issuing a death sentence to murder all the Jewish people.

> *"The king got up in a rage, left his wine and went out into the*
> *palace garden. But Haman, realizing that the king had already*
> *decided his fate, stayed behind to beg Queen Esther for his life"*
> (ESTHER 7:7).

4. Interorganizational Conflict

- A battle or opposing action *between two or more groups* (families, companies, religions, or countries)
- In the book of Esther, because of Haman's surreptitious plot, the Persian nation threatens to annihilate the entire Jewish population—men, women, and children.

> *"Dispatches were sent by couriers to all the king's provinces with*
> *the order to destroy, kill and annihilate all the Jews—young and*
> *old, women and children—on a single day, the thirteenth day of*
> *the twelfth month, the month of Adar, and to plunder their goods"*
> (ESTHER 3:13).

Conflict fills the pages in the book of Esther, just as conflict abounds in many lives. Disharmony in the home, wars in the workplace, the "should I" or "shouldn't I" struggles all try us and ought to lead us to the One to whom Esther will turn for the strength, courage, and resolution she needs. His name isn't even mentioned in the book of Esther, but His sovereignty spreads itself like a shadow over every chapter. The Bible tells us,

"Our God is a God who saves;
from the Sovereign LORD comes escape from death"
(PSALM 68:20).

D. Who Creates Conflict, and Who Keeps It Going?

Drastic times call for drastic measures.

Esther asks Mordecai to gather all of the Jews in Susa, one of the empire's main capitals, and has them go three entire days without food and drink. She and her maids do the same. Esther enlists the people of God to fast and to pray for rescue, and for a resolution to the most formidable conflict of her life.

"Go, gather together all the Jews who are in Susa, and fast for me.
Do not eat or drink for three days, night or day.
I and my attendants will fast as you do.
When this is done, I will go to the king,
even though it is against the law.
And if I perish, I perish"
(ESTHER 4:16).

Esther's act of faith works to open the king's heart. She approaches him without having been summoned, and he graciously extends his golden scepter, granting her an audience. When he inquires about the unannounced visit, the queen makes her request. Esther invites the king and Haman to a banquet, and the king seems eager to fulfill her wishes. Haman is convinced that he is included in the invitation because he is in the queen's favor.

"Haman went out that day happy and in high spirits...
Calling together his friends and Zeresh, his wife,
Haman boasted to them about his vast wealth,
his many sons, and all the ways the king had honored him
and how he had elevated him above the other nobles
and officials...
'I'm the only person Queen Esther invited
to accompany the king to the banquet she gave.
And she has invited me along with the king tomorrow'"
(ESTHER 5:9-12).

Little does Haman know that on this fateful day someone will be honored, but that someone won't be him!

At the advice of his wife and friends, Haman orders a gallows 50 cubits high (75 feet) to be built, on which he intends to have Mordecai hanged. But while Haman's workmen are busily building the gallows, the king has a sleepless night and orders that the book of memorable deeds during his reign be read to him. Found within its pages is the account of Mordecai's heroism in saving the king's life. The following morning Haman arrives at the palace intending to top off his enjoyment of the banquet by manipulating the king to agree to his request to have Mordecai hanged. But the king first asks Haman, "What should be done for the man the king delights to honor?" (Esther 6:6).

Confident the king must be referring to him, Haman proposes placing royal robes and a crown on the man and having a noble official lead him on one of the king's horses through the city square, proclaiming, "This is what is done for the man the king delights to honor!" (Esther 6:9).

While Haman is indeed part of the king's plan, his role is *beside* the horse, not *on* it! Humiliated, Haman leads Mordecai, mounted on a noble steed, through the city streets…for all to see. Entirely mortified by his enemy Mordecai, Haman returns home after the public spectacle. There he receives from his wife and friends a prophetic message, not of hope, but of doom: "Since Mordecai, before whom your downfall has started, is of Jewish origin, you cannot stand against him—you will surely come to ruin!" (Esther 6:13).

Those who create conflict and those who keep it going can generally be divided into two groups—attackers and avoiders.

THREE AGGRESSIVE ATTACKERS [7]

1. Wolves

Wolves are fierce, savage, and cruel animals that make a terrible howling sound and attack even large animals. They possess immense stamina and can travel long distances. They use scent markings to claim their territory, communicating: "This territory is occupied; this territory is mine!"

The word *wolf* is also used in reference to people who are…

- Known to be "wolves in sheep's clothing"—they cloak their harmful intentions behind a harmless facade.
- Known to be forward, direct, and zealous in the seduction of women
- Known to "wolf" down food, eating greedily—devouring their food like prey

The Bible describes the destruction wolves can cause:

> *"Her officials within her are like wolves tearing their prey;*
> *they shed blood and kill people to make unjust gain"*
> (Ezekiel 22:27).

2. Snakes/Serpents/Vipers

These are creeping creatures that can also move rapidly. Although many snakes are harmless, they are most often feared for their hissing, rattling, biting, and striking. They inflict burning pain and cause inflammation where they bite. Considered cunning and subtle, they can also be malicious and deadly.

The word *serpent* is also used in reference to people who are...

- Known to be dangerous and treacherous
- Known to inject injurious venom into people or groups by poisoning their minds, hearts, or reputation
- Known to act silently, secretly, and slanderously to inflict injury on others

The Bible describes the destructive nature of serpents:

> *"They make their tongues as sharp as a serpent's;*
> *the poison of vipers is on their lips"*
> (Psalm 140:3).

3. Hornets

Hornets are any of the larger social wasps that can bite and sting at the same time. Just one hornet can mobilize an entire nest to sting aggressively. In a swarm, they can drive cattle and horses to madness, and their formidable stings can also kill human beings.

The word *hornet* is also used in reference to people who are:

- Known to be excessively angry or "mad as a hornet"
- Known to gather others to "swarm" a person or place, thus creating havoc or harm with "stings" (for example, accusations, threats, attacks, etc.)
- Known to build a "hornet's nest" of angry, assaulting people who can literally be deadly

The Bible depicts their devastating ability in this description:

> *"I sent the hornet ahead of you, which drove them*
> *out before you—also the two Amorite kings. You*
> *did not do it with your own sword and bow"*
>
> (JOSHUA 24:12).

THREE PASSIVE AVOIDERS [8]

1. Tortoises

Tortoises are protected by large, dome-shaped shells that are difficult for predators to crack. They withdraw their necks into their shells by folding them under their spines or folding their necks to the side. Tortoises possess excellent nighttime vision but poor daytime vision because of their color blindness. They have short, sturdy feet and are famous for moving slowly, partly because of their heavy shells, but also because of their relatively inefficient, sprawling gait.

The word *tortoise* (or turtle) is also used in reference to people who are...

- Known for being slow or for being stragglers
- Known for "withdrawing into a shell" when threatened
- Known for dawdling or shirking responsibility

The Bible states this about lizards (which includes tortoises)...

> *"These are unclean for you...any kind of great lizard"*
> (LEVITICUS 11:29).

2. Chameleons

Chameleons can change to a variety of colors—brown, green, blue, yellow, red, black, or white—in response to temperature, light, and mood. A calm chameleon can be green, but when angry, it can turn yellow. Chameleons possess elongated tongues that can reach up to twice the length of their bodies. Their eyes move independently of each other, giving them sharp, stereoscopic vision and depth perception.

The word *chameleon* is also used in reference to people who are...

- Known to change their minds or even their character, but only superficially, merely to be expedient
- Known for their quick or frequent changes, especially in appearance, in order to fit in

- Known to blend in with diverse groups by reflecting each group's look, behavior, and belief when with the group

The Bible states,

> *"These are unclean for you…the chameleon"*
> (Leviticus 11:29-30).

3. Weasels

Weasels have a reputation for cleverness and guile, especially as they perform a "hypnotic dance" in front of their prey. These small, furry animals can twist and burrow down into small holes. They produce a thick, oily, powerful-smelling liquid called musk, used for scent marking and defense.

The word *weasel* is also used in reference to people who are…

- Known to act deviously, unscrupulously, and underhandedly
- Known to use "weasel words" in order to be evasive or insincere
- Known to evade or escape from a situation by "weaseling out" of it

The Bible states,

> *"These are unclean for you…the weasel"*
> (Leviticus 11:29).

E. What Is God's Heart on Conflict Resolution?

During the second feast the next day, at the king's urging, Queen Esther finally makes her request for her people to be spared from annihilation by the crafty *snake* Haman. Not only does the king grant her request, but in his rage he has Haman hanged on the very gallows Haman had built for Mordecai. Haman is indeed elevated, but not in the way he expected! Instead of remaining in power to see the destruction of the Jewish people, Haman had a "short stop and a sudden drop" from grace with the king.

After a time of great conflict, true resolution resonates throughout the land for the Jewish people. If Esther had avoided the conflict (retracting from trouble like a *turtle*), she would not be recognized today as a national heroine and choice servant of God. Instead, she confronted the conflict and rose to the occasion "for such a time as this" (Esther 4:14). The Bible says,

> *"There is a time for everything…a time*
> *to be silent and a time to speak"*
> (Ecclesiastes 3:1,7).

The story of Esther teaches...

- **Conflicts** can be used to accomplish God's purpose.

  Only after becoming queen was Esther able to save the Jewish nation.

  Esther 4:14— *"If you remain silent at this time, relief and deliverance for the Jews will arise from another place, but you and your father's family will perish. And who knows but that you have come to your royal position for such a time as this?"*

  > *"We know that in all things God works for the good of those*
  > *who love him, who have been called according to his purpose"*
  > (ROMANS 8:28).

- **Conflicts** cannot always be avoided.[9]

  Esther and the Jewish people could not escape Haman's threats.

  Esther 4:13— *"He sent back this answer: 'Do not think that because you are in the king's house you alone of all the Jews will escape.'"*

  > *"I have told you these things, so that in me you may*
  > *have peace. In this world you will have trouble.*
  > *But take heart! I have overcome the world"*
  > (JOHN 16:33).

- **Conflicts** that are resolved require advance preparation and planning. At Esther's direction, the Jews fasted before she planned to willingly go before the king on behalf of the Jews.

  Esther 4:16— *"Go, gather together all the Jews who are in Susa, and fast for me. Do not eat or drink for three days, night or day. I and my attendants will fast as you do. When this is done, I will go to the king, even though it is against the law. And if I perish, I perish."*

  > *"The plans of the diligent lead to profit as*
  > *surely as haste leads to poverty"*
  > (PROVERBS 21:5).

- **Conflicts** are not necessarily bad—they can actually sharpen us if we respond correctly.[10] Handled well, they provide an opportunity for role modeling.

For centuries, Esther has been and continues to be a role model of how to make an appeal to a higher authority.

Esther 5:7-8—*"Esther replied, 'My petition and my request is this: If the king regards me with favor and if it pleases the king to grant my petition and fulfill my request, let the king and Haman come tomorrow to the banquet I will prepare for them. Then I will answer the king's question.'"*

> *"Blessed is the one who perseveres under trial because,*
> *having stood the test, that person will receive the crown of*
> *life that the Lord has promised to those who love him"*
> (JAMES 1:12).

- **Conflicts** can sometimes be settled through negotiation.

Esther graciously negotiated with the king.

Esther 7:3-4—*"Then Queen Esther answered, 'If I have found favor with you, Your Majesty, and if it pleases you, grant me my life—this is my petition. And spare my people—this is my request. For I and my people have been sold to be destroyed, killed and annihilated. If we had merely been sold as male and female slaves, I would have kept quiet, because no such distress would justify disturbing the king.'"*

> *"Listen to advice and accept discipline, and at the*
> *end you will be counted among the wise"*
> (PROVERBS 19:20).

- **Conflicts** that are resolved require action toward peace.

Due to Esther's intervention, the king took actions that allowed the Jews to assemble and to defend themselves.

Esther 8:11—*"The king's edict granted the Jews in every city the right to assemble and protect themselves; to destroy, kill and annihilate the armed men of any nationality or province who might attack them and their women and children, and to plunder the property of their enemies."*

> *"Let us therefore make every effort to do what*
> *leads to peace and to mutual edification"*
> (ROMANS 14:19).

II. CHARACTERISTICS OF UNRESOLVED CONFLICT

For 20 years they tussle; their relationship rumbles with turmoil and conflict. After Jacob deceives his aged and blind father, Isaac, into bestowing on him the birthright that belongs to his older brother Esau, he flees to his Uncle Laban's home. When Esau finds out what Jacob has done, he vows to kill him. Laban graciously receives Jacob into his home, but before long the tables are turned and Jacob himself becomes a victim of repeated deception.

The first incident involves Laban's daughters, Leah and Rachel, and a honeymoon hoax. Jacob is deeply in love with Rachel, and he has worked seven years to gain her hand in marriage. But when he wakes up the morning after his wedding night, he doesn't behold the face of his beloved—it's Leah's face he sees!

The command of God is very clear:

> *"Do not deceive one another"*
> (LEVITICUS 19:11).

A. What Are Common Statements Used in Conflict?

> *"What is this you have done to me?*
> *I served you for Rachel, didn't I?*
> *Why have you deceived me?"*
> (GENESIS 29:25).

Jacob is stunned and angered by Laban's deception—he was tricked into marrying Leah instead of Rachel. Laban justifies his behavior in accordance with a local custom, one that calls for the marrying of the eldest daughter before the youngest. But after the bridal week is finished with Leah, Laban vows to give Jacob Rachel as well, yet Jacob will have to work for him another seven years.

Jacob then marries Rachel, and the future patriarch finds himself with two brides in seven days. Laban will soon pull another "switch out" on Jacob, but this time it will involve goats and sheep.

The following Scripture aptly applies to Laban:

> *"Not a word from their mouth can be trusted;*
> *their heart is filled with malice"*
> (PSALM 5:9).

EIGHT FAULTY ACCUSATIONS OF ATTACKERS

- "You'll never change."
- "You challenge me, and I'll pin you to the wall."
- "You don't have what it takes to succeed in this life."
- "You're so stupid that you don't have enough sense to get out of the rain."
- "You failed again—you're just a failure."
- "You're at fault if our relationship fails."
- "You can't even do the simplest things correctly."
- "You're hopeless—there's no hope for you."

Instead of focusing on the faults of others (out of pride), the Bible tells us to bear the burdens of others (out of humility):

> *"Carry each other's burdens, and in this way you will*
> *fulfill the law of Christ. If anyone thinks they are*
> *something when they are not, they deceive themselves"*
> (GALATIANS 6:2-3).

EIGHT FAULTY EXPECTATIONS OF AVOIDERS

- "You should never create conflict in our relationship."
- "You should never get angry with me because I can't handle it."
- "You should always see things my way if you care about my feelings."
- "You should always do things my way if you care about my happiness."
- "You should always trust my judgment if you respect me."
- "You should always depend on me to make you secure."
- "You should always overlook my mistakes if you truly accept me."

- "You should always seek to meet my needs if you want us to have a good relationship."

However, the Bible says we should look to the Lord as our Need-meeter:

> *"My God will meet all your needs according to*
> *the riches of his glory in Christ Jesus"*
> (PHILIPPIANS 4:19).

B. What Is the Appearance of Attackers and Avoiders?

Laban is a wolf among his own sheep and goats, separating the off-colored animals designated for Jacob in hopes of reducing the odds of Jacob's acquiring a large herd.

The off-colored animals that Laban deceitfully hides are supposed to be Jacob's wages, but it's not the first time the dastardly uncle has bilked his nephew over finances. Ten times previously, Laban has cheated Jacob concerning his pay.

But prosperity is in God's hands, not Laban's. Despite the attempt at deceit, Jacob, a shepherd experienced in selective breeding, gets the other sheep and goats in Laban's herd to mate and they bear young that are "streaked or speckled or spotted" (Genesis 30:39). Laban originally thinks he's outwitted Jacob, but Jacob "grew exceedingly prosperous and came to own large flocks, and female and male servants, and camels and donkeys" (Genesis 30:43).

Laban could be included in Paul's audience when the apostle wrote,

> *"You yourselves cheat and do wrong,*
> *and you do this to your brothers and sisters"*
> (1 CORINTHIANS 6:8).

Each of us begins to develop a style of handling conflict at an early age. Our personal ways of "fighting" come from our natural instinct, personality, and early family dynamics. Yet many of us are unable to defuse conflict because we repeat the extreme patterns of childhood, either *attacking* or *avoiding* others.[11]

Considering the characteristics of the six creatures mentioned earlier will help define the personalities of attackers and avoiders. The problem with both styles of handling conflict is that neither one appropriates the grace that is available to a child of God. The Bible says,

> *"See to it that no one falls short of the grace of God*
> *and that no bitter root grows up to cause trouble and defile many"*
> (HEBREWS 12:15).

THREE AGGRESSIVE ATTACKERS

1. The Wolf[12]—alias, "dictator"

This person demands absolute power, insisting on complete autocratic control.

– Authoritative, seeks to control everyone and everything
– Combative, judges the actions and motives of others
– Rigid, refuses to listen to opposing opinions with an open mind
– Disrespectful, uses criticism to cut people down
– Aggressive, engages in power plays

Message: "Give in to me or I'll attack you!"

Goal: To feel powerful

> *"Watch out for false prophets. They come to you in sheep's clothing, but inwardly they are ferocious wolves"*
> (MATTHEW 7:15).

2. The Snake[13]—alias, "backbiter"

This person says mean or spiteful things behind another person's back.

– Strikes when you're not looking
– Uses criticism and put-downs
– Starts false rumors with false accusations
– Pretends to have done nothing wrong
– Gathers allies by distorting the truth

Message: "Don't cross me or you'll regret it later."

Goal: To feel superior

> *"You brood of vipers, how can you who are evil say anything good? For the mouth speaks what the heart is full of"*
> (MATTHEW 12:34).

3. The Hornet[14]—alias, "faultfinder"

This person nags others with persistent questions, petty suggestions, and constant criticism.

- Registers repeated complaints
- Makes negative statements about everything
- Blames others
- Pulls others into disagreements
- Delights in misery

Message: "Don't get on my bad side or I'll talk about you!"

Goal: To feel valuable

> *"The mouths of fools are their undoing, and*
> *their lips are a snare to their very lives"*
> (PROVERBS 18:7).

THREE PASSIVE AVOIDERS

1. The Turtle[15]—alias, "retreater"

This person withdraws from what is perceived as difficult, dangerous, or disagreeable.

- Plays dumb
- Gives one-word answers
- Withdraws from conflicts
- Seeks secrecy
- Tries to make you feel guilty for asking appropriate questions

Message: "Don't confront me because it won't do any good."

Goal: To feel safe

> *"A truthful witness saves lives, but a false witness is deceitful"*
> (PROVERBS 14:25).

2. The Chameleon[16]—alias, "people-pleaser"

This person fears displeasing others and will change anything and everything in order to please.

- Avoids making decisions
- Acts innocent when in the wrong
- Appears to be nice and agreeable

- Recoils from making a commitment
- Downplays differences

Message: "I'm nice to you; you owe it to me to be nice in return."

Goal: To feel accepted

> *"Fear of man will prove to be a snare..."*
> (Proverbs 29:25).

3. The Weasel[17]—alias, "twister"

This person perverts meanings, squirms, is devious, and uses gimmicks.

- Uses clever defenses
- Sidesteps the issue
- Twists and bends the truth
- Blames others
- Avoids taking responsibility or ownership of problems

Message: "I'm not going to get pinned down."

Goal: To feel confident

> *"One whose heart is corrupt does not prosper; one
> whose tongue is perverse falls into trouble"*
> (Proverbs 17:20).

C. What Styles of Conflict Are Found in Scripture, and Who Displays Them?

After years of conflict, Laban, the aggressive attacker, and Jacob, the passive avoider, find resolution through a covenant. They gather a bunch of stones and place them in a pile as a memorial to the oath the two men will share.

Laban then says to Jacob, "This heap is a witness, and this pillar is a witness, that I will not go past this heap to your side to harm you and you will not go past this heap and pillar to my side to harm me" (Genesis 31:52).

The uncle and nephew find a peaceable solution to their conflicts, and Scripture no longer refers to any more struggles between them. The men are obedient to the call of Scripture:

> *"Turn from evil and do good; seek peace and pursue it"*
> (Psalm 34:14).

Given the thousands of narratives throughout the Bible, even the novice reader can see that negative conflict has been alive and well from the beginning of time. For example, Abraham, on two different occasions, lies about his relationship with Sarah, his wife, by passing her off as his sister. Because of her beauty, he fears two different monarchs will kill him in order to take her.

Because of his fear, Abraham acts like a turtle hiding in its shell: "Abraham replied, 'I said to myself, "There is surely no fear of God in this place, and they will kill me because of my wife." Besides, she really is my sister, the daughter of my father though not of my mother; and she became my wife. And when God had me wander from my father's household, I said to her, "This is how you can show your love to me: Everywhere we go, say of me, 'He is my brother'"'" (Genesis 20:11-13).

Which type of *attacker* or *avoider* is each of the following people? Analyze and identify the negative conflict styles in each of the following relationships. (Hint: Read the scripture first, then fill in the blanks.) (Note: Answers are found at the end of Section II, pages 319-320.)

RELATIONSHIP #1

Between the Serpent, Adam, and Eve

- The serpent: He is an attacker, a *snake*. He plays the part of himself!

> *"Now the serpent was more crafty than any of the wild animals the LORD God had made. He said to the woman [Eve], 'Did God really say, "You must not eat from any tree in the garden"?'"*
> (GENESIS 3:1).

- Adam: He is an avoider, a weasel. He tried to weasel out of accepting responsibility for his wrong choices by blaming Eve.

> *"The man [Adam] said, 'The woman you put here with me—she gave me some fruit from the tree, and I ate it'"*
> (GENESIS 3:12).

- Eve: _____

> *"Then the LORD God said to the woman [Eve], 'What is this you have done?' The woman said, 'The serpent deceived me, and I ate'"*
> (GENESIS 3:13).

RELATIONSHIP #2
Cain toward Abel
– Cain: _____

> *"Now Cain said to his brother Abel, 'Let's go out*
> *to the field.' While they were in the field, Cain*
> *attacked his brother Abel and killed him"*
> (GENESIS 4:8).

RELATIONSHIP #3
Between the Philistines, Delilah, and Samson
– The Philistines: _____

> *"The rulers of the Philistines went to her and said, 'See if you can*
> *lure him into showing you the secret of his great strength and how*
> *we can overpower him so we may tie him up and subdue him.*
> *Each one of us will give you eleven hundred shekels of silver'"*
> (JUDGES 16:5).

– Delilah: _____

> *"Then she said to him, 'How can you say, "I love you,"*
> *when you won't confide in me? This is the third time you*
> *have made a fool of me and haven't told me the secret*
> *of your great strength.' With such nagging she prodded*
> *him day after day until he was sick to death of it"*
> (JUDGES 16:15-16).

– Samson: _____

> *"So he told her everything. 'No razor has ever been used on my*
> *head,' he said, 'because I have been a Nazirite dedicated to God*
> *from my mother's womb. If my head were shaved, my strength*
> *would leave me, and I would become as weak as any other man'"*
> (JUDGES 16:17).

RELATIONSHIP #4
King Saul toward David
– King Saul: _____

> *"[Saul] raved within his house while David was playing*
> *the lyre, as he did day by day. Saul had his spear in his*
> *hand. And Saul hurled the spear, for he thought, 'I will*
> *pin David to the wall.' But David evaded him twice"*
>
> (1 SAMUEL 18:10-11 ESV).

RELATIONSHIP #5

King David toward Bathsheba

— King David: _____

> *"This is what the LORD, the God of Israel, says... 'Why did*
> *you despise the word of the LORD by doing what is evil in*
> *his eyes? You struck down Uriah the Hittite with the sword*
> *and took his wife to be your own. You killed him with the*
> *sword of the Ammonites. Now, therefore, the sword will*
> *never depart from your house, because you despised me and*
> *took the wife of Uriah the Hittite to be your own'"*
>
> (2 SAMUEL 12:7,9-10).

RELATIONSHIP #6

The Pharisees toward Jesus

— Pharisees: _____

> *"Then Jesus said to the crowds and to his disciples... 'Woe*
> *to you, teachers of the law and Pharisees, you hypocrites!*
> *You shut the door of the kingdom of heaven in people's*
> *faces. You yourselves do not enter, nor will you let those*
> *enter who are trying to... You snakes! You brood of vipers!*
> *How will you escape being condemned to hell?'"*
>
> (MATTHEW 23:1,13,33).

RELATIONSHIP #7

Pilate toward Jesus

— Pilate: _____

> *"On hearing this, Pilate asked if the man was a Galilean.*
> *When he learned that Jesus was under Herod's jurisdiction, he*
> *sent him to Herod, who was also in Jerusalem at that time"*
>
> (LUKE 23:6-7).

RELATIONSHIP #8

Judas toward Jesus

– Judas: _____

> *"Judas Iscariot...asked, 'What are you willing*
> *to give me if I deliver him over to you?' So they*
> *counted out for him thirty pieces of silver"*
> (MATTHEW 26:14-15).

RELATIONSHIP #9

Martha toward Jesus

– Martha: _____

> *"But Martha was distracted by all the preparations that had to be*
> *made. She came to him and asked, 'Lord, don't you care that my*
> *sister has left me to do the work by myself? Tell her to help me!'"*
> (LUKE 10:40).

RELATIONSHIP #10

Peter toward Jesus

– Peter: _____

> *"Now Peter was sitting out in the courtyard, and a servant girl*
> *came to him. 'You also were with Jesus of Galilee,' she said. But*
> *he denied it before them all. 'I don't know what you're talking*
> *about,' he said. Then he went out to the gateway, where another*
> *servant girl saw him and said to the people there, 'This fellow was*
> *with Jesus of Nazareth.' He denied it again, with an oath: 'I don't*
> *know the man!' After a little while, those standing there went up*
> *to Peter and said, 'Surely you are one of them; your accent gives*
> *you away.' Then he began to call down curses, and he swore to*
> *them, 'I don't know the man!' Immediately a rooster crowed"*
> (MATTHEW 26:69-74).

ANSWERS

Eve: She is an avoider—a *weasel.*

– She tried to weasel out of accepting responsibility for her wrong choices by blaming the serpent.

Cain: He is an attacker—a *wolf*.

- He became angry and killed his brother when God chastised him regarding his offering.

The Philistines: They are attackers—*wolves*.

- They were predators waiting to conquer their prey, Samson.

Delilah: She is an attacker—a *snake*.

- She accepted a bribe from the Philistines to trap Samson.

Samson: He is an avoider—a *chameleon*.

- He told the secret of his strength just to please Delilah.

King Saul: He is an attacker—a *wolf*.

- He was jealous of David.

King David: He is an avoider—a *turtle*.

- He sought to keep his affair with Bathsheba a secret from her husband, Uriah.

The Pharisees: They are attackers—*snakes*.

- They sought to control everyone with laws. They accused Jesus of blasphemy.

Pilate: He is an avoider—a *chameleon*.

- He knew Jesus was innocent, yet condemned Him to death to please the crowd.

Judas: He is an attacker—a *snake*.

- He betrayed Jesus for 30 pieces of silver.

Martha: She is an attacker—a *hornet*.

- She complained to Jesus about her sister Mary.

Peter: He is an avoider—a *turtle*.

- He denied ever knowing Jesus.

An Unparalleled Appeal: The Abigail and David Story

This conflict is ready to become a full-blown catastrophe....

David, God's appointed heir to the throne, has acquired a sizeable army. However, this young warrior is on the run from Israel's current ruler, jealous King Saul, who is chasing his successor through the wilderness and literally trying to kill him.

For a brief time, David and his men set up camp to guard the livestock, possessions, and workers of a wealthy hothead named Nabal. When sheep-shearing season arrives, they expect a "pay day" for the protection they offer to Nabal.

That day finally arrives, and David is in a festive mood. He sends ten of his men to warmly greet Nabal, who happens to be drunk and feasting, and to ask for the well-deserved supplies in exchange for their protection. However, Nabal, known to be "surly and mean in his dealings,"[18] is anything but festive: "Who is this David? Who is this son of Jesse?... Why should I take my bread and water, and the meat I have slaughtered for my shearers, and give it to men coming from who knows where?"[19]

"Who is this David?" What a foolish question! Nabal knows precisely who David is. But then, the name *Nabal* literally means "fool"—and he certainly lives up to his name. In reality, his foolishness is further displayed by a lack of reverence for God.

Outraged and offended by the injustice, David with 400 of his men plans to descend upon Nabal's household, armed to shed the blood of every male. As David embarks on the deadly journey, Nabal's wife, Abigail, becomes aware of what has occurred. Immediately, she begins crafting a shrewd strategy to resolve the conflict.

Described as "intelligent and beautiful," Abigail is also exceptionally wise and diplomatic. She knows she must approach David quickly to plead for mercy and forgiveness. Her first wise move is *sending a peace offering* ahead—a delectable buffet of food and wine in an effort to soften the impact of Nabal's insult. Her second sensible step is *keeping strategically silent* about her plans.

Then *demonstrating humility*, Abigail finally encounters David and bows down with her face to the ground, physically falling at his feet. Though one of the land's wealthiest and most influential women, she also humbles herself verbally. She invites David to place the blame of Nabal's arrogant affront onto her (an offer she likely realizes David will refuse to do).

Then, she asks for permission to speak. This discerning woman calls him "my lord" and refers to herself as his *"servant."* She pleads, "Pardon your servant, my lord, and let me speak to you; hear what your servant has to say. Please pay no attention, my lord, to that wicked man Nabal. He is just like his name—his name means Fool, and folly goes with him."[20]

Some may say Abigail's unvarnished words dishonor her husband, but Scripture offers no such condemnation. Instead she clearly communicates that she understands the enormity of his offense. *Speaking the truth boldly* by neither defending nor downplaying Nabal's unacceptable behavior, Abigail skillfully defuses David's fury. (Many wives unwisely defend their husband's bad behavior, calling it loyalty. However, they completely lose credibility in the eyes of others because they blindly side with wrong, not with right.)

A student of human motivation, Abigail factors into her appeal a keen awareness of David's priorities—*establishing the true priorities*—when she reminds him, "The LORD your God will certainly make a lasting dynasty for my lord, because you fight the LORD's battles, and no wrongdoing will be found in you as long as you live. Even though someone is pursuing you to take your life…the lives of your enemies he will hurl away as from the pocket of a sling."[21]

Another act of wisdom is *remembering God's prior faithfulness*. Abigail's astute analogy further reminds David of how God earlier empowered him to defeat Goliath with a slingshot!

This marvelous mediator is also aware that godly character calls for *considering the long-range consequences* of one's decisions. So Abigail, *appealing to honor and reputation*, suggests that, when David becomes king someday, he won't want to have an avoidable massacre troubling his conscience: "When the LORD has fulfilled for my lord every good thing he promised concerning him and has appointed him ruler over Israel, my lord will not have on his conscience the staggering burden of needless bloodshed or of having avenged himself."[22]

As Abigail makes her plea, grounded in objectivity and reality, the catastrophic conflict is averted. David turns from potential assailant to praising admirer, commending Abigail for her wisdom that leads to a peaceful resolution. "May you be blessed for your good judgment and for keeping me from bloodshed this day and from avenging myself with my own hands...Go home in peace. I have heard your words and granted your request."[23]

In the end, Abigail and Nabal experience two very different destinies. When Abigail tells Nabal all that transpired, "his heart failed him and he became like a stone."[24] Ten days later, God strikes him dead.

When David hears the news, he understands that the Lord has acknowledged his right response. "Praise be to the LORD who has upheld my cause against Nabal for treating me with contempt. He has kept his servant from doing wrong and has brought Nabal's wrongdoing down on his own head."[25]

David's recognition that slaying Nabal in a fit of rage would have been "wrong" demonstrates just how beneficial Abigail's intervention has been—not only for her own household, but for David as well. And it reminds David of God's ability to protect and defend him from his enemies—a timely testimony, given David's status as an innocent fugitive from murderous King Saul.

The unforgettable example of Abigail and David shows us how practicing biblical principles can resolve even the most serious conflict. Through her astute employment of initiative, truth, humility, and diplomacy, Abigail provides a powerful lesson on how to transform a mortal enemy into a merciful ally.

III. CAUSES OF CONFLICT

First comes the affair, then murder—and ultimately, chaos and confusion throughout the kingdom.

David, King of Israel, is described in the Bible as a man after God's own heart, but one very dark season is nothing short of disaster. God forgives David for an affair with a beautiful woman named Bathsheba, and He forgives David for having her husband, Uriah, murdered so that he can take her as his wife, but there are consequences—*catastrophic* consequences—for his sinful behavior.

Through the prophet Nathan, God tells David, "Now, therefore, the sword will never depart from your house, because you despised me and took the wife of Uriah the Hittite to be your own...Out of your own household I am going to bring calamity upon you" (2 Samuel 12:10-11).

A. Why Are Some People Attackers, and Others Avoiders?

A vile deed has been committed, and Absalom vows to attack the attacker.

Tamar, the beautiful sister of Absalom, is raped by their half-brother Amnon, and Absalom's heart becomes filled with hate. King David, their father, is furious over the twisted and tragic family scenario but avoids legal conflict. He does not have Amnon punished as prescribed by the law.

For Absalom, there is only one misguided course to resolve this conflict— *kill Amnon*—which is precisely what he has his trusted men do two years later. Absalom flees and David is overwhelmed with grief concerning the death of his firstborn, but David's continued role as an avoider prompts Absalom to resume the role of an attacker. How different their relationship might have been if only David had reflected the heart of God and reached out to resolve the conflict between him and Absalom:

> *"If it is possible, as far as it depends on you,*
> *live at peace with everyone"*
> (ROMANS 12:18).

Everyone has it, no one wants it, and no one can escape it! What is it? One common denominator for us all is *conflict*. But where does this conflict come from? People act the way they act as a result of a combination of factors. The Bible says,

> *"Whoever loves a quarrel loves sin"*
> (PROVERBS 17:19).

- **Natural temperament** or personality types
    - You were born with a natural bent toward being outgoing or reserved, compliant or defiant, aggressive or passive.
    - Your temperament/personality traits can work to your advantage or disadvantage, depending on whether you learn to use them productively in resolving conflicts or destructively in creating conflicts.

> *"Not that we are competent in ourselves to claim anything*
> *for ourselves, but our competence comes from God"*
> (2 CORINTHIANS 3:5).

- **Early childhood experiences**
    - You were deeply influenced by your early family relationships through words you heard and behaviors you saw, which gave

you messages about who you are and what you do and how to respond to conflict.

– You can change the assumptions you adopted about yourself and about conflict resolution that are influencing your behavior today by identifying the messages you received while growing up in your family and evaluating whether they are helpful or harmful.

> *"Let us discern for ourselves what is right;*
> *let us learn together what is good"*
> (Job 34:4).

• **Physical factors**

– You were born with certain physical characteristics, such as brain chemistry, that may be affecting the way you respond to the rush of adrenaline experienced during times of conflict.

– You can have a thorough medical checkup. When experiencing a conflict, you may even want to have an evaluation performed on your brain chemistry. Did you know that you can learn ways to actually change the chemistry of your brain if it is causing you problems in conflict resolution?

> *"Do not conform to the pattern of this world, but be*
> *transformed by the renewing of your mind. Then you will be*
> *able to test and approve what God's will is—his good, pleasing*
> *and perfect will...Finally, brothers and sisters, whatever is*
> *true, whatever is noble, whatever is right, whatever is pure,*
> *whatever is lovely, whatever is admirable—if anything is*
> *excellent or praiseworthy—think about such things"*
> (Romans 12:2; Philippians 4:8).

• **Learned behaviors**

– You may have *unintentionally* learned negative ways of responding to conflict from the negative people in your life, especially those who are attackers or avoiders.

– You can also *intentionally* "unlearn" negative patterns by learning new behaviors, including learning from those who embrace conflict as a fact of life and who find ways of productively resolving it.

> *"Let the wise listen and add to their learning,*
> *and let the discerning get guidance"*
> (PROVERBS 1:5).

B. What Goals Drive Attackers and Avoiders?

Absalom is away from his home, Jerusalem, for three years, without a single overture from his father, King David.

The dismissing, the devastating abandonment, churns Absalom's emotions into a chaotic concoction of bitterness, anger, and rebellion. The heat is turned up when an official of Israel prompts David to send for Absalom, and upon his return David refuses to see him for another two years. The king's instructions: "He must go to his own house; he must not see my face" (2 Samuel 14:24).

As an attacker, Absalom's foremost goal is to feel significant to his father, but that goal is thoroughly thwarted with David's avoidance of him. The king, on the other hand, manifests a classic goal of an avoider—to feel safe. Rather than responsibly confronting Absalom, David chooses to withdraw like a turtle, to wall himself off emotionally from his estranged son.

Both men would have benefitted from remembering this promise in Scripture:

> *"The LORD will guide you always; he will satisfy your needs [goals]"*
> (ISAIAH 58:11).

Unmet goals become the driving force behind why we act the way we do when we are faced with a conflict. The challenge, of course, is to find a way to get our legitimate goals and needs met legitimately rather than illegitimately. This can be accomplished through a personal, intimate relationship with Jesus Christ. The Bible says,

> *"His divine power has given to us all things that*
> *pertain to life and godliness, through the knowledge*
> *of Him who called us by glory and virtue"*
> (2 PETER 1:3 NKJV).

ATTACKERS FEEL INSIGNIFICANT

- **Wolves** have a goal to feel *powerful.*
  - Children who grow up feeling insignificant within their families typically become driven by the need to feel significant. This drive can result in finding destructive ways of meeting this need.

— Children who feel powerless can develop aggressive tactics to overpower others. These newly developed wolves become fiercely competitive in order to feel like true winners. They become dictatorial in order to feel powerful. Thus, their need to feel significant is met—temporarily.

- **Serpents** have a goal to feel *superior*.

   — Children who grow up experiencing put-downs regularly and are the target of belittling comments may become driven by the need to overcome feelings of inferiority.

   — Children who feel inferior can become behind-the-scenes backbiters. These newly developed serpents spread poisonous rumors in order to feel superior to others—temporarily.

- **Hornets** have a goal to feel *valuable*.

   — Children who grow up being told that "children are to be seen but not heard" or whose opinions and feelings were discounted can become driven by the need to feel valuable, to be heard and understood.

   — Children who feel devalued can develop negative attitudes. Making constant complaints is a way to get the ear of others, leaving these newly developed hornets feeling valuable enough to be heard and understood—temporarily.

Instead of being an unfulfilled attacker, the Bible lets us know that when we yield our will to His will we experience a life of true significance.

> *"Now that you have been set free from sin and have become slaves of God, the benefit you reap leads to holiness, and the result is eternal life"*
> (ROMANS 6:22).

AVOIDERS FEEL INSECURE

- **Tortoises** have a goal to feel *safe*.

   — Children who grow up in homes where anger is unrestrained, where conflict goes unresolved, and where few positive interactive experiences occur typically become driven by the need for peace.

   — Children who don't feel safe typically make being safe their life goal, seeking to protect themselves from dangerous people. By turning inward and emotionally walling themselves off from others, these newly developed tortoises feel a sense of safety—temporarily.

- **Chameleons** have a goal to feel *accepted*.
    - Children who grow up with criticism and negative feedback from significant adults in their lives and who don't receive appropriate compliments and praise can become driven by the need for acceptance.
    - Children starved for acceptance can become classic people-pleasers. They do whatever they think is necessary to make and keep everyone happy and to avoid being criticized or rejected, leaving these newly developed chameleons feeling accepted—temporarily.

- **Weasels** have a goal to feel *confident*.
    - Children who grow up with an overprotective, overcontrolling parent and who have no firm boundaries or personal accountability for their actions typically become driven by the need for confidence.
    - Children who lack courage to take a stand find that becoming shrewd and evasive rather than honest and forthright keeps them "out of trouble." This leaves these newly developed weasels with a sense of confidence and courage—temporarily.

To the person who is an insecure avoider, the Bible says,

> *"The LORD will be your confidence,*
> *And will keep your foot from being caught"*
> (PROVERBS 3:26 NKJV).

C. What Is the Root Cause of Negative Conflict?

A sense of significance…

Absalom doesn't receive it from his father, and he doesn't claim it from his Creator; therefore, he pursues it for himself. After wooing the citizens of Israel by generously dispensing princely kisses and offering to sit as judge of their grievances, Absalom leads a revolt against his father, the king, and a national power play ensues.

A dire message is delivered to King David: "The hearts of the people of Israel are with Absalom" (2 Samuel 15:13). And just as David had fled emotionally from his son, now he flees physically, fearing that Absalom "will move quickly to overtake us and bring ruin on us and put the city to the sword" (2 Samuel 15:14).

But the coup will conclude with God's bringing ruin upon Absalom, who has become a *wolf.*

> *"For the LORD Almighty has purposed, and who can thwart him?*
> *His hand is stretched out, and who can turn it back?"*
> (ISAIAH 14:27).

THREE GOD-GIVEN INNER NEEDS

We have all been created with three God-given inner needs: the needs for love, significance, and security.[26]

- **Love**—to know that someone is unconditionally committed to our best interest

> *"My command is this: Love each other as I have loved you"*
> (JOHN 15:12).

- **Significance**—to know that our lives have meaning and purpose

> *"I cry out to God Most High, to God who fulfills his purpose for me"*
> (PSALM 57:2 ESV).

- **Security**—to feel accepted and a sense of belonging

> *"Whoever fears the LORD has a secure fortress,*
> *and for their children it will be a refuge"*
> (PROVERBS 14:26).

THE ULTIMATE NEED-MEETER

Why did God give us these deep inner needs, knowing that people and self-effort fail us?

God gave us these inner needs so that we would come to know Him as our Need-meeter. Our needs are designed by God to draw us into a deeper dependence on Christ. God did not create any person or position, or any amount of power or possessions to meet the deepest needs in our lives. If a person or thing *could* meet all our needs, we wouldn't need God! The Lord will use circumstances and bring positive people into our lives as an extension of His care and compassion, but ultimately only God can satisfy all the needs of our hearts. The Bible says,

> *"The LORD will guide you always;*
> *he will satisfy your needs in a sun-scorched land*
> *and will strengthen your frame.*
> *You will be like a well-watered garden,*
> *like a spring whose waters never fail"*
> (ISAIAH 58:11).

The apostle Paul revealed this truth by first asking, "What a wretched man I am. Who will rescue me from this body that is subject to death?" He then answers his own question by saying he is saved by "Jesus Christ our Lord!" (Romans 7:24-25).

All along, the Lord planned to meet our deepest needs for…

- **Love**—"I [the Lord] have loved you with an everlasting love; I have drawn you with unfailing kindness" (Jeremiah 31:3).

- **Significance**—"'I know the plans I have for you,' declares the LORD, 'plans to prosper you and not to harm you, plans to give you hope and a future'" (Jeremiah 29:11).

- **Security**—"The LORD himself goes before you and will be with you; he will never leave you nor forsake you. Do not be afraid; do not be discouraged" (Deuteronomy 31:8).

The truth is that our God-given needs for love, significance, and security can be legitimately met—in Christ Jesus! Philippians 4:19 makes it plain: "My God will meet all your needs according to the riches of his glory in Christ Jesus."

The reason we all experience conflict is rooted in a system of wrong beliefs. We assume that what we want is what we need, and that it is up to us to defeat those who oppose us. After all, if we don't protect our interests, who will? This fear-based thinking causes us to respond by either attacking or avoiding people we perceive to be threatening to us.[27]

- **WRONG BELIEF FOR ATTACKERS:**

  "I have the right to have my way by whatever means. In order to feel significant, I must attack and conquer."

- **WRONG BELIEF FOR ATTACKERS:**

"Everyone is out for himself."

- **WRONG BELIEF FOR AVOIDERS:**

"I am afraid of conflict because it makes me feel insecure. In order to feel secure, I must find some way to avoid conflict or get rid of it."

- **WRONG BELIEF FOR AVOIDERS:**

"If I stand up for myself, I won't be loved."

- **RIGHT BELIEF FOR ATTACKERS AND AVOIDERS:**

"I know that conflict is a natural result of living with different types of people. My sense of significance and security are based on the fact that God loves me, He created me with a plan and purpose, and Jesus was willing to die for me."

> *"There is no fear in love. But perfect love drives out fear, because fear has to do with punishment. The one who fears is not made perfect in love"*
> (1 JOHN 4:18).

D. What Causes the Worst Conflict?

The *statement* "I am against you" (Ezekiel 26:3) is among the most frightening phrases uttered by God in all of Scripture.

Whether it be directed toward a person, city, or nation, the implication is that the all-powerful God of the universe is about to execute judgment, and He won't be staved off. Simply put, you don't stand a chance, barring the merciful retrieval of His outstretched hand. But in Absalom's case, there is no merciful retrieval. God's plan is in place "to bring disaster on Absalom" (2 Samuel 17:14).

While riding on a mule in the midst of battle, Absalom's long, flowing hair gets caught in the large branches of an oak tree and the mule rides off, leaving Absalom hanging. He is still alive until David's military commander plunges three javelins into his heart and soldiers strike and kill him. News of Absalom's death stirs even greater disorder in the kingdom, and King David is, once again, awash with grief over the death of a son. "O my son Absalom! My son, my son Absalom! If only I had died instead of you—O Absalom, my son, my son!" (2 Samuel 18:33).

Death, disorder, and disaster—all prophesied by Nathan and all stemming from David's disobedience in having another man killed and then taking his wife for his own.

> *"Obey me, and I will be your God and you will be my people.*
> *Walk in obedience to all I command you,*
> *that it may go well with you"*
> (JEREMIAH 7:23).

Conflict with people is one matter, but conflict with God is another. Why is conflict with God the *worst* conflict? Can you imagine the hands of a watch refusing to function as the watchmaker designed them to function? What if the hands of a watch moved in the opposite direction? The watch would be useless.

You were created by the Master Designer, who has a plan and purpose for you. In fact, His plan and deep desire is to have a meaningful relationship with you. When you enter into a relationship with Him, He will fulfill the very purpose for which you were created. The Lord says,

> *"I know the plans I have for you...*
> *plans to prosper you and not to harm you,*
> *plans to give you hope and a future"*
> (JEREMIAH 29:11).

How to Resolve Your Conflict with God

To resolve your conflict with God, there are four spiritual truths you need to know, which are listed on pages 48-50.

The History of Dueling: The Aaron Burr Story

Today it seems so inconceivable, uncivilized! Yet for a long time, many considered it the "gentlemen's way" to settle differences.

Dueling was all about men defending their honor. From the Roman Empire through the Renaissance to the late 1800s, dueling laws containing specific codes of honor were officially sanctioned. A European document known as the *Code Duello* detailed 25 official rules that governed the one-on-one potentially deadly contest. (The number of rules varied from place to place: the Irish code contained 25, whereas the French code, 84.) Then in 1838,

South Carolina Governor John Lyde Wilson developed an American version of the code.[28]

The man being challenged to duel was typically approached by a "second," a person who served as an intermediary who tried to resolve the conflict peacefully. With the grievance communicated to the single person who offended the challenger, and with the site of the duel established, if the man who was challenged apologized publicly to the offended party through the efforts of the second or if he were to make an acceptable restitution, the conflict would be resolved. But if the recipient of the challenge instead chose to duel, he would select the time and the weapons, as well as agree to a location (the field of honor) for the showdown. Accompanied by a doctor for each side, the seconds of both parties (typically three for each) would continue to seek a peaceful resolution all the way up until the last moment.[29]

Averting a duel wasn't easy, particularly in the South. Men who refused to duel were labeled cowards and their pictures were posted publicly.

Abraham Lincoln received such a challenge. Lincoln had ridiculed James Shields in an Illinois newspaper; therefore, this state auditor challenged Lincoln to a duel. Lincoln even went as far as to select both the dueling site and the sword as his weapon of choice. But then he averted the duel by apologizing to his bitter political rival. Consequently, his apology prevented the potential deadly outcome.[30] This all took place prior to Lincoln's presidency, so you can imagine how the course of American history would have been altered if Lincoln had been killed!

But the duel that shocks the nation is the one between Alexander Hamilton, the United States' first Secretary of the Treasury, and Aaron Burr, vice president under Thomas Jefferson. Like Lincoln and Shields, these two have become bitter political rivals due to several heated battles.

On the morning of July 11, 1804, the two men walk onto the official dueling grounds at Weehawken, New Jersey. Both of their seconds fail to reach a peaceful resolution, so Hamilton and Burr each clutch an official .56 dueling pistol.[31] Undoubtedly both of their minds are rehearsing their sizable history of hostility, dating back to 1791 when Burr won a Senate seat previously held by Hamilton's powerful father-in-law, Philip Schuyler.

Then in 1800, Senator Burr obtains a private document written by opponent Federalist Hamilton, a paper critical of another Federalist, John Adams, who just happened to be the current second president of the United States! Burr publishes Hamilton's sensitive document, which is clearly intended to stay private. Ultimately, this public posting not only becomes embarrassing for Hamilton, but also further splinters the Federalist party.

Four years later Burr runs for governor of New York, a political move that enrages Hamilton. He certainly doesn't want his archenemy running such a powerful state, so Hamilton strongly lobbies against him. But the final straw is the fallout from a dinner conversation.

New Yorker Dr. Charles Cooper attends a dinner where Hamilton is brazenly belittling Burr, whom Dr. Cooper immensely admires. The doctor writes a letter to Hamilton's influential father-in-law criticizing his son-in-law's "despicable opinion" of Burr. All too soon, that fateful letter winds up being published in a New York newspaper.[32]

Shortly afterward, Burr challenges Hamilton to a duel. Each man fires a shot. Burr is unscathed, but Hamilton drops to the ground with a bullet piercing his liver and spine. He dies the next day.

While Burr had hoped a victory on the dueling field would energize his languishing political career, instead, he is charged with two counts of murder.[33] (By this time, dueling had been outlawed in New Jersey and New York.) Later, the charges were dropped.

Ultimately, everyone loses: Burr loses his credibility, and Hamilton loses his life. That is what happens when people refuse to resolve conflict.

So what do you do if someone insults you, slanders you, hounds you? In total truth, have you ever said, "I can't help it! If someone slaps me, I have to slap back! If someone hits me, I have to hit back. If someone strikes me, I have to strike back"? Realize that just because someone *starts* something doesn't mean you have to *finish* it. Just because people take you on doesn't mean you have to accept the challenge.

Think about Hamilton: He was challenged to a duel. He accepted the challenge and needlessly lost his life. Did he think death wasn't a possibility? Oh, assuredly he did! For in 1801—just three years prior—his eldest son Philip had died in a duel.

God's Word is crystal clear: Conflicts should be approached with a heart of peace. Romans 12:18 says, "If it is possible, as far as it depends on you, live at peace with everyone." And 1 Peter 3:9 explicitly states, "Do not repay evil with evil or insult with insult. On the contrary, repay evil with blessing" (1 Peter 3:9). We are then told, "To this you were called." In other words, it's a command. Why are we asked to live this way? "So that you may inherit a blessing."

IV. Steps to Solution

He is a runaway slave, but now he is also a brother.

Operating at first as a *snake*, it appears Onesimus may have taken a swipe at his master's bank account and stolen his money. Philemon, his master and fellow worker with the apostle Paul, most certainly has suffered financial loss. But then Onesimus transforms into a *turtle*, avoiding ownership of any wrongdoing and flees. The name *Onesimus* means "useful, beneficial," but Philemon can testify through what he has experienced that the man doesn't live up to his name.[34]

But that is before Onesimus meets Paul. A divine appointment occurs in Rome, and Philemon's slave becomes sold out for Christ. Now part of the family of God, Onesimus is a spiritual brother to both Paul and Philemon.

The apostle assures Philemon that true spiritual transformation has occurred, that Onesimus indeed is now living up to his name.

> *"Formerly he was useless to you,*
> *but now he has become useful both to you and to me"*
> (Philemon 11).

A. Key Verse to Memorize

Paul recognizes there is a conflict to be resolved, and he becomes the mediator for reconciliation. Onesimus may now be Philemon's brother in Christ, but the absent-without-leave slave has also been a drain on his master's finances. In sending Onesimus back to Philemon, Paul is concerned about how the runaway slave-turned-saint will be received. In a very personal overture, indicative of the deep bond that has formed between the two men, Paul writes, "I am sending him—who is my very heart—back to you" (Philemon 12).

Paul reminds Philemon that, based on Paul's apostolic authority, he could "order you to do what you ought to do" (Philemon 8). But Paul wants to make his appeal in love instead. He entreats Philemon: "So if you consider me a partner, welcome him as you would welcome me" (Philemon 17).

> *"Let us therefore make every effort to do what leads to peace*
> *and to mutual edification"*
> (ROMANS 14:19).

B. Key Passage to Read

The apostle Paul now takes an additional step to resolve the conflict, providing a beautiful illustration of our divine reckoning through Christ.

Paul instructs Philemon, "If he has done you any wrong or owes you anything, charge it to me. I, Paul, am writing this with my own hand. I will pay it back" (Philemon 18-19). Paul's willingness to have Onesimus's debt imputed or reckoned against his own account is a reminder of our sins being imputed or reckoned against Jesus' righteous account, enabling us to stand blameless before the Father in Christ's righteousness.

10 PRINCIPLES FOR FACING CONFLICT

Philemon

1. Appreciation

Acknowledge positive attributes and actions . . . . verses 4-7

2. Humility

Don't speak from a position of power or authority
but of equality. . . . . verse 8

3. Love

Appeal for a resolution on the basis of love. . . . . verse 9

4. Integrity

Be absolutely honest about the problems. . . . . verses 10-11

5. Vulnerability

Share your feelings and your heart's desire . . . . verses 12-13

6. Mutuality

Don't force or coerce but defer and seek agreement . . . . . . verse 14

7. Optimism

Expect the best of another . . . . verse 14

8. Faith

Recognize and trust the sovereign hand of God. . . . . . verses 15-16

9. Forgiveness

Release the past and receive God's plan for
the future. . . . . verses 17-20

10. Exhortation

Express confidence in God's ability to bring
about resolution. . . . . verse 21

C. How to Hit the Target

The scene is chaotic. Confusion reigns as thousands of Ephesians "rushed into the theater" (Acts 19:29), the community gathering place.

They seize Gaius and Aristarchus, Paul's traveling companions, but their primary target is absent from the scene. The assembly is not only unruly, it's illegal, and amidst shouts of one kind or another, the irony is that "most of the people did not even know why they were there" (Acts 19:32).

The city's chief executive officer manages to quiet the crowd and leads the raucous citizens down the road to resolution. He appeals to reason to put a brake on runaway emotions, and immediately thereafter the assembly is dismissed. What did he say? Here are his conflict-solving words:

> *"If, then, Demetrius and his fellow craftsmen have a grievance*
> *against anybody,*
> *the courts are open and there are proconsuls.*
> *They can press charges.*
> *If there is anything further you want to bring up,*
> *it must be settled in a legal assembly.*
> *As it is, we are in danger of being charged with rioting because of*
> *what happened today.*
> *In that case we would not be able to account for this commotion,*
> *since there is no reason for it"*
> (Acts 19:38-40).

HITTING THE TARGET

Target #1—A New Purpose: God's purpose for me is to be conformed to the character of Christ.

> *"Those God foreknew he also predestined to be
> conformed to the image of his Son"*
> (Romans 8:29).

— "I'll do whatever it takes to be conformed to the character of Christ."

Target #2—A New Priority: God's priority for me is to change my thinking.

> *"Do not conform to the pattern of this world, but be
> transformed by the renewing of your mind"*
> (Romans 12:2).

— "I'll do whatever it takes to line up my thinking with God's thinking."

Target #3—A New Plan: God's plan for me is to rely on Christ's strength, not my strength, and to be all He created me to be.

> *"I can do all things through Christ who strengthens me"*
> (Philippians 4:13 nkjv).

— "I'll do whatever it takes to fulfill His plan in His strength."

My Personalized Plan

Conflict—it happens to all of us. Two of God's premier workers in the early days of the church, Paul and Barnabas, have "a sharp disagreement" (Acts 15:39), resulting in each going their separate ways. The cause for contention is that Barnabas wants to take his cousin John Mark along with Paul as they revisit cities where they have ministered.

Paul disagrees, mindful that John Mark deserted them on a previous mission trip. John Mark has obviously regained the trust of Barnabas, but not of Paul. Their differences are resolved by the launching of two separate missionary journeys instead of one, with Barnabas and his cousin going to Cyprus, and Paul and Silas going to Syria and Cilicia. Yet later Paul made this significant statement:

> *"I appeal to you…that all of you agree with one another"*
> (1 Corinthians 1:10).

As you prepare to walk the road to resolution of a conflict, remember to…

- **Pledge** your commitment.

    — "I am committed to this relationship."

    — "I am committed to reconciliation, if at all possible."

> *"If it is possible, as far as it depends on*
> *you, live at peace with everyone"*
> (Romans 12:18).

- **Pray** for yourself and your opposer.

    — "Lord, please show us the true issue."

    — "Reveal any personal errors we need to face."

    — "Prepare both my heart and the heart of (_name_) to be open."

> *"Search me, God, and know my heart; test me and*
> *know my anxious thoughts. See if there is any offensive*
> *way in me, and lead me in the way everlasting"*
> (Psalm 139:23-24).

- **Prepare** before you ask for a meeting.

    — Discern the root cause of the conflict.

    — Examine your expectations, anticipate possible reactions, and plan your responses.

    — Decide on positive solutions, but plan an alternative if negotiations fail.

    — Use the Sandwich Technique (described on page 273).

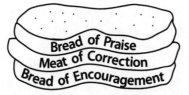

Bread of Praise
Meat of Correction
Bread of Encouragement

> *"Let us examine our ways and test them,*
> *and let us return to the Lord"*
> (Lamentations 3:40).

- **Propose** a time to talk face-to-face.

    — "I care about our relationship. Is it possible for us to have some time to talk?"

    – "I feel that there are some unresolved issues that need to be dealt with positively."

> *"Make every effort to keep the unity of the*
> *Spirit through the bond of peace"*
> (EPHESIANS 4:3).

- **Provide** a private place.
    - Away from people
    - Away from distractions

> *"If your brother or sister sins, go and point out*
> *their fault, just between the two of you. If they*
> *listen to you, you have won them over"*
> (MATTHEW 18:15).

- **Purpose** to be honest.[35]
    - Take responsibility for your actions
    - See the other person's viewpoint

> *"An honest witness tells the truth, but a false witness tells lies"*
> (PROVERBS 12:17).

- **Permit** total forgiveness.
    - Choose to forgive any hurts
    - Don't mentally rehearse the faults of the other person
    - Allow God to reestablish a bond of love

> *"Bear with each other and forgive one another if any*
> *of you has a grievance against someone. Forgive as the*
> *Lord forgave you. And over all these virtues put on love,*
> *which binds them all together in perfect unity"*
> (COLOSSIANS 3:13-14).

- **Perceive** a future harvest.
    - You are sowing seeds that may not take root until later
    - Change is a process

– What you sow, you reap!

> *"Let us not become weary in doing good, for at the proper*
> *time we will reap a harvest if we do not give up"*
> (GALATIANS 6:9).

• **Present** the present conflict.
  – Don't bring up the past
  – Keep the conversation on the present conflict

> *"[Love]…keeps no record of wrongs"*
> (1 CORINTHIANS 13:5).

• **Promote** fairness and objectivity.

  – Avoid generalizations and stick to the facts
  – Mention both positives and negatives

> *"Do not pervert justice; do not show partiality to the poor or*
> *favoritism to the great, but judge your neighbor fairly"*
> (LEVITICUS 19:15).

• **Protect** your privacy.

  – Don't involve outsiders
  – Control your tongue when you are with other people

> *"A gossip betrays a confidence, but a*
> *trustworthy person keeps a secret"*
> (PROVERBS 11:13).

• **Preserve** individuality.

  – Value differences in goals, desires, and priorities
  – Don't demand "like-thinking"

> *"I too will have my say; I too will tell what I know"*
> (JOB 32:17).

- **Project** openness and optimism.

    – Exhibit positive body language

    – Use "I" statements and make good eye contact

    > *"Therefore encourage one another and build each*
    > *other up, just as in fact you are doing"*
    > (1 THESSALONIANS 5:11).

- **Practice** love.

    – End with an appropriate physical expression (a firm handshake, hug, or a pat on the back)

    – Express appreciation, care, and love

    > *"A friend loves at all times, and a brother*
    > *is born for a time of adversity"*
    > (PROVERBS 17:17).

D. How to Apply the "Five W's and an H"

Should they, or shouldn't they?

False teachers in the early church are misguiding new Gentile converts, saying they have to be circumcised in order to be saved. Paul and Barnabas, who planted the churches in which this dissension is stirring, sharply disagree and travel to Jerusalem to settle the issue with church leadership.

After the apostles and elders discuss the divisive matter, the apostle Peter, head of the Jerusalem church, proclaims, "We believe it is through the grace of our Lord Jesus that we are saved, just as they are" (Acts 15:11).

Two church leaders then accompany Paul and Barnabas back to Antioch, carrying an authoritative letter resolving the conflict. They arrived together divided; they left together united. That's what conflict resolution is all about.

> *"How good and pleasant it is when God's*
> *people live together in unity!"*
> (PSALM 133:1).

FIVE W'S AND AN H

Before attempting to resolve a conflict, first answer the following six questions, five of which start with a "W" and one with an "H."

1. **Who?** Who is involved in the conflict?
   - Name those presently involved in the conflict.
   - List those who could be involved to bring about a resolution.

2. **What?** What is your goal?
   - Put into writing what you want to accomplish.
   - Be clear. Is this a onetime goal or a long-term goal?

3. **Why?** Why do you want to do it?
   - List the reasons for taking action.
   - List what will happen if you do not take action.

4. **Where?** Where will it happen?
   - Assess a place where you think the conflict could possibly be resolved.
   - Evaluate whether there is another suitable location where resolution could occur.

5. **When?** When do you want it finished?
   - Establish a time line from beginning to end.
   - List short-term, measurable goals.

6. **How?** How do you want it to be done?
   - List the policies and procedures that need to be put in place.
   - List the guidelines needed to accomplish the goal.

> *"The heart of the discerning acquires knowledge;*
> *for the ears of the wise seek it out"*
> (PROVERBS 18:15).

E. How to Respond When Others Are Critical of You

Conflict comes hurling at Paul one day, one stone at a time.

His Jewish brethren, proponents of legalism and opponents of the gospel of grace, spur a crowd to throw stones at Paul—a crowd that only moments before sought to offer sacrifices to him as to a god for healing a crippled man. After the stoning, Paul is dragged out of their city and left for dead:

> *"When the Jews [in Antioch] saw the crowds,*
> *they were filled with jealousy.*
> *They began to contradict what Paul was saying...*
> *Then some Jews came from Antioch and Iconium*
> *and won the crowd over.*
> *They stoned Paul and dragged him outside*
> *the city, thinking he was dead"*
> (ACTS 13:45; 14:19).

However, after the disciples gather around Paul, he gets up and goes into the city of Lystra and on to Derbe with Barnabas the next day.

As they travel, Paul and Barnabas recognize that opposition is inevitable and reassure the Christians they encounter, "Encouraging them to remain true to the faith. 'We must go through many hardships to enter the kingdom of God'" (Acts 14:22).

It happens all the time—even during the earliest years. One child hits another child...and the other child hits back! Human nature says to respond in kind to others—insult for insult, blow for blow.

Yet one of the clearest challenges mentioned multiple times in the Bible is to not respond in kind, but in the Spirit. To be Spirit-controlled rather than situation-controlled is not *natural* to human nature.

Being Spirit-controlled *becomes natural* because of the new nature a believer receives at salvation—a nature with a new ability to be conformed to the character of Christ (Romans 8:29). Undoubtedly, to counter evil with evil is natural, but to counter evil with good is the supernatural work of the Lord in you. As the apostle Paul said,

> *"Do not be overcome by evil, but overcome evil with good"*
> (ROMANS 12:21).

- **Be discerning** regarding the accuracy of the critical words of others.

  PRAY—"Lord, help me not to accept all critical words as true, nor to reject all words as lies. Enable me to discern the false from the true. Put a hedge of protection around my mind so that I reject the lies. Allow my heart to accept constructive criticism so that You may bring freedom to my life and change me."

> *"The wise in heart are called discerning, and*
> *gracious words promote instruction"*
> (PROVERBS 16:21).

- **Be open** to the slightest kernel of truth when you are criticized.

  PRAY—"Lord, if there is any truth in the critical words said about me, please convict my heart so that I might confess the problem and cooperate with You to bring about change."

> *"A rebuke impresses a discerning person*
> *more than a hundred lashes a fool"*
> (PROVERBS 17:10).

- **Be willing** to consider the criticism. If it is true, this person is God's megaphone to get your attention.

  PRAY—"Lord, I accept this criticism as Your way of teaching me something I need to know. Please reveal to me what it is You are saying to me through the criticism."

> *"The way of a fool seems right to them, but the wise listen to advice"*
> (PROVERBS 12:15).

- **Be able** to receive criticism without being defensive. Admit to any truth in the criticism—agreeing when you are in error, and then asking for further correction.

  PRAY—"Lord, I admit that I (state the offense). I agree that I was wrong. Please continue to use others to put me on a correction course when I'm off track in my attitudes or actions. And please continue to transform me more and more into the likeness of Christ."

> *"Mockers resent correction, so they avoid the wise"*
> (PROVERBS 15:12).

- **Be determined** to speak well of your critic.

  PRAY—"Lord, I yield my tongue to You. I ask that You place a guard over my mouth so that I will speak only the truth in love to (name) and will always speak well of (name) to others. I pledge to focus on the good in (name) and not on the bad."

> *"Bless those who persecute you; bless and do not curse"*
> (ROMANS 12:14).

- **Be dependent** on the Lord's perspective, not on the opinion of others, to determine your worth and value.

  PRAY—"Lord, thank You for establishing my worth and value by dying for me and adopting me into Your family. I will not live for the approval of people because I have Your approval, and that is all I need. Thank You for loving me and accepting me."

> *"Am I now trying to win the approval of human beings, or*
> *of God? Or am I trying to please people? If I were still trying*
> *to please people, I would not be a servant of Christ"*
> (GALATIANS 1:10).

F. How to Follow the "Recipe" for Conflict Resolution

You've heard the saying, "When life hands you lemons, make lemonade!" This simply means that when you find yourself in a contentious situation, a similar kind of transformation can occur as long as you add the right ingredients. By following this simple recipe, you can enjoy the sweet satisfaction of resolving bitter conflicts. The Bible says,

> *"Gracious words are a*
> *honeycomb,*
> *sweet to the soul*
> *and healing to the bones"*
> (PROVERBS 16:24).

Consider a conflict between two people—a hurting struggler and an offender who is willing to listen:

- **Confront your offender.** The struggler feels "sour" (hurt, frustrated, angry) toward the offender and needs to plan a time to get these feelings out.

  - When your relationship has been cut apart, don't hold the pain in—instead, "pour it out."

- Plan a time to meet with your offender in order to "release the juice from your lemon."

"(_Name_), I need to talk with you. Is now a good time? If not, when?"

> *"There is a time for everything, and a season for every activity under the heavens...a time to be silent and a time to speak"*
> (Ecclesiastes 3:1,7).

- **Communicate your feelings.** The struggler "squeezes all the sour juice out of the lemon." Express your feelings by squeezing out your pain in a way that doesn't accuse.

  - Share the problem using "I" statements, not accusatory "you" statements.

    "I'm feeling deeply hurt and betrayed. Would you be willing to listen?"

  - Describe only the upsetting words or behavior without criticizing the person's character.

    "I felt betrayed last night when I wasn't defended."

  - Don't accuse, belittle, or attack.

    > *"Instead, speaking the truth in love... 'In your anger do not sin': Do not let the sun go down while you are still angry"*
    > (Ephesians 4:15,26).

- **Comply by listening.** The offender is an "empty pitcher" willing to collect *all* the sour juice.

  - The person being confronted must be willing to listen to the sour words and to hear the struggler's pain with undivided attention.

    "Yes, I will listen."

  - The listener must hear the problem—without interruption—until the "last drop" goes into the pitcher.

  - Above all, the listener must not make excuses or become angry and defensive.

> *"Submit to one another out of reverence for Christ"*
> (EPHESIANS 5:21).

- **Confirm by repeating.** The offender "fills the pitcher with water" to neutralize the situation without acidic words.

  - The offender now verifies the problem by repeating word-for-word what has been said and then confirms by asking, "Is this correct?"

    "You are saying that you felt betrayed and angry last night when I didn't defend you? Is this correct?"

  - If the problem is not restated correctly, understand what was missed and repeat until it is correct.

  - Then ask, "Is there more?"

    Repeat back, "Yes, I was verbally bashed and I felt humiliated!"

  - Repeat back anything added, and ask this question again until nothing more is added.

  - Agreement with the facts is not necessary; therefore, do not attempt to justify anything.

> *"Whoever heeds life-giving correction will*
> *be at home among the wise"*
> (PROVERBS 15:31).

- **Choose possible changes.** The offender offers several possible changes in behavior, and the struggler will choose one of the changes. Realize that if the offender adds this "sugar to the lemon water," the entire flavor changes!

  - The offender offers possible "sweet solutions."

    "When someone criticizes you in front of me, I would be willing to walk away with you, express emotional support by complimenting you, or ask the person not to speak about you in that way. Which would you prefer?" This displays a willingness to support the struggler by a commitment to change.

  - The hurt struggler identifies one acceptable response to be applied in the future.

- The willingness to listen and change behavior becomes the "sweet ingredient" for developing intimacy in the relationship.

"In humility value others above yourselves, not looking to your own interests, but each of you to the interests of the others"
(PHILIPPIANS 2:3-4).

- **Convey compassionate care.** The offender mixes the sugar and lemon juice so well that there is no hint of distasteful sourness. After the change in behavior has been agreed on, the listener expresses sorrow over the struggler's pain and expresses appreciation for the opportunity to resolve the problem.

  - Address the struggler's pain.

    "I'm so sorry my actions hurt your feelings and caused you to feel betrayed."

  - Thank the struggler for approaching you.

    "Thank you for coming to me directly. I appreciate being given a chance to change my behavior in the future in order to improve our relationship."

  "A word fitly spoken is like apples of gold in a setting of silver"
  (PROVERBS 25:11 ESV).

- **Consider your own condition.** The struggler should consider that the offender could also have been offended. This would be like adding tart lime to the mix. But just as lemonade can be enhanced with the addition of sweet raspberry or mango syrup, so too can relationships be enhanced when both the struggler and the offender acknowledge their own struggles and offenses.

  - Question whether you have caused pain.

    "Have I hurt you by bringing this to your attention?"

  - Apologize and ask forgiveness for contributing to the conflict.

    "I'm sorry I didn't make my feelings clear about this before it became an issue. Would you forgive me, too?"

  - Thank the listener for both accepting and extending mercy.

"Thank you for allowing me to voice my concerns. I'm very grateful we have addressed this issue. Now we can focus on enjoying our time together."

> *"All this is from God, who reconciled us to himself through*
> *Christ and gave us the ministry of reconciliation"*
> (2 CORINTHIANS 5:18).

Thank God for allowing you to participate with Him in turning lemons into lemonade!

> *"Whoever refreshes others will be refreshed"*
> (PROVERBS 11:25).

G. How to Respond to Difficult Personalities

His name is Demetrius, and he most definitely can be described as having a difficult personality.

Paul's words are interfering with the weight of Demetrius's wallet, and he's determined to do something about it. A prosperous silversmith who makes statues of the goddess Artemis, Demetrius wants to muzzle Paul's message that "gods made by human hands are no gods at all" (Acts 19:26). Business is going badly because of Paul's proclamations, and Demetrius says he's concerned that Artemis "will be robbed of her divine majesty" (Acts 19:27).

An attacker who feels he's losing his significance and financial security, Demetrius incites fury in his fellow tradesmen, and "soon the whole city was in an uproar" (Acts 19:29). But the protective hand of God is upon Paul, as promised in Psalm 27:5:

> *"For in the day of trouble he will keep me safe in his dwelling; he will hide me*
> *in the shelter of his sacred tent and set me high upon a rock."*

ATTACKERS WANT TO FEEL SIGNIFICANT

1. **Wolves[30]—Goal: To feel powerful**
   - Let them have their say without interrupting.
   - Get their attention with praise.
   - Hold your ground (match strength with strength).
   - Avoid arguments.
   - Don't put yourself down.

> *"Don't have anything to do with foolish and stupid*
> *arguments, because you know they produce quarrels"*
> (2 TIMOTHY 2:23).

2. Snakes[31]—Goal: To feel superior

    – Be aware of their power to destroy.

    – Catch them in a lie.

    – Enlist someone to help you confront them in private.

    – Expect them to deny what they have done.

    – Don't let them get away with an attack.

> *"If your brother or sister sins, go and point out their fault,*
> *just between the two of you. If they listen to you, you have*
> *won them over. But if they will not listen, take one or two*
> *others along, so that 'every matter may be established by the*
> *testimony of two or three witnesses.' If they still refuse to listen,*
> *tell it to the church; and if they refuse to listen even to the*
> *church, treat them as you would a pagan or a tax collector"*
> (MATTHEW 18:15-17).

3. Hornets[32]—Goal: To feel valuable

    – Learn to cut off negative conversation.

    – Respond only to what is important.

    – Confront their game-playing.

    – Encourage a look at solutions.

    – Don't reinforce their complaints.

> *"Do not let any unwholesome talk come out of your mouths,*
> *but only what is helpful for building others up according*
> *to their needs, that it may benefit those who listen"*
> (EPHESIANS 4:29).

AVOIDERS WANT TO FEEL SECURE

1. Turtles[33]—Goal: To feel safe

    – Ask questions that can't be answered with *yes* or *no*.

    – Seek to help them express their feelings.

— Hang in there until you get a response.

— Be positive, not critical, with them.

— Don't answer for them.

> *"A person is praised according to their prudence,*
> *and one with a warped mind is despised"*
> (Proverbs 12:8).

2. Chameleons[34]—Goal: To feel accepted

— Make it okay for them to disagree with you.

— Help them to identify priorities.

— Learn their hidden fears.

— Reinforce their decisions.

— Don't accept their *yes* as complete agreement with you.

> *"Anxiety weighs down the heart, but a kind word cheers it up"*
> (Proverbs 12:25).

3. Weasels[35]—Goal: To feel confident

— Avoid accusations.

— Don't let yourself be drawn into arguments.

— Be strong and steadfast.

— Be forgiving.

— Be consistently encouraging.

> *"As servants of God we commend ourselves in every way:*
> *in great endurance; in troubles, hardships and distresses...*
> *in truthful speech and in the power of God; with weapons*
> *of righteousness in the right hand and in the left"*
> (2 Corinthians 6:4,7).

H. How to Turn Foes into Friends

Imagine the angst. It hurts when your own people are talking against you. His foes are from his family lineage, and Paul's heart is pained by their persecution.

Paul longs to see his Jewish brethren come to faith in Christ, to soften their hearts toward the true Messiah and Savior. But they are his major opposition, as he aptly testifies: "I served the Lord with great humility and with tears and in the midst of severe testing by the plots of my Jewish opponents" (Acts 20:19).

Eventually Paul's prayers, love, and faithful proclamation of the gospel turn some of the Jews from foes into friends—they become fellow believers in the Lord Jesus. Paul's tender care reflects the compassion of Christ, and that makes all the difference.

> *"I have great sorrow and unceasing anguish in my heart.*
> *For I could wish that I myself were cursed*
> *and cut off from Christ for the sake of my people,*
> *those of my own race"*
> (Romans 9:2-3).

Rather than resolving conflicts by treating your opposer as a foe, follow the steps in this F-R-I-E-N-D-S acrostic.

F—Find ways to compliment your opposer.

- Look for and express positive character traits that your opposer possesses.
- Don't focus on complimentary externals such as clothes, hair, or good looks.
- Express a sincere compliment at an appropriate time. "I've noticed how effectively you (_spoke/worked/sang_), and I really admire that."

> *"The mouths of the righteous utter wisdom,*
> *and their tongues speak what is just"*
> (Psalm 37:30).

R—Repay your opposer's evil with good.

- Look for and extend acts of kindness.
- Commit to God that you will not act negatively, like your opposer.
- Do not talk about your opposer in a demeaning way to others.

> *"Do not repay anyone evil for evil. Be careful to*
> *do what is right in the eyes of everyone"*
> (Romans 12:17).

I—Intercede in prayer for your opposer.

   – Ask God to reveal your opposer's genuine needs.

   – Seek the Lord's perspective on the differences between you and your opposer.

   – Commit to praying for your opposer every time the person comes to mind.

> *"As for me, far be it from me that I should sin*
> *against the LORD by failing to pray for you. And I*
> *will teach you the way that is good and right"*
> (1 SAMUEL 12:23).

E—Empathize with your opposer.

   – Learn about the past hurts and hardships that your opposer has experienced.

   – Get in touch with your feelings as you think about your own hurts and hardships.

   – Allow yourself to feel compassion as you identify with your opposer.

> *"Finally, all of you, be like-minded, be sympathetic,*
> *love one another, be compassionate and humble"*
> (1 PETER 3:8).

N—Nurture a forgiving heart toward your opposer.

   – Realize that you, too, have wounded others.

   – Remember that you, too, stand in need of forgiveness.

   – Pray for God to give you a willingness to forgive just as He was willing to forgive you.

> *"And when you stand praying, if you hold anything*
> *against anyone, forgive them, so that your Father*
> *in heaven may forgive you your sins"*
> (MARK 11:25).

D—Decide to love your opposer.

- See yourself as a conduit of God's love. (The Greek word *agape* refers to the kind of love that seeks the highest good of another person.)
- Look for tangible ways to express *agape* love on a continual basis.
- Keep focusing on what is in the best interest of your opposer, and then do it.

"Let no debt remain outstanding, except the continuing debt to love one another, for whoever loves others has fulfilled the law"
(ROMANS 13:8).

S—Seek to meet the needs of your opposer.

- Reach out by looking for what is especially meaningful to your opposer (such as reaching out to one of that person's loved ones).
- Reach out by inviting your opposer to attend an event with you that you know that person would like.
- Reach out by taking food to your opposer when you hear that person is sick or has lost a loved one.

"If your enemy is hungry, feed him; if he is thirsty, give him something to drink. In doing this, you will heap burning coals on his head"
(ROMANS 12:20).

When you are faced with conflict, passivity is not the path to peace. Conflict resolution lies in reaching out to your opposer with the love of Christ.

—JUNE HUNT

Conflict Resolution: Answers in God's Word

Question: "When conflict is present, how much effort should I personally make?"

Answer: *"Let us therefore make every effort to do what leads to peace and to mutual edification"* (Romans 14:19).

Question: "Does God hold me accountable to live at peace with everyone?"

Answer: *"If it is possible, as far as it depends on you, live at peace with everyone"* (Romans 12:18).

Question: "What should I do when someone sins against me?"

Answer: *"If your brother or sister sins, go and point out their fault, just between the two of you. If they listen to you, you have won them over. But if they will not listen, take one or two others along, so that 'every matter may be established by the testimony of two or three witnesses' "* (Matthew 18:15-16).

Question: "What should I do if someone starts foolish arguments?"

Answer: *"Don't have anything to do with foolish and stupid arguments, because you know they produce quarrels"* (2 Timothy 2:23).

Question: "Do I appeal to others in a spirit of unity?"

Answer: *"Make every effort to keep the unity of the Spirit through the bond of peace"* (Ephesians 4:3).

Question: "In the midst of conflict, what should I think about? Should I think the best of others?"

Answer: *"Finally, brothers and sisters, whatever is true, whatever is noble, whatever is right, whatever is pure, whatever is lovely, whatever is admirable—if anything is excellent or praiseworthy—think about such things"* (Philippians 4:8).

Question: "Do I avoid taking revenge and allow God to fight my battles?"

Answer: *"Do not take revenge, my dear friends, but leave room for God's wrath, for it is written: 'It is mine to avenge; I will repay,' says the Lord"* (Romans 12:19).

QUESTION: "Am I more interested in stating my own opinion than understanding another's viewpoint?"

ANSWER: *"Fools find no pleasure in understanding but delight in airing their own opinions"* (Proverbs 18:2).

QUESTION: "Do I pray for those who are my enemies?"

ANSWER: *"I tell you, love your enemies and pray for those who persecute you"* (Matthew 5:44).

QUESTION: "Do I have a heart that is quick to forgive?"

ANSWER: *"Bear with each other and forgive one another if any of you has a grievance against someone"* (Colossians 3:13).

FORGIVENESS
The Freedom of Letting Go

6

FORGIVENESS
The Freedom of Letting Go

The year is 1944. Nazi Germany occupies Holland. An elderly watchmaker and his family are actively involved in the Dutch Underground. By hiding Jewish people in a secret room in their home, members of the ten Boom family courageously help men, women, and children escape Hitler's roll call of death.[1] Yet one fateful day, their secret is discovered. The watchmaker is arrested, quickly imprisoned, and soon after, he dies. His tenderhearted daughter Betsie also fails to escape the clutch of death at the hands of her cruel captors. In a Nazi concentration camp, she perishes.

And what about Corrie, the watchmaker's youngest daughter, now middle-aged? Will she live...and, if so, will she ever be able to forgive her captors, those who caused the deaths of both her father and sister? As she struggles to survive the ravages of Ravensbruck, one of Hitler's most horrific death camps, can anything sustain Corrie ten Boom? To what can she cling? Indeed, Corrie does survive. Her God and His Word sustain her. She lives the truth of these verses:

"False witnesses rise up against me, spouting malicious accusations.
I remain confident of this:
I will see the goodness of the Lord in the land of the living.
Wait for the Lord;
be strong and take heart and wait for the Lord"
(Psalm 27:12-14).

I. Definitions of Forgiveness

Two years after the war, Corrie is speaking at a church in Munich. She has come from Holland to a defeated Germany, bringing with her the message that God does indeed forgive. There in the crowd, a solemn face stares back at her. As the people file out, she notices "a balding heavyset man in a gray overcoat, a brown felt hat clutched between his hands." Suddenly a scene flashes back in her mind: "A blue uniform and a visored cap with its skull and crossbones...the huge room with its harsh overhead lights...the shame of walking naked past this man"—this man who is now standing before her.

"You mentioned Ravensbruck in your talk. I was a guard there," he says. "But since that time I have become a Christian. I know that God has forgiven me for the cruel things I did there, but I would like to hear it from your lips as well." He extends his hand toward her and asks, "Will you forgive me?" Corrie stares at the outstretched hand. The moment seems to stretch into hours as she struggles with the most difficult decision she has ever made.[2] Corrie knows Scripture well, but applying this passage seems to be too much:

> *"If your brother or sister sins against you, rebuke them;*
> *and if they repent, forgive them.*
> *Even if they sin against you seven times in a day*
> *and seven times come back to you saying 'I*
> *repent,' you must forgive them"*
> (Luke 17:3-4).

A. What Is Forgiveness?

Assume you need to borrow $100 to pay a medical bill. You ask a friend for a loan and promise to pay it back at the end of the month. But when the time comes for repayment, you don't have the money. In fact, for the next three months, you still don't have the money. Then unexpectedly, out of a kind heart, your friend *chooses* to *forgive the debt*! This is one facet of forgiveness. The Bible says,

> *"Let no debt remain outstanding,*
> *except the continuing debt to love one another"*
> (Romans 13:8).

- **Forgiveness** is the dismissing of a debt.[3]

    In the New Testament, the Greek noun *aphesis* denotes a "dismissal" or "release."[4]

— When you grant forgiveness, you dismiss the debt owed to you.

— When you receive forgiveness, your debt is dismissed. (You are released from any requirement for repayment.)

— When you grant forgiveness, you dismiss the debt from your thoughts.

Jesus expressed the heart of forgiveness when He said,

> *"Love your enemies, do good to those who hate you"*
> (LUKE 6:27).

- **Forgiveness** is dismissing your demand that others owe you something, especially when…

  — They fail to meet your expectations.

  — They fail to keep a promise.

  — They fail to treat you justly.

Jesus said,

> *"If anyone slaps you on the right cheek,*
> *turn to them the other cheek also"*
> (MATTHEW 5:39).

- **Forgiveness** is dismissing, canceling, or setting someone free from the consequence of falling short of God's standard.

  — The holy standard of God is perfection, yet we all have sinned.

  — The penalty for our sins is spiritual death (separation from God).

  — The penalty for our sins (our debt) was paid by Jesus through His sacrificial death on the cross. Therefore, instead of being separated from God, we can have our debt dismissed by God and experience eternal life in heaven. That's because

> *"everyone who believes in him [Jesus]*
> *receives forgiveness of sins through his name"*
> (ACTS 10:43).

God's Ability to Forgive

QUESTION: "Is it possible to sin beyond God's ability to forgive?"

ANSWER: No. God promises to purify us from all unrighteousness, not just specific sins, but we need to first confess our sins. (*Confess* means literally "to agree"—to agree with God.)[5] And if we agree with God about our sins, we not only admit we have sinned, but we also turn from our sins and turn to Jesus, entrusting our lives to the One who died for our sins.

> *"I acknowledged my sin to you and did not cover up my iniquity.*
> *I said, 'I will confess my transgressions to the LORD.'*
> *And you forgave the guilt of my sin"*
> (PSALM 32:5).

B. What Forgiveness Is Not[6]

Misconceptions abound when the word *forgiveness* is mentioned. Some think forgiveness is the equivalent of *excusing* sin—saying that what was wrong is now okay. Yet this is not the example of forgiveness Jesus displayed. When He encountered the mob of men eager to stone a woman caught in adultery, He chose not to stone her; however, never did He excuse her. Instead, He said, "Go, and sin no more" (John 8:11 KJV). To help correct any confusion about what forgiveness is, you need to know what forgiveness is *not*! Proverbs says,

> *"Let the wise listen and add to their learning,*
> *and let the discerning get guidance"*
> (PROVERBS 1:5).

- *Forgiveness is not* circumventing God's justice.
  - It is allowing God to execute His justice in His time and in His way.

- *Forgiveness is not* waiting for "time to heal all wounds."
  - It is clear that time does not heal wounds—some people will not allow healing.

- *Forgiveness is not* letting the guilty "off the hook."
  - It is moving the guilty from your hook to God's hook.

- *Forgiveness is not* the same as reconciliation.
  - It takes two for reconciliation to occur, but only one for forgiveness.

- *Forgiveness is not* excusing unjust behavior.

– It is acknowledging that unjust behavior is without excuse, while still forgiving.

- *Forgiveness is not* explaining away the hurt.
  - It is working through the hurt.

- *Forgiveness is not* based on what is fair.
  - It was not "fair" for Jesus to hang on the cross, but He did so that we could be forgiven.

- *Forgiveness is not* being a weak martyr.
  - It is being strong enough to be Christlike.

- *Forgiveness is not* stuffing your anger.
  - It is resolving your anger by releasing the offense to God.

- *Forgiveness is not* a natural response.
  - It is a supernatural response, empowered by God.

- *Forgiveness is not* denying the hurt.
  - It is feeling the hurt and releasing it to God.

- *Forgiveness is not* being a doormat.
  - It is seeing that if this were so, Jesus would have been the greatest "doormat" of all!

- *Forgiveness is not* conditional.
  - It is unconditional, a mandate from God to everyone.

- *Forgiveness is not* forgetting.
  - It is necessary to remember before you can forgive.

- *Forgiveness is not* a feeling.
  - It is a choice—an act of the will.

A loose woman is caught "in the act," and the stone-throwers are ready. The penalty for adultery is clear—stone the guilty person to death! But Jesus challenges the stone-throwers to examine their own hearts before condemning the woman. "Let any one of you who is without sin be the first to throw a stone at her" (John 8:7). No one moves. Then, after all the stones drop—one by one—and the stone-throwers leave—one by one—Jesus focuses His attention on the woman. He looks beyond her fault and sees her need. She needs to know the life-changing love of God. Unexpectedly, Jesus gives her a priceless gift—His merciful favor and forgiveness.

> *"'Neither do I condemn you,' Jesus declared.*
> *'Go now and leave your life of sin'"*
> (JOHN 8:11).

Fact not Feeling

QUESTION: "If I don't feel like forgiving, how can I be asked to forgive? That doesn't seem right."

ANSWER: Forgiveness is not based on a *feeling*, but rather on the fact that we—all of us—are called by God to forgive. Forgiveness is not an *emotion*, but rather an act of the *will*, a *choice*. Therefore, what seems right based on feelings can easily be wrong! Remember:

> *"There is a way that appears to be right,*
> *but in the end it leads to death"*
> (PROVERBS 14:12).

C. What Does It Mean to Forgive Others?

Imagine you are a runner and the race is an event in the Olympics. You have the right shoes, right shorts, right shirt. Yet something is desperately wrong. Locked on your ankle is a heavy black ball and chain! This weight is too heavy—you can't run the distance; you can't even qualify. If only you could free yourself! But you don't have the key to unlock the chain.

Then, on the day of the qualifying run, you are told you already possess the key to freedom. Quickly, you retrieve it from its hiding place, free yourself, and, oh, what freedom! It is as though that black ball miraculously becomes a big helium balloon. The balloon is released. The load is lifted. The weight is sent away. Previously, no one told you your unforgiveness was the black ball weighing you down. Now that you know forgiveness is one of the major keys to freedom, you can run the race…and cross the finish line with freedom. The Bible says,

*"Let us throw off everything that hinders and the
sin that so easily entangles. And let us run with
perseverance the race marked out for us"*
(HEBREWS 12:1).

- **To forgive** means to *release your resentment* toward your offender.

In the New Testament, the Greek verb *aphiemi* primarily means "to send away"—in other words, "to forgive, send away or release" the penalty when someone wrongs you.[7] This implies that you need...

- *To release* your right to hear "I'm sorry"
- *To release* your right to be bitter
- *To release* your right to get even

*"Do not repay anyone evil for evil.
Be careful to do what is right in the eyes of everyone"*
(ROMANS 12:17).

- **To forgive** is to *release your rights* regarding the offense.

- *To release* your right to dwell on the offense
- *To release* your right to hold on to the offense
- *To release* your right to keep bringing up the offense

*"Whoever would foster love covers over an offense,
but whoever repeats the matter separates close friends"*
(PROVERBS 17:9).

- **To forgive** is to *reflect the character of Christ.* Just as God is willing to forgive us, we are called to forgive others.

- *To forgive* is to extend mercy
- *To forgive* is to give a gift of grace
- *To forgive* is to set the offender free

Jesus taught His disciples to pray,

"Forgive us our debts, as we also have forgiven our debtors"
(MATTHEW 6:12).

═══════ *Examine Your Thoughts* ═══════

QUESTION: "What can I do when I don't feel like forgiving?"

ANSWER: Whenever you don't feel like doing something you should do, examine your thoughts.

- *You can't control* what your offenders do, but you can control what you think about your offenders.

    God gives us much counsel about what we should sift out from our thinking. Imagine that the Bible is a "thought-sifter"—a tool that helps us sift the thoughts that should not go into our minds.

- *Evaluate your thoughts* about those who offend you.

    Remember: Your thoughts produce your feelings. Do your thoughts naturally flow through the "thought-sifter" in the scripture below? If not, catch them before they pass through and sift them out.

When you carefully choose what you will dwell on, your emotions will begin to line up and you will gradually even feel like forgiving those you don't want to forgive.

> *"Whatever is true, whatever is noble, whatever is right,*
> *whatever is pure, whatever is lovely, whatever is admirable—*
> *if anything is excellent or praiseworthy—*
> *think about such things"*
> (PHILIPPIANS 4:8).

D. Is Forgiveness the Same As Reconciliation?[8]

No. Forgiveness is not the same as reconciliation. Forgiveness focuses on the offense, whereas reconciliation focuses on the relationship. Forgiveness requires no relationship. However, reconciliation requires a relationship in which two people, in agreement, are walking together toward the same goal. The Bible says,

> *"Do two walk together unless they have agreed to do so?"*
> (AMOS 3:3).

- *Forgiveness* can take place with only one person.
    - *Reconciliation* requires at least two people.

- *Forgiveness* is directed one-way.
  - *Reconciliation* is reciprocal...occurring two ways.

- *Forgiveness* is a decision to release the offender.
  - *Reconciliation* is the effort to rejoin the offender.

- *Forgiveness* involves a change in thinking about the offender.
  - *Reconciliation* involves a change in behavior by the offender.

- *Forgiveness* is a free gift to the one who has broken trust.
  - *Reconciliation* is a restored relationship based on restored trust.

- *Forgiveness* is extended even if it is never, ever earned.
  - *Reconciliation* is offered to the offender because it has been earned.

- *Forgiveness* is unconditional, regardless of a lack of repentance.
  - *Reconciliation* is conditional, based on repentance.

After Forgiving

QUESTION: "After we forgive someone, must we also *try* to be reconciled?"

ANSWER: The answer to this question is sometimes *yes* and sometimes *no*.

- Most of the time God's desire for us is reconciliation. Second Corinthians 5:18 says, "God...reconciled us to himself through Christ and gave us the ministry of reconciliation."

- However, sometimes encouraging the restoration of a relationship is not always wise, as with an unrepentant, recurrent abuser. First Corinthians 15:33 says, "Do not be misled: 'Bad company corrupts good character.'" For instance, if a husband's anger is out of control and he refuses to get help for his violent temper, the wife needs to take this scripture to heart and move out of harm's way until counseling and lasting changes are a part of his lifestyle. The Bible gives this instruction:

> *"Do not make friends with a hot-tempered person,*
> *do not associate with one easily angered"*
> (PROVERBS 22:24).

E. What Is Divine Forgiveness?

Do you sometimes struggle with forgiving others? Understand that your awareness of how much God loves you and continually forgives you can be the catalyst that compels you to forgive. You can actually forgive others with the Lord's "divine forgiveness." The Bibles says,

> *"The LORD our God is merciful and forgiving,*
> *even though we have rebelled against him"*
> (DANIEL 9:9).

- **Divine forgiveness** is the fact that God, in His mercy, chose to release you from the penalty for your sins. (Unfortunately, some people refuse to receive this gift from God.)

> *"The LORD is compassionate and gracious, slow to anger,*
> *abounding in love...he does not treat us as our sins deserve or*
> *repay us according to our iniquities...as far as the east is from*
> *the west, so far has he removed our transgressions from us"*
> (PSALM 103:8,10,12).

- **Divine forgiveness** was extended by Jesus, who paid the penalty for our sins in full—He died on the cross as payment for the sins of all people. While we owed a debt we could not pay, He paid a debt He did not owe. One of the many messianic prophecies in the Old Testament states,

> *"We all, like sheep, have gone astray, each of us has*
> *turned to our own way; and the LORD has laid on*
> *him [Christ, the Messiah] the iniquity of us all"*
> (ISAIAH 53:6).

- **Divine forgiveness** is an extension of grace as seen in the Greek word *charizomai*, which is translated "forgive" and means "to bestow a favor unconditionally."[9] The Greek word *charis* means "grace."[10] You are an expression of God's grace when you forgive others with divine forgiveness.

> *"Be kind and compassionate to one another, forgiving*
> *each other, just as in Christ God forgave you"*
> (EPHESIANS 4:32).

═══ *Forgiveness Is a Gift* ═══

QUESTION: "When Jesus was on the cross, He prayed
Does that mean *everyone* received salvation?"

ANSWER: No. Realize that forgiveness is a gift, and the forgiver is blessed in g
ing it whether the person being forgiven benefits from it or not. Many refuse forgiveness because accepting it requires acknowledging the need for forgiveness.
Being forgiven by having your sins paid for is one matter. Receiving and benefit-
ing from being forgiven is entirely another. It is our part to give forgiveness, and
it is the offender's part to receive that forgiveness. So it is with a thankful heart
that you can say,

> *"You, Lord, are forgiving and good,*
> *abounding in love to all who call to you"*
> (PSALM 86:5).

A BIBLICAL EXAMPLE OF FORGIVENESS—JOSEPH AND HIS BROTHERS[11]

What could erupt in more resentment than friction within the family? Joseph
is a prime example of someone who could have chosen to be vindictive rather
than forgiving. (See Genesis chapters 37–45.) He is the favorite son of his father,
Jacob. Joseph's ten older brothers are so bitter and jealous that they sell him into
slavery. Later, he is falsely accused of attempted rape, unjustly imprisoned, and
forgotten by a royal official who promised to help him. Joseph has every reason to sever ties with his family, vent hatred on humanity, and slam the door on
God...but he doesn't.

Later when Joseph becomes the prime minister of Egypt, severe famine
plagues the land. But through God's involvement with Joseph, Egypt is well
prepared. When Joseph's brothers hear of Egypt's abundance, they make a long
journey from Canaan in order to obtain food. While in Egypt, they encounter
their brother Joseph, whom they think is dead but has become the prime minister of Egypt. What an opportunity for Joseph to take revenge! But instead of
settling the score, Joseph speaks kindly to them and recounts the way God used
their treatment of him for his good, for their good, and for the good of the Jewish people:

> *"Do not be distressed and do not be angry with yourselves for selling*
> *me here, because it was to save lives that God sent me ahead of*
> *you...to preserve for you a remnant on earth*

and to save your lives by a great deliverance...
He made me father to Pharaoh,
lord of his entire household and ruler of all Egypt...
You intended to harm me, but God intended it for good
to accomplish what is now being done, the saving of many lives"
(GENESIS 45:5-8; 50:20).

Even though Joseph had been tossed into the deepest of pits, he emerged with extraordinary forgiveness toward those who wronged him. What was his secret?

THE SECRET TO JOSEPH'S SUCCESS—ACCEPTING GOD'S SOVEREIGNTY

- *"Do not be distressed and do not be angry."*
  When you realize that God, in His sovereignty, will bring good out of the wrongs done to you, you will have an attitude of forgiveness.

- *"God sent me."*
  When you realize that God, in His sovereignty, will use your location (wherever you are placed) for good, you will have an attitude of forgiveness.

- *"He made me."*
  When you realize that God, in His sovereignty, will make your every circumstance result in good because He created you purposefully, you will have an attitude of forgiveness.

- Conclusion:
  When you are able to accept God's sovereignty over your location, your circumstances, even the wrongs done to you, and when you trust Him to use them one day for good, you will have both success and freedom—through having an attitude of forgiveness!

  "We know that in all things God works for the good of those
  who love him, who have been called according to his purpose"
  (ROMANS 8:28).

=========== *Enduring Unjust Treatment* ===========

QUESTION: "How can I respond in a Christlike way when I'm being treated so unjustly?"[12]

ANSWER: Realize, Christ suffered unjustly and horrendously to pay the penalty for your sins—to make possible the forgiveness of your sins. Therefore, after you become a true Christian, you rely on Christ (who lives in you) to enable you to endure unjust suffering—but even more so, to forgive those who mistreat you. Be clear about this point: Every Christian is called to suffer, but with suffering comes a blessing.

> *"It is commendable if someone bears up under the pain of unjust*
> *suffering because he is conscious of God...*
> *To this you were called, because Christ suffered for you,*
> *leaving you an example, that you should follow in his steps.*
> *'He committed no sin, and no deceit was found in his mouth.'*
> *When they hurled their insults at him, he did not retaliate;*
> *when he suffered, he made no threats.*
> *Instead, he entrusted himself to him who judges justly"*
> (1 PETER 2:19,21-23).

F. What Is God's Heart on Forgiveness?

THE NEED FOR A HEART OF FORGIVENESS

The obvious answer to the question "Why forgive?" is this: Because God says so! But *why does God say so?* First, because *others* need it. And second, because *we* need it! Long ago, poet and priest George Herbert said the person who cannot forgive "breaks the bridge over which all must pass if they would ever reach heaven; for everyone has need to be forgiven."[13] Jesus Himself said,

> *"We also forgive everyone who sins against us"*
> (LUKE 11:4).

GOD'S HEART ON FORGIVENESS

1. God commands that we forgive each other.

*"Be kind and compassionate to one another, forgiving
each other, just as in Christ God forgave you"*
(EPHESIANS 4:32).

2. **God wants** us to forgive others because He forgives us.

*"Bear with each other and forgive one another if any of you has
a grievance against someone. Forgive as the Lord forgave you"*
(COLOSSIANS 3:13).

3. **God wants** us to see unforgiveness as sin.

*"If anyone, then, knows the good they ought to
do and doesn't do it, it is sin for them"*
(JAMES 4:17).

4. **God wants** us to get rid of unforgiveness and to have a heart of mercy.

"Blessed are the merciful, for they will be shown mercy"
(MATTHEW 5:7).

5. **God wants** us to do our part to live in peace with everyone.

*"If it is possible, as far as it depends on
you, live at peace with everyone"*
(ROMANS 12:18).

6. **God wants** us to overcome evil with good.

"Do not be overcome by evil, but overcome evil with good"
(ROMANS 12:21).

7. **God wants** us to be ministers of reconciliation.

*"God…reconciled us to himself through Christ and gave us the
ministry of reconciliation: that God was reconciling the world
to himself in Christ, not counting people's sins against them.
And he has committed to us the message of reconciliation"*
(2 CORINTHIANS 5:18-19).

II. CHARACTERISTICS OF UNFORGIVENESS AND FORGIVENESS

Here stands the enemy, the former Nazi SS officer. His very presence embodies cruelty and the stench of crematoriums. As Corrie ten Boom stares at the rough hand extended by her former captor, she knows in her head what she has to do—*forgive*! But her emotions violently engage her will. The very message she has been sharing with the victims of Nazi brutality emphasizes that she must forgive those who persecuted her. Forgiveness is a necessity. But Corrie stands paralyzed as the battle rages between her mind and her emotions:

> And I stood there—I whose sins had again and again to be for-given—and could not forgive. [My sister] Betsie had died in that place—could he erase her slow terrible death simply for the asking?[14]

Imagine Corrie's dilemma. She knows those who have forgiven their enemies have experienced deep spiritual and emotional healing and have found what eludes the unforgiving—peace. And those who continue to nurse their bitterness remain imprisoned, not in Hitler's horrid concentration camps, but within their own wounded souls. The Nazi officer's presence brings to the surface what perhaps has been deep-seated bitterness in Corrie's soul, something perhaps even Corrie hadn't been cognizant of until her captor stretched out his hand. Corrie knows the cost of bitterness—the very bitterness she is now battling—because the Bible says,

> *"See to it that no one falls short of the grace of God*
> *and that no bitter root grows up to cause trouble and defile many"*
> (HEBREWS 12:15).

A. What Characterizes the Unforgiving Heart?

When you refuse to forgive, your unforgiveness keeps you *emotionally bound to both the offense and the offender. A continual* refusal to forgive digs a deeper hole in which you can easily hide your hardened heart. Blaming others is a favorite tactic to justify unforgiveness. You can become too comfortable in the sinful habitat of self-righteousness and self-pity. Your past hurts, though buried, are still very much alive. And because they are not released God's way, oddly enough, you unknowingly *become like your offender* by becoming offensive yourself. Not forgiving your offender is an offense to God, thereby making you an offender to God as well! The Bible says to confess and renounce this sin:

> *"Whoever conceals their sins does not prosper,*
> *but the one who confesses and renounces them finds mercy"*
> (PROVERBS 28:13).

THE UNFORGIVING HEART IS...

- **Judgmental**—focusing on the past wrongs the offender has committed

THE UNFORGIVING HEART HAS...

- **Condemnation**—being intolerant of any present failures of the offender

"Do not judge...Do not condemn... Forgive, and you will be forgiven"
(LUKE 6:37).

- **Merciless**—rehearsing the reasons why the offender does not deserve mercy

- **Contempt**—looking down without mercy on the offender

"Judgment without mercy will be shown to anyone who has not been merciful. Mercy triumphs over judgment"
(JAMES 2:13).

- **Resentful**—begrudging the successes of the offender

- **Envy**—coveting the accomplishments of the offender

"Resentment kills a fool, and envy slays the simple"
(JOB 5:2).

- **Vengeful**—rejoicing when the offender experiences failure, difficulty, or hurt

- **Retaliation**—desiring to get even with the offender

"Do not gloat when your enemy falls; when they stumble, do not let your heart rejoice"
(PROVERBS 24:17).

- **Maligning**—talking to others about the faults of the offender with the intent to hurt

- **Slander**—sharing unnecessary negatives about the offender

"Whoever conceals hatred with lying lips and spreads slander is a fool"
(PROVERBS 10:18).

- **Prideful**—elevating self above the offender, who is considered less deserving

- **Haughtiness**—acting with arrogance toward the offender

"Pride goes before destruction, a haughty spirit before a fall"
(PROVERBS 16:18).

- **Profane**—verbally abusive toward the offender

- **Bitterness**—harboring hostility toward the offender

"Their mouths are full of cursing and bitterness"
(ROMANS 3:14).

- **Complaining**—quick to quarrel, grumble, and blame others for own choices, words, and deeds

- **Resistance**—arguing about any advice or constructive criticism regarding the offender

"Do everything without grumbling or arguing"
(PHILIPPIANS 2:14).

- **Impatient**—exhibiting little patience while being easily provoke

- **Annoyance**—feeling easily irritated by the offender

"A person's wisdom yields patience; it is to one's glory to overlook an offense"
(PROVERBS 19:11).

- **Bitter**—feeling weighed down with unresolved anger

- **Negativity**—feeling no joy and no approval concerning the offender

"I will give free rein to my complaint and speak out in the bitterness of my soul"
(JOB 10:1).

Because of unforgiveness, the offended person becomes spiritually dry—perhaps desiring to feel connected with God but lacking spiritual vitality and growth. As a direct result of unforgiveness, the offender's prayer life is blocked.

> *"If you do not forgive others their sins,*
> *your Father will not forgive your sins"*
> (MATTHEW 6:15).

Extending Forgiveness

QUESTION: "How can I forgive someone who has not apologized or shown any kind of repentance?"

ANSWER: Forgiveness has nothing to do with repentance. Forgiveness is not based on what the offender does or deserves, but rather on giving the gift of grace to your offender—a gift that is not deserved. The real question is, Do you want to be Christlike? When Jesus was being crucified on the cross, His enemies had neither apologized nor repented, yet He extended His heart of forgiveness by praying,

> *"Father, forgive them, for they do not know what they are doing"*
> (LUKE 23:34).

Forgiving Is Not Enabling

QUESTION: "If I forgive those who offend me, I'll be a classic enabler. Why should offenders bother to change if there is no consequence for their offensive behavior?"

ANSWER: To forgive is *not* to enable. If a man borrows money from you and later refuses to repay you, still, you should forgive him. Release both him and the offense to God—for your sake, if for no other reason, so that you do not become bitter. But you should not enter into another monetary relationship with him.

Do not give irresponsible people more opportunities to be irresponsible toward you. Enabling includes not establishing a boundary or not implementing a consequence when others violate a boundary. Only then do you enable an offender to continue in his or her bad behavior.

- *Enabling* puts you in a position of being offended again and again.

- *Enabling* never helps offenders change, but further ingrains their bad habits. However, establishing consequences communicates to offenders that they will not have other opportunities to offend again.

- *Enablers* are classic people pleasers who do not sa
  should say *no*. If you say *yes* to irresponsible people v
  say *no*, you are actually saying *no* to Christ.

The apostle Paul said,

> *"Am I now trying to win the approval of human beings, or of God?*
> *Or am I trying to please people?*
> *If I were still trying to please people, I*
> *would not be a servant of Christ"*
> (GALATIANS 1:10).

B. What Does the Forgiving Heart Look Like?

When the Spirit of Christ is rooted within you, He produces fruit consistent with the character of Christ. The moment you entrust your life to Jesus, you are "sealed" with the Holy Spirit, who dwells within you for the rest of your life (see Ephesians 1:13-14). Just as orange trees produce oranges and banana trees produce bananas, the Spirit of Christ produces the character of Christ in a Christian. Therefore, the next time you are wronged, allow the Holy Spirit the freedom to produce His fruit of forgiveness in you.

> *"The fruit of the Spirit is love, joy, peace, patience, kindness,*
> *goodness, faithfulness, gentleness, self-control…"*
> (GALATIANS 5:22-23 ESV).

THE FORGIVING HEART IS…

- **Loving**—not keeping a record of bad things the offender has done

THE FORGIVING HEART HAS…

- A **loving spirit**, allowing for the possibility that the offender can change

> *"Above all, love each other deeply, because*
> *love covers over a multitude of sins"*
> (1 PETER 4:8).

- **Joyous**—taking to heart the goodness of God and His sovereignty over all events in life, even the painful ones

- A **joyful awareness** that God will use trials to bring triumph

"I will continue to rejoice, for I know that through...
God's provision of the Spirit of Jesus Christ
what has happened to me will turn out for my deliverance"
(PHILIPPIANS 1:18-19).

- **Peaceful**—seeking to resolve any difficulty, hurt, or division, and wanting the offender to be right with God and to be blessed by Him

- A **peaceful demeanor** that lowers the guard of the offender and paves the way for reconciliation

"Peacemakers who sow in peace reap a harvest of righteousness"
(JAMES 3:18).

- **Patient**—giving God time to work in the heart of the offender to bring about possible change

- A **patient commitment** to wait for God's perfect timing in dealing with difficulties and resolving them

"Love is patient"
(1 CORINTHIANS 13:4).

- **Kind**—looking for and acting in practical ways to express kind deeds and to meet needs

- A **kind deed** that is unexpected on behalf of the offender

"Those who are kind benefit themselves, but
the cruel bring ruin on themselves"
(PROVERBS 11:17).

- **Good**—holding to moral principles and purity even in the midst of conflict

- A **good heart**, reflecting the highest moral character—the character of Christ

"Give an answer...do this with gentleness and respect,
keeping a clear conscience, so that those who
speak maliciously against your good behavior in
Christ may be ashamed of their slander"
(1 PETER 3:15-16).

- **Faithful**—praying that those who have caused much pain might have changed lives

- A **faithful commitment** to pray for those who have been hurtful

"Be joyful in hope, patient in affliction, faithful in prayer"
(ROMANS 12:12).

- **Gentle**—taking into account the woundedness of the offender and responding to harshness with gentleness

- A **gentle response**, understanding that often "hurt people hurt people"

*"A gentle answer turns away wrath, but
a harsh word stirs up anger"*
(PROVERBS 15:1).

- **Self-controlled**—deciding ahead of time how to respond when conflict arises

- A **controlled response** that is Christlike so that no matter what is said or done, there is a loving attitude toward the offender

"Think clearly and exercise self-control"
(1 PETER 1:13 NLT).

Forgiveness Test

QUESTION: "How do I know whether I have genuinely forgiven someone?"

ANSWER: After someone has offended you, you can test the "quality" of your forgiveness by asking yourself the following questions:

- Do I still expect my offender to "pay" for the wrong done to me?
- Do I still have bitter feelings toward my offender?
- Do I still have vengeful thoughts toward my offender?

Forgiving someone does not in any way mean that you do not want justice. It simply means you are leaving the offense entirely in God's hands. You are refusing to harbor hateful feelings toward your offender.

Remember, forgiveness is an ongoing process that requires you to choose to forgive every time the offense comes to mind. Likewise, you must choose to pray for the offender every time the offense crosses your mind.

> *"Far be it from me that I should sin against the LORD by failing to pray for you. And I will teach you the way that is good and right"*
> (1 SAMUEL 12:23).

C. What Is the High Cost of Unforgiveness Versus the High Reward of Forgiveness?[15]

Carrying around unforgiveness is like carrying a sack of cement all day long. If you hold unforgiveness in your heart, you are walking around with a weight God never intended for you to carry. Unforgiveness becomes a burden, and Jesus says, "Come to me, all you who are weary and burdened, and I will give you rest" (Matthew 11:28).

> *"Cast all your anxiety on him because he cares for you"*
> (1 PETER 5:7).

UNFORGIVENESS	FORGIVENESS
• **Unforgiveness** blocks the door to salvation and God's forgiveness.	• **Forgiveness** opens the door to salvation and God's forgiveness.

> *"If you forgive other people when they sin against you, your heavenly Father will also forgive you. But if you do not forgive others their sins, your Father will not forgive your sins"*
> (MATTHEW 6:14-15).

• **Unforgiveness** allows a root of bitterness to grow.	• **Forgiveness** keeps a root of bitterness from growing.

> *"See to it that no one falls short of the grace of God and that no bitter root grows up to cause trouble and defile many"*
> (HEBREWS 12:15).

• **Unforgiveness** opens a door to Satan in your life.	• **Forgiveness** closes a door to Satan in your life.

"I have forgiven in the sight of Christ for your sake,
in order that Satan might not outwit us. For
we are not unaware of his schemes"
(2 CORINTHIANS 2:10-11).

- **Unforgiveness** causes you to walk in darkness.

- **Forgiveness** brings you into the light.

"Anyone who claims to be in the light but hates a brother or sister is
still in the darkness...anyone who hates a brother or sister is in the
darkness and walks around in the darkness.
They do not know where they are going, because
the darkness has blinded them"
(1 JOHN 2:9-11).

- **Unforgiveness** is of Satan.

- **Forgiveness** is of God.

"If you harbor bitter envy and selfish ambition in your hearts...
Such 'wisdom' does not come down from heaven
but is earthly, unspiritual, demonic"
(JAMES 3:14-15).

- **Unforgiveness** reflects a godless heart.

- **Forgiveness** reflects a godly heart.

"The godless in heart harbor resentment"
(JOB 36:13).

- **Unforgiveness** makes you captive to sin.

- **Forgiveness** frees you.

"I see that you are full of bitterness and captive to sin"
(ACTS 8:23).

- **Unforgiveness** grieves the Spirit of God.

- **Forgiveness** is empowered by the Spirit of God.

"Do not grieve the Holy Spirit of God, with whom you were sealed
for the day of redemption.
Get rid of all bitterness, rage and anger, brawling
and slander, along with every form of malice"
(EPHESIANS 4:30-31).

Welcome Home! The Prodigal Son Story

He personifies the young and the restless...

Living at home with his dad and brother is simply too much of a bore—routine days with routine chores that have become more than mundane.

"It's time to live it up," he says to himself. "I want what I'm entitled to—*now*! I want to see the world—*now*! I will get the cash to do it—*now*!"

Filled with presumption, he insists on having his inheritance, insinuating to his father, "I can't wait around for you to die so I can get what's coming to me. Give it to me *now*!"

Incredibly, the father grants the son's request, distributing his property between his two boys in accord with the law: two-thirds to the elder, one-third to the younger. The impetuous son eagerly packs his bags. So much to do...so much to experience...and now, with so much to do it with!

This self-centered son moves far away from home—far from the familiar, far from his father. Enchanted by his new environment and free from the confines of family, he quickly loses self-control and squanders all "his" money. All too soon, every last dollar disappears—spent on the lure of wild living. Destitute, the brazen boy begins a downward spiral toward total depravity, falling faster and further until he hits rock bottom.

Meanwhile, hard times have hit the whole land and a famine further compounds his plight. Not only is all his money gone, but so are all his "friends," along with all his options.

He's hungry. He has to find a job. And, somehow, he has to find food. At last he locates a farmer looking for a hired hand to feed pigs—dirty, disgusting, smelly pigs! For a Jew even to touch a pig, much less feed them, is beyond disgrace. (He will be cursed, according to Old Testament law.) Yet with no other choice available, this broken, humiliated young man finds himself working in the fields, where "he longed to fill his stomach with the pods that the pigs were eating, but no one gave him anything."[16]

The work is hard on both his body and his pride, yet it also leaves plenty of time for something vital: much thinking and rethinking. He thinks of all the money he's squandered, thinks of all the time he's wasted, thinks of all the blessings he's lost. And he wonders, *What was I thinking?*

Finally, when he comes to his senses, he remembers that even his father's lowest-ranking servants—the day laborers—always have food to spare. He realizes how foolish he'd be to remain in his current condition. So he decides to return home. His new plan comes with a complete change of heart and a humble, contrite confession.

Likewise, his father has a plan. Since his boy's painful departure, not a day has gone by that he hasn't yearned to see his son back home—to see that face he dearly loves, to welcome his son with open arms. Every day he aches with anticipation, and every day he watches with a hopeful heart.

Then one day, *that* day arrives. Jesus describes the scene. The father saw his son off in the distance, "and was filled with compassion for him; he ran to his son, threw his arms around him and kissed him."[17]

Dispensing with all dignity, the dad races to his boy. Immediately, with no sense of entitlement, the son humbles himself and admits, "Father, I have sinned against heaven and against you. I am no longer worthy to be called your son."[18]

But the father, instead of treating his son as a servant, he treats him like a king! He calls out to the servants to hurry and bring new clothes and shoes, and to prepare a meal with the finest meat. He puts his ring of authority on his son and declares it's time to celebrate the son's return.

Meanwhile, through the entire time of estrangement, the older son has remained at home, fully supportive of his father. And now, as he returns from the field, he hears music and dancing and asks a servant, "What's the revelry all about?" Upon discovering his reckless brother not only has the audacity to return home but is also being honored, he fumes with resentment and refuses any part of the festivities.

"Unfair...unjust...it's just not right!" he protests to his father. "Look at *my loyalty*! Look—I've done *my duty*!" He demands an explanation from his dad for his undeserved display of affection, his irrational response, his unjustified joy. Although the father reasons as to why his older son should also rejoice, deep-rooted jealousy bars him from doing so. How ironic it is that he remains resentful, for he, too, had received a portion of the inheritance—a portion *twice* as large as his brother's!

"He doesn't deserve a party! He deserves *nothing*!" Self-righteous indignation blinds him from seeing his own hardened heart.

Yet his father, whose heart is always filled with kindness, responds, "I *will* give him what he doesn't deserve—a feast, festivities, and a renewed relationship." (That's grace.) And, with a caring spirit marked by determined strength, he added, "I absolutely *refuse* to give him what he does deserve—rejection, condemnation, and a renunciation of him as my son." (That's mercy.)

In truth, the father has extended the gifts of grace and mercy to both of his sons. Beyond the financial inheritance the father had already bestowed, he presents both sons with a coin of compassion. This precious coin cannot be purchased—it's priceless. This coin cannot be earned—it's unmerited. One side is engraved with grace; the other is minted with mercy.

How can such a wrongly treated father respond with such tender generosity? He himself gives the explanation: "Let's have a feast and celebrate. For this son of mine was dead and is alive again; he was lost and is found."[19] The father reminds his eldest that it's precisely because the relationship is broken that reconciliation is needed; thus, by extending forgiveness, the relationship can be restored.

But from where did this father's forgiveness originate? The strong foundation of an unbreakable bond of grace and mercy resides in the deepest part of his heart. And forgiveness is the external expression, the outflowing of both mercy and grace.

- *Giving grace* means his son is given a priceless gift he could never, ever deserve: full forgiveness and a reconciled relationship.
- *Granting mercy* means his son is not given the repercussion he most definitely deserves: not being rejected, even though he callously rejected his father.

What the father bestows upon both of his unworthy sons is a poignant picture of what our heavenly Father bestows upon us—on all of us who are most unworthy. Like the younger son, we've all rebelled, we've all rejected His rightful rule, we've all strayed and gone our own way. And like the older son, we've all stayed physically close, yet maintained a cold, distant heart. Yet our Father yearns for us to turn to Him, and to yield our will to His.

A humble, contrite heart always stirs the heart of God. Then from that strong foundation, that unbreakable bond of His grace and His mercy, He overflows forgiveness into our hearts. And finally, one day we realize we really are forgiven—fully, freely, forever.

"Let us then approach God's throne of grace with confidence,
so that we may receive mercy and find grace
to help us in our time of need"
(HEBREWS 4:16).

III. CAUSES OF UNFORGIVENESS

Amazingly, the ten Boom's little home became the hub of the underground network. From their secret hiding place the fingers of the underground reached into the farthest corners of Holland. As members of the ten Boom family lived their double lives, they shuffled hunted Jews into their one-room hiding place for sometimes up to two weeks, while members of the underground sought to slip the stowaways out of the country to safety.

Meanwhile, Corrie lived with the constant fear they could be caught—and with good reason. The family was eventually betrayed by a man who posed as a friend in order to determine their involvement in the underground movement.[20] As a result of this deadly treachery, Corrie never again embraced her father or delighted in the presence of her beloved sister Betsie. How could Corrie not be consumed with bitterness toward this "friend" whose betrayal cost the lives of the two people she loved most in the world? She suffered the severity of these words:

"Even my close friend, someone I trusted,
one who shared my bread, has turned against me"
(PSALM 41:9).

A. Why Is It So Difficult to Forgive?

People fail to forgive others for a variety of reasons. For example, when you have been deeply offended by a friend, forgiveness can leave you feeling emotionally deflated, draining you of emotional vitality.

In contrast, withholding forgiveness can initially cause you to feel emotionally invigorated. Therefore, you may refuse to forgive the friend who offended you because of pride or the need to feel powerful.[21]

The Bible states it this way:

"A brother wronged is more unyielding than a fortified city"
(PROVERBS 18:19).

BARRIERS TO FORGIVENESS

- *No modeling* of forgiveness from parents
  - "I don't know how to forgive."

- *Denying* the offense ever occurred
  - "I don't want to think about it."

- *Fearing* to hold the guilty accountable
  - "It's really all my fault." (This kind of thinking short-circuits the reality and the pain of being wronged.)

- *Not feeling* that you can forgive yourself
  - "No mercy for me; no mercy for you."

- *Not being forgiven* for your past offenses
  - "They didn't forgive me. Why should I forgive them?"

- *Not understanding* God's forgiveness
  - "God will never forgive me. I will never forgive her."

- *Believing* bitterness is a required response to betrayal
  - "God knows my feelings are normal."

- *Thinking* forgiveness is excusing unjust behavior
  - "I'm not about to say what she did was okay!"

- *Requiring* an apology or show of repentance
  - "He shouldn't be forgiven because he's not really sorry."

- *Feeling* a sense of power by hanging on to unforgiveness
  - "He needs to see how wrong he is!"

- *Refusing* to let go of the desire for revenge
  - "He should pay for what he's done."

- *Harboring* a prideful, hardened heart that becomes a spiritual stronghold
  - "I refuse to forgive."

> *"Blessed is the one who always trembles before God,*
> *but whoever hardens their heart falls into trouble"*
> (Proverbs 28:14).

Results of Unforgiveness

QUESTION: "What should I do if I don't want to reap the damaging results of unforgiveness?"

ANSWER: Choose to change your thinking and seriously ask God to soften your heart so that you will be willing to forgive. Unforgiveness can turn into an emotional stronghold that can damage many areas of your life. You *do* have control of what you dwell on. That is why the Bible says we are to

> *"take captive every thought to make it obedient to Christ"*
> (2 Corinthians 10:5).

B. Why Does the Need for Justice Contribute to Unforgiveness?

We feel outraged when justice is denied. Thus, the cry for justice is common from everyone—that is, everyone except the guilty person waiting to *receive* justice! For that person, the cry is not for justice, but for *mercy.*

> *"Have mercy on me, O God, according to your unfailing love;*
> *according to your great compassion blot out my transgressions"*
> (Psalm 51:1).

Why is the human desire for justice so strong and natural, and why is forgiveness so difficult and unnatural?

There are three reasons:

1. **God has instilled** within every human heart a sense of right and wrong. Therefore, we feel a need for justice when we are wronged.

> *"The requirements of the law are written on their*
> *hearts [on the hearts of even the heathen]"*
> (Romans 2:15).

2. **Based on the law**, forgiveness seems inappropriate and unnatural.

> *"Show no pity: life for life, eye for eye, tooth for*
> *tooth, hand for hand, foot for foot"*
> (Deuteronomy 19:21).

3. **Because God is a God of justice**, someone has to pay for all the wrongs, all the offenses committed by people. That Someone is Jesus. The death of Jesus on the cross fulfilled the justice of God (see Romans 3:25-26).

In the same way that God needed to have His justice satisfied by Jesus' dying on the cross, shouldn't we expect justice before we extend mercy and forgiveness? The truth is, although everyone must face *God's justice*, Jesus was the payment for *everyone's* wrongs. While governments execute justice, *individually* we are to extend mercy. We are to leave individual justice to God. The Bible exhorts us to

> *"be merciful, just as your Father is merciful"*
> (Luke 6:36).

C. Why Does Unforgiveness Spiral into a Spiritual Stronghold?

In times of war, if your enemy gains a foothold, your enemy has gained some ground. He has taken some of your territory. Now, with that foothold, your foe has a secure base from which to further advance.

If you have been hurt and as a result harbor anger in your heart, realize your *unresolved anger* can be a foothold for the enemy. The Bible says,

> *" 'In your anger do not sin':*
> *Do not let the sun go down while you are still angry,*
> *and do not give the devil a foothold"*
> (Ephesians 4:26-27).

The Development of a Spiritual Stronghold

1. *When you refuse* to forgive your offender, you have unresolved anger.
2. *Unresolved anger*, in turn, allows Satan the opportunity to tempt you into greater sin.
3. *Giving Satan greater room* to operate in your life means you will face more "flaming arrows of the evil one" (Ephesians 6:16).

4. *These flaming arrows of accusation* and unforgiveness can continue to burn in your heart and keep you captive to do the enemy's will.

At this point you are engaged in spiritual warfare. In order to win the spiritual war, recognize that the battle for freedom is fought in your mind. You need to take captive every thought of unforgiveness and release your unresolved anger to God. The Bible says,

"You must also rid yourselves of all such things as these:
anger, rage, malice, slander, and filthy language from your lips"
(COLOSSIANS 3:8).

The following spiritual warfare prayer will help you to honestly confront and release your anger to God, and thereby rid yourself of such damaging habits.

SPIRITUAL WARFARE PRAYER

"Dear heavenly Father…

- *"I don't want to be defeated* in my life. Thank You that Jesus, who lives in me, is greater than Satan, who is in the world (read 1 John 4:4).

- *"I know I have been bought* with the price of Christ's blood, which was shed at Calvary. My body is not my own—it belongs to Christ (read 1 Corinthians 6:19-20).

- *"Right now,* I refuse all thoughts that are not from You (read 2 Corinthians 10:3-5).

- *"I choose to forgive* those who have hurt me, and I choose to release each one of them along with all of my pain and anger into Your hands (read Colossians 3:13).

- *"I resist Satan* and all his power (read James 4:7).

- *"As I stand in the full armor of God,* I ask You to bind Satan and his demonic forces from having any influence over me (read Ephesians 6:11).

- *"From now on, with the shield of faith,* I will deflect and defeat every unforgiving thought that could defeat me (read Ephesians 6:16).

- *"And I yield my life to Your plan* and Your purpose (read Jeremiah 29:11).

"In the holy name of Jesus I pray. Amen."

D. What Is the Root Cause of Unforgiveness?

Many people who have been hurt feel insignificant and powerless; therefore, they try to get their need for significance met by withholding forgiveness. Unforgiveness gives them a sense of power and superiority.

If you have ever been betrayed by a friend, you may have felt powerless to stop the pain for a time. Since no one likes to feel powerless, unforgiveness provides an illusion of power. By refusing to forgive, you feel a sense of control. By holding on to hatred, you feel infused with strength. By retaliating with revenge, you carry out a power play.

THREE GOD-GIVEN INNER NEEDS

We have all been created with three God-given inner needs: the needs for love, significance, and security.[22]

- **Love**—to know that someone is unconditionally committed to our best interest

    "My command is this: Love each other as I have loved you"
    (JOHN 15:12).

- **Significance**—to know that our lives have meaning and purpose

    "I cry out to God Most High, to God who fulfills his purpose for me"
    (PSALM 57:2 ESV).

- **Security**—to feel accepted and a sense of belonging

    *"Whoever fears the LORD has a secure fortress,
    and for their children it will be a refuge"*
    (PROVERBS 14:26).

THE ULTIMATE NEED-MEETER

Why did God give us these deep inner needs, knowing that people and self-effort fail us?

God gave us these needs so that we would come to know Him as our Need-meeter. Our needs are designed by God to draw us into a deeper dependence upon Christ. God did not create any person or position or any amount of power or possessions to meet the deepest needs in our lives. If a person or thing *could* meet all our needs, we wouldn't need God! Now, the Lord will use circumstances and bring positive people into our lives as an extension of His care and compassion, but ultimately, only God Himself can satisfy all the needs of our hearts. The Bible says,

> *"The LORD will guide you always;*
> *he will satisfy your needs in a sun-scorched land*
> *and will strengthen your frame.*
> *You will be like a well-watered garden,*
> *like a spring whose waters never fail"*
> (ISAIAH 58:11).

The apostle Paul revealed this truth by first asking, "What a wretched man I am. Who will rescue me from this body that is subject to death?" He then answers his own question by saying he is saved by "Jesus Christ our Lord!" (Romans 7:24-25).

All along, the Lord planned to meet our deepest needs for…

- **Love**—"I [the Lord] have loved you with an everlasting love; I have drawn you with unfailing kindness" (Jeremiah 31:3).

- **Significance**—"'For I know the plans I have for you,' declares the LORD, 'plans to prosper you and not to harm you, plans to give you hope and a future'" (Jeremiah 29:11).

- **Security**—"The LORD himself goes before you and will be with you; he will never leave you nor forsake you. Do not be afraid; do not be discouraged" (Deuteronomy 31:8).

The truth is that our God-given needs for love, significance, and security can be legitimately met in Christ Jesus! Philippians 4:19 makes it plain:

> *"My God will meet all your needs according to*
> *the riches of his glory in Christ Jesus."*

WRONG BELIEF:
"It's natural for me to resent those who have wronged me. If I forgive them, they will get away with it. My offenders need to pay for the wrongs committed against me."

RESULT:
This belief reflects an attitude of pride that sets you up as a judge higher than God Himself, who is willing to forgive and forget.

> *"I, even I, am he who blots out your transgressions, for*
> *my own sake, and remembers your sins no more"*
> (ISAIAH 43:25).

RIGHT BELIEF:

"Because God has totally forgiven me, I can release my resentment and choose to forgive others. I will rely on Christ, who is living within me, to forgive through me."

RESULT:

This belief reflects a heart of humility that results in a desire to forgive others in the same way God forgives you.

> *"If you forgive other people when they sin against you, your*
> *heavenly Father will also forgive you. But if you do not forgive*
> *others their sins, your Father will not forgive your sins"*
> (MATTHEW 6:14-15).

E. Why Can You Be Totally Forgiven by God?

You can't truly forgive others until you have God's forgiveness in your own life. Of all the world's religions, only biblical Christianity teaches that God forgives sin completely.[23] God is ready to forgive each and every one of our offenses.

Yet many refuse His forgiveness because they don't understand mercy and grace. Grace is getting what you don't deserve (forgiveness and heaven). Mercy is not getting what you do deserve (unforgiveness and hell). Right now, God wants to show you His mercy and grace.

Through Jesus Christ, God wants to give you His forgiveness—forgiveness that is found only in a secure relationship with Him.

> *"It [salvation] does not, therefore, depend on human desire*
> *or effort, but on God's mercy…Let us then approach God's*
> *throne of grace with confidence, so that we may receive*
> *mercy and find grace to help us in our time of need"*
> (ROMANS 9:16; HEBREWS 4:16).

HOW CAN YOU FIND GOD'S FORGIVENESS?

To experience God's forever forgiveness in your life, there are four points you need to know, which are listed on pages 48-50.

===== *Forgiving Yourself* =====

QUESTION: "I know God has forgiven me of my sins, myself?"

ANSWER: Have you ever considered that being unwilling to forgive what God has forgiven is to discredit God's gift of mercy toward you? It is placing yourself as a higher judge than God Himself. It is saying,

- "God, You are wrong in forgiving me because I don't deserve to be forgiven."
- "Christ's sacrifice on the cross must not be sufficient to cleanse me of my sins."
- "Something else must be done to make up for what is lacking in Jesus' sacrifice."

While not forgiving yourself may make you *feel* like you are being humble before God, realize in such a situation your focus is not on God, but on yourself.

Humility is bowing your knee to God, and submitting to His authority and right to declare righteous whomever He chooses. After all, who are you to overrule God?

Since Satan is the "accuser" of Christians (Revelation 12:10), when you continue blaming yourself, you align yourself with Satan, whose goal is to keep you feeling defeated. Instead, humbly thank God for His undeserved mercy. Thank Him for His undeserved grace and live in His undeserved forgiveness!

> *"He saved us, not because of righteous things we had done,*
> *but because of his mercy.*
> *He saved us through the washing of rebirth*
> *and renewal by the Holy Spirit"*
> (TITUS 3:5).

A Prisoner Twice Set Free: The Louie Zamperini Story

Prepare to crash…

The nose and left wing hit at high speed. The piercing impact with the cold ocean water thrusts his body forward, and the plane breaks apart. Debris from the decimated plane begins to float around him.

Darkness surrounds the submerged soldier and he is sure he is experiencing…death.

Miraculously, Louie Zamperini survives the plunge into the Pacific, but little does he know it will be the first of many horrors that will test and try him to his very core. This American Olympic runner found his life drastically altered by Adolf Hitler's deadly march across Europe. With draft papers delivered at Louie's door, dreams of competing in the 1940 Olympics immediately disappeared.

Trained as a World War II bombardier, Louie is on a rescue mission when his dilapidated plane dives into the ocean, leaving just three survivors.

Bloodied and dazed, the trio manages to climb aboard a pair of rafts, where thoughts of rescue keep their spirits afloat. Louie, Phil, and Mac expect to be discovered in a day or two, but the sky remains deafeningly silent. Days turn into weeks, and the once-beloved outdoors becomes their fierce enemy.

Not only does the sun burn and scald their skin; the salt water pours pain onto every inch of cracked flesh. Blinding sunlight sears their eyes.

And another deadly threat torments the men night and day. Sharks continually circle the rafts, some as long as 12 feet. At any given moment they can leap and land on the rafts, with gaping mouths hoping to devour their human prey. The men fight them off with their oars. Yet the sharks persistently wait for another opportune time to attack.

Rations on the rafts, so minimal, have now disappeared. The weakened men must rely on their survival instincts. While Louie lies still and lifeless, a huge albatross lands on his raft. Slowly moving his hands, Louie grabs its legs. The giant bird pecks at his knuckles, tearing away skin.

To finish the battle, Louie breaks the bird's neck, but the prospect of a meal soon turns repugnant. Upon slicing the bird open, a putrid odor fills the air, and the men find themselves gagging on the raw meat. They simply cannot swallow it, but they do use the bird's bones to make small fishing poles and use the meat as bait to catch fish.

On the morning of the twenty-seventh day at sea, a roar fills the sky. It's a plane! Louie wastes no time sending up flares. The plane circles back and races low toward the men; then suddenly pock marks spray across the ocean's surface. Gunners are shooting at the three men, forcing them to jump into the ocean for refuge underneath the rafts. After the firing stops, the three weary men struggle back into their rafts, grateful to be alive.

But then the roar returns along with another barrage of bullets from the Japanese fighters. This time, only Louie jumps back into the water because Phil and Mac are too exhausted to fend for themselves.

Seven times the Japanese attack. Worse yet, Louie finds himself fighting battles both above and below the surface. While underwater, a shark repeatedly lunges at him. A survival instructor's recommendation of showing teeth and the whites of his eyes didn't do the trick, but "a straight-arm to the snout did."[24]

Incredibly, neither Louie nor his besieged buddies are harmed. Puncture wounds riddle the rafts, even in the tiny spaces between Phil and Mac, but not a single bullet has touched any of them.

Soon after, Mac begins slipping away, dehydration and starvation devouring his body. On day 33, Mac takes his last breath.

One week later, Louie experiences what seems to be a divine reprieve, a moment of hope from above. Suddenly, he hears singing—voices from a magnificent choir. Louie looks up to the sky and sees human silhouettes, floating in a cloud and singing a song so divine that it had to come from heaven above. Phil is oblivious; it's a moment meant solely for Louie.

Meanwhile, the two skeletal men continue their perilous journey across the water, eating fish when they can catch them and drinking rainwater when they can catch it. Finally, after 47 days, they spot land—a joyous sight after drifting across 2000 miles of ocean! A typhoon propels the pair even faster toward the shore, but they never make it out of the raft to climb onto the Marshall Islands.

Japanese military on a boat spot them, and before long the two are hauled off to an internment camp. The filthy conditions are repulsive, with wiggling maggots infesting the cells and flies and mosquitoes filling the air.

After being on the vast ocean for almost two months, Louie is totally disoriented in his cramped "new home." His new reality is life in a wooden cell about the length of an average man and no wider than his shoulders. Adding to his emotional pain is separation from Phil. Louie wonders if he'll ever see his dear friend again.

The stench of human waste permeates the air. A window in the cell door proves frightening as Japanese guards use it to pummel him with rocks and poke him with sticks. Then one day, while laying in misery, he hears the magnificent voices again. He sees nothing, but relishes every word of the heavenly hymn. The divine encounter prompts Louie to pray for hours.

Louie eventually receives news that he is being transferred from Ofuna to a POW camp in Omori, where conditions are considered more favorable for prisoners. But for Louie, his nightmare grows even darker, for there he encounters…*a monster.*

Louie's Japanese military nemesis, Mutsuhiro Watanabe, is a finely crafted man, notably handsome with a perfectly proportioned physique. He exudes confidence and power. No one will tell him what to do, or not to do. An impressive sword dangles off his hip, and a belt with a huge metal buckle stretches across his waist. Louie meets a sadist who finds his greatest delight in breaking POWs.

Perhaps because Louie is a famous Olympian, Watanabe, otherwise known as The Bird, swoops upon him daily and beats him relentlessly. Fists, clubs, sticks, and even the shiny belt buckle become weapons intended to demoralize Louie. The Bird disgraces Louie every chance he can get, including making him clean a pigsty with his hands.

For two-and-a-half more years Louie endures cruelty at the hands of Japanese military officers. But on August 6, 1945, an atomic bomb is dropped on the city of Hiroshima, and the course of the war turns decisively for the Allies. Then the Japanese surrender and a formal ceremony marks the end of the war on September 2, 1945.

After the war's conclusion, Louie returns home to California to resume a "normal life," but it turns out he doesn't return alone. The Bird accompanies him in flashbacks, nightmares, and haunted memories. Louie obsesses about him—even to the point of planning a trip to Japan to murder his tormentor. One night Louie finds himself straddled over his victim, choking him with all of his might, but the victim isn't The Bird—*it's his wife.*

Shortly thereafter, Louie's wife, Cynthia, hears a neighbor talking about a famous man coming to town, a man by the name of Billy Graham. She attends the crusade and comes home a changed woman, a *born-again* woman, who had planned on divorcing Louie but now vows to stay married. On another evening, Louie reluctantly attends the crusade with his wife but storms out, enraged. Graham insists no one is inherently good, although deep down Louie recognizes that about himself.

Due to Cynthia's persistence, Louie again attends the crusade on yet another evening. His memory begins recounting all the miracles in his life, including surviving the plane crash and escaping harm's way from Japanese bullets. Suddenly he remembers a broken promise, one lifted up to heaven with sunburned, swollen lips—"If I get home through all this…I'll serve You for the rest of my life."[25]

Louie's spirit warms and he senses his heavy burden lifting. Hearing that he could receive a new life in Christ, he accepts the invitation and walks out a changed man. For five years after the war had ended, The Bird haunted Louie's dreams. After Louie's salvation experience, he never reappears.

The change in Louie's life is profound. He still plans to return to Japan—but now not to murder The Bird, but to make amends with him. With Christ as his example, Louie wants to extend forgiveness to The Bird along with the other brutal Japanese guards who so tormented his life. After traveling back to Sugamo Prison, he encounters some of the same guards, but The Bird is nowhere to be found. As it turns out, Louie was told his chief torturer took his own life by committing hari-kari.[26]

To his amazement, Louie finally realizes true freedom—the freedom of forgiveness…and real peace.

Ultimately, forgiveness has the power to end the war within everyone, lighting the darkness, liberating the mind, lifting the spirit. And for all

ceived freedom through the forgiveness of Christ, this same
s meant to be shared with others who also need to be set

> *"Be kind and compassionate to one another,*
> *forgiving each other, just as in Christ God forgave you"*
> (EPHESIANS 4:32).

IV. STEPS TO SOLUTION

After surviving the suffering of concentration camps (living in flea- and rat-infested barracks, losing her father and sister to inhumane treatment, facing death on a daily basis, and coping with what seemed to be the triumph of evil), wouldn't Corrie's future problems pale in comparison to the horrors of her past? Could she possibly ever truly wrestle with anything again? But by her own admission, Corrie could not sleep at night—until she made the determined decision to *choose* forgiveness on a daily basis and then to act on that decision each day. Corrie's admission is amazingly honest:

> I wish I could say that after a long and fruitful life, traveling the world, I had learned to forgive all my enemies. I wish I could say that merciful and charitable thoughts just naturally flowed from me and on to others. But they don't. If there is one thing I have learned… it's that I can't store up good feelings and behavior—but only draw them fresh from God each day.[27]

Corrie ten Boom learned that she not only needed to be forgiven by God, but she also needed to forgive as God forgives. She needed to show mercy, for Jesus said,

> *"Go and learn what this means: 'I desire mercy, not sacrifice.'*
> *For I have not come to call the righteous, but sinners"*
> (MATTHEW 9:13).

A. Key Verse to Memorize

Have you ever prayed "the model prayer," or what is often called the Lord's Prayer? If so, did you mean it? Think about it—did you *really* mean it? Jesus said, "Forgive us our debts, *as we also have forgiven our debtors*" (Matthew 6:12). If you really meant these words, then you are asking God to forgive you in *the exact same way* you have forgiven those who have wronged you. That is why the Bible says,

"Bear with each other and forgive one another
if any of you has a grievance against someone.
Forgive as the Lord forgave you"
(COLOSSIANS 3:13).

B. Key Passage to Read

The standard is set, the command is clear, the mandate has been made: Forgiveness is not optional! Not only did Jesus say it in the model prayer; He illustrated it by use of a parable—if we want to be forgiven, we must forgive. It is as simple and as difficult as that. But it is also as easy as that if we allow Him to do it for us and through us.

MATTHEW 18:23-35

The Parable of the Unmerciful Servant

Jesus told a parable about a servant who owed the king ten thousand talents (about $50,000,000 today). The king ordered the servant and his family to be sold—literally—along with all they had. The servant fell to his knees begging for mercy: "I will pay back everything." The king extended mercy and forgave the entire debt.

- The king represents our heavenly Father, who *forgives all of our debt of sin* when we sincerely come to Him for forgiveness and mercy.
  .... verses 23-27

  Later, this same servant grabbed one of his fellow servants who owed him a hundred denarii (about $50 today) and demanded repayment. His fellow servant fell to his knees begging for mercy: "I will pay it back." Instead, the first servant had the man thrown into prison until he could pay the debt.

- The servant who had his debts removed was *not willing to forgive the debts* of another servant who sought forgiveness.
  .... verses 28-30

  When the other servants saw what happened, they were greatly distressed and told the king about it. The cruel servant was called by the king, who was angered that his servant had not extended the mercy he himself had received from the king. The servant was then thrown into jail to be tortured until he could pay all he owed.

...on't extend *true forgiveness to others*, our Father in heaven will ...rgive us . . . . verses 31-35

> *"This is how my heavenly Father will treat each of you*
> *unless you forgive your brother or sister from your heart"*
> (Matthew 18:35).

C. How to Hit the Target

Have you ever said, "I have been severely wronged. People want me to forgive, but how can I simply forget what happened?" If these words have passed your lips or even crossed your mind, be assured you are not alone.

Hitting the Target

Target #1—A New Purpose: God's purpose for me is to be conformed to the character of Christ.

> *"Those God foreknew he also predestined to be*
> *conformed to the image of his Son"*
> (Romans 8:29).

- "I'll do whatever it takes to be conformed to the character of Christ."

Target #2—A New Priority: God's priority for me is to change my thinking.

> *"Do not conform to the pattern of this world, but be*
> *transformed by the renewing of your mind"*
> (Romans 12:2).

- "I'll do whatever it takes to line up my thinking with God's thinking."

Target #3—A New Plan: God's plan for me is to rely on Christ's strength, not my strength, to be all He created me to be.

> *"I can do all things through Christ who strengthens me"*
> (Philippians 4:13 nkjv).

- "I'll do whatever it takes to fulfill His plan in His strength."

My Personalized Plan

Through the strength of Christ, I will take the follow..
to forgive. I will give the offender and each offense to God be..
to continue to carry the pain from my past any longer. I will release it
to the Lord. I choose to forgive!

- *I will face* the truth of the offense.
- *I will allow* myself to feel the anger and unfair pain of the offense.
- *I will make* a list of wrongs and forgive the offender for each and every one.
- *I will seek* oneness and restoration, without resentment, if reconciliation is possible.

D. How to Complete the Four Stages of Forgiveness

Have you ever noticed the word *forgiveness* has the little word *give* in it? When you choose to forgive, you give someone a gift—the gift of freedom from having to pay the penalty for offending you, the gift of dismissing the debt owed to you. Because this can be a difficult gift to give, you may need to travel through the four stages of forgiveness before you are able to extend this gift to certain hurtful people. Realize that you are also giving yourself a gift—the gift of grudge-free living. That is true freedom. And that is why the Bible says,

> *"Do not seek revenge or bear a grudge against anyone*
> *among your people, but love your neighbor as yourself"*
> (Leviticus 19:18).

1. Face the Offense [28]

When you feel pain that is personal, unfair, and deep, you have a wound that can be healed only by forgiving the one who wounded you. First you must face the truth of what has actually been done and not hinder true healing by rationalizing and false thinking.

– **Don't minimize** the offense by saying. "No matter how badly he treats me, it's okay."

Truth: Bad treatment is not okay. There is no excuse for bad treatment of any kind—any time.

> *"Have nothing to do with the fruitless deeds of darkness,*
> *but rather expose them"*
> (EPHESIANS 5:11).

– **Don't excuse** the offender's behavior by saying, "He doesn't mean to hurt me. I shouldn't feel upset with him—he's a member of my family!"

TRUTH: No matter our relationship or the age of the offender, we need to call sin "sin." We need to face the truth instead of trying to change it. There must first be a *guilty* party in order to have someone to forgive.

> *"Whoever says to the guilty, 'You are innocent,' will*
> *be cursed by peoples and denounced by nations"*
> (PROVERBS 24:24).

– **Don't assume** that quick forgiveness is full forgiveness by saying,[29] "As soon as that horrendous ordeal occurred, I quickly and fully forgave him. That's what I've been taught to do!"

TRUTH: Many well-intentioned people feel guilty if they don't extend immediate forgiveness, so they "forgive" quickly. Yet they have neither faced the full impact of the offense nor grieved over what actually happened.

Rarely is the full impact of sin felt at the moment it occurs. Rather, it is felt at different levels over a period of time. Therefore, forgiveness needs to be extended at each of these levels.

"Quick forgiveness" over deep hurts may seem sufficient, but it is not "full forgiveness"—not until it has been fully extended at each level of impact. Before complete forgiveness can be extended, you must face the truth about the gravity of the offense and its extended impact on you.

> *"You [God] desired faithfulness even in the womb;*
> *you taught me wisdom in that secret place"*
> (PSALM 51:6).

2. Feel the Offense[36]

We usually do not hate strangers or acquaintances; we just "get angry" with them. But author and theologian Lewis Smedes writes, "When a person

destroys what our commitment and our intimacy created, some
is destroyed."[37] Then anger or even hatred may be our true feeling
to deep, unfair pain. Hatred toward an offender needs to be broug
the basement of our souls and dealt with. However, not all hatred is wrong. For
example, God *hates* evil, and we should too. The Bible says,

> *"There is a time for everything,*
> *and a season for every activity under the heavens…*
> *a time to love and a time to hate"*
> (ECCLESIASTES 3:1,8).

Failing to feel the offense results in…

- **Denying your pain:** "I don't blame her for always criticizing
  me…She is under a lot of pressure. And besides, it doesn't hurt
  me."

  TRUTH: Being mistreated by someone you love is painful. Feeling
  the pain must take place before healing can occur.

  > *"The LORD is close to the brokenhearted and*
  > *saves those who are crushed in spirit"*
  > (PSALM 34:18).

- **Carrying false guilt:** "I feel guilty if I hate what was done to
  me. I'm never supposed to have hatred."

  TRUTH: God hates sin. You too can hate sin. You are to hate the
  sin, but not the sinner.

  > *"To fear the LORD is to hate evil; I hate pride and*
  > *arrogance, evil behavior and perverse speech"*
  > (PROVERBS 8:13).

3. Forgive the Offender[38]

"To err is human, to forgive, divine."[39] This famous quote by English poet
Alexander Pope is a heavenly reminder to all of us. However, the earthly reality
is more like this: "To err is human, to blame it on someone else is more human!"

Oh, how much easier it is to blame than to forgive. But we are called by God
to forgive! And when you do forgive, genuine forgiveness draws you into the
heart of God and your life takes on the divine character of Christ.

– **Argument:** "I don't think it is right to forgive just anyone and everyone no matter the offense."

Answer: Jesus established what was right when He said,

> *"When you stand praying, if you hold anything*
> *against anyone, forgive them, so that your Father*
> *in heaven may forgive you your sins"*
> (MARK 11:25).

– **Argument:** "I can forgive everyone else, but I don't have the power to forgive *that* person."

Answer: The issue is not your lack of power to forgive, but rather how strong God's power is within you to forgive any sin committed against you.

> *"His divine power has given us everything we need*
> *for a godly life through our knowledge of him who*
> *called us by his own glory and goodness"*
> (2 PETER 1:3).

– **Argument:** "Forgiveness isn't fair. She ought to pay for her wrong!"

Answer: God knows how to deal with each person fairly—and He will, in His own time.

> *"Do not take revenge, my dear friends, but leave*
> *room for God's wrath, for it is written: 'It is mine*
> *to avenge; I will repay,' says the Lord"*
> (ROMANS 12:19).

– **Argument:** "I have forgiven, but it doesn't do any good. He keeps doing the same thing over and over."

Answer: You cannot control what others do, but you can control *how you respond* to what others do. Jesus said you are to respond with forgiveness no matter the number of times you have been wronged. The apostle Peter asked Jesus,

> *" 'Lord, how many times shall I forgive my brother*
> *when he sins against me? Up to seven times?' Jesus a...*
> *'I tell you, not seven times, but seventy-seven times' "*
> (Matthew 18:21-22).

— **Argument:** "I cannot forgive and forget. I keep thinking about being hurt."[40]

Answer: When you choose to forgive, you don't get a case of "holy amnesia."[41] However, after facing the hurt and confronting the offender, close off your mind to rehearsing the pain of the past. Forget about your pain by refusing to focus on your hurt.

> *"Brothers and sisters, I do not consider myself yet to have taken*
> *hold of it. But one thing I do: Forgetting what is behind and*
> *straining toward what is ahead, I press on toward the goal to win*
> *the prize for which God has called me heavenward in Christ Jesus"*
> (Philippians 3:13-14).

4. Find Oneness[36]

Relationships filled with resentment ultimately perish. Relationships filled with forgiveness ultimately prevail. However, reconciliation in a relationship—the restoration of oneness—is contingent on several vital factors. When these conditions are met, when both parties are committed to *honesty in the relationship*, there is real hope that the two can be of one mind and one heart again. The Bible says,

> *"If you have any encouragement from being united with Christ,*
> *if any comfort from his love, if any common sharing in the Spirit,*
> *if any tenderness and compassion,*
> *then make my joy complete by being like-minded,*
> *having the same love, being one in spirit and of one mind"*
> (Philippians 2:1-2).

Honesty Required for Restoring Oneness

To help restore oneness, follow the steps outlined in this H-O-N-E-S-T-Y acrostic.

H–Honestly evaluate yourself and your relationships.

God intends to use your relationships to reveal your weaknesses and to strengthen your relationship with Him. The first step toward reconciliation is to honestly evaluate your own weaknesses and the weaknesses within your relationships so that you can know where change needs to take place.

> *"Search me, God, and know my heart; test me and*
> *know my anxious thoughts. See if there is any offensive*
> *way in me, and lead me in the way everlasting"*
> (PSALM 139:23-24).

O–OPEN your heart and share your pain.

Have a candid conversation with your offender. Fully explain the pain you have suffered and the sorrow in your heart. Don't attack your offender. Instead, address the offense and share how it made you feel.

> *"If your brother or sister sins, go and point out*
> *their fault, just between the two of you. If they*
> *listen to you, you have won them over"*
> (MATTHEW 18:15).

N–NOTICE whether your offender takes responsibility.

Offenders need to know their actions struck like an arrow into your heart. They need to *feel* your hurt. If offenders ignore your pain and respond with how much you have hurt them, they are not ready for reconciliation because they are not ready to take responsibility. They need to care about your pain as much as they care about their own pain. They need to indicate a godly sorrow.

> *"Godly sorrow brings repentance that leads to salvation*
> *and leaves no regret, but worldly sorrow brings death"*
> (2 CORINTHIANS 7:10).

E–EXPECT your offender to be completely truthful.

Promises need to be made regarding honesty, support, and loyalty within the relationship. Although you cannot guarantee someone else's dependability, you should be able to discern whether there is sincerity and truthfulness.

> *"Truthful lips endure forever, but a lying*
> *tongue lasts only a moment"*
> (PROVERBS 12:19).

S–SET appropriate boundaries for the relationship.

You may have a heart for reconciliation; however, you need to evaluate the situation and ask: Has my offender crossed the line regarding what is appropriate (excessively angry, possessive, demeaning, insensitive, irresponsible, prideful, abusive)?

If so, explain what the boundary line is, what the repercussion is for crossing the boundary (a limited relationship), and what the reward is for staying within the boundary (increased trust). You need to be disciplined enough to hold your offender accountable, and your offender needs to become disciplined enough to stop hurting the relationship.

> *"Whoever heeds discipline shows the way to life, but*
> *whoever ignores correction leads others astray"*
> (PROVERBS 10:17).

T–TAKE time, cautiously ponder, and sincerely pray before you let your offender all the way back into your heart.

When trust has been trampled, time, integrity, and consistency are needed to prove your offender is now trustworthy. Change takes time. Therefore, don't rush the relationship. Confidence is not regained overnight. Trust is not given, but earned.

> *"Above all else, guard your heart, for*
> *everything you do flows from it"*
> (PROVERBS 4:23).

Y–YIELD your heart to starting over.

God wants you to have a heart that is yielded to His perfect will for your life. Serious offenses will reshape your future, and you will not be able to come back together with your offender as though nothing ever happened.

You personally change through pain. You take on new roles, and you cannot simply abandon new commitments and activities the moment a friend is forgiven and is invited back into your heart and life. Leave negative patterns in the past and establish positive patterns of relating.

> *"Forget the former things; do not dwell on the past. See, I am*
> *doing a new thing! Now it springs up; do you not perceive it? I am*
> *making a way in the wilderness and streams in the wasteland"*
>
> (ISAIAH 43:18-19).

E. How to Actually Forgive

Have you ever said, "I have been severely wronged. People want me to forgive, but how can I simply let my offender off the hook?" If these words have passed your lips or even crossed your mind, be assured you are not alone. That is precisely why you need to know...

HOW TO HANDLE "THE HOOK"

Make a list of all the offenses caused by your offender.

Imagine right now a meat hook strapped around your neck and a burlap bag hanging from the hook, laying against your chest. And imagine all the pain caused by the offenses against you represented as 100 pounds of rocks dropped into the burlap bag. Now you have 100 pounds of heavy rocks—rocks of resentment—hanging from the hook around your neck.

Ask yourself, *Do I really want to carry all that pain with me for the rest of my life?* Are you willing to take the pain from the past and release it into the hands of the Lord?

If so, lift up your pain and release it all to Jesus.

Then also take the one who offended you off of your emotional hook and place your offender onto God's hook. The Lord will deal with your offender—in His time and in His way. God says,

> *"It is mine to avenge; I will repay"*
> (DEUTERONOMY 32:35).

A PRAYER TO FORGIVE YOUR OFFENDER

After you have given your pain to the Lord, pray...

> "Lord Jesus, thank You for caring about
> how much my heart has been hurt.
> You know the pain I have felt because of (list every offense).
> Right now I release all that pain into Your hands.
> Thank You, Jesus, for dying on the cross for me and extending
> Your forgiveness to me.

As an act of my will, I choose to forgive (_name_).
Right now, I move (_name_) off of my emotional hook
to Your hook.
I refuse all thoughts of revenge.
I trust that in Your time and in Your way
You will deal with my offender as You see fit.
And Lord, thank You for giving me Your power to forgive
so that I can be set free.
In Your holy name I pray. Amen."

F. How You Can Sustain a Forgiving Spirit

In the Olympics a boxer doesn't simply step into the ring and register a knockout with the first punch. Generally, it takes several rounds of exchanging many blows before a winner is announced. Likewise, forgiveness is not a one-time event.[37] You may need to go through many bouts of forgiving as part of the *process* of forgiveness. And it's likely you will suffer some emotional bruising along the way as you confront your deep hurts.

But eventually, as you consistently release each recurring thought of an offense, the thoughts will stay away. The process will be complete; the fight will be won. Jesus emphasized the again-and-again nature of forgiveness when He said,

> *"Even if they sin against you seven times in a day*
> *and seven times come back to you saying,*
> *'I repent,' you must forgive them"*
> (LUKE 17:4).

HOW TO FORGIVE...AGAIN

Sustain a forgiving spirit by following the steps outlined in this acrostic on the word F-O-R-G-I-V-E:

F–FORBID recurring thoughts of wrongs to enter your mind.
Stop them as soon as they occur. Boldly say to yourself, "I refuse to keep a record of this. I refuse to keep a ledger."

> *"[Love] keeps no record of wrongs"*
> (1 CORINTHIANS 13:5).

O–OVERCOME the temptation to bring up the matter again.
After an honest confrontation with the offender and both sides of the

situation have been dealt with, or if the other person refuses to talk about the problem, let the Holy Spirit do His work of conviction. Ecclesiastes 3:7 says, "*[There is] a time to be silent and a time to speak.*" Pray this passage:

> "*Set a guard over my mouth, LORD; keep*
> *watch over the door of my lips*"
> (PSALM 141:3).

R–REPEAT Scripture in your mind.

Allow God's perspective to change your perspective. Allow God's heart to permeate your heart. At times of testing, repeat over and over, "Love covers this wrong. Lord, may I be an expression of Your love. May I reflect Your love that covers over all wrongs."

> "*Hatred stirs up conflict, but love covers over all wrongs*"
> (PROVERBS 10:12).

G–GIVE the situation to God.

Jesus understands how much you have been wronged. When He was being persecuted, He knew the heavenly Father would judge justly—in His way and in His time. And you can know the same. Your trial will make you either bitter or better. Say to the Lord, "I put my heart into Your hands; I entrust myself to You. I know You will judge this situation justly." These words were said about Jesus:

> "*When they hurled their insults at him, he did not*
> *retaliate; when he suffered, he made no threats. Instead,*
> *he entrusted himself to him who judges justly*"
> (1 PETER 2:23).

I–INTERCEDE on behalf of your offender.

God does not present prayer as merely optional; it is a command. When you have been wronged, pray, "Lord, give me eyes to see this person through Your eyes. May I care for my offender with Your care."

> "*As for me, far be it from me that I should sin*
> *against the LORD by failing to pray for you*"
> (1 SAMUEL 12:23).

V–VALUE what you can give rather than what you can receive.
Pray for God to help you understand the offender's past and how his
pain has contributed to the injury you are now experiencing. Focus on
how you might meet some of these inner needs, for it is more blessed to
give than to receive.

> *"The Lord Jesus himself said: 'It is more*
> *blessed to give than to receive' "*
> (ACTS 20:35).

E–EXTEND God's grace, mercy, and forgiveness.
Forgiveness is a direct expression of both God's grace and God's mercy.
Grace is getting what you don't deserve (pardon). Mercy is not getting
what you do deserve (punishment). Pray often, "Lord, may my life be an
expression of Your grace and an extension of Your mercy."

> *"The Lord is full of compassion and mercy"*
> (JAMES 5:11).

G. How to Protect Your Heart from Bitterness

Jesus said, "Love your enemies." Impossible! Unrealistic! No way! People *can't*
love their enemies—at least that's the assumption. Yet the Greek word *agape*,
translated "love" in this passage, means a commitment to seek the highest good of
another person. The highest good for those who are genuinely *wrong* is that their
hearts become genuinely *right*. What can be one major catalyst for this change?
Jesus provides the answer:

> *"Love your enemies and pray for those who persecute you"*
> (MATTHEW 5:44).

If you are saying, "But they really aren't enemies," realize that if someone
evokes resentment, bitterness, or hatred, that person is an enemy to your spirit.
Because praying for your enemy is commanded by Christ, believers should obey
this directive and not regard this kind of prayer as optional.

And because praying for your enemy protects your heart from bitterness, you
should *want* to obey this directive in heart and in deed. One approach is to pray
"the fruit of the Spirit" for your offender. And because you are willing to bless
your enemy, the Bible says you will inherit a blessing:

"Do not repay evil with evil or insult with insult.
On the contrary, repay evil with blessing,
because to this you were called so that you may inherit a blessing"
(1 Peter 3:9).

How to Pray for Those Who Hurt You

"The fruit of the Spirit is love, joy, peace, forbearance,
kindness, goodness, faithfulness, gentleness and self-control.
Against such things there is no law"
(Galatians 5:22-23).

"Lord, I pray (__name__) will be filled with *the fruit of*...

- *love* by becoming fully aware of Your unconditional *love* and, in turn, will share your *love* with others.

- *joy* because of experiencing Your steady *joy* and, in turn, will radiate that inner *joy* to others.

- *peace*—Your inner *peace*—and, in turn, will have a *peace* that passes all understanding toward others.

- *forbearance* because of experiencing Your *forbearance* and, in turn, will extend that same extraordinary *forbearance* to others.

- *kindness* because of experiencing Your *kindness* and, in turn, will extend that same undeserved *kindness* to others.

- *goodness* because of experiencing the genuine *goodness* of Jesus and, in turn, will reflect the moral *goodness* of Jesus before others.

- *faithfulness* because of realizing Your amazing *faithfulness* and, in turn, will be *faithful* to You, to Your Word, and to others.

- *gentleness* because of experiencing Your *gentleness* and, in turn, will be *gentle* with others.

- *self-control*—the *control of self* by Christ—and, in turn, will rely on His *control* to break out of bondage and to be an example before others.

In the name of Jesus I pray. Amen."

> *"The wisdom that comes from heaven is first of all pure;*
> *then peace-loving, considerate, submissive, full of mercy*
> *and good fruit, impartial and sincere"*
> (JAMES 3:17).

Releasing Bitterness

QUESTION: "How can I release bitterness toward my offender when he or she is dead?"

ANSWER: When you are unable to confront your offender in person, you can confront indirectly by saying what you would want to say or need to say as though your offender were in front of you.

- **Consider** the often helpful and commonly used "chair technique."
    - *Imagine* your offender seated in a chair placed in front of you. Say the things you would say if the person were actually seated across a table from you.
    - *Express* your feelings about what was done to you and the painful ramifications those events have had on your life.
    - *Extend* forgiveness and explain that you have taken the person off of your emotional hook and placed the person onto God's hook.

- **Write** a letter to your offender, stating every painful memory.
    - *Read* it over the person's grave or at a place where you can openly speak as though you were in each other's presence.
    - *Choose*—at the close of your letter—to forgive by releasing your offender into God's hands.

- **Make** a list of all painful—as well as positive—memories.
    - *Go back* to the beginning—after completing the list—and write the word *past* by each memory.
    - *Acknowledge* and accept that the past is in the past.
    - *Release* all the pain, as well as the person, into the hands of God.

The fact that your offender has died does not mean you cannot forgive and thereby release bitterness that may have established a foothold in your heart and mind.

The Bible says,

> *"See to it that no one falls short of the grace of God*
> *and that no bitter root grows up to cause trouble and defile many"*
> (Hebrews 12:15).

H. How to Lighten Your Scales of Blame[38]

"To err is human. To blame someone else is more human."

SCALE OF JUSTIFICATION[39]

PLAYING THE BLAME GAME

Often people justify acting badly toward others by focusing on the guilt of others. These offenders will blame you for *your* guilt in order to relieve them of *their own* guilt. Even if they are 98 percent wrong, they feel justified and their "scale of justification" is balanced by blaming you for your 2 percent. This means they will not feel the full weight (conviction) of their sin.

Your offenders may attempt to balance their scale by focusing heavily on your guilt, but they still haven't emptied the scale of their guilt. And every time they begin to feel guilty for whatever wrong *they* have done, they will blame you for what *you* have done. As a result, they end up staying in bondage to this unhealthy method of keeping their scales balanced. Realize, however, that even if you are not the major guilty party, you are still responsible before God for your percentage of wrong—even if it is only 2 percent!

"If we claim to be without sin,
we deceive ourselves and the truth is not in us"
(1 JOHN 1:8).

ENDING THE BLAME GAME

Regardless of how much blame someone else bears for doing wrong, you are responsible to ask forgiveness for your own amount of wrong. Jesus said, "If you are offering your gift at the altar and there remember that your brother or sister has something against you, leave your gift there in front of the altar. First go and be reconciled to them; then come and offer your gift" (Matthew 5:23-24).

- *When you humbly ask* forgiveness for your sin and forgiveness is extended, your guilt is removed and the blame game is over.

- *When your blame is lifted* off the other person's justification scale, the weight of that person's guilt comes crashing down! This is why when one person asks "Will you forgive me?" often the other person responds with "Yes, but will you also forgive me?"

- *When you have a spirit of humility,* the Spirit of God can use your humble heart to bring godly conviction to your offender's heart.

True freedom can be found only by keeping the scale of justification empty. So, ask for forgiveness from those you have wronged, and extend forgiveness to those who have wronged you.

"I strive always to keep my conscience clear before God and man"
(ACTS 24:16).

I. How the Story Ends

The horrors of World War II are now far behind Corrie, but the intense battle between forgiveness and unforgiveness still rages within her heart. How can she find the strength to take the hand of someone who embodies the evil that destroyed two of her beloved family members? How can she forgive this man? To Corrie's dismay, she discovers she cannot!

> His hand was thrust out to shake mine. And I, who had preached so often...the need to forgive, kept my hand at my side.
>
> Even as the angry, vengeful thoughts boiled through me, I saw the sin of them. Jesus Christ had died for this man; was I going to ask for more? Lord Jesus, I prayed, forgive me and help me to forgive him.
>
> I tried to smile. I struggled to raise my hand. I could not. I felt nothing, not the slightest spark of warmth or charity. And so again I breathed a silent prayer. Jesus, I cannot forgive him. Give me Your forgiveness.
>
> As I took his hand, the most incredible thing happened. From my shoulder along my arm and through my hand a current seemed to pass from me to him, while into my heart sprang a love for this stranger that almost overwhelmed me.
>
> And so I discovered that it is not on our forgiveness any more than on our goodness that the world's healing hinges, but on His. When He tells us to love our enemies, He gives, along with the command, the love itself.[40]

Jesus would never tell you to "love your enemies, do good to those who hate you" (Luke 6:27) without giving you the power to do it. And Corrie ten Boom was living proof of this love until her death in 1983. Perhaps no words reflect Corrie's heart of forgiveness and life of love more than these: "My friends, I want you to know that through Jesus the forgiveness of sins is proclaimed to you" (Acts 13:38).

Jesus would never tell you to forgive and love your enemies
without empowering you to do it.

—JUNE HUNT

FORGIVENESS: ANSWERS IN GOD'S WORD

QUESTION: "Does God expect me to continue to forgive those who repeatedly sin against me?"

ANSWER: *"Peter came to Jesus and asked, 'Lord, how many times shall I forgive my brother or sister who sins against me? Up to seven times?' Jesus answered, 'I tell you, not seven times, but seventy-seven times'"* (Matthew 18:21-22).

QUESTION: "Is my forgiveness toward others related to my heavenly Father's forgiveness of me?"

ANSWER: *"If you forgive other people when they sin against you, your heavenly Father will also forgive you. But if you do not forgive others their sins, your Father will not forgive your sins"* (Matthew 6:14-15).

QUESTION: "To what degree or in what way am I to be forgiving of others?"

ANSWER: *"Be kind and compassionate to one another, forgiving each other, just as in Christ God forgave you"* (Ephesians 4:32).

QUESTION: "If I forgive others, is there any guarantee that I will be forgiven as well?"

ANSWER: *"Do not judge, and you will not be judged. Do not condemn, and you will not be condemned. Forgive, and you will be forgiven"* (Luke 6:37).

QUESTION: "Are there times when it is loving to 'cover over an offense'?"

ANSWER: *"Whoever would foster love covers over an offense, but whoever repeats the matter separates close friends"* (Proverbs 17:9).

QUESTION: "How does God expect me to act toward those who persecute me?"

ANSWER: *"Love your enemies and pray for those who persecute you"* (Matthew 5:44).

QUESTION: "Does being reconciled to someone who has something against me have any effect on my offering gifts to God?"

ANSWER: *"If you are offering your gift at the altar and there remember that your brother or sister has something against you, leave your gift there in front of the altar. First go and be reconciled to them; then come and offer your gift"* (Matthew 5:23-24).

QUESTION: "Does justice not require that I take revenge and repay evil for evil?"

ANSWER: *"Do not repay anyone evil for evil...Do not take revenge, my dear friends, but leave room for God's wrath, for it is written: 'It is mine to avenge; I will repay,' says the Lord"* (Romans 12:17,19).

QUESTION: "If I should refuse to forgive an offense, will that cause me to miss the grace of God in any way or cause trouble for me and for others whom I love?"

ANSWER: *"See to it that no one falls short of the grace of God and that no bitter root grows up to cause trouble and defile many"* (Hebrews 12:15).

QUESTION: "Does God expect me to continue to bear with those who sin against me by forgiving whatever grievances I have against them?"

ANSWER: *"Bear with each other and forgive one another if any of you has a grievance against someone. Forgive as the Lord forgave you"* (Colossians 3:13).

Epilogue:

THE BRIDGE BUILDER

Bridging the gaps that separate us—gaps that keep us from close relationships. How we wish we could! If we really want peace and happiness (and everyone does), then quality relationships are a must. Building a bridge from heart to heart requires investing *intentional* time, which means both *quality* time and *quantity* time.

In reality, all bridges require regular maintenance. Along the way, we can do much to nurture meaningful relationships, including mastering the foundational principles found in this book. But even when we use our best tools, implementing the best plan and exerting our best effort, there's no guarantee that the bridges we extend will be secured on the other side.

Jesus provides the ultimate example for this principle. He died on the cross for our sins in order to bridge the gap that separates us from Him. And He lovingly invites *"whosoever will"* to cross over the bridge and enter into a rich, rewarding relationship with Him. Yet, that word *will* is the key—*whosoever will.*

God doesn't force us to love Him—or even to relate to Him. The Creator of love knows that loving relationships can never be mandated. The only way they occur is when two *willing* people decide to do the hard work necessary to build a relationship of reciprocal respect and mutual commitment.

When it comes to building your own personal relationships, you want to construct the safest and most stable bridge. You can invite someone to meet you on that bridge, but you must allow that person to join you...*or not*! And if it's a not, then you need to commit that person's rejection and your own personal pain to God. Allow Him to comfort you, and look to Him to meet your deepest inner needs.

As you hone your bridge-building skills, you will enjoy more and more success, satisfaction, and trust in God's sovereign plan (regardless of rejection or reconciliation). Yet realize that you won't be building strong relationships solely for your benefit. Your most meaningful relationships are part of God's unseen plan to offer the blessing of safety and security to others. In truth, everyone's heart yearns to feel completely safe—to feel emotionally secure, without a speck of worry.

Imagine a young boy approaching a bridge. He totally trusts the bridge to hold him securely—he assumes he will be completely safe. That's simply not an issue for him.

At times your role in life will be to be a bridge builder for someone else—perhaps even someone much younger. Years ago, I read an unforgettable poem that helped me value the bridge builders in my life.

The Bridge Builder[1]

An old man, walking on a lone highway,
Came in the evening, cold and gray,
To a chasm—
vast and deep and wide—
Through which was flowing a rapid tide.

As the old man crossed in the twilight dim,
That deep stream held no fear for him.
But he turned after reaching the other side,
Slowly building a bridge to span the tide.

"Old man," said a fellow traveler near,
"You're wasting your strength by building here.
Your journey will stop at the end of the day.
You never again will pass this way.
You have crossed the chasm, deep and wide,
Why build the bridge at eventide?"

The builder lifted his old grey head.
"Good friend, as I've walked this path," he said,
"A boy is following me today—
A youth whose feet must pass this way."

"This chasm that hasn't been hard for me,
To that fair boy may a pitfall be.
He, too, must cross in the twilight dim.
My friend, I'm building the bridge for him."

Adapted by June Hunt
from a poem (circa 1900)
by Will Allen Dromgoole

Bridging the Gap

1. At http:www.dailymail.co.uk/news/article-2035520/Meghalaya-villagers-create-living-bridges-training-roots-river.html.

Critical Spirit: Confronting the Heart of a Critic

1. Timothy Friberg, Barbara Friberg, and Neva F. Miller, *Analytical Lexicon of the Greek New Testament* (Grand Rapids: Baker Books, 2000), #238.

2. See *Merriam Webster Online Dictionary*, s.v. "Criticism," http://www.m-w.com.

3. See *Merriam Webster Online Dictionary*, s.v. "Care," http://www.m-w.com.

4. See also *The New Shorter Oxford English Dictionary*, vol. 1 ed. Lesley Brown (Oxford: Clarendon Press, 1993), s.v. "Encourage."

5. For this section see W.E. Vine, Merrill F. Unger, and William White, *Vine's Complete Expository Dictionary of Biblical Words*, elec. ed. (Nashville: Thomas Nelson, 1996), s.v. "Encourage."

6. H.P. Thien, M.A. Moelyadi, and H. Muhammad, "Effects of Leaders' Position and Shape on Aerodynamic Performances of V Flight Formation," *Proceedings of the International Conference on Intelligent Unmanned System* (Bali, Indonesia: ICIUS, 2007), 1.

7. Elizabeth Day, "I'll Never Forgive Mommie," *The Observer,* May 24, 2008 (London: Guardian News and Media Limited), http://www.guardian.co.uk/film/2008/may/25/biography.film.

8. Day, "I'll Never Forgive Mommie," *The Observer*, http://www.guardian.co.uk/film/2008/may/25/biography.film.

9. Day, "I'll Never Forgive Mommie."

10. Day, "I'll Never Forgive Mommie."

11. Day, "I'll Never Forgive Mommie."

12. Stephanie Jones, "America's Real Sweetheart: A Biography of Joan Crawford, Part 3," http://joancrawfordbest.com/biowarnersfreelance.htm.

13. Day, "I'll Never Forgive Mommie."

14. Peter B. Flint, "Joan Crawford Dies at Home," *NYTimes.com,* May 11, 1977.

15. Stephanie Jones, "America's Real Sweetheart: A Biography of Joan Crawford, Part 4," http://joancrawfordbest.com/biography.htm.

16. Stephanie Jones, "America's Real Sweetheart: A Biography of Joan Crawford, Part 4," http://joancrawfordbest.com/biography.htm.

17. For this section see David Field, *Family Personalities* (Eugene, OR: Harvest House, 1988), 19-29.

18. On the three God-given inner needs, see Lawrence J. Crabb, Jr., *Understanding People: Deep Longings for Relationship* (Grand Rapids: Zondervan, 1987), 15-16; Robert S. McGee, *The Search for Significance,* 2d ed. (Houston, TX: Rapha, 1990), 27-30.

19. See also William D. Backus, *Telling Each Other the Truth* (Minneapolis: Bethany House, 1985), 106-8.

20. On the three God-given inner needs, see Crabb, *Understanding People,* 15-16; McGee, *The Search for Significance,* 27-30.

21. See Susan Forward, *Toxic Parents: Overcoming Their Hurtful Legacy and Reclaiming Your Life* (New York: Bantam, 1989), 236-74.

Manipulation: Cutting the Strings of Control

1. Lori Thorkelson Rentzel, *Emotional Dependency* (Downers Grove, IL: InterVarsity, 1990), 14; *Merriam Webster Online Dictionary*, s.v. "Manipulate," http://www.m-w.com.

2. See *American Heritage Electronic Dictionary*, 4th ed. (Boston: Houghton Mifflin, 2000), s.v. "Persuade."

3. Frank W. Abagnale and Stan Redding, *Catch Me If You Can* (New York: Simon & Schuster, 1989), 4.

4. Abagnale and Redding, *Catch Me If You Can*, 16.

5. Abagnale and Redding, *Catch Me If You Can*, 16.

6. Abagnale and Redding, *Catch Me If You Can*, 12.

7. Abagnale and Redding, *Catch Me If You Can*, 25.

8. A&E Networks, "Bio.True Story: Frank Abagnale," http://www.biography.com/people/frank-abagnale-20657335?page=1.

9. A&E Networks, "Bio.True Story: Frank Abagnale."

10. A&E Networks, "Bio.True Story: Frank Abagnale."

11. Abagnale and Associates, "Comments," http://www.abagnale.com/comments.htm.

12. Francis Brown, Samuel Rolles Driver, Charles Augustus Briggs, *Enhanced Brown-Driver-Briggs Hebrew and English Lexicon*, elec. ed. (Oak Harbor, WA: Logos Research Systems, 2000), s.v. "Jacob."

13. See Tim Kimmel, *Powerful Personalities* (Colorado Springs: Focus on the Family, 1993), 29-42.

14. See Kimmel, *Powerful Personalities*, 64-66.

15. See Everett Shostrom and Dan Montgomery, *The Manipulators* (Nashville, TN: Abingdon, 1990), 12.

16. See Kimmel, *Powerful Personalities*, 36-39.

17. See Kimmel, *Powerful Personalities*, 37-38; Jan Silvious, *Please Don't Say You Need Me: Biblical Answers for Codependency* (Grand Rapids: Pyranee Books, 1989), 56.

18. See Kimmel, *Powerful Personalities*, 48, 143-44; Barbara Sullivan, *The Control Grip: A Woman's Guide to Freedom from the Need to Manage People and Circumstances* (Minneapolis: Bethany House, 1991), 67-69.

19. See Kimmel, *Powerful Personalities*, 46-48, 97.

20. See Kimmel, *Powerful Personalities*, 61-62, 64-66.

21. See Kimmel, *Powerful Personalities*, 64-66; Sullivan, *Control Grip*, 64-68.

22. See Kimmel, *Powerful Personalities*, 53-54.

23. See Kimmel, *Powerful Personalities*, 46-48.

24. See Sullivan, *Control Grip*, 67-68; See Kimmel, *Powerful Personalities*, 61-62; Paul F. Schmidt, *Coping with Difficult People*, Christian Care Books, ed. Wayne E. Oates, vol. 6 (Philadelphia: Westminster, 1980), 100-1.

25. Edward Camella, "Religious Abuse," *The Remuda Review* (Spring 2005), 17-23.

26. Story Source: MEDIA 7, Tirana, Albania.

27. James S. Messina, "Eliminating Manipulation," Livestrong.com, http://Jamesjmessina.Com/Tools-forcontrolissues/Eliminatemanipulation.html.

28. See Silvious, *Please Don't Say You Need Me*, 31; Kimmel, *Powerful Personalities*, 202-3.

29. See Henry Cloud and John Townsend, *Boundaries: When to Say Yes, When to Say No, To Take Control of Your Life* (Grand Rapids: Zondervan, 1992), 199-201.

30. Macmillan Dictionary, *Online English Dictionary* (New York: Macmillan, 2009), s.v. "Brainwash."

31. For the three God-given inner needs, see Lawrence J. Crabb, Jr., *Understanding People: Deep Longings for Relationship* (Grand Rapids: Zondervan, 1987), 15-16; Robert S. McGee, *The Search for Significance*, rev. and exp. ed. (Nashville: Word, 1998), 27-29.

32. See Crabb, *Understanding People*, 15-16; McGee, *The Search for Significance*, 27-30.

33. See Crabb, *Understanding People*, 15-16; McGee, *The Search for Significance,* 27-30.
34. See McGee, *Search for Significance*, 65-67, 73.
35. Jo Coudert, "Nice Ways to Say No," *Reader's Digest* (January 1993), 135-37.
36. See Crabb, *Understanding People*, 15-16; McGee, *The Search for Significance*, 27-30.
37. See Crabb, *Understanding People*, 15-16; McGee, *The Search for Significance*, 27-30.
38. See Crabb, *Understanding People*, 15-16; McGee, *The Search for Significance*, 27-30.
39. See Crabb, *Understanding People*, 15-16; McGee, *The Search for Significance*, 27-30.

Codependency: Balancing an Unbalanced Relationship

1. For this section see Robert Hemfelt, Frank Minirth, and Paul Meier, *Love Is a Choice* (Nashville: Thomas Nelson, 1989), 11-12.
2. For this section see Melody Beattie, *Codependent No More: How to Stop Controlling Others and Start Caring for Yourself* (New York: Harper, 1987), 29-30; Jan Silvious, *Please Don't Say You Need Me* (Grand Rapids: Pyranee, 1989), 9-10.
3. See also Silvious, *Please Don't Say You Need Me,* 73-75.
4. For this section see *Beattie, Codependent No More*, 37-39.
5. For this section see Hemfelt, Minirth, and Meier, *Love Is a Choice*, 28.
6. For this section see John Bradshaw, *How Childhood Development Stages Effect [sic] Adult Relationships*, VHS, Part 1 and 2, Linkletter Films (Nimco, 2000), distributed as *The Sources of Love*, vol. 1 and *The Work of Love*, vol. 2.
7. On the three God-given inner needs, see Lawrence J. Crabb, Jr., *Understanding People: Deep Longings for Relationship* (Grand Rapids: Zondervan, 1987), 15-16; Robert S. McGee, *The Search for Significance*, 2d ed. (Houston, TX: Rapha, 1990), 27-30.
8. For this section see Pia Mellody, Andrea Wells Miller, and J. Keith Miller, *Facing Love Addiction: Giving Yourself the Power to Change the Way You Love* (New York: Harper San Francisco, 1992), 21.
9. For this section see Mellody, Miller, and Miller, *Facing Love Addiction*, 50.
10. For the three God-given inner needs, see Lawrence J. Crabb, Jr., *Understanding People: Deep Longings for Relationship* (Grand Rapids: Zondervan, 1987), 15-16; Robert S. McGee, *The Search for Significance*, 2d ed. (Houston, TX: Rapha, 1990), 27-30.
11. W. E. Vine, Merrill F. Unger, and William White, Jr., *Vine's Expository Dictionary of Biblical Words* (Nashville: Thomas Nelson, 1985), s.v., "Burden, Burdened, Burdensome."
12. Vine, Unger, and White, *Vine's Expository Dictionary of Biblical Words*, s.v., "Burden, Burdened, Burdensome."
13. For this section see Hemfelt, Minirth, and Meier, *Love Is a Choice*, 180-84.
14. For this section see Mellody, Miller, and Miller, *Facing Love Addiction*, 78-79.
15. For this section see Mellody, Miller, and Miller, *Facing Love Addiction*, 166-69, 196-98.
16. For this section see Mellody, Miller, and Miller, *Facing Love Addiction*, 90-92.
17. For this section see Mellody, Miller, and Miller, *Facing Love Addiction*, 86-92.
18. For this section see also Mellody, Miller, and Miller, *Facing Love Addiction*, 102-8.
19. For this section see also Mellody, Miller, and Miller, *Facing Love Addiction*, 108-13.
20. For this section see Mellody, Miller, and Miller, *Facing Love Addiction*, 94-100; Valerie J. McIntyre, *Sheep in Wolves' Clothing*, 2d ed. (Grand Rapids: Baker, 1996), 137-44; Hemfelt, Minirth, and Meier, *Love Is a Choice,* 177-91; Rich Buhler, *Pain and Pretending,* rev. and exp. ed. (Nashville: Thomas Nelson, 1991), 160-64.
21. Hemfelt, Minirth, and Meier, *Love Is a Choice*, 258.

Confrontation: Challenging Others to Change

1. Leslie Brown, ed., *The New Shorter Oxford English Dictionary on Historical Principles,* 2 vols. (Oxford: Clarendon, 1993), s.v. "Confrontation."

2. Richard Whitaker, *Whitaker's Revised Brown-Driver-Briggs Hebrew-English Lexicon,* elec. ed. (Norfolk: BibleWorks, 1995), s.v. "Tokhot."

3. Timothy Friberg and Barbara Friberg, *Analytical Lexicon to the Greek New Testament,* elec. ed. (Grand Rapids: Baker, 2000), s.v. "Parable."

4. W.E. Vine, Merrill F. Unger, and William White, *Vine's Complete Expository Dictionary of Old and New Testament Words,* elec. ed. (Nashville: Thomas Nelson, 1996), s.v. "Admonish."

5. Vine, Unger, and White, *Vine's Complete Expository Dictionary,* s.v. "Rebuke."

6. Vine, Unger, and White, *Vine's Complete Expository Dictionary,* s.v. "Rebuke."

7. John Nieder and Thomas M. Thompson, *Forgive & Love Again: Healing Wounded Relationships* (Eugene, OR: Harvest House, 1991), 151-55.

8. Deborah Smith Pegues, *Confronting Without Offending* (Tulsa, OK: Vincom, 1995), 3.

9. Nieder and Thompson, *Forgive & Love Again,* 156-60.

10. For this section see Josh McDowell, *Resolving Conflict* (Pomona, CA: Focus on the Family, 1989), 6-8; Ken Sande, *The Peacemaker,* 3d ed. (Grand Rapids: Baker, 2004), 22-29.

11. Josh McDowell, *Resolving Conflict* (Pomona, CA: Focus on the Family, 1989), 6-8; Ken Sande, *The Peacemaker,* 22-29.

12. On the three God-given inner needs, see Lawrence J. Crabb, Jr., *Understanding People: Deep Longings for Relationship* (Grand Rapids: Zondervan, 1987), 15-16; Robert S. McGee, *The Search for Significance,* 2d ed. (Houston, TX: Rapha, 1990), 27-30.

13. Vision.org, "William Wilberforce: The Persevering Parliamentarian," *Vision,* Winter 2007 (Pasadena, CA: Church of God, an International Community, 2012), http://www.vision.org/vision media/article.aspx?id=2266.

14. Cathy Gorn, *Triumph and Tragedy* (College Park, MD: University of Maryland, 2006), 50.

15. Smithsonian Institutes, *Smithsonian Timelines of History* (New York: DK Publishing, 2001), 286.

16. Gorn, *Triumph and Tragedy,* 52.

17. Gorn, *Triumph and Tragedy,* 53.

18. Gorn, *Triumph and Tragedy,* 55.

19. Eric Metaxas, *Amazing Grace: William Wilberforce and the Heroic Campaign to End Slavery* (New York: HarperCollins, 2007), 136.

20. Nieder and Thompson, *Forgive & Love Again,* 161-62.

21. For this section see McDowell, *Resolving Conflict,* 8-10.

22. Nieder and Thompson, *Forgive & Love Again,* 162-63.

23. Nieder and Thompson, *Forgive & Love Again,* 162-63.

24. See also Nieder and Thompson, *Forgive & Love Again,* 164-65.

25. For this section see Nieder and Thompson, *Forgive & Love Again,* 164-66.

26. Nieder and Thompson, *Forgive & Love Again,* 166-170; Duke Robinson, *Too Nice for Your Own Good* (New York: Warner, 1997), 80-83, 217-28.

27. Pegues, *Confronting Without Offending,* 34-35.

28. For this section see David Augsburger, *Caring Enough to Confront,* rev. ed. (Ventura, CA: Regal, 1981), 17-21; Pegues, *Confronting Without Offending,* 8-31.

29. For this section see Stephen Van Cleave, Walter Byrd, and Kathy Revell, *Counseling for Substance Abuse and Addiction,* ed. Gary R. Collins, vol. 12 (Dallas: Word, 1987), 83-86; Carolyn Johnson, *Understanding Alcoholism* (Grand Rapids: Zondervan, 1991), 145-50; Christina B. Parker, *When Someone You Love Drinks Too Much* (New York: Harper & Row, 1990), 55-56.

30. For this section see Van Cleave, Byrd, and Revell, *Counseling for Substance Abuse and Addiction*, 87.

31. Carole Mayhall, *Words That Hurt, Words That Heal* (Colorado Springs: NavPress, 1986), 88-90.

32. Sande, *The Peacemaker*, 92-98.

Conflict Resolution: Solving Your People Problems

1. See *Merriam-Webster Collegiate Dictionary* (2001), http://www.m-w.com, s.v. "Conflict."

2. *Merriam-Webster Collegiate Dictionary*, s.v. "Conflict."

3. See H.G. Liddell, *A Lexicon: Abridged from Liddell and Scott's Greek-English Lexicon*, elec. ed. (Oak Harbor, WA: Logos Research Systems, Inc., 1996), s. #10.

4. Marvin Richardson Vincent, *Word Studies in the New Testament*, vol. 3 (Bellingham, WA: Logos Research Systems, Inc., 2002), 481.

5. On the differences between resolution and reconciliation, see also L. Randolph Lowry and Richard W. Meyers, *Conflict Management and Counseling*, ed. Gary R. Collins, vol. 29 (Waco, TX: Word, 1991), 26-29.

6. For types of conflict see G. Brian Jones and Linda Phillips-Jones, *A Fight to the Better End* (Wheaton, IL: Victor, 1989), 16.

7. See also Will Cunningham, *How to Enjoy a Family Fight* (Phoenix, AZ: Questar, 1988), 151-66; Cunningham characterizes "attacking" fighting styles as the skunk and the shark.

8. See also Cunningham, *How to Enjoy a Family Fight*, 167-80; Cunningham characterizes "avoiding" fighting styles as the turtle and the chameleon.

9. See also Jones, *Fight to the Better End*, 16.

10. See also Jones, *Fight to the Better End*, 17.

11. See also Cunningham, *How to Enjoy a Family Fight*, 145-48.

12. Cunningham, *How to Enjoy a Family Fight*, 159-66; Bramson calls this style "the Sherman Tank." Robert M. Bramson, *Coping with Difficult People* (Garden City, NY: Doubleday, 1981), 13.

13. See Bramson, *Coping with Difficult People*, 26-29.

14. See Bramson, *Coping with Difficult People*, 44-52; Cunningham calls this style of conflict the skunk. Cunningham, *How to Enjoy a Family Fight*, 151-58.

15. Cunningham, *How to Enjoy a Family Fight*, 167-76; see also Bramson, *Coping with Difficult People*, 70-73.

16. Bramson, *Coping with Difficult People*, 85-90.

17. See Cunningham, *How to Enjoy a Family Fight*, 177-80. Cunningham calls this style the chameleon.

18. 1 Samuel 25:3.

19. 1 Samuel 25:10-11.

20. 1 Samuel 25:24-25.

21. 1 Samuel 25:28-29.

22. 1 Samuel 25:30-31.

23. 1 Samuel 25:33-35.

24. 1 Samuel 25:37.

25. 1 Samuel 25:39.

26. On the three God-given inner needs see Larry Crabb, Jr., *Understanding People: Deep Longings for Relationship* (Grand Rapids: Zondervan, 1987), 15-16; McGee, *The Search for Significance* (Houston, TX: Rapha, 1990), 27-30.

27. See Terry Hershey, *Intimacy: The Longing of Every Human Heart* (Eugene, OR: Harvest House, 1984), 147-48.

28. The American Experience, "The History of Dueling in America" (Boston: PBS online and WGBH, 2000), http://www.pbs.org/wgbh/amex/duel/sfeature/dueling.html.

29. The American Experience, "The History of Dueling in America."

30. The American Experience, "The History of Dueling in America."

31. The American Experience, "The History of Dueling in America."

32. The American Experience, "The History of Dueling in America."

33. The American Experience, "The History of Dueling in America."

34. R.G. Bratcher and E.A. Nida, *A Handbook on Paul's Letters to the Colossians and to Philemon* (New York: United Bible Societies, 1993), 124-25.

35. See Josh McDowell, *Resolving Conflict* (Pomona, CA: Focus on the Family, 1989), 11.

36. Bramson, *Coping with Difficult People*, 14-25.

37. See Bramson, *Coping with Difficult People*, 29-34.

38. Bramson, *Coping with Difficult People*, 52-64.

39. Bramson, *Coping with Difficult People,* 74-84.

40. See Bramson, *Coping with Difficult People*, 90-97.

41. See Cunningham, *How to Enjoy a Family Fight*, 177-80.

Forgiveness: The Freedom of Letting Go

1. For this and all sections on the Corrie ten Boom story, see *Corrie ten Boom*, John L. Sherrill and Elizabeth Sherrill, *The Hiding Place* (Washington Depot, CT: Chosen, 1971); Corrie ten Boom and Jamie Buckingham, *Tramp for the Lord* (Fort Washington, PA: Christian Literature Crusade, 1974).

2. For the account of Corrie and the Ravensbruck guard and all quotations in this section see Corrie ten Boom, *I'm Still Learning to Forgive* (Wheaton, IL: Good News Publishers, 1995), http://www.gnpcb.org/product/663575723080; ten Boom and Buckingham, *Tramp for the Lor*d, 54-55.

3. Robert Jeffress, *When Forgiveness Doesn't Make Sense* (Colorado Springs: WaterBrook, 2000), 47-49.

4. W.E. Vine, Merrill F. Unger, and William White, Jr., *Vine's Expository Dictionary of Biblical Words* (Nashville: Thomas Nelson, 1985), s.v. "Forgive, Forgave, Forgiveness."

5. Vine, Unger, and White, *Vine's Expository Dictionary of Biblical Words*, s.v. "Confess, Confession."

6. For this section see Jeffress, *When Forgiveness Doesn't Make Sense*, 46-51.

7. Vine, Unger, and White, *Vine's Expository Dictionary of Biblical Words*, s.v. "Forgive, Forgave, Forgiveness."

8. For this section see also John Nieder and Thomas M. Thompson, *Forgive & Love Again: Healing Wounded Relationships* (Eugene, OR: Harvest House, 1991), 173-85; Jeffress, *When Forgiveness Doesn't Make Sense*, 107-23.

9. Vine, Unger, and White, *Vine's Expository Dictionary of Biblical Words*, s.v. "Forgive, Forgave, Forgiveness."

10. Vine, Unger, and White, *Vine's Expository Dictionary of Biblical Words*, s.v. "Grace."

11. Robert Jeffress, *Choose Your Attitudes, Change Your Life* (Wheaton, IL: Victor, 1992), 102-7; see also Chuck Swindoll, "I Am Joseph!" *Insight*, Winter 1986, 3-9.

12. See also Nieder and Thompson, *Forgive & Love Again*, 30.

13. David Augsburger, *The Freedom of Forgiveness*, rev. and exp. ed. (Chicago: Moody, 1988), 18.

14. Ten Boom and Buckingham, *Tramp for the Lord*, 54.

15. Nieder and Thompson, *Forgive & Love Again*, 47-51.

16. Luke 15:16.

17. Luke 15:20.

18. Luke 15:21.

19. Luke 15:23-24.

20. Ten Boom and Buckingham, *Tramp for the Lord*, 49.

21. See also Lewis B. Smedes, *Forgive and Forget: Healing the Hurts We Don't Deserve* (San Francisco, CA: Harper & Row, 1984), 138.

22. For the three God-given inner needs, see Lawrence J. Crabb, Jr., *Understanding People: Deep Longings for Relationship* (Grand Rapids: Zondervan, 1987), 15-16; Robert S. McGee, *The Search for Significance*, 2d ed. (Houston, TX: Rapha, 1990), 27-30.

23. J.K. Grider, "Forgiveness," in *Evangelical Dictionary of Theology*, ed. Walter A. Elwell, 2d ed. (Grand Rapids: Baker Academic, 2001), 460.

24. Louis Zamperini and David Rensin, *Devil at My Heels: A Heroic Olympian's Astonishing Story of Survival as a Japanese POW in World War II* (New York: William Morrow, 2011), 110. Excerpts from *Devil at My Heels* © 2003 by Louis Zamperini, by permission of HarperCollins Publishers.

25. Zamperini, *Devil at My Heels*, 99.

26. Zamperini, *Devil at My Heels*, 265.

27. Ten Boom and Buckingham, *Tramp for the Lord*, 181.

28. See Smedes, *Forgive and Forget*, 3-19.

29. See Augsburger, *The Freedom of Forgiveness*, 47-50.

30. See Smedes, *Forgive and Forget*, 21-26.

31. Smedes, *Forgive and Forget*, 23.

32. See Smedes, *Forgive and Forget*, 27-30.

33. Alexander Pope, *Essay on Criticism*, part 2, line 325.

34. For this section see Augsburger, *The Freedom of Forgiveness*, 44-46.

35. Augsburger, *The Freedom of Forgiveness*, 46.

36. For the following section see Smedes, *Forgive and Forget*, 31-37.

37. Augsburger, *The Freedom of Forgiveness*, 42; Smedes, *Forgive and Forget*, 111-13.

38. For this section see Bill Gothard, *Rebuilder's Guide* (Oak Brook, IL: Institute in Basic Life Principles, 1991), 92. Used by permission.

39. For this image see Bill Gothard, *Rebuilder's* Guide (Oak Brook, IL: Institute in Basic Life Principles, 1991), 92. Used by permission.

40. Ten Boom, Sherrill, and Sherrill, *The Hiding Place*, 238.

Epilogue: The Bridge Builder

1. Adapted by June Hunt from the poem "The Bridge Builder" by Will Allen Dromgoole. Interesting tidbit: This poet laureate was a female whose father wanted a son, so he named her William.

Other Harvest House Books by June Hunt

Counseling Through Your Bible Handbook

The Bible is richly relevant when it comes to the difficult dilemmas of life. Here are 50 chapters of spiritual wisdom and compassionate counsel on issues such as anger, adultery, depression, fear, guilt, grief, rejection, and self-worth.

How to Rise Above Abuse

Compassionate, practical, hands-on guidance for the toughest issues to talk about—childhood sexual abuse, spiritual abuse, verbal and emotional abuse, victimization, and wife abuse. Filled with the hope and healing only Christ can give.

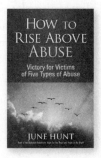

How to Handle Your Emotions

In Scripture, God gives counsel that helps us process our full range of emotions in a healthy way. Learn how to better navigate your emotions by understanding their definitions, characteristics, and causes, as well as the solutions that lead to emotional growth.

How to Deal with Harmful Habits

June Hunt provides compassionate biblical guidance to help readers recognize addictive impulses, set boundaries, seek help, and trust the power of Christ and God's Word to release them from the hold of addictions and embrace healing God's way.

How to Forgive... When You Don't Feel Like It

Though we know God has called us to forgive, we find ourselves asking hard questions: What if it hurts too much to forgive? What if the other person isn't sorry? How can I let the other person off the hook for doing something so wrong? June Hunt speaks from experience as she offers biblical answers, hope, and true freedom through forgiveness.

Keeping Your Cool... When Your Anger Is Hot!

This book explores the causes and kinds of anger and the biblical steps toward resolution. You will learn how to identify the triggers of anger, ways of dealing with past angers, what the Bible says about righteous and unrighteous anger, and how to bring about real and lasting change.

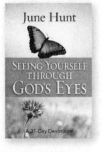

Seeing Yourself Through God's Eyes

How you view yourself can have a profound effect on your everyday living. The key is to see yourself through God's eyes. Discover the great riches of your identity in Christ in the 31 devotions in this book.

About the Author

June Hunt is founder and CEO of **Hope For The Heart** (www.HopeForTheHeart.org) and is a dynamic Christian leader who has yielded landmark contributions to the field of Christian counseling. Hope For The Heart provides biblically based counsel in 24 languages and has worked in 60 countries on six continents. June, who celebrated 25 years of ministry in 2011, is also an author, speaker, musician, and has served as guest professor to a variety of colleges and seminaries.

Early family pain shaped June's heart of compassion. Her bizarre family background left her feeling hopeless and caused June to contemplate "drastic solutions." But when June entered into a life-changing relationship with Jesus Christ, the trajectory of her life was forever altered. As a result, she grew passionate about helping people face life's tough circumstances.

As a youth director, June became aware of the need for real answers to real questions. Her personal experiences with pain and her practical experience with youth and parents led June into a lifelong commitment to *Providing God's Truth for Today's Problems*. She earned a master's in counseling at Criswell College in 2007 and has been presented with two honorary doctorates.

Between 1989 and 1992, June Hunt developed and taught *Counseling Through the Bible*, a scripturally based counseling course addressing 100 topics in categories such as marriage and family, emotional entrapments and cults, as well as addictions, abuse, and apologetics. Since then, the coursework has been continuously augmented and refined, forming the basis for the *Biblical Counseling Library*. Her *Biblical Counseling Keys* became the foundation of the ministry's expansion, including the 2002 creation of the *Hope Biblical Counseling Institute* (BCI) initiated by Criswell College to equip spiritual leaders, counselors, and people with hearts to help others with practical solutions for life's most pressing problems.

The *Biblical Counseling Keys* provide a foundation for the ministry's two daily radio programs, *Hope For The Heart* and *Hope In The Night*, both hosted by June. *Hope For The Heart* is a half-hour of interactive teaching heard on over 100 radio outlets across America, and *Hope In The Night* is June's live two-hour call-in counseling program. Together, both programs air domestically and internationally on more than 1000 stations. In 1986, the National Religious Broadcasters (NRB) honored *Hope For The Heart* as "Best New Radio Program" and awarded it Radio Program of the Year in 1989. Women in Christian Media presented June Hunt with an Excellence in Communications award in 2008. The ministry received NRB's Media Award for International Strategic Partnerships in 2010.

As an accomplished musician, June has been a guest on numerous national TV and radio programs, including NBC's *Today*. She has toured overseas with the USO and has been a guest soloist at Billy Graham Crusades. June communicates her message of hope on five music recordings: *The Whisper of My Heart, Hymns of Hope, Songs of Surrender, Shelter Under His Wings*, and *The Hope of Christmas*.

June Hunt's numerous books include *Seeing Yourself Through God's Eyes, How to Forgive...When You Don't Feel Like It, Counseling Through Your Bible Handbook, How to Handle Your Emotions, How to Rise Above Abuse, Bonding with Your Teen through Boundaries, Keeping Your Cool...When Your Anger Is Hot, Caring for a Loved One with Cancer* (June is a cancer survivor), and *Hope for Your Heart: Finding Strength in Life's Storms*. She is also a contributor to the *Soul Care Bible* and the *Women's Devotional Bible*.

June Hunt resides in Dallas, Texas, home of the international headquarters of Hope For The Heart.